DISSENT AFTER DISRUPTION

Scottish Religious Cultures *Historical Perspectives*

Series Editors: Scott R. Spurlock and Crawford Gribben

Religion has played a key formational role in the development of Scottish society shaping cultural norms, defining individual and corporate identities, and underpinning legal and political institutions. This series presents the very best scholarship on the role of religion as a formative and yet divisive force in Scottish society and highlights its positive and negative functions in the development of the nation's culture. The impact of the Scots diaspora on the wider world means that the subject has major significance far outwith Scotland.

Available titles

George Mackay Brown and the Scottish Catholic Imagination
Linden Bicket

Poor Relief and the Church in Scotland, 1560–1650
John McCallum

Jewish Orthodoxy in Scotland: Rabbi Dr Salis Daiches and Religious Leadership
Hannah Holtschneider

Miracles of Healing: Psychotherapy and Religion in Twentieth-Century Scotland
Gavin Miller

George Strachan of the Mearns: Seventeenth-Century Orientalist
Tom McInally

Scottish Liturgical Traditions and Religious Politics: From Reformers to Jacobites, 1560–1764
Edited by Allan I. Macinnes, Patricia Barton and Kieran German

Dissent after Disruption: Church and State in Scotland, 1843–63
Ryan Mallon

Forthcoming titles

The Scot Afrikaners: Identity Politics and Intertwined Religious Cultures
Retief Muller

Dugald Semple and the Life Reform Movement
Steven Sutcliffe

Scottish Presbyterianism Re-established: The Case of Dunblane and Stirling, 1687–1710
Andrew Muirhead

The Catholic Church in Scotland: Financial Development 1772–1930
Darren Tierney

The Dynamics of Dissent: Politics, Religion and the Law in Restoration Scotland
Neil McIntyre

William Guild and Moderate Divinity in Early Modern Scotland
Russell Newton

edinburghuniversitypress.com/series/src

DISSENT AFTER DISRUPTION

Church and State in Scotland, 1843–63

RYAN MALLON

EDINBURGH
University Press

Edinburgh University Press is one of the leading university presses in the UK. We publish academic books and journals in our selected subject areas across the humanities and social sciences, combining cutting-edge scholarship with high editorial and production values to produce academic works of lasting importance. For more information visit our website: edinburghuniversitypress.com

© Ryan Mallon, 2021, 2023

First published in hardback by Edinburgh University Press 2021

Edinburgh University Press Ltd
The Tun – Holyrood Road
12 (2f) Jackson's Entry
Edinburgh EH8 8PJ

Typeset in 10/12 ITC New Baskerville by
Servis Filmsetting Ltd, Stockport, Cheshire

A CIP record for this book is available from the British Library

ISBN 978 1 4744 8279 0 (hardback)
ISBN 978 1 4744 8280 6 (paperback)
ISBN 978 1 4744 8281 3 (webready PDF)
ISBN 978 1 4744 8282 0 (epub)

The right of Ryan Mallon to be identified as author of this work has been asserted in accordance with the Copyright, Designs and Patents Act 1988 and the Copyright and Related Rights Regulations 2003 (SI No. 2498).

Contents

Abbreviations vi
Acknowledgements vii

Introduction 1

Part One   Dissent and Disruption

1 New Lights: The Growth of Dissent and Voluntaryism in Scotland, 1712–1843 21
2 A National or Voluntary Church? The Free Church and the Establishment Principle 38

Part Two   Co-operation and Incorporation

3 'Co-operation without Incorporation': Dissenting Relations after the Disruption 67
4 The Age of Unions? Dissenting Church Reunion, 1847–63 87

Part Three   Politics and Anti-popery

5 Truth, Error and Principle: Anti-Catholicism in Presbyterian Dissent 115
6 Bigotry or Liberalism? Dissenting Politics and the Liberal Party 152

Part Four   Reforming Scotland: Social Reform and National Education

7 Recreating the Godly Commonwealth: Urban Mission and Social Reform 191
8 Scottish Education and Dissenting Division 219

Conclusion 262

Appendix 273
Bibliography 274
Index 299

Abbreviations

AGAFC	*Acts of the General Assembly of the Free Church of Scotland*
FCM	*Free Church Magazine*
HFRFC	*Home and Foreign Record of the Free Church of Scotland*
NCL	New College Library, Edinburgh
NEA	National Education Association of Scotland
NLS	National Library of Scotland
NYPL	New York Public Library
OSM	*Original Secession Magazine*
PGAFC	*Proceedings of the General Assembly of the Free Church of Scotland*
RSCHS	*Records of the Scottish Church History Society*
SRS	Scottish Reformation Society
UPM	*United Presbyterian Magazine*
USM	*United Secession Magazine*
USRM	*United Secession and Relief Magazine*

Acknowledgements

The monograph in your hands (or on your computer screen) is not, despite all appearances, my first book. My debut 'book' was actually a review of Manchester United's 1999–2000 season, written – and illustrated – on my grandparents' living-room floor and using my Granda's newspapers as my source material (some of the analysis in it holds up well: seven-year-old me was right about United needing a dependable 'keeper). It's quite surreal, then, to be writing the acknowledgements for a proper, published book with a cover not hand-drawn by myself. So you can forgive me if they're a touch indulgent.

The majority of the research for this book was undertaken during my doctoral studies at Queen's University Belfast, which were funded by the Arts and Humanities Research Council through its Northern Bridge Doctoral Training Partnership. I gratefully acknowledge the assistance and helpfulness of the staff and librarians at New College Library, the University of Edinburgh; the National Library of Scotland; the McClay Library at Queen's; and the Gamble Library, Union Theological College, Belfast. I'd like to express my thanks to the staff at Edinburgh University Press, particularly Jen Daly, Sarah Foyle and Eddie Clark, for their encouragement, patience and support through the publishing process, and to the anonymous readers for their comments and suggestions on the manuscript. The series editors, Crawford Gribben and Scott Spurlock, have been fantastic sources of guidance for many years, and I'm grateful to Crawford, who also examined the thesis on which this book is based, for encouraging me to 'get the proposal in'.

I am exceptionally grateful to my doctoral supervisors, Andrew Holmes and Graham Walker, for almost a decade (gulp) of support, guidance and encouragement. Andrew has always been patient and generous with his advice and expertise, and helped me fully understand what I was actually writing about, as well as the meaning of deadlines! Just don't let him drive you to historic landmarks without a map. Graham's help and enthusiasm has been invaluable during the last ten years, and I have learnt a lot from our frequent tea- and coffee-fuelled discussions on everything from Scottish and Irish politics to Bob Dylan and the Northern Ireland and Scotland football teams. I like to think Andrew and Graham have also learnt a lot about professional cycling from me, whether they wanted to or not. I especially thank them for their comments and feedback on drafts of this work, and for their unwavering support and friendship. I've also known Colin Kidd for ten years now, from my first class at Queen's to my MLitt at the University of St Andrews and beyond, and I should thank him for always being generous with his time, guidance and good humour. S. J. Brown examined my doctoral thesis, and I thank him for his ever-insightful feedback and advice. I'd like to record my thanks to brilliant colleagues at Queen's who have helped and supported me in a variety of ways, including Marie Coleman, James Davis, Margaret O'Callaghan, Sean O'Connell and Olwen Purdue. I thank Daniel Ritchie for his insight into the topic and for generously sharing his research. Any errors of fact or the interpretation contained in this book are of course my own

I was lucky to share my PhD experience with a number of people I now count as friends, and I thank the following colleagues for their help, ideas and camaraderie, not to mention all the tea breaks, lunches, walks around Scrabo and games of two tap (yes, we invented a sport – anything to distract you from writing a chapter): Matthew Bingham and all the Bingham clan, Mark Benson, Morris Brodie, Conor Campbell, Jack Crangle, Ruairí Cullen, Laura Gillespie, Pete Hodson (and Chalky), Bridget Harrison, Benjamin Huskinson, Stuart Irwin, Sam Manning, Stuart Mathieson, Eliza McKee, Claire McNulty, Jamie Pow, Lucy Wray and everyone else who helped along the way. Outside of Queen's I've been fortunate to get to know a number of new, exciting scholars whose work has greatly influenced my own understanding of this book's subject area and of the broader history of religion in Scotland, including but not limited to Andrew Jones, Clare Loughlin, Felicity Loughlin, Russell Newton and Piotr Potocki. Jack Gebhard was also extremely helpful discussing ideas for this topic when we were Masters students.

I completed the book while working for the Estates Directorate at Queen's. I'd like to thank Lorraine McCallum, Richard McElnay and John Nugent for accommodating my teaching, writing and research, and for encouraging me along the way. I'd like to thank the whole of the Estates Directorate for being so welcoming, and by the time this book is published Chris Johnston might have convinced me to do a cycling tour of the Highlands with him! I'd also like to thank Junction café's largest shareholder, Paddy Brannigan, for his unfailing enthusiasm and first-class conversation skills, as he celebrates his retirement this year after over forty years at Queen's. I'm extremely grateful to my school History teachers, Catherine Loney and Ronnie McMullan, for fostering and encouraging my love for the subject

Finally, I should thank my friends, Ben Oliver, Georgia Brame, Thomas and Rebecca Greenaway, James Wilson and Michael Magennis, for providing a welcome distraction from writing and editing, though most of them are still bemused by the book's subject area. I'm very grateful to my parents, Tony and Angela, my brother Connor and all the Mallons, Faulkners, Magills and Brownlees for their support over the last few years (I'm sure Alfie could write this book's sequel!), and to the dogs, Tommy and Bonnie, for always being there when we need them. I'd like to especially thank the 'wee cousins', Finley, Dylan, Regan and Freya, for the hours of fun, wonder and enjoyment – I can't wait to read their own books. Most of all, I'd like to thank Chelsea Brownlee for putting up with me throughout the duration of this project, helping compile this book's bibliography, and for sharing in all the graft, trips (both research and leisure), gigs, gegs and all the fun of the last six years. I know the next few years will be even more exciting

This book is dedicated to my Granda Seamus, who gave me my first sources.

Ryan Mallon
Dromore, March 2021

Introduction

On 18 May 1843, following a lengthy protest read by the retiring moderator David Welsh, a group of evangelical Presbyterian ministers filed out of the General Assembly of the Established Church of Scotland and walked in solemn procession to Tanfield Hall, Edinburgh, where they formally constituted themselves as the Free Protesting Church of Scotland. Out of a total of 1,195 ordained ministers, 474 seceded from the national church during the 'Great Disruption' and they were followed by 192 probationary ministers and roughly half of the laity. They did so in protest against the perceived intrusion of the British state in the spiritual affairs of the Scottish Kirk. According to these evangelical 'non-intrusionists', led by the most influential churchman of his age, Thomas Chalmers, the 'spiritual independence' of the Presbyterian Church was under threat from an alien and largely Anglican government in London. Erastian British statesmen, claimed the non-intrusionists, did not understand Presbyterianism – and in particular its adherence to the doctrine of the 'two kingdoms', which stipulated that Christ, not the monarch, was the head of the Church and that the church and state each had complete sovereignty over their own province – and appeared to be actively subverting it, in direct contravention of the terms of the 1707 Treaty of Union. The Disruption marked the climax of over a decade of ecclesiological conflict not only between the non-intrusionists and the government, but also within the Church of Scotland itself and wider Presbyterianism in general. By leaving the state church, the non-intrusionist ministers voluntarily gave up their manses and stipends, and the security associated with life in the establishment, in exchange for a precarious future, with many preaching to their congregations the following Sunday in fields, barns and public halls. The schism in the national church dominated national discourse in Scotland, divided families and had a lasting influence on Scottish religious, political and social life.

The Disruption was the most important event in Victorian Scotland, and had a profound effect on the future of British religion.[1] S. J. Brown described the Disruption as a 'tragedy for organised religion in Scotland',

---

1. S. J. Brown and Michael Fry (eds), *Scotland in the age of the Disruption* (Edinburgh, 1993), vii–xi; W. M. Hetherington, *History of the Church of Scotland; from the introduction of Christianity to the period of the Disruption in 1843* (New York, 1856), 467; D. J. Withrington, 'The Disruption: a century and a half of historical interpretation', *RSCHS*, xxv (1993), 118–53.

with the remainder of the nineteenth century characterised by competition between the various Presbyterian denominations, which 'thwarted the revival of any national feeling of Christian community'.[2] Beyond its impact on the ecclesiastical make-up of Scotland, the Disruption was, according to James Kellas, also instrumental in reshaping Scottish politics, education, society and national identity.[3] The historians and Church of Scotland ministers Andrew Drummond and James Bulloch have argued that the Disruption marked both the 'birth of Victorian Scotland' and the end of Scotland's national history, as the traditions and distinctive character of Scottish life and its old national institutions slowly began to give way to the bureaucracy of centralised government in London.[4] John McCaffrey has also termed it the beginning of Scotland's 'modern era', while Michael Fry has gone so far as to claim that the political and ecclesiastical events of the 1830s and 1840s amounted to a 'Scottish Revolution'.[5]

The events of May 1843 also resulted in, to all intents and purposes, the creation of a new and powerful dissenting church in Scotland at a time when England, Ireland and Scotland's state churches were coming under threat from an increasingly influential nonconformist campaign for disestablishment.[6] As S. J. Brown has recently noted, despite the wealth of scholarship on the Disruption and the 'Ten Years' Conflict' that preceded it, little has been written on the Disruption's turbulent aftermath.[7] This book will focus on the relationship between the two major Scottish non-established churches after 1843: the newly formed Free Church of Scotland, which emerged out of the Disruption, and the United Secession and Relief churches which would unite in 1847 to form the United Presbyterian Church, the third-largest Presbyterian church in Scotland behind the state and Free churches. While the Free Church was formed out of the politico-ecclesiastical struggle of the previous decade's 'Ten Years' Conflict', the United Presbyterian Church represented an amalgamation of the various strands of Scotland's eighteenth-century secessions from the Established Church.

Though after 1843 these two churches nominally formed the bulk of an enlarged Scottish Presbyterian dissenting contingent (together they accounted for roughly half of Scotland's churchgoing population), they

---

2. S. J. Brown, *Thomas Chalmers and the Godly Commonwealth in Scotland* (Oxford, 1982), 337, 374.
3. James G. Kellas, 'The Liberal Party and the Scottish Church Disestablishment Crisis', *English Historical Review*, lxxix (1964), 31.
4. A. L. Drummond and James Bulloch, *The Church in Victorian Scotland 1843–1874* (Edinburgh, 1975), 4.
5. J. F. McCaffrey, *Scotland in the Nineteenth Century* (Basingstoke, 1998), 38; Michael Fry, *Patronage and Principle* (Aberdeen, 1987), 59.
6. S. J. Brown, *The National Churches of England, Ireland, and Scotland, 1801–46* (Oxford, 2001).
7. S. J. Brown, 'Religion and Society to c.1900', in T. M. Devine and Jenny Wormald (eds), *The Oxford Handbook of Modern Scottish History* (Oxford, 2014), 92.

advocated very different visions of Presbyterianism. Despite seceding from the national kirk, the Free Church, which maintained after 1843 that it represented the 'true' Church of Scotland free from government intrusion and the corruptions of the current state church, initially at least retained its adherence to the establishment principle and believed that the state should endow and recognise the church but not interfere in its affairs. The United Presbyterians on the other hand advocated the voluntary principle in religion and called for the disestablishment of the Church of Scotland, a belief that led them to engage in a bitter dispute, known as the 'Voluntary Controversy', in the decade before the Disruption with those ministers who would go on to form the Free Church. Ecclesiastical establishments, formed in the wake of the Protestant Reformation to assert doctrinal and disciplinary uniformity on the existing churches by the English, Irish and Scottish monarchical states, were anathema to the voluntaries' ideal of religious liberty. However, despite these differences in principle and the lingering hostility of the pre-Disruption period, by 1863 the Free and United Presbyterian churches had begun negotiations for the union of their two denominations, a remarkable turnaround that Iain Hutchison has described as akin in ecclesiastical terms to the Nazi–Soviet pact of 1939.[8] This book aims to assess this dramatic shift in dissenting relations by placing it within the context of a Scotland that was changing religiously, politically and socially.

Following the major upheaval of the Disruption, the two decades between 1843 and 1863 represent a transitional period for both Presbyterianism and wider Scottish society. This study examines how the major dissenting churches reacted to the uncertainty of this period and how they attempted to shape the changing character of post-Disruption Scotland. It explores the kind of Presbyterianism that emerged from the disparate elements of Scottish nonconformity and whether a unified dissenting identity emerged within the Free and United Presbyterian churches before 1863. Were the establishmentarian and voluntary strands of Presbyterian dissent able to find common ground that would allow the two churches to effectively challenge the Established Church, and if so, was this common purpose based upon a positive affirmation of dissent or did it rely solely upon a shared opposition to the existing establishment? To answer this question the book assesses the attempts at co-operation between the Free and United Presbyterian churches concerning the major ecclesiastical, political and social issues of the period. By doing so, it will trace the path that led to the union negotiations of the 1860s, placing them within the context of the previous twenty years of dissenting relations.

Perhaps most broadly, the book will attempt to ascertain what the term 'dissent' actually meant in post-Disruption Scotland. The term 'dissenting'

---

8. I. G. C. Hutchison, *Industry, Reform and Empire: Scotland, 1790–1880* (Edinburgh, 2020), 140.

will be used throughout to refer to those Presbyterian churches which existed outside of the Established Church.[9] However, how the Free and United Presbyterian churches viewed themselves under the wider umbrella of Scottish dissent – and whether the Free Church can even be described as a dissenting church at all – is an entirely different matter. As we have seen, the Free Church (initially at least) viewed itself as Scotland's true national kirk and the majority, though not all, of its members hotly repudiated the term 'dissenter' in the years after the Disruption. After 1843, as the Free Kirk sought to elevate itself above Scotland's older seceding churches by claiming to be the rightful heir of the country's Presbyterian heritage, it therefore occupied a state of 'principled denial' that it even existed as a dissenting body, let alone a voluntary one.[10] However, as this book demonstrates, in the two decades following the Disruption the Free Church increasingly joined its voluntary dissenting counterparts in championing the shared principles of unendowed or non-established Presbyterianism, including evangelicalism, spiritual independence and anti-erastianism. Though they may have rejected the dissenting tag and remained committed to pro-establishment principles, from the outset members of the Free Church were quasi-dissenters, standing between the extremes of voluntaryism and a sham establishment but increasingly embodying the sprit and character, if not the label, of Scottish Presbyterian dissent. Therefore, despite the denials of its leadership, in a practical sense the Free Kirk can be viewed as advocating a softer version of dissent, which criticised the existing state church but not necessarily the principle of religious establishments, while the United Presbyterians are generally viewed as representing the more radical elements of anti-state church voluntaryism. One of the major points of this study is to assess how these seemingly disparate ideological stances developed following the Disruption and if a single united vision of mainstream Presbyterian 'dissent', regardless of how it was labelled, formed within the two churches by 1863.

A Period of Transition: Scottish Presbyterianism in the Aftermath of the Disruption

The twenty years between the Disruption of 1843 and the commencement of negotiations for dissenting union between the Free and United Presbyterian churches in 1863 was a period of transition for Scottish Presbyterianism. The Disruption marked the first time, since the Revolution Settlement at least, that the Church of Scotland failed to account for a

---

9. The description will also apply to non-Presbyterian Scottish Protestants, such as the Baptist and Congregational churches, who found common cause with their non-established Presbyterian counterparts in dissenting, evangelical, political or anti-Catholic societies.
10. Colin Kidd and Valerie Wallace, 'Biblical Criticism and Scots Presbyterian Dissent in the age of Robertson Smith', in Scott Mandelbrote and Michael Ledger-Thomas (eds), *Dissent and the Bible in Britain* (Oxford, 2013), 235.

majority of the Scottish people. It was estimated that in the year after the Disruption, of 2.6 million Scots, only 900,000 belonged to the establishment.[11] By the 1851 Religious Census, just over 32 per cent of churchgoers on census Sunday were part of the Established Kirk; in contrast, the combined total of the Free and United Presbyterian churches amounted to roughly half of all churchgoers (with a further 2 per cent attending the Reformed Presbyterian and Original Secession churches). In Glasgow and Edinburgh the impact of the Disruption was even starker. In both cities the Established Church represented less than 20 per cent of the population, while in Edinburgh the Free and United Presbyterian churches together accounted for two-thirds of the Scottish capital's churchgoers.[12]

The numerical impact of the events of May 1843 was compounded by major social and political changes from the mid-1840s that further weakened the national influence of the now minority state Kirk. In 1845 Robert Peel's Tory government introduced the Poor Law Amendment Act that removed the national church's traditional control over the administration of poor relief and placed it in the hands of the state. A dissenting campaign to enact a similar change in education by resituating the Church of Scotland's parish schools as part of a state-run national system also began to gather momentum by the end of the decade. More broadly, the decision by Peel in 1845 to increase the annual stipend afforded to the Roman Catholic seminary at Maynooth redefined the relationship between Britain's Protestant established churches and the state at a time when the Established Church of Scotland appeared increasingly vulnerable.[13] The developments of the mid-1840s were in many respects a culmination of the earlier reforms of the late 1820s and early 1830s, and underlined the emergence of a new 'script' in Scottish society in which the Kirk had an increasingly peripheral role.[14] According to Lindsay Paterson, any arguments in support of the state-like authority of the Church of Scotland, under threat from the rise of dissent before 1843, had been dismantled at the Disruption.[15] The cataclysmic events of May 1843, combined with the subsequent secularisation of the Kirk's traditional civil responsibility for poor relief and education, were integral to the emergence of a more pluralist denominational landscape in Scotland and spelled the end of the religious, political and social hegemony of a monolithic state church. However, though the Disruption heralded the waning influence of the Kirk upon the life of the common Scot, as Callum Brown and others have observed, Presbyterianism, and

11. *FCM*, i (January 1844), 9–13.
12. Callum G. Brown, *The Social History of Religion in Scotland since 1730* (Cambridge, 1987), 61; Graeme Morton, *Ourselves and Others: Scotland 1832–1914* (Edinburgh, 2012), 208.
13. Jonathan Parry, *The Rise and Fall of Liberal Government in Victorian Britain* (New Haven, 1993), 163.
14. T. C. Smout, *A Century of the Scottish People 1830–1950* (London, 1986), 181–4.
15. Lindsay Paterson, *The Autonomy of Modern Scotland* (Edinburgh, 1994), 56.

religion in general, remained robust and significant in a changing society, though the reasons for that significance would be fundamentally altered.[16]

For instance, Presbyterianism remained integral to conceptions of Scottishness and national identity, but the variety of these identities and how they were expressed irrevocably changed. Though it had not been the case for over a century, the myth of the synonymous relationship between the Established Church of Scotland and Scottish identity was shattered by the Disruption, and replaced by a multitude of denominational identities that each claimed ownership of Scotland's Presbyterian history and national character. In a recent essay on the denominational press, Colin Kidd and Valerie Wallace have argued that in the nineteenth century Scottishness was related 'not in terms of national grievance or nationalist assertion, but according to distinctive denominational perspectives. Confessional allegiances – rather than nationhood per se – framed the national story.'[17] Therefore, as James Coleman and Neil Forsyth have argued, the period after 1843 was marked by attempts by the three major Presbyterian denominations to assert their own denominational identity and its association with Scottish history, in essence claiming Scotland's Presbyterian past for their church.

During a period in which the position and identity of Scotland's national church was highly ambiguous, by claiming to be the legitimate 'true' Church of Scotland, the Scottish churches, whether established or dissenting, could attempt to control the future of Scottish Presbyterianism. According to Craig Beveridge, Ronnie Turnbull and others, the Church of Scotland and its history was the primary 'source of inspiration for a Scottish liberal-democratic ideology' steeped in myth and tradition and tailored to suit the needs of churches desperate to assert their validity on a national scale.[18] This was especially true for the Free Church, which consciously embodied a Presbyterian Whig interpretation of Scottish history centred upon what Coleman has termed the mythological 'leitmotif' of civil and religious liberty stretching back as far as the Culdees and incorporating the Reformation and covenanting movement.[19] For instance, the open-air worship employed by the protesting Evangelicals at Strathbogie

---

16. Brown, 'Religion and Society'; Alice Brown, David McCrone and Lindsay Paterson, *Politics and Society in Scotland* (London, 1996), 1.
17. Colin Kidd, 'Union and the ironies of displacement in Scottish literature', Valerie Wallace and Colin Kidd, 'Between Nationhood and Nonconformity: The Scottish Whig-Presbyterian novel and the denominational press', in Gerard Carruthers and Colin Kidd (eds), *Literature and Union: Scottish texts, British contexts* (Oxford, 2018), 28, 197.
18. Craig Beveridge and Ronnie Turnbull, *Scotland after Enlightenment: Image and Tradition in Modern Scottish Culture* (Edinburgh, 1997), 96; Colin Kidd and James Coleman, 'Mythical Scotland', in Devine and Wormald, *The Oxford Handbook of Modern Scottish History*, 63.
19. James Coleman, *Remembering the Past in Nineteenth-century Scotland: Commemoration, Nationality and Memory* (Edinburgh, 2014), 130, 133.

during the Ten Years' Conflict recalled similar methods employed by the later Covenanters and allowed the non-intrusionists to identify directly with their Presbyterian forbears, and present themselves as the 'true successors' of the covenanting era by fighting for the Kirk's religious and constitutional liberty. On the other hand, those who remained in the state church after the Disruption, especially its majority Moderate party, were identified with the 'discredited' Restoration settlement of 1660.[20] The narrative constructed by the non-intrusionists that they, and they alone, represented the historic Church of Scotland would become an important component of evangelical propaganda and formed the ideological basis of the Free Church after 1843.[21]

While the voluntaries in the United Presbyterian Church also adopted this rhetoric, Forsyth and most recently Coleman have emphasised the Free Church's status as the 'mother lode of the Scottish Whig interpretation of British history' and its 'triple association' between the people of Scotland, the Kirk, and civil and religious liberty.[22] The events of 1843 would have a profound effect on the reimagining and redefining of Scotland's nineteenth-century interpretation of its religious, political and national history. Marinell Ash argued that diverging interests within the middle class after the Disruption ended any authoritative Kirk-driven vision of the Scottish past, though as Coleman has acknowledged, in order to claim its place as Scotland's true national church, the Free Church 'positioned itself as the church most closely aligned with the mainstream of Scottish Presbyterian history'.[23]

Yet the desire to represent the true national Church of Scotland was not limited to the Free Kirk and would prove central to the formation of a distinctly dissenting identity within Scottish Presbyterianism after 1843. While Scottish Presbyterian history has been intrinsically linked with secessions from the national church, the Disruption was the first schism to place dissent truly on an equal footing with the establishment in religious, political and social matters. Though Seceders believed that they represented the pure and uncorrupted Church of Scotland after 1733, the period after 1843 called into question where that church was actually situated and what it represented in an industrial, pluralist Scotland. This study will assess how the impact of the Disruption allowed for a common ground to emerge between Scotland's major non-established Presbyterian churches, and overturned the roles of Scotland's churches and their place in society. It will

20. Thomas Smith, *Memoirs of James Begg* (2 volumes, Edinburgh, 1885), ii, 17; Hetherington, *History of the Church of Scotland*, 205–7.
21. Ryan Mallon, 'A church for Scotland? The Free Church and Scottish Nationalism after the Disruption', *Scottish Church History*, 49 (2020), 1–24.
22. Neil Forsyth, 'Presbyterian historians and the Scottish invention of British liberty', *RSCHS*, xxxiv (2004), 104, 109–10.
23. Marinell Ash, *The Strange Death of Scottish History* (Edinburgh, 1980), 13–15, 124–52; Coleman, *Remembering the Past*, 93–4.

question the extent to which this common ground developed and if and how a 'dissenting' identity emerged in the Free and United Presbyterian churches between 1843 and 1863 to challenge the Established Church and in effect create a de facto non-established Church of Scotland after the Disruption.

The twenty years between 1843 and 1863 also witnessed a period of transition and immense change within Scottish dissent. As will be outlined in Chapter One, the non-intrusionists who would go on to form the Free Church in May 1843 and the 'old' dissenters in the United Secession and Relief churches had been engaged throughout the 1830s in a bitter dispute over the future of the church–state connection. In the aftermath of the Disruption, the traditional lines of division between the voluntaries and the newly formed Free Church remained intact. Though they had quit what Chalmers had described as a 'vitiated' national church, the Free Kirk, like the majority of eighteenth-century Seceders, retained their belief in the principle of a religious establishment, but one that was spiritually independent, 'pure' and free from state intrusion. Despite the sanguine hopes of their new dissenting colleagues, they were not, as Chalmers famously declared at the Free Church's inaugural assembly, voluntaries.[24] While the Free Kirk nominally occupied the same position of dissent as their counterparts in the voluntary United Secession and Relief churches (which had been engaged in ever-closer co-operation from the early 1830s), ecclesiastically they, initially at least, stood on opposite ends of the Scottish Presbyterian ideological spectrum. Unlike the proud voluntaryism of what would become the United Presbyterians, the Free Church carried a somewhat awkward quasi-dissenting stance, detached from both the Established Church and the overt anti-establishment principles of mainstream Presbyterian dissent. The awkwardness of the Free Church position was most neatly encapsulated by the staunchly establishmentarian Edinburgh minister James Begg, who claimed that 'no church in Christendom is more deeply committed to the principle of a Church Establishment' than the nominally dissenting Free Church.[25]

However, by 1863 a new era had emerged within the dissenting churches, led by a generation of ministers too young to have been involved in the bitter ecclesiological struggles of the Ten Years' Conflict and the Voluntary Controversy. This new era began with the commencement of negotiations between the Free and United Presbyterians regarding the possibility of church union, which continued intermittently between 1863 and 1873. These negotiations were originally based on a policy of mutual forbearance on the divisive issues of voluntaryism and the establishment principle. However, after a decade of negotiations and following an often hostile campaign by an increasingly marginal conservative and establishmentar-

24. *PGAFC, May 1843* (Edinburgh, 1843), 11–13, 99.
25. James Begg, *The Union Question* (Edinburgh, 1868), 3.

ian wing of the Free Church, largely based in the Highlands and led by Begg and John Kennedy, the potential union was 'wrecked on the reefs of the establishment principle'.[26] Nevertheless the union negotiations, which took place amid a campaign for the abolition of patronage in the state church and the wider context of disestablishment rhetoric in Britain and Ireland, underlined the growing influence of voluntaryism in the Free Church under the leadership of Robert Rainy, especially in the Lowlands. Rainy would prove instrumental in securing the Free Church's support for Scotland's own disestablishment campaign from the 1870s.[27]

Kidd and Wallace have noted the ironies evident in the dramatic shift in Free Church attitudes only two decades after the Disruption. Voluntaryism, instead of seeking to destroy Scottish Presbyterianism, was now viewed by Free Church leaders such as Robert Rainy as an opportunity to unite the fragments of Scotland's religious community, in effect rewriting the church's own history.[28] These developments were reinforced by the decision by both the United Presbyterian and Free churches, in 1879 and 1893 respectively, to qualify their commitment to the Westminster Confession of Faith. The modification and effective 'liberalisation' of one of the hitherto fundamental tenets of Scottish Presbyterianism provoked a schism within the Free Church, as the conservative establishmentarian wing seceded to form the Free Presbyterian Church. It also paved the way for the union of the Free and United Presbyterian churches, and the creation of the United Free Church in 1900.[29] As excellent recent scholarship by S. J. Brown and Andrew Jones has shown, the period after 1863 also witnessed a remarkable rejuvenation of the Established Kirk itself. The upturn in fortunes of the so-called 'residual' establishment was successful in halting the dissenting challenge that dominated the twenty years after the Disruption, and would ultimately prove the ruin of the disestablishment campaign.[30]

---

26. Kidd and Wallace, 'Biblical Criticism and Scots Presbyterian Dissent', 244.
27. J. P. Parry, *Democracy and Religion: Gladstone and the Liberal Party 1867–1875* (Cambridge, 1986), 103–4, 220; Ewen A. Cameron, *Impaled upon a thistle: Scotland since 1880* (Edinburgh, 2010), 64–5; Kellas, 'The Liberal Party and Scottish Disestablishment', 32.
28. Kidd and Wallace, 'Biblical Criticism and Scots Presbyterian Dissent', 241–4; Drummond and Bulloch, *The Church in Victorian Scotland*, 329–37.
29. J. L. McLeod, *The Second Disruption: the Free Church in Victorian Scotland and the origins of the Free Presbyterian Church* (East Linton, 2000); Morton, *Ourselves and Others*, 211–12; Cameron, *Impaled upon a thistle*, 25; G. I. T. Machin, 'Voluntaryism and Reunion 1874–1929', in Norman Macdougall (ed.), *Church, Politics and Society: Scotland 1408–1929* (Edinburgh, 1983), 221–38.
30. S. J. Brown, 'After the Disruption: the recovery of the national Church of Scotland, 1843–1874', *Scottish Church History*, 48 (2019), 103–25; Andrew Jones, 'The Continuation, Breadth, and Impact of Evangelicalism in the Church of Scotland, 1843–1900', unpublished PhD thesis, University of Edinburgh (2018).

Outline of Contents

If 1843 marked the final death blow of the vision of Scotland as a covenanted, godly nation led by the Kirk, 1863 represented the start of a new era for Presbyterianism, which began with negotiations for dissenting union, the campaign for disestablishment, and culminated in the 1929 reunion of the Church of Scotland. The disparity between these two distinct phases of Scottish Presbyterian history underlines the necessity of a study of the intervening period. By focusing on the ecclesiastical, political and social co-operation of the Free and United Presbyterian churches between 1843 and 1863, this book will assess the reaction of Scottish Presbyterian dissent to the changing landscape of post-Disruption Scotland and question to what extent the distinctly dissenting identity that dominated the years after 1863 emerged in this period.

The book consists of four sections, each containing two chapters, which assess the ideological, ecclesiastical, political and social development of Scottish dissent in the twenty years after Disruption. These sections question whether dissenting co-belligerence, where it existed, was based upon common principles or common opponents. While the Free and United Presbyterians shared an antagonism for both state intrusion in the affairs of the Kirk and the perceived hegemony of the Established Church, they were divided by their conflicting views on the church–state relationship. The first section therefore addresses the shifting and malleable character of dissent before and after 1843. Chapter One provides an overview of how dissent emerged and changed throughout Scottish Presbyterian history up to the Disruption, and in doing so outlines the provenance of the Free and United Presbyterian churches. The chapter details the origins of the eighteenth-century secessions from the Kirk and the reasons for these schisms, assesses the changing identities of the seceding churches during the late eighteenth and early nineteenth centuries, and evaluates the role of the Voluntary Controversy and the Ten Years' Conflict in the formation of the Free Church.

The second chapter examines the role of the establishment and voluntary principles in the Free Kirk's attempt to cement their position as the 'true' national Church of Scotland in the immediate years after the Disruption. It assesses the extent of the Free Kirk's success in creating a truly national church from scratch through voluntary methods, an achievement which has been the subject of some scholarly debate.[31] However, the methods utilised by the Free Church as it attempted to gain national standing in the immediate aftermath of the Disruption, either through voluntary funding

---

31. Drummond and Bulloch, *The Church in Victorian Scotland*, 33; Brown, *National Churches*, 359; Gerald Parsons, 'Church and State in Victorian Scotland: Disruption and Union', in Gerald Parsons (ed.), *Religion in Victorian Britain, Volume II: Controversies* (Manchester, 1988), 115–16.

or church union, have never been fully examined. This study addresses this gap by analysing both the national rhetoric and success of the new church, and will attempt to answer Brown's question – how did the Free Church become a 'national' church after 1843?

The Free Kirk's relationship with voluntaryism, and its compatibility with its 'national' outlook, is equally ambiguous. During the Voluntary Controversy, future Free Churchmen denounced voluntaryism as atheistic and averse to the principle of national religion. While the Free Church retained its stated abhorrence of the voluntary principle after the Disruption (a stance that significantly cooled dissenting support for the new church), outside of the establishment they now adopted a position of 'practical' voluntaryism, relying on the contributions of their own members to create a new national church. However, whether it embraced voluntaryism as an ideal upon which Presbyterian church government should be based is an entirely different and much more problematic issue. According to Drummond and Bulloch, their new dissenting stance and the changing beliefs of their own members meant that the Free Church drift to the voluntary principles of the United Presbyterians was 'inevitable'.[32] The chapter discusses if this was indeed true, and whether the new church experienced an ideological as well as a practical shift to voluntaryism after 1843, particularly as the realities of their new dissenting position came into conflict with the insistence on maintaining a national character. For instance, Andrew Muirhead pointed out that the practical restraints of voluntary funding, which emphasised the need to provide for the local church, hindered the Free Kirk's national ambitions.[33] Did the practical realities and challenges of the Free Church's new dissenting position make their deeply entrenched establishment and 'national' principles a 'dead letter'?[34]

While the first section assesses whether the churches' respective adherence to the establishment and voluntary principles could coexist within the new dissenting framework in Scotland, the second section questions how this impacted co-operation between the Free and United Presbyterian churches and their challenge to the Established Kirk. While the Free Church had to adapt to the practicalities associated with voluntary-funded religion, the Disruption also ensured that, regardless of its ideological stance, it now joined an increasingly strong group of Presbyterian dissenting churches in Scotland. Prior to 1843, Presbyterian dissent was generally a unified force working together to challenge the Church of Scotland. Did the Free Church join this united front, based on a common evangelical and dissenting stance, to create a non-established and national alternative to the Church of Scotland? Or were any attempts at finding a middle ground

32. Drummond and Bulloch, *The Church in Victorian Scotland*, 14–15.
33. A. T. N. Muirhead, *Reformation, Dissent and Diversity: The Story of Scotland's Churches, 1560–1960* (London, 2015), 129.
34. Drummond and Bulloch, *The Church in Victorian Scotland*, 21.

overshadowed by lingering animosity and ideological divisions that saw the Free and United Presbyterian churches each lay their own claim to represent Scotland's national church? Chapter Three examines the working relationship between the churches after 1843, including the tentative attempts at ecclesiastical co-operation in the immediate aftermath of the Disruption and their dual role in the early years of the Evangelical Alliance, the grand confederation of Protestants established in 1846. The fourth chapter assesses how closer relations between Scotland's non-established Presbyterians opened the door for the dissenting church unions of 1847 and 1852, and the attempts in the mid-1850s to create a 'national dissenting church' through union between the Free and United Presbyterian churches.

This period has tended to be characterised in the historiography as one of sectarian animosity. Lindsay Paterson's depiction of the inter-church conflict of the period as one of 'petty jealousies' is echoed in Donald Withrington and Michael Fry's characterisation of the Free Church's 'proud and arrogant' sectarianism after 1843, which Fry claims indirectly led to the United Presbyterian union of 1847.[35] The fourth chapter assesses the 1847 union of the United Secession and Relief churches and the kind of Presbyterianism it espoused. Was the 1847 union a 'voluntary' union, and how did the Disruption and the nominally establishmentarian Free Church affect the new church's outlook? The Free Church attempt to 'renew the national Church' through the 1852 union with the Original Secession Church was also indicative of the new body's establishmentarian principles and 'principled denial' of its new-found dissenting position in its formative years.[36] Though historians have generally tended to overlook these church unions, they offer valuable insight into the development of Presbyterian dissent after 1843. For instance, was Scottish dissent in the decades after the Disruption defined by its adherence to voluntary principles or did it allow for a range of interpretations that would influence the future ideology and shifting character of Scottish Presbyterianism?

The following two sections examine how similar themes developed beyond the church walls and into political and social concerns. The third section focuses on the common thread of anti-Catholicism within the churches, and analyses their various responses to the controversial Maynooth endowment and the electoral alliance it produced. Chapter Five outlines the dissenting churches' reaction to the Maynooth controversy, the restoration of the Roman Catholic hierarchy in England during the so-called 'papal aggression', and the anti-popery movement that dominated British public discourse in the late 1840s and 1850s. In many respects anti-Catholicism was historically synonymous with Scotland's Presbyterian iden-

---

35. Paterson, *Autonomy of Modern Scotland*, 57–8; Fry, *Patronage and Principle*, 53; D. J. Withrington, 'Towards a New Social Conscience?', *RSCHS*, xix (1976), 160.
36. Kidd and Wallace, 'Biblical Criticism and Scots Presbyterian Dissent', 234–5, 240.

tity and had been a central feature of the defence of Britain's Protestant liberties from the Reformation. As Frank Wallis has argued, the rise of more modern religious movements such as evangelicalism underpinned the 'endemic' nature of mid-nineteenth-century British anti-popery, and shaped the response within the Free and United Presbyterian churches.[37] While the Maynooth controversy and the papal aggression appeared to offer a shared common enemy against which Scotland's dissenters could unite, the chapter questions how far this dissenting co-operation moved beyond simple anti-popery and allowed for a dissenting and anti-erastian vision of Protestantism to emerge within the churches.

Historians have been divided as to the extent to which anti-Catholicism played a role in fostering dissenting co-operation. Though Steve Bruce and Kenneth Boyd have questioned the prevalence of anti-Catholicism within Presbyterian dissent, Michael Dyer has argued that the increased state endowment of Maynooth brought Scotland's dissenters together as it offended the voluntaryism of the United Presbyterians and the anti-Catholicism of both churches.[38] Jonathan Parry has also claimed that anti-Catholicism acted as a unifier for nonconformists against the state church, which they believed lacked the zeal necessary to fight popery effectively.[39] Tom Gallagher, on the other hand, has claimed that the majority of Presbyterians were more concerned with 'their own internal schisms' than with tackling 'the menace of Rome'.[40] This view can be broadened to include the relevant inability to create a combined British Protestant movement as a bulwark against the perceived aggression of Roman Catholicism, with Kidd arguing that the differences between Scottish Presbyterianism and Anglican Episcopacy could not be so easily reduced to allow for a united British effort.[41] Chapter Five assesses how far a united dissenting effort against popery and Maynooth in particular was able to be maintained despite differences in principle. It also questions whether dissenting unity in the anti-popery movement of the mid-nineteenth century was based simply on a narrow opposition to Roman Catholicism or a more positive assertion of Protestant dissenting identity.

Chapter Six also shows how anti-Catholicism and dissenting co-operation played a major role in altering the complexion of Scottish electoral politics

37. G. I. T. Machin, *Politics and the Churches in Great Britain, 1832 to 1868* (Oxford, 1977), 100, 108–9; Frank Wallis, 'The Revival of the Anti-Maynooth Campaign in Britain, 1850–52', *Albion*, xix (1987), 528–9.
38. Dyer, *Men of Property and Intelligence: The Scottish Electoral System prior to 1884* (Aberdeen, 1996), 55; Steve Bruce, *No Pope of Rome: Anti-Catholicism in modern Scotland* (Edinburgh, 1985), 31–6; Kenneth Boyd, *Scottish church attitudes to sex, marriage and the family, 1850–1914* (Edinburgh, 1980), 19.
39. Parry, *Democracy and Religion*, 220.
40. Tom Gallagher, *Glasgow, The Uneasy Peace: Religious tension in modern Scotland* (Manchester, 1987), 34–5.
41. Colin Kidd, *Union and Unionisms: political thought in Scotland, 1500–2000* (Cambridge, 2008), 212.

for over a decade.[42] It examines the political alliance forged within the Liberal party by the Free and United Presbyterian churches based largely if not solely on a shared opposition to Maynooth. Throughout Scotland the alliance allowed middle-class radical dissenters to wrest control of the Liberal party from the ruling Whig elite. As was the case during the Voluntary Controversy, religion and politics were intertwined in Scotland and across Britain in the mid-nineteenth century. As Lindsay Paterson and Callum Brown have argued, politics was a means by which Scotland's churches could retain their power and influence within Scottish society after the Disruption.[43] Jonathan Parry and Boyd Hilton have observed the relationship between British nonconformity and the wider liberal political agenda, both of which aimed to combat the civil, political and economic discrimination of dissenters.[44] S. J. Brown, Machin, Timothy Larsen and more recently Valerie Wallace have acknowledged the often synonymous relationship between politically liberal and religious dissenting values, with Machin describing voluntaryism as 'a branch of civil liberty' and as 'springing from the same liberal, individualistic root as Free Trade'. Brown in particular has emphasised the influence of political liberalism upon Scottish voluntary thought and the role it played in cultivating among dissenters a vision of an egalitarian and individualistic Scotland that emphatically overturned the paternalism of Chalmers' godly commonwealth. This vision, Brown argued, appealed most convincingly to the liberal and dissenting heartlands, the merchants and manufacturers of the cities.[45] The growth of militant political radicalism in both England and Scotland, particularly from the 1830s, had sprung out of the religious agitations of voluntary churchmen against the established churches.[46] According to H. J. Hanham, this legacy of shared religious and political grievances against the establishment ensured that the United Presbyterians were generally more radical than their Free Church counterparts.[47] However, Larsen has argued that

42. I. G. C. Hutchison, *A Political History of Scotland 1832–1924, Parties, Elections and Issues* (Edinburgh, 1986), 61.
43. C. G. Brown, 'Religion and Secularism', in A. Dickson and J. H. Treble (eds), *People and Society in Scotland, Vol. III, 1914–1990* (Edinburgh, 1992), 65; Paterson, *Autonomy of Modern Scotland*, 57–9.
44. Parry, *Democracy and Religion*, 200, 255–7; Boyd Hilton, *The Age of Atonement: the Influence of Evangelicalism on Social and Economic Thought, 1785–1865* (Oxford, 1988), 342.
45. Stewart J. Brown, 'Religion and the Rise of Liberalism: The Disestablishment Campaign in Scotland, 1829–1843', *Journal of Ecclesiastical History*, xlviii (1997), 682–4; Machin, *Politics and the Churches in Great Britain*, 100, 108; Timothy Larsen, *Friends of Religious Equality: nonconformist politics in mid-Victorian England* (Woodbridge, 1999); Valerie Wallace, 'Benthamite Radicalism and its Scots Presbyterian Contexts', *Utilitas*, xxiv (2012), 1–25.
46. Larsen, *Friends of Religious Equality*, 257; Brown, 'Religion and the Rise of Liberalism', 682–704; R. J. Morris, *Class and Class Consciousness in the Industrial Revolution 1780–1850* (London, 1979), 38.
47. H. J. Hanham, 'Mid-Century Scottish Nationalism: Romantic and Radical', in Robert Robson (ed.), *Ideas and Institutions of Victorian Britain: Essays in honour of George Kitson Clark* (London, 1967), 156.

mid-Victorian English militant voluntaries were successful in shifting the political centre of gravity among their fellow moderate dissenters in a more radical direction.[48] Did this shift also occur within Scottish Presbyterian dissent? This chapter assesses if the Free Church, by engaging in an electoral alliance based on the anti-Maynooth campaign, embraced the dissenting and liberal-radical political values of the United Presbyterians.

The anti-Maynooth campaign would have a profound impact on the relationship between Scottish liberalism and Presbyterian dissent. According to I. G. C. Hutchison and Gordon Millar, Free Church and voluntary leaders such as Duncan McLaren, for a brief period at least, utilised the agitation as a 'dynamo of resistance' to 'refashion Scottish political representation more to their taste'. Millar has suggested that the prominence of Maynooth in Scottish political debate during the 1840s and 1850s highlighted the increasingly harmonious relations and desire for united action within Scottish nonconformity.[49] Chapter Six explores the extent to which this dissenting alliance allowed for a unified political vision that moved beyond Maynooth and articulated a broader anti-Whig and radical agenda. However, as Karly Kehoe and John Wolffe have argued, this new-found cordiality among Scotland's dissenters was 'more apparent than real', with deeply rooted ideological, ecclesiastical and often personal divisions once again threatening to overshadow the flimsy foundations of a shared anti-Catholicism.[50] Michael Fry has elaborated on this point, claiming Scottish dissenting radicals politically capitalised on the anti-Catholic fervour gripping Scotland after 1845 by playing up their perceived opposition to popery in an attempt to attract the electoral support of militant Protestant Free Churchmen.[51] Did a liberal-radical vision of dissenting Presbyterian politics emerge in the years after 1843, or was the electoral alliance of the 1840s and 1850s simply a marriage of convenience based on the narrow platform of opposition to Maynooth?

The final section assesses the changing social role of Presbyterianism after the Disruption. Chapter Seven examines the social activism of the dissenting churches both within Scotland's cities and in reform societies, in particular focusing on how Chalmers' ideal of a godly commonwealth of kirk-centred religious communities was reinterpreted in its new voluntary context, following the Poor Law Amendment Act of 1845. For instance, Callum Brown has argued that the Free Church increasingly became dominated by the upwardly mobile middle class of Scotland's major cities.[52] The

---

48. Larsen, *Friends of Religious Equality*, 11, 262–3.
49. G. F. Millar, 'Maynooth and Scottish Politics: the role of the Maynooth Grant issue, 1845–1857', *RSCHS*, xxvii (1997), 227.
50. S. K. Kehoe, *Creating a Scottish Church: Catholicism, gender and ethnicity in nineteenth-century Scotland* (Manchester, 2010), 59; John Wolffe, *The Protestant Crusade in Great Britain 1829–1860* (Oxford, 1991), 249.
51. Fry, *Patronage and Principle*, 38.
52. Brown, *Social History of Religion*, 38.

chapter questions whether this new urban middle-class character, traditionally associated with the older dissenting churches such as the United Presbyterians, hampered Chalmers' aim to instil the godly commonwealth ideal throughout Scotland and create a national church that appealed to all classes. To Kenneth Boyd, the Disruption killed Chalmers' communal dream.[53] Nevertheless, others have highlighted the more socially aware plans of the Free Church after 1843, with territorial operations such as in the West Port of Edinburgh emphasising communal responsibility as well as individual salvation.[54] However, Smout has claimed that few heeded Chalmers' social message after 1843, while Drummond and Bulloch argued that the new system of territorial churches was merely 'a sop to conscience' in a rapidly changing ecclesiastical and social landscape.[55] Others, such as the Marxist historian Allan MacLaren, have agreed, claiming that the Free Kirk slowly submerged into the middle-class voluntaryism traditionally associated with the United Presbyterians, which lessened the national and social influence of the self-proclaimed 'church of the people'.[56] However, Donald Withrington and Smout have praised the 'Christian morality' of the United Presbyterian social mission, which acted both as a spur to contemporary movements in the Free Church and also in later political and labour movements.[57] This chapter examines the attempts of the dissenting churches to reclaim Scotland's 'sunken' masses, and whether a dissenting social vision was possible in the post-godly commonwealth period of the mid-nineteenth century.

The final chapter assesses the role of the Free and United Presbyterian churches in the campaign for national education. From the early 1830s, the questions regarding the position of national education in Britain and Ireland formed part of the broader battle between Church and dissent in the mid-nineteenth century.[58] Increasingly, debates on the future of national education in Britain were viewed as a struggle between the established churches and an apparently unified dissenting interest growing in confidence and aiming to challenge the national churches' statutory supremacy in education and privileged position in British society in general.[59] This was

53. Boyd, *Scottish Church Attitudes*, 15.
54. S. J. Brown, 'The Christian Socialist movement in Scotland c. 1850–1930', *Political Theology* (November 1999), 63; W. G. Enright, 'Urbanisation and the Evangelical Pulpit in Nineteenth-Century Scotland', *Church History*, xlvii (1978), 405.
55. Smout, *A Century of the Scottish People*, 183; Drummond and Bulloch, *The Church in Victorian Scotland*, 20.
56. Allan MacLaren, *Religion and Social Class: The Disruption Years in Aberdeen* (London, 1974), 30; Enright, 'Urbanisation and the Evangelical Pulpit', 400–2; Boyd, *Scottish Church Attitudes*, 16.
57. Withrington, 'Towards a New Social Conscience?', 159–60; Smout, *A Century of the Scottish People*, 188–9, 206.
58. Machin, *Politics and the Churches in Great Britain*, 165.
59. D. G. Paz, *The Politics of Working-Class Education in Britain, 1830–50* (Manchester, 1980), 142–3; John Stevenson, 'Scottish Schooling in the Denominational Era', in Robert

most evident in the 1843 defeat of Sir James Graham's Factory Education Bill, which has been viewed as a resounding dissenting victory against government plans to legislate for the expansion of the Church of England's education provision.[60] In Scotland, the national education debates offered Scotland's dissenters a similar opportunity to attack the perceived privilege of the Established Church and its control over the parish schools. Organisations such as the National Education Association of Scotland that called for a state-run non-denominational system to replace the parish schools were primarily under the influence of Scottish dissent and were viewed by those in the Church of Scotland as vehicles formed simply to harm the establishment. However, Withrington has acknowledged that the future direction of education in Scotland divided not only the dissenting churches, but the Free Church itself.[61] This chapter examines the extent to which the national education debates unified Scotland's dissenters in a common goal against the Established Kirk's parish schools, or whether they simply highlighted the existing divisions within Scottish dissent.

In many respects, the education debates, like the other aspects of ecclesiastical, political and social co-operation covered in this book, provide an interesting snapshot of Presbyterian dissenting relations in the transition period between 1843 and 1863. Though the Free and United Presbyterian churches may have been united in their opposition to a residual and erastian establishment, the formation of a common dissenting agenda and identity to effectively challenge the Church of Scotland and take advantage of the changing ecclesiastical, political and social context of post-Disruption Scotland remained under threat from sectarian jealousies and inter-church conflict. The extent to which this dissenting identity was created in the aftermath of the Disruption will be the subject of this study.

Anderson, Mark Freeman and Lindsay Paterson (eds), *The Edinburgh History of Education in Scotland* (Edinburgh, 2015), 135–40; Gerald Parsons, 'Reform, Revival and Realignment: The Experience of Victorian Anglicanism', in Gerald Parsons (ed.), *Religion in Victorian Britain, Volume I: Traditions* (Manchester, 1988), 59–60.
60. David Hempton, *Methodism and Politics in British Society 1750–1850* (London, 1984), 149–78.
61. D. J. Withrington, 'Adrift among the reefs of conflicting ideals? Education and the Free Church, 1843–55', in S. J. Brown and Michael Fry (eds), *Scotland in the age of the Disruption* (Edinburgh, 1993), 92.

PART ONE

Dissent and Disruption

CHAPTER ONE

New Lights:
The Growth of Dissent and Voluntaryism in Scotland, 1712–1843

Unlike in England, Wales and Ireland, where dissent from the established churches centred upon differences in theology and liturgy, from the end of the seventeenth century the majority of Scots adhered to Presbyterianism.[1] Therefore, secessions from the Scottish Kirk were largely based on divergent views on the meaning of Presbyterian ecclesiastical polity and church government, and divisions over what Presbyterianism represented in Scotland.[2] Seceders departed from the national church in the eighteenth and nineteenth centuries generally because they believed that it was not Presbyterian enough and did not represent the principles and ideals of the Kirk's founding fathers. The desire to advocate the 'purest' form of Presbyterian church government in Scotland, and a willingness to depart from a church that failed to live up to these standards, was evident from the earliest days of the Kirk. From the sixteenth-century Reformation and under the leadership of Andrew Melville, Scotland had adopted a Calvinist and 'Presbyterian' church structure distinct from and in opposition to the Episcopalian tradition implemented in England and Wales. While the Established Church of England was governed by bishops, Scottish Presbyterians took great pride in the theoretically more 'democratic' character of their system of church government.[3] Influenced by developments from the 1570s within the Reformed churches in continental Europe, the Presbyterian system was composed of an internal hierarchy of ecclesiastical courts. These ranged from the local parish kirk session to the district presbytery, which consisted of ministers and lay elders of the neighbouring parishes, and culminated in the General Assembly which met once a year and acted as the Church's national court. In this system, elders and parish ministers were supposed to be elected by their congregations, and all ministers and elders had, in theory, an equal status and say in the affairs of the Kirk.

The ability of congregations to choose their own ministers and the

---

1. Erik Routley, *English Religious Dissent* (Cambridge, 1960); Doreen Rosman, *The Evolution of the English Churches 1500–2000* (Cambridge, 2003), 117–46.
2. Kidd and Wallace, 'Biblical Criticism and Scots Presbyterian Dissent', 234.
3. C. G. Brown, *The People in the Pews: Religion and Society in Scotland since 1780* (Glasgow, 1993), 9–10.

theoretical parity of these ministers, seemingly stipulated in the First and Second Books of Discipline (1560 and 1578), would prove a fundamental feature of Presbyterianism's defence against the authoritarian structure of episcopacy.[4] According to Jane Dawson, the absorption of the pre-existing territorial parish system into the Scottish Kirk, combined with the organisational strength afforded by the hierarchy of ecclesiastical courts, helped to underline the assumption that it represented a truly national church with spiritual jurisdiction over the whole of Scotland. The local parish system would prove integral to the reformers' intention to create a morally pure godly commonwealth in Scotland modelled on small continental city-states such as John Calvin's Geneva and centred upon sermons, scripture, education, discipline and the provision of poor relief.[5] The Presbyterian Church also emphasised its 'spiritual independence' from the state in matters of religion, including its sole authority over its sacraments, liturgy and the ordination of ministers. Though these Presbyterians in theory did not accept the sovereign as head of the church and believed in the coexistence of two separate ecclesiastical and civil kingdoms within the realm, many in the Kirk expected the state to work together with the church to create the godly commonwealth in Scotland.[6]

The seventeenth century witnessed a period of intense struggle between the competing models of presbytery and episcopacy. Despite early Presbyterian hopes for James VI to act as a 'godly king', the Stuart monarchy's desire to impose episcopal church government upon Scotland and therefore control the Kirk culminated in a popular revolt that included the drafting of a National Covenant in 1638 calling for the restoration of Presbyterianism. This was followed by the 1643 Solemn League and Covenant, entered into with English parliamentarians against the Crown, and the Covenanters' adoption later in that decade of the Westminster Confession of Faith, the rigid Calvinism of which dominated Presbyterian thought in Scotland for much of the next century.[7] These Covenanters wished to install a uniform Presbyterian system in Britain and Ireland, and viewed themselves as a national movement representing the Scottish people against the combined threats of popery, prelacy and royal suprem-

---

4. John McKerrow, *History of the Secession Church* (2 volumes, Edinburgh, 1839), i, 36–8; Jane Dawson, *Scotland Re-formed, 1488–1587* (Edinburgh, 2007), 223; Alan MacDonald, *The Jacobean Kirk, 1567–1625: sovereignty, polity and liturgy* (Aldershot, 1998), 15.
5. Dawson, *Scotland Re-formed*, 216–17; Margo Todd, *The culture of Protestantism in early modern Scotland* (London, 2002), 22; James Kirk, *Patterns of Reform: continuity and change in the Reformation Kirk* (Edinburgh, 1989); Jenny Wormald, 'Reformed and Godly Scotland?', in Devine and Wormald, *Modern Scottish History*, 213–14.
6. John Young, 'The Covenanters and the Scottish Parliament, 1639–51: the rule of the godly and the "Second Scottish Reformation"', in Elizabethanne Boran and Crawford Gribben (eds), *Enforcing Reformation in Ireland and Scotland, 1550–1700* (Aldershot, 2006), 131–2.
7. Ian Cowan, *The Scottish Covenanters, 1660–1688* (London, 1976), 17–34; Alan Macinnes, *Charles I and the Making of the Covenanting Movement, 1625–1641* (Edinburgh, 1991), 155–82.

acy over the church.⁸ During the Restoration period, armed Presbyterian revolts in 1666 and 1679 were swiftly suppressed by the government, and in the 1680s a number of covenanting rebels were summarily executed during an infamous period which became somewhat exaggeratedly known as the 'killing times'.⁹

After almost a century of often bloody conflict with the Crown, the Revolution Settlement of 1688–90 finally re-established and cemented the Presbyterian system in Scotland. This was confirmed by the 1707 Acts of Union between Scotland and England, which pledged to guarantee the integrity of the Scottish Presbyterian Church from interference by a predominantly Anglican Union parliament in London.¹⁰ By the early decades of the eighteenth century the Presbyterian system, with its hierarchy of church courts and parish-based focus on Christian community, was in operation throughout Scotland and could claim the support of the majority of Scots (notwithstanding Catholic and Episcopalian support for the failed Jacobite risings of 1715 and 1745–6). A small group of extreme Covenanters, known variously as Cameronians or the 'anti-government party', also refused to join the re-established Presbyterian Kirk at the Revolution because it was not founded on the covenants of 1638 and 1643. To the Cameronians, the pluralist union of 1707 appeared to contradict further the Presbyterian Britain envisioned by the Solemn League and Covenant.¹¹ The belief by the anti-government party, who would become known as the Reformed Presbyterian Church after 1743, that the Treaty of Union was an 'open violation' of the covenants ensured that they remained outside the mainstream Presbyterian denominations until 1876, when a majority of Reformed Presbyterians joined the Free Church.¹²

While the Cameronians refused to join the post-Revolution Kirk due to its incompatibility with their version of Presbyterianism and its relationship with the state, similar ideological divisions also emerged within the Church of Scotland itself which threatened the apparent unity of the Presbyterian commonwealth and would be exacerbated by developments after 1707. The early decades of the eighteenth century witnessed the rise of an important group of clergymen known as 'Moderates' within the Established Kirk. Though they never secured a dependable majority in the lower church courts, from the 1750s an organised Moderate party, under the leadership of the influential minister and Enlightenment figure William Robertson, enjoyed a prolonged period of ascendancy in the General Assembly over

---

8. Robert McCorkle, *The Scottish Reformation: its testimony against popery and prelacy* (Edinburgh, 1863), 86–8.
9. Cowan, *Scottish Covenanters*, 120–33; Alasdair Raffe, 'Scotland Restored and Reshaped: politics and religion, c. 1660–1712', in Devine and Wormald, *Modern Scottish History*, 252–3.
10. Jeffrey Stephen, *Scottish Presbyterians and the Act of Union, 1707* (Edinburgh, 2007).
11. Colin Kidd, 'Conditional Britons: the Scots Covenanting tradition and the eighteenth-century British state', *English Historical Review*, cxvii (2002), 1147–76.
12. Kidd, *Union and Unionisms*, 222–3.

their opponents in the so-called 'Popular', or Orthodox, party. Unlike the Popular party, who eulogised the seventeenth-century martyrs, these Moderates largely repudiated the dogmatism and intolerance associated with the strict Calvinism of the covenanting movement. Intent on moving Presbyterianism away from the fanaticism and narrow sectarianism of the previous century, they instead embraced the intellectual, political and cultural developments of the eighteenth-century 'age of improvement' and advocated a more broadly based and tolerant vision of the Kirk, which would represent and interact with all aspects of modern Scottish society.[13] Though their opponents in the Popular party also gradually came under the influence of the Enlightenment later in the century, a number of conservative and orthodox members of the Kirk (including their descendants in the Free Church) were fierce critics of the apparent worldliness and doctrinal laxity of the Moderates, which they believed was moving the Church away from its reformed heritage.[14]

Divisions between the Moderate and Popular parties also centred on their contrasting definitions of how the Church of Scotland should be managed. While the Popular party owed its name to its apparent defence of popular rights, the Moderate regime under Robertson emphasised the importance of law, order and discipline within the Established Kirk, derived from the supreme authority of the General Assembly. Though they asserted their independence from secular interference, the Moderates recognised the need to co-operate with the London government to manage a 'strong, unified, and orderly national church'.[15] The Moderate–Popular divide and their competing interpretations of Scottish Presbyterianism would define the tensions surrounding the reimposition of lay patronage in the appointment of ministers after 1712. Introduced alongside the Toleration Act, which granted legal rights to Scottish Episcopalians, the 1712 Patronage Act served as the focal point around which these contrasting definitions of

13. Ian D. L. Clark, 'From Protest to Reaction: the Moderate regime in the Church of Scotland, 1752–1805', in N. T. Phillipson and Rosalind Mitchison (eds), *Scotland in the Age of Improvement: essays in Scottish history in the eighteenth century* (Edinburgh, 1970), 200–23; Richard B. Sher, *Church and University in the Scottish Enlightenment: the Moderate literati of Edinburgh* (Princeton, 1985).

14. John McIntosh, *Church and Theology in Enlightenment Scotland: the Popular party, 1740–1800* (East Linton, 1998); S. J. Brown, 'Protestant Dissent in Scotland', in Andrew C. Thompson (ed.), *The Oxford History of Protestant Dissenting Traditions, Volume II: The Long Eighteenth Century, c. 1689–c. 1828* (Oxford, 2018), 145–6; D. C. Lachman, *The Marrow Controversy 1718–1723* (Edinburgh, 1988), 409–75; Henry Sefton, 'Neu-lights and Preachers Legall: some observations on the beginnings of Moderatism in the Church of Scotland', in Norman Macdougall (ed.), *Church, Politics and Society: Scotland 1408–1929* (Edinburgh, 1983), 186–96.

15. Richard Sher and Alexander Murdoch, 'Patronage and party in the Church of Scotland, 1750–1800', in Macdougall, *Church, Politics and Society*, 212; Andrew L. Drummond and James Bulloch, *The Scottish Church 1688–1843: The age of the Moderates* (Edinburgh, 1973), 64–5; S. J. Brown, 'William Robertson (1721–1793) and the Scottish Enlightenment', in S. J. Brown (ed.), *William Robertson and the expansion of empire* (Cambridge, 1997), 13–14.

Presbyterianism were debated within the Kirk and acted as the catalyst for the growth of Presbyterian nonconformity during the eighteenth century.[16] The medieval system of lay patronage, which enabled the legal patron of a parish (usually the Crown or landowner) to present a minister to a vacancy, had been abolished at the religious settlement of 1690 in favour of a more popular system of election. The British government's decision to restore this patronage right was viewed by many within the Church of Scotland as both a threat to the Kirk's spiritual independence and an attack on the Presbyterian system by a largely Anglican parliament aiming to impose religious conformity throughout Britain in 'flagrant contravention of the Union' of 1707.[17]

Though the Kirk as a whole issued an annual protest to parliament against the Patronage Act for much of the eighteenth century, confusion over how best to respond to the law highlighted the growing divide between the Church's Moderate and Popular factions and brought into question where sovereignty lay within the Kirk. This would prove especially the case after 1730, when both the Crown and the landed aristocracy began to exercise fully their right of presentment to further their own political and ecclesiastical agendas.[18] As has been shown, while the more orthodox members of the Church favoured some form of popular and supposedly 'democratic' alternative to patronage (though they were divided regarding the details of any alternative), Moderates especially from the 1750s viewed patronage as a legitimate Presbyterian option designed to instil ecclesiastical law and order and to garner the support of the nobility and government to serve the interests of the Kirk and Scotland.[19] Unsurprisingly, lay patrons tended to favour these Moderate ministers, who often reflected the political ambitions of the anglicising landed class, shared similar cultural and intellectual interests, and partook in the same liberal and 'enlightened' social circles.[20] As Sher and Murdoch have argued, opposition by presbyteries and parishioners to the presentation of unpopular ministers was sporadic and usually formed part of broader ecclesiastical and political crises. Nevertheless, when disorder over controversial patronage settlements did occur, mob violence was common and tended to harden pre-existing divisions within the Kirk.[21]

16. Paterson, *Autonomy of Modern Scotland*, 57.
17. S. J. Brown, *National Churches*, 29–30; Kidd, *Union and Unionisms*, 221; Christina Christie Lumsden, 'Class, gender and Christianity in Edinburgh 1850–1905: a study in denominationalism' (unpublished PhD thesis, University of Edinburgh), 2012, 80; Callum G. Brown, *Religion and Society in Scotland since 1707* (Edinburgh, 1997), 18.
18. Brown, *People in the Pews*, 10; S. J. Brown, 'Religion and Society to c. 1900', in Devine and Wormald (eds), *Modern Scottish History*, 89; Stephen G. Myers, *Scottish Federalism and Covenantalism in Transition: the theology of Ebenezer Erskine* (Cambridge, 2016), 117–18.
19. Sher and Murdoch, 'Patronage and party', 215; Brown, 'William Robertson and the Scottish Enlightenment', 13–14.
20. Sher, *Church and University in the Scottish Enlightenment*, 121.
21. Sher and Murdoch, 'Patronage and party', 201; Brown, 'William Robertson and the Scottish Enlightenment', 12; Drummond and Bulloch, *The Scottish Church*, 40.

The first significant crisis concerning patronage and the diverging views of Presbyterianism occurred in the 1730s and produced a major secession from the Established Church. In 1732 the Stirling minister Ebenezer Erskine launched a blistering attack on the General Assembly's decision, against the will of the presbyteries, to confine the power of election in the event of a patron failing to present a ministerial candidate to the elders and Protestant heritors and town council members, thereby effectively ending the role of congregations in the selection of their ministers.[22] Along with three other ministers, Erskine was removed as a minister of the Church of Scotland for his insubordination and a year later formed the Associate Presbytery, which would later become known as the Secession Church. According to Erskine and his supporters, the ministers of the Associate Presbytery adhered to true Presbyterian principles and, in a markedly similar manner to the non-intrusionists at the Disruption, believed that they were not seceding from the national kirk, but from 'the prevailing party in this established Church', who they regarded as having diverted from Scotland's Reformed and covenanting heritage.[23] Erskine and the Seceders maintained their support for the establishment principle and a pure and spiritually independent national church. Despite concessions offered by the General Assembly in an attempt to induce the ministers back into the Church, the sympathy generated by the Seceders as martyrs across the Lowlands ensured their church's continued growth as numerous ministers and congregations from the Kirk joined the Secession in protest over the abuse of patronage.[24] Within seven years of the foundation of the Associate Presbytery, there were thirty-six Secession congregations, rising to forty-five by 1746.[25]

However, divisions remained even among the Seceders regarding their definitions of Presbyterianism and the role of the Secession in Scotland. In 1747 a split occurred over the controversial burgess oath in Edinburgh, Perth and Glasgow, which some Seceders viewed as an oath of loyalty to a 'corrupt' Established Kirk. The nineteen ministers who broke away in opposition to the oath formed the General Associate Synod and would become commonly known as the 'Anti-Burghers', while the remaining twelve, who believed the oath referred to Protestantism in general, would be known as the 'Burghers'. While the Anti-Burghers were undoubtedly the more uncompromising of the two Secession groups, in the mid-eighteenth century both remained committed to the establishment principle and viewed themselves as the true Church of Scotland and the descendants of the Covenanters of the 1630s.[26]

22. McKerrow, *History of the Secession Church*, i, 50–3; Drummond and Bulloch, *The Scottish Church*, 40; Kidd, *Union and Unionisms*, 223.
23. McKerrow, *History of the Secession Church*, i, 59–63.
24. Drummond and Bulloch, *The Scottish Church*, 42–4; Brown, *People in the Pews*, 10.
25. Drummond and Bulloch, *The Scottish Church*, 51.
26. Christopher Harvie, *Scotland and Nationalism: Scottish Society and Politics, 1707–1977* (London, 1977), 70–1; Brown, 'Religion and Society', 89.

The second major Secession of 1761 also emerged out of a crisis concerning church polity and once again centred on the diverging views of Presbyterianism and opposition to lay patronage within the Church of Scotland. However, it marked a distinct break from the covenanting puritanism associated with the first Secession and set the tone for the development of Presbyterian dissent into the nineteenth century. In 1752 the newly ascendant Moderate leadership, led by the young William Robertson, acted to reassert the authority of the General Assembly in the matter of patronage.[27] After the Dunfermline presbytery, acting on the wishes of the local parish, refused to ordain the patron's candidate at Inverkeithing, the Assembly decided to set an example to the rest of the church by deposing from the ministry one of the offending presbytery's 'disobedient' members, Thomas Gillespie, the minister of Carnock. Though Gillespie accepted the Assembly's punishment with humility, the decision angered many within and without the Kirk, including George Whitefield, who criticised the Moderate leadership as Presbyterian popes.[28]

Preferring not to follow the rigidity of the Seceders, Gillespie continued to minister to his congregation in a Dunfermline meeting house purchased by his supporters. He was soon joined by other like-minded Church of Scotland ministers who opposed patronage and what they regarded as the erastianism of the Moderates, yet favoured a more inclusive form of Reformed Presbyterianism than what was practised in the Secession Church. By 1761, along with two other ministers, Gillespie formed a new presbytery 'for the relief of Christians oppressed in their Christian privileges' by patronage and the Moderates, which would become known as the Relief Church.[29] The new Relief Church was noted, according to Kenneth Roxburgh, for its 'commitment to religious liberty, open communion, and tolerant attitudes towards other churches', while R. M. Smith has described the denomination as being 'in the vanguard of toleration' in Scotland.[30] As the debate over patronage and ecclesiastical sovereignty dominated the Church of Scotland in the two decades after Gillespie's dismissal, the Secession churches went from strength to strength. By the time of Gillespie's death in 1774, the Relief Church constituted nineteen congregations organised into two presbyteries, mostly based in the central and southern Lowlands of Scotland.[31] Despite the schism over the burgess

---

27. Brown, 'William Robertson and the Scottish Enlightenment', 12–15; Clark, 'From Protest to Reaction', 208–9.
28. Gavin Struthers, *The History, of the rise, progress, and principles of the Relief Church* (Glasgow, 1843), 95–9.
29. Struthers, *History of the Relief Church*, 164; Brown, 'Protestant Dissent', 151–2; Kidd, *Union and Unionisms*, 226.
30. Kenneth B. E. Roxburgh, *Thomas Gillespie and the origins of the Relief Church in eighteenth-century Scotland* (Bern, 1999), ii; R. M. Smith, 'The United Secession Church in Glasgow 1820–1847', *RSCHS*, xxxiv (2004), 48.
31. Roxburgh, *Thomas Gillespie*, 237; Brown, *People in the Pews*, 11.

oath, the Secession churches also continued to grow, and by the 1770s had roughly 170 congregations between them.[32]

Though it still professed a Reformed theological outlook, the second Secession differed from the first, perhaps most significantly, in its approach to the church–state connection.[33] Unlike the founding fathers of the Secession Church who upheld the establishment principle outside of the Kirk, the Relief Church believed that 'the church of Christ is entirely distinct from the kingdoms of this world, and no civil magistrate has any right to interfere with it, or to attempt to establish it'.[34] By the turn of the nineteenth century, the voluntaryistic principles of the Relief Church had gained a foothold in the other fragments of Scottish Presbyterian dissent. The Seceders' adherence to the church–state connection slowly receded as the evangelical awakening, with its emphasis on personal conversion and voluntary association of the faithful, took hold in Scotland during the eighteenth century.[35] Combined with the political and religious ferment of the French Revolution, and its ideals of liberty and egalitarianism, the new evangelicalism of the late eighteenth century transformed both Scottish Presbyterian dissent and the Kirk's Popular party. As David Bebbington has outlined in his definitive study on British evangelicalism, the transatlantic movement was rooted in the authority of the Bible, the atoning death of Christ on the cross, the necessity of personal conversion, and religious activism.[36] More stress was placed on the individual's personal relationship with Christianity and the assurance of salvation through faith, while less attention was paid to the structures of the parish church as a model of religiosity.

The new religious environment of the 1790s saw a number of Scotland's dissenters embrace what they described as 'new light' (or 'new licht' in its Scots form) ways of thinking which called into question the continuing relevance of the seventeenth-century covenants and the teachings of the Westminster Confession regarding the relationship between church and state. These New Licht dissenters advocated religious toleration and the voluntary principle, arguing that the church should be separated from the state, and that all churches should be supported by the voluntary contributions of their adherents. While the majority of both the Burgher and Anti-Burgher factions of Scottish dissent embraced the New Licht ecclesiology, smaller 'Auld Licht' groups formed rumps of both churches, who preferred the traditional Presbyterian belief in the covenants and the ideal of a pure religious establishment. The emerging gulf between Auld and New Lichts resulted in the further fragmentation of the Scottish secession

32. Brown, 'Protestant Dissent', 148–9; Kidd, *Union and Unionisms*, 224–5.
33. Kidd, *Union and Unionisms*, 226.
34. Struthers, *History of the Relief Church*, 272–3.
35. Brown, 'Protestant Dissent', 149.
36. D. W. Bebbington, *Evangelicalism in Modern Britain: a history from the 1730s to the 1980s* (London, 1989), 2–17.

as the old lights, including influential churchmen such as Thomas McCrie, seceded from both the Burgher and Anti-Burgher synods in 1799 and 1806 respectively.[37]

As S. J. Brown has argued, the emergence of the New Licht movement witnessed a major shift in the aims, attitudes and social and political profile of Presbyterian dissent. While eighteenth-century dissent was marked by a willingness to return to a purified Established Church, from the early nineteenth century Presbyterian dissenters were intrinsically linked to voluntaryism and the rejection of the church–state connection.[38] The New Licht–Auld Licht splits of 1799 and 1806 were also the last in a period of schisms within Presbyterian dissent that was replaced by co-operation and union based on the common ground of evangelical voluntaryism. Though the New Lichts retained the Calvinist and Presbyterian doctrine of the Secession's founding fathers, their defining characteristic became the campaign for denominational equality under the law.

The geographic, social and economic make-up of these dissenters also changed around the turn of the nineteenth century. Before 1790, Seceders were largely drawn from the rural lowlands, and were comprised of small landowners, craftsmen and skilled farm servants. However, by the early 1800s they became increasingly identified with the rising and aspirant middle class in newly industrialised urban areas, who were attracted to the individualism and egalitarianism associated with voluntary religion, and its challenge to the traditional control of the religious, social and political establishment.[39] Church historians and historians of Scotland in general have tended to characterise perhaps unfairly the eighteenth-century Seceders as provincial, reactionary and employing an outdated Calvinism, while the rest of Scotland embraced enlightened Moderatism; Presbyterian dissenters after 1800 became intrinsically linked to movements for liberal democratic reform, and the modern restructuring of Scotland's society away from the old landed elite during the Industrial Revolution.[40]

Religiously, Scotland was also changing in the early nineteenth century. Denominational pluralism became increasingly pronounced and created a competitive dynamic that characterised Scottish religion throughout the century.[41] Callum Brown has estimated that by 1800 Presbyterian dissenters represented over a fifth of Scotland's total population, rising to roughly

---

37. Brown, 'Protestant Dissent', 157–8; Brown, *National Churches*, 44; Kidd, *Union and Unionisms*, 227; Drummond and Bulloch, *The Scottish Church*, 150–1; Brown, *People in the Pews*, 11.
38. Brown, *National Churches*, 44.
39. Brown, *Religion and Society*, 19–24.
40. Brown, *People in the Pews*, 12; Drummond and Bulloch, *The Scottish Church*, 51; T. C. Smout, *A History of the Scottish People 1560–1830* (Glasgow, 1972), 218; Stewart J. Brown, 'Religion and the Rise of Liberalism: The First Disestablishment Campaign in Scotland, 1829–1843', *Journal of Ecclesiastical History*, xlviii (1997), 682–4.
41. Brown, 'Protestant Dissent', 158–9.

one-third by 1830, the majority of whom were based in Lowland Scotland. This rapid increase in and diversity of Presbyterian dissent highlighted the new multidenominational character of Scottish society, which was consolidated by pockets of Episcopalians, Methodists, Quakers and Glasites, and a growing Roman Catholic minority caused by immigration from Ireland to the west of Scotland, as well as the Baptists and Congregationalists that had formed in the wake of the Evangelical Revival.[42] These dissenting churches gained most of their support from the skilled artisans and manufacturing and commercial middle class of Scotland's major towns and cities.[43] In the 1830s, Presbyterian, Baptist and Congregationalist dissenters made up over two-fifths of the populations of Edinburgh and Glasgow, and together they accounted for roughly equal the number of churchgoers as the Church of Scotland.[44] S. J. Brown has noted that by the end of the eighteenth century the strength of Scottish dissent reflected the increasing prosperity of the country. Leaving the Established Church no longer reflected the loss of social position or respectability that it may have earlier in the century. Instead it highlighted the ambitions of a largely urban and aspiring class who were outside the traditional social structures of rural Scotland and able to pay for the maintenance of their own churches, and possessed the independence and conscientious conviction to challenge what they regarded as the errors of the national kirk.[45]

The growing confidence within Scottish dissent was reflected in the formation of the United Secession Church in 1820. Following the abolition of the controversial burgess oath by the town councils in 1819, the New Licht Burgher and New Licht Anti-Burgher strands of the Secession reunited after seventy-three years apart.[46] Within twenty years the new United Secession Church had roughly 250,000 members and over 350 congregations, and represented 10 per cent of the Scottish population.[47] Of the smaller old light groups that formed the first Secession, the Burghers rejoined the Church of Scotland in 1839, while the majority of Anti-Burghers, known as the Original Secession Church, would eventually unite with the Free Church in 1852. Writing in 1840, the Secession historian John McKerrow claimed that the New Licht union of 1820, based on voluntaryism and toleration, gave 'increased energy and influence to the Secession Church' and ensured it was 'better prepared for acting a prominent and decided part' in the religious controversies that would dominate Scottish civic life

---

42. Brown, *Religion and Society*, 20, 61–2; Brown, 'Religion and Society', 89.
43. Brown, 'Religion and the Rise of Liberalism', 686.
44. Brown, *Social History of Religion*, 61.
45. Brown, 'Protestant Dissent', 158–9.
46. McKerrow, *History of the Secession Church*, ii, 397–413; James Cleland, *Enumeration of the inhabitants of the city of Glasgow and county of Lanark for the government census of 1831* (Glasgow, 1832), 73–4; Smith, 'United Secession Church in Glasgow', 48; Brown, 'Protestant Dissent', 157–8.
47. Machin, *Politics and the Churches in Great Britain*, 114.

in the 1830s.⁴⁸ More broadly, the presence of two significant Presbyterian dissenting churches, the United Secession and the Relief Synod, represented a major blow to the belief that the Church of Scotland represented the Scottish nation. Though their growth would slow from the 1840s, the increasing influence of the dissenting churches and their challenge to the establishment in the changing Scotland of the early nineteenth century would prove an integral feature of the religious controversies of the 1830s and beyond.

The Voluntary Controversy and the Ten Years' Conflict

The rapid growth of Presbyterian dissent in the early nineteenth century coincided with the rise to power of the Evangelical, or Popular, party within the Church of Scotland. Re-energised by the Evangelical Revival and faced with the apparent decline of the Kirk's position owing to Moderatism and various secessions, the Evangelicals, led by the most impressive churchman of the nineteenth century, Thomas Chalmers, set about rebuilding the Established Church's status as a national institution. They also sought to respond to the challenges of industrialisation and urbanisation that had further revealed the Kirk's weaknesses. The rapid growth of the cities and large towns had left Scotland's parish system outdated and meant that the churches could no longer fulfil their duty of pastoral care to every resident. The so-called 'chapels of ease', established by private enterprise in overcrowded parishes to ease the burden on the parish church and lacking full recognition by the Moderate-dominated General Assembly, failed to fully address the scale of the issue. Chalmers' attempt to reinvent the rural parish structure and godly commonwealth ideal in the new urban context at his St John's parish in Glasgow between 1819 and 1823 was only a partial success.⁴⁹ The failure of the Kirk to adapt to the changing social circumstance in pastoral care can also be applied to its control of national education. The equality of opportunity associated with the parish school system evaporated with the Industrial Revolution as the children of the poor went to work in the fields and factories. The mythology attached to Scottish education also began to be questioned, as standards fell, teachers' salaries remained pitifully low, and the country began to be described even by members of the Church of Scotland itself as a 'half educated nation'.⁵⁰

The challenges faced by the Established Kirk in this period were compounded by the major political reforms of the late 1820s and early 1830s. The repeal of the Test and Corporation Acts in 1828 granted dissenters in England and Wales full civil and political rights, while the 1829 Catholic

---

48. McKerrow, *History of the Secession Church*, ii, 413.
49. Drummond and Bulloch, *The Scottish Church*, 184–8; Brown, *Thomas Chalmers*, 91–151.
50. George Lewis, *Scotland a Half Educated Nation, both in the quantity and quality of her educational institutions* (Glasgow, 1834).

Emancipation Act gave British and Irish Catholics the right to sit in parliament and hold most positions in government. The 1832 Reform Acts increased parliamentary representation in the new industrial cities and opened up the franchise to the urban middle class that formed the basis of Scottish dissent. In Scotland, which before 1832 resembled 'one vast, rotten borough', the Reform Act expanded the franchise from only 4,500 to approximately 65,000, moving the control of its representation beyond a narrow corrupt oligarchy and granting the country, in the words of the Solicitor-General Henry Cockburn, 'a political constitution for the first time'. In doing so it offered dissenters the chance to wrest electoral control from the Tory establishment.[51] This period of reform, as S. J. Brown has argued, transformed the nature of the British state, ushering in a 'sudden, almost revolutionary end' to what J. C. D. Clark termed Britain's *ancien régime*, and galvanised the dissenting opposition to the established churches in England and Ireland.[52]

The impact of the new political order also prompted Scotland's dissenters to actively campaign for the disestablishment of the Established Church of Scotland, in what became known as the 'Voluntary Controversy'. While reformers in Scotland utilised Presbyterian covenanting language to pursue parliamentary reform, in many respects the voluntary agitation of the 1830s was rooted in the wider secular liberal agenda that emerged during and following the Reform Act campaign.[53] The controversy, which dominated Scottish public debate in the mid-1830s, brought Scotland's Presbyterian voluntaries in the United Secession and Relief churches closer together, widened divisions within the Kirk, and cultivated a unified dissenting and radical-liberal political agenda in Scotland. According to Brown, these voluntaries, and their campaign against the Established Church, were the 'makers of the Disruption'.[54] Instigated by the firebrand United Secession minister Andrew Marshall's April 1829 sermon, the voluntary campaign intended to abolish all church establishments and aimed to create a religious free market based on individual choice that Marshall claimed would galvanise true religion by liberating the Gospel from unwarranted state intrusion. State endowments, Marshall argued, tended to 'secularise the church' and made it a mere 'political institution'.[55] The political impact of

---

51. Pentland, 'Scotland and the creation of a National Reform Movement', 999; William Ferguson, 'The Reform Act (Scotland) of 1832: intention and effect', *Scottish Historical Review*, xlv (1966), 105; McCaffrey, *Scotland in the Nineteenth Century*, 48; Norman Gash, *Politics in the age of Peel* (London, 1969), 35–6.
52. Stewart J. Brown, 'The Ten Years' Conflict and the Disruption of 1843', in Brown and Fry, *Scotland in the age of the Disruption*, 2–3.
53. Gordon Pentland, *Radicalism, reform, and national identity in Scotland, 1820–1833* (Woodbridge, 2008), ch. 6; Pentland, 'Scotland and the creation of a National Reform Movement', 1018–22.
54. Brown, 'Religion and the Rise of Liberalism', 683.
55. Andrew Marshall, *Ecclesiastical establishments considered: a sermon, preached on the evening of Thursday, 9th April, 1829, in Greyfriars Church, Glasgow* (Glasgow, 1829), 20.

the campaign was such that in an 1838 speech in the House of Lords regarding the dissenting campaign against the establishment, Lord Aberdeen claimed that 'never had any question of domestic policy so much agitated the people of Scotland since the union of the two kingdoms'.[56]

Throughout Scotland, radical politicians and dissenting churchmen united to establish voluntary societies with the aim of propagating dissenting principles and securing the disestablishment and disendowment of the Kirk. Notable voluntary organisations included the Voluntary Church Associations of Edinburgh and Glasgow, and the Edinburgh-based Scottish Central Board for Vindicating the Rights of Dissenters, which was led by the influential Edinburgh merchant and politician Duncan McLaren.[57] Radicals such as McLaren viewed the disestablishment campaign as one plank of the wider liberal programme to tackle the political, social, economic and religious hegemony of the landed establishment.[58] This broader agenda was perhaps most evident in the prolonged dissenting campaign for the abolition of the controversial Annuity Tax in Edinburgh. The campaign against the tax, a 6 per cent levy on house and shop rentals used in part to pay the city's parish clergy, resembled the concurrent Tithe War in Ireland and, McLaren claimed, pitted the 'guardians of the public interest' against the 'representatives of privilege and monopoly'.[59] Along with its assault on the privilege and rank of the establishment, the voluntary agitation also highlighted what its supporters viewed as the evangelical fervour of the dissenting churches in comparison to the stale, Moderate Kirk, with Marshall claiming that 'the dissenters and they alone had kept religion alive in this country'.[60]

The voluntary campaign's attack on the church–state connection proved instrumental in securing for the Evangelical party the leadership of the General Assembly. After decades of Moderate rule, the Popular party, under Chalmers' leadership, transformed the national kirk. Seeking to revive the establishment, counteract the voluntaries' increasing social strength in the cities, and answer the dissenting taunts of erastianism, the evangelicals pursued a programme that included an 'aggressive' church extension policy and sweeping reform of the patronage system. In 1834 the evangelical-dominated General Assembly passed two highly significant measures which ultimately led to the beginning of the Ten Years' Conflict with the state: the Chapels Act and the Veto Act. The Chapels Act, which established the chapels of ease as *quoad sacra* parish churches, formed a central part of Chalmers' broader church extension policy. Under the auspices of

56. *Hansard's Parliamentary Debates*, 3rd series, xliii (30 March 1838), col. 112.
57. Scottish Central Board for Vindicating the Rights of Dissenters, *Statement relative to Church Accommodation in Scotland* (Edinburgh, 1835).
58. J. B. Mackie, *The Life and Work of Duncan McLaren* (2 volumes, London, 1888), ii, 29.
59. Duncan McLaren, *Substance of a speech regarding the Bishops' Teinds, delivered at a public meeting of the Central Board of Dissenters* (Edinburgh, 1838), 11.
60. *Caledonian Mercury*, 6 January 1838.

the Church Extension Committee, this national campaign aimed to revitalise the ecclesiastical, social and moral influence of the Kirk in the face of voluntary pressure, and expand the communal ideals of Chalmers' St John's experiment.[61] Unsurprisingly, Chalmers' church extension scheme, and its request for state subsidies, was vociferously opposed by dissenters, who regarded the Kirk's 'unjust' and 'injurious' attempts to secure public funds as 'an infringement of [dissenting] rights'.[62] The pronounced and often bitter voluntary opposition to the church extension scheme would ultimately prove successful. In 1838, following the initial reports of a Royal Commission of Inquiry on church accommodation in Scotland, the Whig government announced that it would not endow the new parish churches. This 'betrayal' by the state towards one of its established churches dealt a major blow to Chalmers' vision of a unified godly commonwealth.[63]

The influence of the voluntary campaign on other aspects of the relationship between the Kirk and the government was also evident in the renewed furore over patronage. The Veto Act can be partly viewed as the Established Kirk's attempt to diminish the voluntaries' increasing influence, in a similar vein to the church extension policy.[64] The Act, which allowed the male heads of family in a parish to veto the patron's nominee, represented a compromise between the extreme anti-patronage and pro-patronage wings of the church, and addressed the major issue of the eighteenth-century Secessions by restoring the place of the popular 'call' in the selection of ministers. Though the new policy initially appeared to work well, the emergence of instances in which the aggrieved candidate appealed against the veto in the civil courts, most notably in the case of the young probationer minister Robert Young at Auchterarder, drew into question the legality of the evangelicals' position and the very essence of the relationship between the church and state.[65]

The House of Lords' confirmation in 1839 of the Court of Session's decision to pronounce the Veto Act illegal highlighted the increasingly divergent views of church and state regarding the role and status of the national kirk. While the British government viewed the Church of Scotland as a creation of the state and therefore subservient to its laws, the 'non-intrusionist' party in the church (containing the majority of evangelicals) defended the 'spiritual independence' of the Kirk from the intrusion of both the state and lay patronage. They also reasserted the doctrine of the 'two king-

---

61. Brown, 'The Ten Years' Conflict', 7–9; Smith, 'The United Secession Church in Glasgow', 58; Kidd, *Union and Unionisms*, 233.
62. Scottish Central Board for Vindicating the Rights of Dissenters, *Remarks on the First Report of the Commissioners of Religious Instruction, Scotland* (Edinburgh, 1837), 10–12; Mackie, McLaren, i, 170, 172; Scottish Central Board, *Statement relative to Church Accommodation*, 2.
63. Brown, *Thomas Chalmers*, 273–5.
64. R. M. W. Cowan, *The Newspaper in Scotland, 1815-60* (Glasgow, 1947), 227; D. J. Withrington, 'The making of the Veto Act, 1833-34, *RSCHS*, xxviii (1998), 122.
65. Kidd, *Union and Unionisms*, 230.

doms', in which the church and state had complete sovereignty over their own province with Christ as the head of the Church. The Moderates, on the other hand, though maintaining the independence of the church in spiritual matters, respected the jurisdiction of the state when the civil and ecclesiastical courts came into conflict, and therefore agreed with the withdrawal of the Veto Act. The growing tensions between not only the Kirk and the government but also the Moderate and non-intrusionist factions within the establishment were heightened by the General Assembly's suspension of seven Moderate ministers at Strathbogie for ordaining a vetoed candidate, a decision infamously overturned by the Court of Session.[66]

Tensions were further compounded by the emergence after 1838 of a new generation of militant young non-intrusionists known as the 'Wild Party' who openly challenged the state's conduct and interference in the Kirk's affairs, and defended popular rights. This group of ambitious evangelicals included Robert Smith Candlish, James Begg, Thomas Guthrie and William Cunningham, and would go on to dominate affairs in the Free Church after 1843.[67] Writing after the Disruption, one of the Wild Party's members, Robert Buchanan, argued that if the state's intrusion into the church's affairs was the price to pay for the temporal benefits of being part of the establishment, then it was preferable to be a 'rebel against Caesar', by 'dissolving her union with the state', rather than be a 'rebel against Christ'.[68] With the support of Chalmers, who was initially expected to mollify the extremes of the Wild Party, this attitude characterised the 1842 General Assembly, during which the non-intrusionists adopted the 'Claim of Right'. Penned by the influential lawyer Alexander Dunlop, the Claim of Right emphasised the 'sole Headship of Christ over the Church' and argued that, as a church of Christ and under the terms of the 1707 Treaty of Union, the state could not interfere in its ecclesiastical affairs. Following the Claim of Right, the increasing number of patronage cases in the church courts (totalling thirty-nine by the end of 1842) and the seeming reticence of parliament and the Tory Prime Minister Robert Peel to intervene made the prospect of secession increasingly likely. In November 1842, a convocation was held in Edinburgh to prepare plans for the creation of a new, voluntary-funded church. The Peel government's dismissal of the Claim of Right as 'unreasonable' in January 1843, along with the Court of Session's decision to render the Chapels Act illegal and thus deprive the mostly evangelical *quoad sacra* churches of representation in the church courts, made disruption inevitable.

When it finally occurred on 18 May 1843, the Disruption incited great excitement in Scotland and dominated public discourse. It was a truly national movement that touched almost every area of the country, though

---

66. Brown, 'Ten Years' Conflict', 16-7.
67. Brown, *Thomas Chalmers*, 303.
68. Buchanan, *Ten Years' Conflict*, ii, 494-5.

reasons for seceding varied across different regions of Scotland. In urban areas the Disruption marked a form of religious and social 'self-determination' by the upwardly mobile middle class who would go on to dominate the Free Church, while in the piously Calvinist Highlands the strength of the secession owed much to the evangelical missions of the early nineteenth century and anti-government sentiment in the wake of the Clearances. On all sides of the debate many viewed the actions of Chalmers and his colleagues as a triumph of sacrifice and principle over personal interest.[69] In the accounts of the Disruption written by Free Churchmen after 1843, most notably those by Robert Buchanan, William Maxwell Hetherington and Thomas Brown, the events of May 1843 represented the latest defence of Scotland's historic Presbyterian principles and posed broader interpretative questions regarding the relationship between church and state throughout the United Kingdom and beyond.[70] Though many within the Free Church, which in principle remained committed to the ideal of a 'pure' religious establishment, lamented the bitterness of the conflict and the tragic break-up of both the church and the national vision of a godly commonwealth, they heroically depicted themselves as Israelites escaping the bonds of Egypt.[71]

This triumphalist rhetoric reverberated throughout Scotland's older dissenting churches. While the non-intrusionists claimed to go out as the 'true' Church of Scotland, the Disruption was nevertheless a momentous occasion for Scottish dissent, and seemed to mark the culmination of the Voluntary Controversy and over a century of secessions from the establishment. As the procession of new Free Church ministers streamed into Tanfield Hall on the day of the Disruption, the leading United Secession minister, John Brown, a veteran of the previous decade's voluntary campaign, waited to greet them into the dissenting fold. His gesture was lost in the fervent atmosphere of the occasion, and ignored by ministers who refused to acknowledge the voluntaries' role in splitting their national church, but the symbolism remained.[72] For Scotland's voluntary Presbyterians, the Disruption was viewed as 'strengthening the principle of protest against all connection of Church with State', an assessment that was shared by anti-state church campaigners in Europe and the United States.[73] 'The separation of such a large number of ministers and people

---

69. Brown, *Thomas Chalmers*, 333–6; Brown, *Social History of Religion*, 38–9.
70. Robert Buchanan, *The Ten Years' Conflict: being the history of the Disruption of the Church of Scotland* (2 volumes), vol. i, 4; Hetherington, *History of the Church of Scotland*, 473–4; Thomas Brown, *Annals of the Disruption* (Edinburgh, 1884), 2.
71. [James Hamilton], *Farewell to Egypt: or, the departure of the Free Church of Scotland out of the Erastian Establishment* (London, 1844), 3–12.
72. Brown, 'Religion and the Rise of Liberalism', 682–3.
73. *Morning Chronicle*, 29 May 1843; J. J. Gurney to Thomas Chalmers, 15 December 1843, NCL, CHA.4.308.64; Princeton Theological Seminary to New College Missionary Association, 30 September 1843, NCL, New College Missionary Association correspondence, AA.3.3.32.

from the communion of the National Church', wrote the editor of the *United Secession Magazine*, 'we hail as an event good in itself, and one which will be productive of beneficial results.'[74] In a letter to a Free Church minister, the moderator of the Relief Synod, Peter Brown, argued that the 'bold and decisive step' taken by the Free Church at the Disruption had removed 'a great stumbling block out of the way' of the ultimate goal of complete disestablishment. The 'great principles' of the Disruption – in so far as they could be interpreted as an attack on the church–state system – were viewed by voluntary ministers as consistent with the historical testimony of the Secession church.[75] Speaking nine years later at an event to mark the centenary of Gillespie's deposition from the Established Church, the United Presbyterian minister David Anderson claimed that, just as Erskine and the first Seceders had paved the way for Gillespie, so too was it 'comparatively easy' for the Free Church to secede 'with the example and encouragement of Dissent flourishing and in honour all around'.[76] Whether the new Free Church would answer such encouragement was another matter, which will be discussed in the next chapter. In any case, Scotland's national church, and the very nature of Scottish Presbyterianism itself, had irrevocably changed.

74. *USM*, xi (September 1843), 43.
75. Peter Brown, private letter to a Free Church Minister, dated 18 March 1844, in J. A. Wallace (ed.), *Testimonies in favour of the principles and procedure of the Free Church of Scotland* (Edinburgh, 1844); Archibald Baird, Speech at Paisley, May 1843, in Wallace, *Testimonies in favour*, 31–3; *PGAFC, October 1843*, 49; *Caledonian Mercury*, 21 October 1843.
76. *Gillespie centenary: report of the centenary meeting held in Tanfield Hall, Edinburgh* (Edinburgh, 1852), 26.

CHAPTER TWO

A National or Voluntary Church? The Free Church and the Establishment Principle

'The voluntaries mistake us, if they conceive us to be voluntaries', Thomas Chalmers announced to his fellow Free Churchmen gathered in Tanfield Hall, Canonmills, on 18 May 1843. Earlier that morning, Chalmers had led 450 non-intrusionist ministers from St Andrew's Church, Edinburgh, home of the Established Church of Scotland's General Assembly, to an uncertain future without state endowments and seemingly reliant on the voluntary financial contributions of their congregations. However, the Free Church leader made clear, in what would become an infamous and divisive speech, that they were doing so on the grounds of the establishment principle. Chalmers and his Free Churchmen had claimed to have quit a 'vitiated Establishment, but would rejoice in returning to a pure one'. According to Chalmers, the Free Church remained committed advocates for 'national recognition and national support of religion', holding that 'every part and every function of a commonwealth should be leavened with Christianity'.[1] This belief in a truly national church, encompassing the entirety of Scotland, would be carried by the non-intrusionists after the Disruption. To Free Churchmen, the national character of Presbyterianism, in and out of the Established Church, remained a central tenet of their denominational identity. The success of the Disruption, in which over a third of the ministers and half the laity departed the Church of Scotland, appeared to cement the Free Church's claim to be the 'national-church-in-waiting'.[2] The Free Church, in the eyes of its adherents, would not be a mere seceding sect like Scotland's older voluntary churches, but a national church in its own right, a people-endowed Church of Scotland.

This chapter will discuss how the Free Churchmen attempted to reconcile their bid to create a truly national kirk with their new reliance on voluntary methods. It will first explore the theoretical tension between the Free Church's seemingly unflinching establishmentarianism and its new role as a dissenting and voluntary-funded church. The Free Church leadership's stated support for the national recognition of religion not only attracted

---

1. *Proceedings of the General Assembly of the Free Church of Scotland, May 1843* (Edinburgh, 1843), 12.
2. Kidd and Wallace, 'Biblical Criticism and Scots Presbyterian Dissent', 240.

criticism from Scotland's voluntary churches, it also threatened to divide the new church, as certain sections were not as committed as Chalmers to the establishment principle. The chapter will then examine the practicalities of the Free Church's attempt to create a voluntary Church of Scotland. The introduction of a 'new' brand of voluntaryism, focused on a centralised, national structure, epitomised the Free Church's bid to reconcile the competing ideals of the voluntary and establishment principles, but also highlighted, by Chalmers' death in 1847, the apparent inefficiencies of voluntaryism on a national level. The ambiguous interrelationship between national, establishment and voluntary principles in the Free Church after 1843 dominated ecclesiastical discourse within Scottish dissent and acted as both a benefit and hindrance to the Free Kirk's bid to usurp the Church of Scotland as Scotland's national church. While the Ten Years' Conflict and Disruption have dominated the scholarship of this period, S. J. Brown has recently pointed out the historiographical gap surrounding events immediately after the schism of May 1843. Brown urged further exploration of how the Free Church appeared to create a national church, in theory and in practice, despite the severe economic downturn of the 1840s.[3] This chapter will examine the Free Church's ambition to become a 'people-endowed' national church. This aim was predicated on maintaining both the rhetoric of a national church, through the ideal of a 'pure' establishment, while delivering through voluntary means the practicalities of one. To what extent did the Free Kirk, as Brown suggests, effectively manage to retain the theoretical and practical stature of a national church after May 1843?

A People-endowed National Church: The Disruption and Voluntaryism

The desire to affirm its establishmentarian principles, while undermining the theoretical significance of its new voluntary position, characterised the Free Church's official stance at the Disruption. The protest laid on the table of the Church of Scotland's General Assembly by David Welsh maintained the principle of a 'pure' establishment free from unwarranted civil intrusion and agreeable to Scripture while also attacking the state's conduct during the Ten Years' Conflict. It firmly asserted 'the right and duty of the civil magistrate to maintain and support an establishment of religion in accordance with God's word'. While the Free Church fathers could no longer comply with the 'conditions' they deemed were now attached to membership of the state church, they nevertheless lamented 'our enforced separation from an Establishment which we loved and prized'.[4] This position was underscored two years after the Disruption by the moderator Patrick Macfarlan at the Free Church General Assembly. Macfarlan

---

3. Brown, 'Religion and Society', 92.
4. 'Protest by those Commissioners to the General Assembly appointed to meet on 18 May 1843, by whom this Assembly was constituted', *AGAFC, 1843* (Edinburgh, 1843), 8.

emphasised the church's principles 'respecting the duty of nations and their rulers, as bound, in their national and official character, to own Christ, and to aim at the advancement of his cause', and dismissed 'any reason to apprehend a change of sentiment on this subject'. However, as the 1843 Protest made clear, he also maintained that 'we cannot approve of existing Establishments, in which the countenance of the State is purchased by the subserviency of the Church'.[5] This criticism of the Church of Scotland's relationship with the state drew inevitable hostility from supporters of the Kirk, who cited a lack of principle from ministers who had pledged to 'be true to the Establishment'. Speaking in the House of Lords days before the Disruption, Lord Campbell highlighted what he regarded as the inconsistency of 'those who had eagerly supported the Establishment, had expressed themselves hostile to all voluntary churches, and shown a great antipathy to Dissenters' yet who were now 'not only determined to leave the Church themselves', but to 'utterly overturn and subvert it'.[6] The official Free Church belief that 'Christ is Head over the nations' and that 'it is lawful and right to employ the national resources' in support of the Gospel – a stance, according to the non-intrusionists, denied by 'merely voluntary societies' – was counterbalanced by a resolute unwillingness to maintain the existing Scottish establishment that fuelled the Disruption.[7] The duality of the Free Church position, national and establishmentarian yet hostile to the national establishment as it currently stood, placed the church between and against both the voluntaryism of Scotland's other secessionist bodies and the perceived erastianism of the Church of Scotland.

The ambiguity surrounding the Free Church's attitude towards the voluntary principle and its future position as a self-proclaimed 'national church' operating outside of the national establishment was evident long before the events of May 1843. In a series of letters to the Scots-American philanthropist James Lenox and his brother John, Chalmers confidently asserted that the national role and character of the Kirk would not diminish in the event of a rupture with the state, and that it would 'persevere unimpaired her moral weight in the country'. This 'Non-Erastian Church of Scotland', Chalmers predicted, would have 'the great bulk and body of the common people with a goodly proportion of the middle classes upon our side'.[8] While Chalmers appeared confident in preserving the national characteristics of his church, the potential role of the establishment and voluntary principles in a disendowed Church of Scotland proved a much more complex question. Chalmers' correspondence offers insight into

---

5. Free Church of Scotland, *Pastoral Address of the General Assembly, met at Edinburgh, in the year 1845, to the people under their charge* (Edinburgh, 1845), 5–6.
6. *Hansard's Parliamentary Debates*, 3rd series, vol. lxix (9 May 1843), cols 12–15.
7. *Catechism on the principles and constitution of the Free Church of Scotland* (Edinburgh, 1845), 12–13; *Pastoral Address*, 6.
8. Thomas Chalmers to James Lenox, 17 January 1842; Chalmers to James Lenox, 4 May 1842; Chalmers to James Lenox, 19 April 1843, NYPL, James Lenox Papers, MssCol 1732.

the conflicting arguments proffered to the evangelical leader in the pre-Disruption period and emphasises how the voluntary question in the Free Church extended far beyond that of a parochial Scottish debate. Samuel Hanna – the first moderator of the Presbyterian Church in Ireland, formed in 1840, and father of William Hanna, Chalmers' son-in-law and future biographer – urged Chalmers and his followers not only to quit the establishment, but in doing so to dissolve the church–state connection completely, therefore making it 'difficult to say that those who remain really be called *the* Church of Scotland'.[9]

In contrast, Hanna's colleague Henry Cooke, the most influential Irish Presbyterian of the nineteenth century, was a prominent defender of Britain and Ireland's ecclesiastical establishments and felt 'crushed' by the events of May 1843. Though he was a key supporter of Chalmers and the non-intrusionists' struggle against state control, Cooke tried desperately to divert the Disruption, even appealing two days before it took place to the Prime Minister Robert Peel to acquiesce to non-intrusionist demands by abolishing patronage and granting full spiritual independence. He told Peel that the Disruption 'is felt by every Presbyterian as an injury inflicted upon himself'.[10] The sacrifice inherent in any secession from the national kirk was emphasised by James McCosh, a non-intrusionist minister at Brechin, who questioned the soundness of any voluntary disestablishment policy, which by late 1842 was being debated within evangelical circles in Edinburgh. McCosh upheld the establishment principle even in the face of disendowment and argued that 'an important place has been given to us in the constitution of the kingdom, which we are no more at liberty to abandon hastily or rashly, than the House of Lords or the House of Commons, or the court of session is at liberty to abandon its peculiar privileges'.[11] Belfast minister Josias Wilson also argued in favour of the establishment principle, claiming that if the Kirk's non-intrusionist faction plunged over the precipice into voluntaryism, 'the glory of the Church of Scotland as an Establishment is gone'.[12]

While an outspoken champion of ecclesiastical establishments, Chalmers himself recognised the potential for voluntary contributions within a state church framework. He claimed on multiple occasions before 1843 that his own interpretation of establishments 'has never been to the exclusion of the voluntary principle, which I hold to be of the greatest practical benefit both for supplementing and for stimulating the National Church'.[13] This belief would evolve as the Ten Years' Conflict progressed. During a meeting at

9. Samuel Hanna to Thomas Chalmers, 12 January 1843, NCL, Chalmers Papers, CHA.4.308.74; Hanna to Chalmers, 19 January 1843, NCL, CHA.4.308.76.
10. J. L. Porter, *Life and Times of Henry Cooke, D.D., LL.D* (London, 1871), 432.
11. James McCosh to Thomas Chalmers, 11 November 1842, NCL, CHA.4.304.35.
12. Josias Wilson to Thomas Chalmers, 23 August 1841, NCL, CHA.4.301.70.
13. Thomas Chalmers, *Lectures on the Establishment and Extension of National Churches, delivered in London, from April 25 to May 12, 1838* (Glasgow, 1838), 88–9; Chalmers to James Lenox,

Glasgow City Hall immediately prior to the Disruption, Chalmers claimed that this fusion of 'the legal with the voluntary principle' was a consistent feature of his ecclesiastical policy, citing the Church Extension scheme of the previous decade as evidence of this approach. He declared that 'my invariable sentiment all along has been that both are best'. Chalmers argued that the policy of 'external voluntaryism', in which contributions are centralised in a general fund and distributed throughout the country according to need, was 'in precise consistency with the principle of a national establishment'.[14] Chalmers' equation of state endowments to a voluntarily supported general fund was critical in his reconciliation of the voluntary principle and the maintenance of a 'national' church in the period leading up to the Disruption. While many within the evangelical faction of the Established Kirk feared a transition 'from endowments to voluntaryism', at the November 1842 Edinburgh convocation of non-intrusionist ministers Chalmers was able to pitch the coming schism as a simple conversion from 'a state-endowed church to a nationally-endowed church'.[15]

The rhetoric of a voluntarily endowed national church only increased in the aftermath of the Disruption in May 1843. By emphasising the national character of the Disruption the Free Church could theoretically distance itself from its new position as a seceding body. A catechism on the principles and constitution of the Free Church, issued by the General Assembly in 1845, presented the anti-erastian ideals of the Disruption as an integral component of the history of the Church of Scotland. In doing so, the Free Church emphasised its claim to be the rightful heir of the historic church and the 'true' national church.[16] At the inaugural Free Church General Assembly, Robert Smith Candlish reminded his colleagues of the 'high position' they had occupied during the Ten Years' Conflict and warned of the 'danger, that when the excitement is over, we shall settle down into a mere Scottish protesting and seceding sect'.[17] To Candlish, anything other than presenting the Free Church as the 'real national Church of Scotland' and as a 'Kingdom', superior to all other dissenting denominations, was absurd.[18] The *Belfast News-Letter* claimed that the 'prestige' of the establishment had 'not departed' from the Free Church, and that it remained

    n.d. (c. March 1840), NYPL, James Lenox Papers, MssCol 1732; James Lenox to Chalmers, 27 January 1841, NCL, CHA.4.299.42.
14. *Great Church Meetings in Glasgow. Addresses delivered at the formation of a Young Men's Evangelical Church of Scotland Society and address of the Rev. Dr Chalmers on the Free Presbyterian Church in Scotland* (Glasgow, 1843), 22–3.
15. Thomas Chalmers, *Sermon preached before the Convocation of Ministers in St George's Church, Edinburgh, on Thursday the 17 of November, 1842* (Edinburgh, 1842), 2–3.
16. *Catechism on the principles and constitution of the Free Church*, 61–81.
17. PGAFC, May 1843, 36–7.
18. PGAFC, May 1844 (Edinburgh, 1844), 202; *Christian Witness, and Church Member's Magazine*, i (London, 1844), 149.

the 'true Church of Scotland, and not a mere dissenting communion'.[19] The Presbyterian Church in Ireland, of which the *News-Letter* was the most prominent organ, solidified this stance by officially recognising the Free Church as Scotland's national church. The first Irish General Assembly to follow the Disruption described the Free Church 'alone as the legitimate representative of those from whom the Presbyterian Church in Ireland has always regarded it the noblest distinction to be descended'.[20] Alexander Goudy, minister at Strabane, told the Free Kirk's Glasgow General Assembly that there was never any doubt among Irish Presbyterians that the new body was the 'supreme judicatory of the ancient Church of Scotland', a view he argued was confirmed by the actions of both the Free Church and the establishment in the months following the Disruption.[21] Indeed, such was the support within Ulster Presbyterianism for the Disruption and Free Church principles that formal links between the Presbyterian Church in Ireland and the Established Church of Scotland were only resumed in 1885. In keeping with the triumphalist rhetoric of the Disruption, the Church of Scotland was ridiculed by one Free Churchman, Jonathan Anderson, as a 'residuary Corporation' and an 'Anti-Christian community'.[22]

These attacks were based on the fact that the Church of Scotland was now a minority establishment. While it remained the single largest Presbyterian denomination in Scotland, the effects of the Disruption ravaged the Established Kirk. By the time of the 1851 religious census, only 32 per cent of churchgoers on census Sunday attended the Church of Scotland. In Aberdeen, one of the areas where the Disruption was most keenly felt, Free Church attendance was double that of the establishment.[23] In 1844 the *Free Church Magazine* calculated that of 2.6 million Scots, 700,000 attended the Free Church, while 900,000 remained in the 'Auld Kirk', as it was becoming increasingly known. This albeit rough estimate allowed William Maxwell Hetherington, the magazine's editor, to commend the 'numerical and moral strength of the Free Church'. However, with considerably more tact than his colleague Anderson, Hetherington also acknowledged that the Free Church had not 'left behind all that was bad in the Establishment'.[24] In their report on the first General Assembly, *The Times* echoed this sentiment, highlighting the large yet 'discordant' nature of the secession, and claimed that despite an almost universal deference to Chalmers, 'we cannot

---

19. *Belfast News-Letter*, 14 November 1843.
20. Andrew R. Holmes, *The Irish Presbyterian Mind: Conservative Theology, Evangelical Experience, and Modern Criticism, 1830–1930* (Oxford, 2018), 49.
21. *PGAFC, held at Glasgow, October 17, 1843* (Glasgow, 1843), 55.
22. *Edinburgh Advertiser*, 2 January 1844; *Glasgow Courier*, 1 January 1844.
23. S. J. Brown, *National Churches*, 406–7; Robert Currie, Alan Gilbert and Lee Horsley, *Churches and Church-Goers: Patterns of Church Growth in the British Isles since 1700* (Oxford, 1977), 219; Brown and Fry, *Scotland in the age of the Disruption*, viii; MacLaren, *Religion and Social Class*, 44–5.
24. *FCM*, i (January 1844), 9–13.

help suspecting that they are destined, and that before long, to undergo another subdivision'.[25] Nevertheless, the national character of the Free Church in 1843 cannot be disputed. Despite not completely emptying the Established Church of its members, as many in the Free Church might have hoped, the numerical harm inflicted on the Church of Scotland ensured it at least could no longer identify as the 'Church of the Nation'.[26]

As we saw in the first chapter, despite an unwillingness to identify with Scotland's other seceding bodies, the Free Church was welcomed with open arms into the dissenting fold. The Free Church minister Thomas Guthrie praised the 'kind and cordial support' offered by Scottish dissenters in the wake of the Disruption, a sharp contrast to the 'inveterate hostility' that characterised the Voluntary Controversy and had marred relations between the two groups right up until the Disruption.[27] Acknowledging the previous bitterness between Scotland's Presbyterian denominations, the United Secession leader John Brown described the Disruption as 'a display of the force of principle' that 'even the bitterest of their opponents are constrained in their hearts to do homage'.[28] Much of the positive voluntary response to the Disruption was centred on the serious wounds it inflicted on the Established Church, and the establishment principle in general. Leading Congregationalist Ralph Wardlaw claimed that the non-intrusionists had embodied the spirit of dissent within the establishment, and had effectively become 'Dissenters *in* the Church'. Despite their insistence on upholding the principle of national religion, Wardlaw suggested that, due to their repeated attacks on the Established Church as it stood, Chalmers and his adherents were 'contending for right principles in a wrong place'.[29] James Harper, speaking as part of a United Secession deputation to the Free Church General Assembly of October 1843, emphasised the importance of the Disruption to Scotland's dissenters, claiming that 'the emancipation from State control achieved by you none can rejoice in more fervently than we'.[30]

Dissenting support for the Disruption, based on the belief that the Free Church, consciously or otherwise, was working towards the historic aims of the Scottish voluntaries, was almost immediately derailed by Chalmers' infamous inaugural address at the May Assembly. The speech, in which Chalmers vigorously upheld the establishment principle while criticising the voluntaries as the 'corrupters' and 'tyrants' of the Scottish Church,

---

25. *The Times*, 29 May 1843.
26. Edward Royle, *Modern Britain: a social history, 1750–2011* (London, 2012), 374; MacLaren, *Religion and Social Class*, 55.
27. *PGAFC, May 1843*, 98–9.
28. John Brown, Speech at Canonmills Hall, Edinburgh, 14 December 1843, in Wallace, *Testimonies in favour*, 30.
29. Ralph Wardlaw, *The Sentiments and Conduct of Dissenters towards their Non-Intrusion Brethren in the Established Church* (Edinburgh, 1843), 2.
30. *PGAFC, October 1843*, 47.

was ridiculed by the *United Secession Magazine* as 'illiberal, anti-popular, and sectarian'. While the magazine conceded that 'honesty required' the Evangelical leader 'to declare that they were not voluntaries', the association, 'in one well-conned sentence', of voluntaries 'with "demagogues", "agitators", and "anarchists"' was deemed particularly offensive and 'unworthy of a man occupying his position'.[31] The Free Church immediately went on the defensive and claimed that the offensive nature of the address was simply due to a newspaper 'misreport'. Less than a week after the speech, Welsh wrote to the leading dissenting politician and Congregationalist Adam Black to explain that Chalmers was merely stating the Free Kirk's continued attachment to the establishment principle, and was not attacking the right of voluntaries to oppose the church–state connection.[32] Despite Chalmers' attempt to repair the damage himself through an amended report in the following week's *Witness*, the 'general current' of the speech, claimed the *Nonconformist*, 'no subsequent explanations can change'.[33] The speech was greeted with the 'profoundest distress' among Edinburgh dissenters, while in England, the Congregational Union described Chalmers' 'pretensions' on ecclesiastical establishments as 'somewhat alarming'.[34] The reverberations spread across the Atlantic. In a debate on slavery in Cincinnati, the pro-slavery Presbyterian minister Nathan Rice claimed that Chalmers was 'blinded by his prejudices' on the subject of establishments.[35]

Though Chalmers bore the brunt of dissenting criticism in the aftermath of his speech, the hostility to voluntaryism in the Free Church did not stop at its leader. Candlish, the rising star of the new body, was perhaps even more forceful in his denunciation of the voluntary principle, stating his desire to 'maintain uncompromised our principle of a religious establishment'. In response to letters from English dissenters expressing their hope that the formation of the Free Church was a move towards voluntaryism, he retorted 'that we do not see, we have never seen, and trust that we will never see, that the movement we have made is at all a step in advance of the Voluntary principle'.[36] The reaction by the voluntaries to these respective declarations by the two leading Free Church ministers is noteworthy as it indicates the shifting positions within the new kirk's hierarchy after May 1843. While the Disruption was undoubtedly the defining moment of Chalmers' public life, it was becoming clear by this point that Candlish was

---

31. *PGAFC, May 1843*, 11–13, 99; *USM*, xi (August 1843), 38–9.
32. David Welsh to Adam Black, 23 May 1843, NLS, Black and Tait Letters, MSS 3713.
33. *Witness*, 30 May 1843.
34. *PGAFC, May 1843*, 99; *Christian Witness*, 30 April 1844.
35. Jonathan Blanchard and N. L. Rice, *A debate on slavery: held in the city of Cincinnati, on the first, second, third, and sixth days of October, 1845, upon the question: is slave-holding in itself sinful, and the relation between master and slave, a sinful relation?* (Cincinnati, 1846), 241–2.
36. *PGAFC, May 1843*, 37; *PGAFC, October 1843*, 38; R. S. Candlish, *Notes on Rev. John Cumming's letter to the Marquis of Cholmondeley on the present state of the Church of Scotland* (London, 1843), 5.

swiftly positioning himself as his heir apparent – and the voluntaries knew it. 'A speech from Dr Chalmers, though an element in the case, is a very trifling one', claimed the *United Secession Magazine*, 'it has distressed us much more to observe Dr Candlish frequently manifesting a similar exclusive and repellent spirit'.[37]

Nevertheless, it was Chalmers who was initially charged with the task of steering the disparate components of the Free Church in such an unprecedented direction. His General Assembly address pitched the Free Church as an ultra-establishmentarian body outside of the establishment, a stance, *The Times* claimed, that placed Chalmers in an uncomfortable position. Rather ominously, the article remarked that 'there are others [within the Free Church] who are not at all uncomfortably placed' and that 'he and his will, before long, find themselves at issue with them and theirs'.[38] The *Morning Chronicle* echoed this sentiment: 'the zealous advocate of Church Establishments, he has become the leader of a Voluntary Association – of a Free Church; and yet the reasons on which he defends the course he has taken have a certain kind of awkwardness, which can hardly be read without a feeling of pain'.[39] While Chalmers' maiden address as Moderator appeared to definitively place him as the 'zealous' anti-voluntary, his earlier discourses on the benefits of voluntaryism within a national system indicate that the reality was much more complex. Nevertheless, it opened a public debate between the churches on the respective virtues of the establishment and voluntary principles within Scotland's new dissenting framework.

This debate often centred on the suitability of both principles on a national scale. To the Free Church, which continued to place emphasis on a nation's obligation to promote religion, voluntaryism on its own was an ineffective tool in the struggle to build a godly nation.[40] The leading Free Church writer and geologist Hugh Miller argued that Scotland's voluntary clergy 'act but feebly on the mass to which they are attached, and not at all good on the formidable masses beyond'. He claimed that the 'religious men of the party are comparatively few', a view echoed by one contributor to the *Free Church Magazine*, who described voluntaryism as 'purely political, and a very hollow and hypocritical thing'. Miller, the editor of the Free Church-supporting newspaper the *Witness*, believed that a 'Voluntary triumph' would prove 'the bane of the country', claiming that 'it is not the spirit of modern Voluntaryism . . . which is to re-establish the old character' of Scotland and 'save our country'.[41] The national pretensions of the early Free Church, so strikingly evident in Chalmers' and Candlish's vision of a 'people-endowed' Church of Scotland, were heavily criticised by the *United*

37. *USM*, xi (August 1843), 39.
38. *Times*, 29 May 1843.
39. *Morning Chronicle*, 29 May 1843.
40. *PGAFC*, May 1844, 67–8.
41. Hugh Miller, 'The Position and Duty of the Free Church', *Free Church Tracts No. 11* (1872), 3–4; *USM*, iii (July 1846), 44.

Secession Magazine. The Free Church, which the magazine argued maintained the establishment principle with an 'unnecessary degree of warmth', was styling itself as 'the sole and honoured instrument of evangelising the nation'. The 'free and easy manner' in which the new body was building places of worship throughout Scotland after 1843, as if 'the whole country had hitherto been in a state of perpetual darkness', was viewed by the voluntaries as the foundation of a merely divisive, not national, church.[42] The Free Church's rejection of voluntary ideology also led others to question their new position as a dissenting body. At the inaugural conference of the British Anti-State Church Association, held in London in May 1844, Ralph Wardlaw argued that though they were seceders from the Church of Scotland, the Free Church's continued adherence to the establishment principle ensured they could not be regarded as true dissenters. In a stirring defence of voluntaryism as the sole criterion for a dissenting church, Wardlaw claimed that 'there was no consistent half-way house between Dissent and Establishment'.[43] However, the Free Church's willing embrace of 'practical' voluntaryism after the Disruption ensured that, consciously or otherwise, they indeed occupied this half-way house.

Practical Voluntaries?

Following the events of May 1843, the clergy and members of the Free Church of Scotland were by and large practical voluntaries. Outside of the state-funded establishment, they were voluntaries of necessity, but not of theory. Though the reality was more complex and prone to shift over time, this would prove the de facto official position of the Free Church for most of the following thirty years. While voluntaries like Wardlaw were quick to point out the duplicity evident in the concurrent establishmentarian and voluntary stance of Chalmers and the Free Church, this position was certainly not new.[44] The Tractarian movement in the Church of England, Irish Presbyterians, Wesleyans and Welsh Calvinistic Methodists all adhered to the Free Church ideal of spiritual independence long before the Disruption, advocating a 'pure', self-governing religious establishment free from state interference.[45] Like the Free Church in Scotland, in the initial period after the Disruption at least, the Wesleyans were traditionally the largest yet most unrepresentative in principle of England's dissenting

---

42. *PGAFC, October 1843*, 126; *USM*, xi (September 1843), 495.
43. British Anti-State Church Association, *Proceedings of the first Anti-State–Church Conference, held in London, April 30, May 1 & 2* (London, 1844), 25–6.
44. *Morning Chronicle*, 29 May 1843.
45. G. I. T. Machin, 'The Disruption and British politics 1834–43', *Scottish Historical Review*, li (1972), 20; Geoffrey Rowell, 'The ecclesiology of the Oxford Movement', in Stewart J. Brown, Peter B. Nockles and James Pereiro (eds), *The Oxford Handbook of the Oxford Movement* (Oxford, 2017), 216–30; A. R. Holmes, 'Presbyterian religion, historiography, and Ulster Scots identity, c. 1800 to 1914', *Historical Journal*, lii (2009), 624.

factions. They did not regard themselves as either churchmen or dissenters, and stood in 'relation to both these parties as neither of them does to the other'.[46] Timothy Larsen portrayed Wesleyan Methodism's position of dissent as 'more an unfortunate (but perhaps necessary) circumstance rather than a point of principle to be trumpeted', a description that resonates heavily with the Free Church position after 1843. However, as Machin has illustrated, it is worth noting that Wesleyan adherence to this third way in ecclesiastical politics loosened in much the same manner as the Free Church towards the end of the nineteenth century, as disestablishment became a national issue in Britain from the 1870s.[47] Nevertheless, for most of the 1840s and 1850s the Free Church reflected the ambiguity between dissent and establishment evident in E. P. Thompson's withering depiction of the Wesleyans, who he argued did 'their utmost to make the worst of both worlds'.[48] Yet the placid Methodist approach alluded to by Thompson was certainly less forthright and self-assured than the Free Church's predominant position in the years following the Disruption. As practical voluntaries committed to the establishment principle, they appeared to be apologists for an institution they believed was corrupt, and practitioners of a method they solemnly detested.

Nevertheless, the Free Church's new position as 'practical voluntaries' fostered a spirit of cordiality and co-operation between the dissenting churches, which will be discussed further in the next chapter. Most importantly in the short term, the duality of the Free Church's ideological position allowed it to adopt a chameleon-like form outside of Scotland, which became particularly useful during the 'begging' missions to England and America.[49] These deputations were essential to the Free Church drive to achieve Chalmers' projected annual target of £100,000 to sustain the clergy. At the time of the Disruption, Scotland was in the midst of a severe economic depression. Widespread unemployment, and therefore less money for congregational offerings, was coupled with the hostile reception from landlords to the new church. This ensured that the influence and financial aid of supporters in England, Ireland and the United States was deemed necessary to secure the funds lacking from a suffering Scottish population.[50]

Buoyed by the generally enthusiastic response to the Disruption from

---

46. 'The Common Enemy', *Wesleyan Methodist Magazine*, x (June 1854), 536.
47. Larsen, *Friends of Religious Equality*, 17; Machin, *Politics and the Churches in Great Britain*, 247, 345–6.
48. E. P. Thompson, *The Making of the English Working Class* (London, 1963), 350–1.
49. *USM*, xi (September 1843), 46–7.
50. Daniel Ritchie, 'Antislavery Orthodoxy: Isaac Nelson and the Free Church of Scotland, c. 1843–65', *Scottish Historical Review*, xciv (2015), 77; Brown, *Thomas Chalmers and the Godly Commonwealth*, 336–46; George Thompson and Henry C. Wright, *The Free Church of Scotland. Substance of speeches delivered in the Music Hall, Edinburgh, during May and June 1846* (Edinburgh, 1846), 50.

English dissenters, as well as a minority within the Church of England, the Free Church devised an ambitious scheme to raise £50,000 for church-building through a series of calculated mission trips. The ministers venturing south of the Tweed were also expected to uphold the Free Church's founding principles of national religion and spiritual independence, while there were whispers of a 'grand project of union' with England's dissenters conceived by Candlish.[51] While early deputations may have been 'soliciting the *voluntary* contributions of the English public', as pointed out by the *Bradford Observer*, they took 'care to let it be known that they were not in the slightest degree tinctured with voluntaryism'.[52] To do otherwise, claimed the *Witness*, would be 'unbrotherly and unchristian'.[53] However, the failure of the deputations to raise the General Assembly's ambitious target – £27,689 was raised in England in the year after the Disruption, including money donated by the Free Church's London Committee – saw subsequent deputations markedly change their tone to suit their dissenting audiences.[54] In a letter to a Bradford Baptist minister, Patrick Macfarlan claimed that while 'we have not changed our principles ... we never were opposed' to voluntaryism, and expressed a desire for voluntary contributions 'to enable us to prosecute the glorious end of making the Free Church commensurate with the boundaries of our beloved country'.[55] Other delegates were much more forthright in their denunciation of their former principles. In Bristol, Nathaniel Paterson, who in that year's forthcoming General Assembly would argue that English dissenters were warming to Free Church principles, attested that the Free Church 'were, practically, voluntaries, and would be to the end of their days'. He claimed to believe that 'they were sailing in the same ship with the Dissenters and the Free Church had no other dependence than on the providence of God and the voluntary principle'.[56] Another minister, Robert Forbes of Aberdeen, professed to a Bury congregation that the principles of the Free Church and English nonconformists were practically the same.[57] These assertions led one Baptist minister, H. I. Roper, to affirm that 'it was clear they of the Free Church of Scotland were in the high road to the voluntary principle'.[58]

However, around the same time as the 'Send Back the Money' campaign began to shed light on the church's acceptance of donations from American slave-owners, the Free Church fundraising campaign in England

---

51. Wallace, *Testimonies in favour*, 60–5; *PGAFC, October 1843*, 84–6; *Dumfries Herald*, 16 January 1844.
52. *Bradford Observer*, 9 November 1843.
53. *Witness*, 13 January 1844.
54. *PGAFC, May 1844*, 110–15.
55. *Leeds Times*, 20 December 1843.
56. *Bristol Mercury*, 20 January 1844; *PGAFC, May 1844*, 115.
57. *Bury and Norwich Post, and East Anglican*, 13 March 1844.
58. *Bristol Mercury*, 27 January 1844.

suffered a setback in 1844.⁵⁹ This was due to the hostile reaction within English dissent to the Free Church's expulsion of the young voluntary preacher at Girvan, Peter Hately Waddell, a move that emphasised the new church leadership's strident defence of establishmentarianism, which stood in stark contrast to their voluntary posturing in England at the same time. Waddell, only twenty-six years old and a probationer for ordination when the Disruption occurred, represented a new generation of Free Church preachers more detached from the bonds of the church–state relationship and confessional orthodoxy, and increasingly inclined to favour their new voluntary position in both theory and practice. Through a series of pamphlets published throughout 1843, he outlined his opposition to any future plans for re-establishment and expressed his belief that evangelical dissent was the only means available for purifying religion.⁶⁰ In a public letter to Chalmers and Thomas Guthrie, Waddell criticised the Free Church leader's speech at the Disruption Assembly, and instead demanded that 'we must be voluntaries', insisting that 'the question of voluntaryism cannot be buried' until 'the Establishment has been destroyed'.⁶¹ These deliberate provocations brought him under the scrutiny of local church authorities, and he was moved from the parish of Rhynie, Aberdeenshire, to Girvan in the hope that he 'would follow a more calm and discreet course'.⁶²

Within weeks of his appointment at Girvan in October 1843, Waddell courted more controversy by issuing two petitions to the Free Church General Assembly, then sitting at Glasgow. The first petition, signed by three-quarters of the Girvan congregation, moved for the General Assembly, among other considerations such as the admittance of female voters on matters of church governance, to 'repudiate and renounce' not only the present Church of Scotland, but also the church–state connection itself. The petition argued that 'the connection of a Christian Church with the State is dangerous and fatal to the cause of true, vigorous, and undefiled religion'. In the second even more inflammatory petition, attributed solely to Waddell, he claimed that closer dissenting relations could be achieved by revising or rejecting most of the twenty-third chapter of the Westminster Confession of Faith, which upheld the role of the civil magistrate to enforce national religion and, according to Waddell, acted as a 'bar of separation' between the Free Church and voluntaries. This chapter, part of a doctrine

---

59. Iain Whyte, *Send back the money: the Free Church of Scotland and American slavery* (Cambridge, 2012).
60. P. H. Waddell, *Orthodoxy is not Evangelism: being a letter of remonstrance, in the name of Christ, to all Orthodox ministers, preachers, and professors of the Gospel, in the Establishment, or out of it* (Glasgow, 1843), 6; Waddell, *Protestant Delusion in the Nineteenth Century; being another letter of remonstrance to all Orthodox ministers, preachers, and professors of the Gospel* (Glasgow, 1843), 7.
61. P. H. Waddell, *A Letter to Thomas Chalmers, D.D., and Rev. Thomas Guthrie, on the question of co-operation with Dissenters* (Glasgow, 1843), 6–7, 15–16.
62. *Caledonian Mercury*, 20 May 1844.

Waddell rather sensationally claimed that 'the great bulk of the professing Christian world has never read, does not understand, and far less believes', was described in the petition as 'a serious stumbling-block to many conscientious adherents of the Free Church' and that 'does not appear to them to be consistent with itself, or with the present position of the Free Church'.[63]

Unsurprisingly, the General Assembly disagreed and a case of discipline was brought against Waddell. To Free Church traditionalists, Waddell was advocating national atheism that was, according to the Committee of Bills which forwarded the case to the General Assembly, a deviation from the standards of the church and enough to discipline the young probationer.[64] Following some confusion, during which Waddell was unable to defend his case in person, the Acting Committee of the General Assembly's Special Commission, of which Candlish was convenor, withdrew Waddell from his charge at Girvan and barred him from future employment in the Free Church. Waddell duly protested this sanction and compared Candlish's actions to a transaction 'managed by the inferior judicatories of the Papal House, for the suppression of heresy, in the fifteenth century'.[65] After two months of often hostile back and forth with the Ayr presbytery, Waddell along with the majority of his congregation left the Free Church in early January 1844 to eventually form an independent 'Church of the Future' at Girvan, though he would spend most of that summer on a much ridiculed lecture tour of Scotland criticising the Free Church.[66]

Though Waddell appears to have been simply a firebrand attracted to agitation and controversy, the overt expression of establishmentarianism evident in the treatment of him by Candlish and other Free Church leaders, described as 'tyrannical' by the *Caledonian Mercury*, severely hindered otherwise constructive attempts at cordial co-operation with Scotland's voluntaries, and offered dissenting newspapers a stick with which to beat the perceived hypocrisy of Chalmers and his adherents.[67] The contrast between the Girvan case and the friendly assertions of voluntary co-operation by the

63. P. H. Waddell, *The Girvan Petitions; or the Voluntary Question in the Free Church: being an account of the recent schism in the Free Church congregation at Girvan* (Glasgow, 1844), 3–5; *Scheme of a Confession of Faith and Church Government, adopted by a Reforming Protestant Congregation at Girvan* (Glasgow, 1844), 3.
64. Waddell, *Girvan Petitions*, 2, 6. For examples of Free Church rhetoric on voluntaryism and atheism, which would later play a major role in the opposition to union between the United Presbyterians and the Free Kirk, see William Balfour, *The Establishment Principle Defended: a reply to the statement by the Committee of the United Presbyterian Church on Disestablishment and Disendowment* (Edinburgh, 1873), vi.
65. Waddell, *Girvan Petitions*, 6–7.
66. P. H. Waddell, *Church of the Future; arguments and outlines* (Edinburgh, 1861); *Northern Warder*, 4 June 1844. Concerns about Waddell's divisive and confrontational character were underlined by the United Secession Church's decision to reject his application to join their denomination during the controversy, despite his obvious voluntary credentials (*Caledonian Mercury*, 20 May 1844).
67. *Caledonian Mercury*, 2 May 1844.

deputations in England proved a consistent feature in the press coverage of Waddell's dismissal. According to nonconformist writers in Scotland and England, the controversy at Girvan emphasised what they regarded as the duplicity and dishonesty of the Free Church deputations and their 'unprincipled' attempts to garner both English and American money by concealing their establishment principles 'under the cloak of Voluntaryism'. This position, exploited by the likes of Paterson in England, increasingly became tinged with cynicism by voluntaries and significantly hampered plans for future Free Church co-operation with English dissenters. The *Bradford Observer* compared the Free Church to a man, who in society 'is all smiles and courtesy; at home, a surly tyrant', and suggested that it 'was a very fortunate circumstance for the Free Churchmen that they made their appearance in England before the English public were aware of their home-tricks'.[68] The Free Church for its part remained unapologetic. Shortly after the controversy, Waddell's replacement Ebenezer Wallace dismissed the voluntary issue as a 'very inferior one' and professed the Free Church belief that 'Church and State are authorities co-equal, co-ordinate, the two arms of God's power in the government of the world, mutually independent, but when acting in concord, affording prodigious aid to each other'.[69] The lasting irony of the Girvan controversy would be felt in the coming decades: while the Free Church increasingly adopted the practicalities and principles of voluntaryism in the years after the Disruption, Waddell rejoined the Church of Scotland in 1888.[70] Despite what would emerge in later years, the maintenance in 1844 of the principle of national religion remained a cause of grave concern within the Free Church hierarchy.

Despite their establishmentarian rhetoric, it is unfair to conclude that the Free Church failed to grasp fully the nettle of practical voluntaryism after the Disruption. In fact, as one United Secession minister openly feared, they set out to 'silence our Voluntary boastings by quite transcending our Voluntary exertions'.[71] In order to do so, the Free Church had to reconcile their national and establishmentarian ethos with the practicalities of voluntary religion. Chalmers' biographer William Hanna asserted that the Free Church leader 'threw his mind open to any new convictions which the history of the Free Church might originate or confirm', and while 'he was not prepared at the instant to cast his old convictions away', he was nevertheless 'ready to admit whatever light this new experience might supply'.[72] The purely practical and necessary nature of the Free Church's voluntary experiment was emphasised by both Chalmers and Candlish, who described the question of voluntaryism within the new

68. *Bradford Observer*, 18 April 1844.
69. *Scotsman*, 27 April 1844; E. B. Wallace, *A Lecture on the Right Relation between Church and State; delivered to the Girvan Mechanics' Institution* (Ayr, 1844), 1, 13, 17.
70. *Glasgow Herald*, 6 May 1891.
71. PGAFC, October 1843, 52.
72. William Hanna, *Memoirs of Thomas Chalmers* (4 volumes, Edinburgh, 1852), iv, 477.

church as one of 'Christian economics' and not of 'Christian doctrine' or principle.[73]

Chalmers, at a July 1843 meeting in Edinburgh to celebrate the bicentenary of the Westminster Assembly of the Divines, expressed his willingness to ensure that voluntaryism was 'fully put upon its trial' and vowed to draw upon its resources and capabilities 'to the uttermost'. In a bid to perhaps repair the damage of his opening speech at the May General Assembly, and fully aware of the realities of the new practical situation, Chalmers insisted that 'I for one should most heartily rejoice if Voluntaryism, playing upon us in every direction, shall make such demonstrations of its exuberance and its power as well-nigh to submerge myself, and utterly to overwhelm my argument'. However, he made it clear that the success of voluntaryism within the Free Church was reliant upon its ability to function nationally. If the 'utmost efforts' of voluntaryism, Chalmers suggested, 'shall fall short of a full provision for the Christian instruction of the people, so as to leave thousands and thousands more unreached and unclaimed', the Free Church leader – rather naively – opened the door to the acceptance of a governmental endowment, similar to the *regium donum* in Ireland, which would leave the church 'unfettered' from state interference and free to service the Christian need of the country.[74] Chalmers' speech, though nominally an acceptance of full voluntary methods within the new body, offers an insight into the realities of early Free Church voluntaryism: first, its purely practical and potentially transient nature; second, the requirement of a successful national system, in which the Free Church could maintain its claim to be the 'true' Church of Scotland.

The need for the Free Church to resemble a national church was evident in the support for a 'General Fund', a national system outlined by Chalmers as early as 1841, which would be comprised of a Building Fund supported by congregational donations, and a Sustentation Fund upheld by payments to a local association.[75] The Sustentation Fund would provide the Free Church with a centralised administration free from the whims and fluctuating wealth of individual congregations and presbyteries. By doing so, this 'common store for all' attempted to provide ministers with the advantages of establishment – a steady income – while losing its disadvantages such as the perceived gulf between state-endowed ministers and their congregations.[76] In theory at least, it would ensure that the strong could support the weak and enable the Free Church to operate an ambitious development programme effectively

73. *PGAFC, October 1843*, 37, 39.
74. *Bicentenary of the Assembly of Divines at Westminster, held at Edinburgh, July 12 and 13, 1843* (Philadelphia, 1845), 179–80; *Aberdeen Journal*, 19 July 1843.
75. Hanna, *Memoirs of Thomas Chalmers*, iv, 564–5.
76. William K. Tweedie to Thomas Chalmers, 14 May 1845, NCL, CHA 4.320.52; *Dundee Warder*, 5 September 1843; Chalmers to Tweedie, 14 May 1845, NCL, CHA 3.17.93.

and efficiently throughout Scotland, not just in small pockets of wealthy districts.[77]

The General Fund was based on Chalmers' interpretation of 'external voluntaryism', which he believed to be compatible with the Free Kirk's national vision and an able, if only necessary, replacement for state endowments. External voluntaryism, Chalmers explained prior to the Disruption, was a process in which 'a congregation extends its liberality to other and poorer congregations around it'.[78] The General Fund, by dispensing equal ministerial stipends across the country, would facilitate and centralise this process. The fifth act of the October 1843 General Assembly stipulated that every minister on the Sustentation Fund would receive a minimum yearly income regardless of the amount offered by their local congregation, set by Chalmers and the Financial Committee at the ambitious national target of £150.[79] According to Robert Buchanan, a future convenor of the Sustentation Fund, this 'equal dividend' would enable the Free Church, 'though disestablished, to maintain the standing and character of a National Institution'.[80] Additionally, a local or supplementary fund, utilising internal voluntaryism – in which a congregation supports its own minister – would coexist with the General Fund. These congregational funds, usually derived from pew-rents and church-door collections, could be used to provide ministers with an additional stipend and to support other local activities, such as the funding of Sabbath schools, at the discretion of the individual congregations.[81] As James McCosh noted in a letter to the Free Church leader in September 1843, the 'local' principles of internal voluntaryism would aim to complement, and possibly advance, the efficiency of the General Fund's 'patriotic' principles, though McCosh did warn of the necessity for every congregation to actively support the national fund. Despite advocating that 'both are best' when used together, Chalmers also stressed the dangers of uninhibited internal voluntaryism on a national church system.[82]

He dismissed the 'inherent feebleness' and 'utter inefficiency' of a pure internal system for 'covering the whole land', and warned, with a particular eye to the wealthier areas, that 'we shall fall to pieces if we leave each congregation to shift for itself'.[83] To Chalmers, the national church was

---

77. Drummond and Bulloch, *The Church in Victorian Scotland*, 15; 'Regulations and Resolutions as to the Administration of the Funds for supplying ordinances', *AGAFC, October 1843*, 51–2.
78. *Great Church Meetings in Glasgow*, 20–3.
79. *AGAFC, October 1843*, 51; *PGAFC, October 1843*, 123
80. *Remarks on the Sustentation Fund of the Free Church of Scotland, including a plan for promoting church extension without encroaching on the Equal Dividend Fund* (Edinburgh, 1855), 7–8.
81. *AGAFC, October 1843*, 51.
82. James McCosh to Thomas Chalmers, 19 September 1843, NCL, CHA 4.335.33; *Great Church Meetings in Glasgow*, 22.
83. *PGAFC, October 1843*, 125.

paramount: 'If your care for your own minister shall lead you to neglect the general fund, then, in virtue of this neglect, we shall lose all title to be a national, or compact, or extended Church.'[84] In order to combat any potential neglect from wealthier yet more selfish congregations, the Financial Committee possessed a discretionary power to 'withhold a portion of the dividend' in cases in which 'it may clearly appear to them that the congregations are improperly diverting their whole means to their own local objects, and wilfully withholding their due contributions from the General Fund, of which they share the benefit'.[85]

The object of the General Fund was to 'Christianize the whole of Scotland', and was deemed a 'greater and patriotic good' than the local fund, which as the Free Churchman James Lewis argued, was prone to vast inequalities even within the same city. The free market of internal voluntaryism did not appeal to Chalmers' paternal and national instincts. He argued, with more than a slight reference to the urban-centric nature of Scottish dissent, that internal voluntaryism, through its 'vitiating flaw of a partial or personal interest', would 'speedily degenerate' the Free Church's system 'into a mere economy of rare and isolated congregations, flourishing it may be in towns, but dying by inches, and at length fading utterly away, throughout the main length and breadth of the Scottish territory'.[86] The external voluntaryism of Chalmers' General Fund, on the other hand, would embody the 'Christian Patriotism' evident in the Disruption and aim to provide for the 'moral and religious good' of the entire country, from 'the poor Highland parishes of the west' to the 'innumerable putrid, wretched lanes of our great cities'.[87] It also appeared to provide the most direct replacement to national state funding. A 'fountain of all supplies', the Sustentation Fund would, Lewis claimed, 'alone uphold the executive power and administrative vigour' of the Free Church.[88] Most crucially to Free Churchmen, the centralised character of the General Fund, as McCosh argued, not only constituted 'the grand distinction betwixt the Free Church and every other body of Dissenters' but also, 'if well maintained', entitled the new body to the status of 'the national church'. The only change after May 1843, McCosh claimed, was that Scotland's national kirk was now a people-endowed rather than state-endowed church.[89]

On the surface, the Free Church embrace of practical voluntaryism was

---

84. *Great Church Meetings in Glasgow*, 20–3.
85. *AGAFC, October 1843*, 51.
86. Free Church of Scotland, *Report of the Financial Committee to the General Assembly of 1843* (Edinburgh, 1843), 2–4; James Lewis, *Finance of the Free Church of Scotland: Suggestions on the principles of distribution, for the consideration of the fathers and brethren of the Free Assembly* (Edinburgh, 1843), 5.
87. *Dundee Warder*, 5 September 1843; *Great Church Meetings in Glasgow*, 23.
88. Lewis, *Finance of the Free Church of Scotland*, 6.
89. James McCosh to Thomas Chalmers, 19 September 1843, NCL, CHA 4.335.33.

a success. While Drummond and Bulloch have highlighted that from the very beginning the system was overstrained, in the initial years at least, zeal went a long way.[90] Church extension was rapid; in the decade following the Disruption, an average of twenty-one additional congregations was established every year.[91] Accordingly, the building of churches, rather than the sustentation of ministers, was identified early by Chalmers as the principal objective of the General Fund.[92] In its first four years, the Free Church had 730 churches and claimed to have raised £450,000 for the erection of new buildings across Scotland, £100,000 for ministers' manses and £50,000 to build 500 schoolhouses. The Free Church's own New College for training ministers, with nine professorships, was established in Edinburgh in 1843 and two other theological colleges were soon founded in Aberdeen and Glasgow. The foundation stone of New College, located on the Mound in Edinburgh city centre, was laid by its first Principal, Chalmers, in June 1846 and the building was completed in November 1850, a year after the erection of the Aberdeen college building.[93] The funds secured to enable this ambitious building programme, according to the *Free Church Magazine*, were 'far beyond what even the most sanguine would have anticipated'.[94] S. J. Brown has described the Free Church's building scheme as one of Victorian Britain's greatest achievements.[95]

Despite the apparent success story of the zealous new Free Church, there were early murmurs of discontent. The 'indefinite power' of external voluntaryism with its equal dividend, much vaunted by Chalmers in 1843, failed almost immediately to live up to expectations. The Sustentation Fund proved particularly inadequate in providing satisfactory ministerial stipends. At the October 1843 General Assembly the Financial Committee recommended an interim payment of £40 to be granted to ministers for the half-year following the Disruption, an allowance far short of the projected annual target of £150. The committee claimed that the underperformance of the Sustentation Fund was a result of the church's focus being diverted to other pertinent objects such as the Building Fund and the church extension scheme.[96] According to Chalmers, once 'our buildings are completed and the organization of the country is set fully at work', then attention

---

90. Drummond and Bulloch, *The Church in Victorian Scotland*, 15.
91. *Remarks on the Sustentation Fund*, 5.
92. Thomas Chalmers to James Lenox, 28 July 1843, NYPL, James Lenox Papers, MssCol 1732; Building Committee of the Free Church of Scotland, *Communication to the friends of the Free Church of Scotland* (Edinburgh, 1845).
93. Hanna, *Memoirs of Thomas Chalmers*, iv, 473; Parsons, 'Church and State in Victorian Scotland', 116; S. J. Brown, 'The Disruption and the Dream: the making of New College 1843–1861', in David Wright and Gary Badcock (eds), *Disruption to Diversity: Edinburgh Divinity 1846–1996* (Edinburgh, 1996), 29–52.
94. *FCM*, iii, no. 30, June 1846, 168.
95. Brown, *Thomas Chalmers and the Godly Commonwealth*, 344–5.
96. *PGAFC, October 1843*, 123–4;

could turn to the sustentation of the ministry.[97] Nevertheless, to rectify the existing shortfall, in 1844 the Free Church leader controversially deviated from the equal dividend principle, introducing a new system termed the 'half-more scheme', a kind of mixed internal voluntaryism tenuously proposed by James Lewis a year earlier.[98] Designed to combat what many in the Free Church hierarchy deemed as the inherent selfishness of certain wealthier congregations who supplemented their own minister at the expense of the national objectives of the church, the 'half-more' offered an incentive for these congregations to donate the entirety of their collections to the General Fund.[99] According to this incentive-based scheme, the General Fund promised to supplement the original contributions of individual congregations by a further 50 per cent. A congregation raising £60, for instance, would receive an additional £30 from the General Fund, totalling £90. This would apply up to the predetermined minimum ministerial stipend of £150, an amount that, though championed by Chalmers in 1843, was not reached nationwide until 1868.[100] While this divisive system only lasted until 1848, when the principle of an equal dividend was reinstated, its very implementation highlighted the deficiencies of the Free Church's effort to create a national and centralised voluntary church through the General Fund.[101]

Despite incentivised schemes such as the half-more, the national income of the Sustentation Fund alone was insufficient to providing an equal dividend of £150 for all Free Church ministers. As Table 2.1 shows, throughout the 1840s the number of ministers receiving a stipend from the General Fund expanded at a much greater rate than those collecting a full equal dividend, which invariably fell far below its projected target in the church's formative years. This was largely due to the rapid expansion of the Free Church ministry after 1843 and the inadequate amounts raised by the Sustentation Fund to facilitate this growth. In the seven years following the Disruption, an approximate average of £18,000 a year extra in contributions would have been required for every Free Church minister on the Sustentation Fund to receive an annual salary of £150.

Chalmers' aim to cover the entirety of Scotland, from the Highlands to the cities, with an equal dividend also appeared under scrutiny as early

97. Thomas Chalmers to James Lenox, 16 January 1844, NYPL, James Lenox Papers, MssCol 1732.
98. Thomas Chalmers, *Considerations on the economics of the Free Church for 1844* (Glasgow, 1844), 6–7; 'Act anent the future arrangements of the Sustentation Fund', *AGAFC 1844*, 16; Lewis, *Finance of the Free Church of Scotland*, 4–5.
99. W. K. Tweedie to Thomas Chalmers, 17 June 1845, NCL, CHA.4.320.56; Thomas Chalmers, *On the Economics of the Free Church of Scotland* (Glasgow, 1845), 25.
100. Robert Buchanan, *The Finance of the Free Church of Scotland: its origins, objects, methods, and results* (London, 1870), 90; Thomas Chalmers to Peter Henderson, 13 December 1845, in William Hanna (ed.), *A selection from the correspondence of the late Thomas Chalmers, D.D., LL.D.* (New York, 1853), 400–1.
101. 'Act anent the appropriation of the Sustentation Fund', *AGAFC 1848*, 14.

Table 2.1 Development of the Equal Dividend, 1843–50

Year	Ministers on Sustentation Fund	Ministers on Equal Dividend	Equal Dividend (£)	Sustentation Fund income (£)	Amount required for all ministers to receive £150 (£)
1843–4	583	470	105	61,513	87,450
1844–5	627	557	122	76,180	94,050
1845–6	657	580	122	80,290	98,550
1846–7	673	590	120	82,166	100,950
1847–8	684	596	128	84,051	102,600
1848–9	694	623	122	87,519	104,100
1849–50	706	647	123	89,649	105,900

Source: Buchanan, *Finance of the Free Church of Scotland*, p. 106.

as January 1844. The *Dumfries Herald*, in an article entitled 'Flaws in the Free Church', listed ten cases in which the new body had deviated from its stated objectives. Among these was the lack of uniformity across Scotland evident in both the building of places of worship and individual salaries. For instance, Candlish's initial church at Castle Terrace in Edinburgh, deemed by the *Herald*'s writer as an example of the 'cheap City simplicity' to be imitated in the country parishes, soon made way for an apparently 'more showy new church' on the Lothian Road.[102] At the same time, one Free Church minister, described by the *Scottish Guardian* as 'a most respectable country clergyman', complained in a letter to Chalmers of the disparity in the Sustentation Fund between country and city ministers.[103] According to the minister, while Edinburgh and Glasgow ministers, many of whom were 'mere chapels of ease and *quoad sacra* men' prior to the Disruption, received three to five hundred pounds annually from the fund and their more wealthy congregations, country clergymen were 'left to pine' on a 'stinted' allowance of £40. Chalmers' 'testy' retort to this complaint epitomised the rapid shift in his and his church's practical position, demanding that the country ministers 'work up each their own association to the uttermost'. In essence, the Free Church leader was actively promoting the kind of personal interest, through internal voluntaryism, he had vehemently opposed only seven months before. To his detractors, it was becoming apparent within a year of the Disruption that Chalmers, for all of his previous talk about a superior, national form of Free Church voluntaryism, was ushering his kirk 'head over heels' into a system he purportedly despised.[104]

This development was, of course, welcomed by the United Secession and

102. *Dumfries Herald*, 16 January 1844.
103. *Scottish Guardian*, 8 January 1844.
104. *Reformers' Gazette*, 9 January 1844.

Relief churches as evidence of the increasing influence of Scottish voluntaryism. A January 1845 article in the *United Secession Magazine* praised their 'new allies in the field of practical voluntaryism' for subscriptions raised to establish the Free Church training college in Glasgow.[105] However, the speed with which the Free Church embraced its voluntary experiment significantly slowed, at least in certain sections of its leadership, by the mid-1840s. Amid a backdrop of economic depression and an overt reliance on diminished zeal among its adherents – or as the Sustentation Committee termed it in 1846, 'relaxed effort' – Free Church voluntaryism was generally condemned as a failed experiment.[106] This perceived failure centred on the very issues initiatives such as the General Fund had attempted to avoid – the inequality and inadequacy of ministerial stipends, the emergence of a local or 'selfish' congregational mentality and a lack of national character. Despite his best efforts to galvanise his church's voluntary efforts, Chalmers was most critical of its lack of success. In his 1845 essay on Free Church economics, he claimed 'his hopes of an extended Christianity from the efforts of voluntaryism have not been brightened' since the Disruption. Voluntaryism, in both its internal and external forms, was condemned by the Free Church leader, despite 'all its high-sounding pretensions', as 'an impotent and most inoperative theory'.[107] At the 1853 General Assembly, Candlish was even more critical, claiming that voluntaryism had revealed itself to be 'an infinitely worse thing than we ever thought it looked before the Disruption'.[108]

The failure of voluntaryism on a national level in the years following the Disruption was most galling to Chalmers' establishmentarian ethos and hopes of cementing the Free Kirk's position as the true Church of Scotland. In an interview with the Parliamentary Committee on Sites shortly before his death in 1847, Chalmers asserted that the voluntary principle 'does not overtake the masses'.[109] Between 1843 and 1845, while the number of Free Church ministers increased from 470 to 625, the actual number of church associations had fallen to 750 from 800. One of the most prevalent causes given for this failure to permeate Scotland, despite the rapid church extension and increase in 'ecclesiastical labourers', was the promulgation of what Candlish would later describe as 'local and territorial' habits among individual congregations.[110] Chalmers reminded

---

105. *USM*, ii (January 1845), 48.
106. Free Church of Scotland Sustentation Fund Committee, *To the office-bearers of the Free Church* (Edinburgh, 1846); *Earnest Appeal in Behalf of the Sustentation Fund* (Edinburgh, 1849).
107. Chalmers, *On the Economics of the Free Church*, 39–40.
108. *Statement explanatory and defensive of the position assumed by certain ministers and elders of the Free Church of Scotland: in consequence of the decision of last General Assembly in regard to the present scheme of union* (Edinburgh, 1867), 34.
109. *Reports from Committees: Sites for Churches (Scotland)*, H.C. 1847 (9), xiii, 131.
110. Chalmers, *On the Economics of the Free Church*, 23; *Witness*, 17 November 1855; Thomas Chalmers to James Lenox, 29 April 1847, NYPL, James Lenox Papers, MssCol 1732.

his fellow Free Church leaders that voluntaryism would fail as a national project if they became 'too much occupied with the affairs of the inner department to look abroad on the outfields of Scotland'. According to Chalmers in 1845, the habit of maintaining 'a wide and watchful eye over the spiritual necessities of Scotland', in essence the Central Fund, had still to be formed.[111]

This lack of national character was attributed to 'congregational selfishness' in many districts throughout Scotland. While Chalmers vowed not to abandon the poorer localities, wealthier congregations were condemned for not contributing their full potential to the General Fund, and thus placing a heavier burden on their country brethren and retarding the progress of the church's development.[112] In 1848 Buchanan complained in a letter to John Bonar of the 'extremely small' contributions to the fund, and stressed the need for a 'prompt and vigorous effort in all our congregations' to address the deficiency.[113] In many instances, congregational supplements to ministers outweighed, and in some cases doubled, donations to the national fund, prompting one observer to argue that 'it is evident that our People do not heartily approve of this system, for a large proportion of them contribute nothing at all to the fund'.[114] The Free Church minister David Thorburn complained of congregations supplementing their own minister 'at the expense of the Fund or of the poorer congregations', asserting that this inward-looking mentality was the antithesis of the spirit of the fund and the principles upon which it was founded. Most alarmingly to Chalmers, in the year following the Disruption only one-quarter of the Free Church's congregations contributed more than what they received from the fund, with the contributions of a mere fifteen congregations accounting for 20 per cent of its entire income. By contrast, over 150 congregations donated less than £20, while more than 350 offered less than £50.[115] Even poverty was not considered a sufficient excuse by Chalmers for this poor showing. At the General Assembly of May 1844, he noted that while the rural and Highland ministers readily accounted the small offerings as a natural consequence of their poorer congregations, £6,000 a year was spent on tobacco on the island of Islay alone. Chalmers claimed that 'if we got but a tenth of the snuff used by the Highlanders' it would support the church's entire ecclesiastical system in that part of Scotland.[116]

While Chalmers was quick to ridicule his rural brethren, one prominent

---

111. Chalmers, *On the Economics of the Free Church*, 22, 26.
112. Hugh Handyside, *To the Office-bearers of the congregations of the Free Church* (Edinburgh, 1845).
113. Robert Buchanan to J. J. Bonar, 18 February 1848, NCL, Z.h.43/80.
114. [Adelphos], *The Common Fund versus the Sustentation Fund: earnestly addressed to all those who desire the stability of the Free Church of Scotland* (Edinburgh, 1847), 4, 7.
115. Hanna, *Memoirs of Thomas Chalmers*, iv, 364.
116. *PGAFC, May 1844*, 252–3.

Table 2.2 Donations to the general and local funds, 1843–9

Year	Sustentation Fund (£)	Congregational Fund (£)	General Building Fund (£)	Local Building Fund (£)
1843–4	61,513	41,540	85,238	142,598
1844–5	76,180	69,986	34,206	97,532
1845–6	80,290	70,675	23,774	66,066
1846–7	82,166	78,227	38,920	46,446
1847–8	84,051	71,850	23,269	34,566
1848–9	87,519	71,379	22,011	43,981
Total	471,719	403,657	227,418	431,189

Source: Buchanan, *Finance of the Free Church of Scotland*, p. 109.

example of a city congregation more concerned with its own affairs than the national welfare of the church was that of the popular Edinburgh minister James Begg at Newington. Between March 1844 and March 1845, Begg's adherents donated approximately £200 to the Sustentation Fund; by contrast, over £512 was raised for congregational supplements. This remained the case five years later, with the Newington local effort once again more than double the contribution to the central fund.[117] As Table 2.2 highlights, the example of Newington was replicated, though to a much lesser degree, across Scotland with congregational supplements almost equalling and, in the case of the Building Fund, exceeding the national totals raised for the General Fund. The figures for the Building Fund in particular suggest that the initial success of the Free Church's building and extension scheme owed more to localised efforts than any organised national vigour. However, even the stated figures for the Sustentation Fund often do not tell the full story. In 1846, for example, over £80,000 was directed from the General Fund to the sustentation of ministers. However, as stipulated in Act V of the October 1843 General Assembly, £4,395 of that figure was derived from the local supplements of 'self-sustaining' congregations adjudged to have failed in their duty to the General Fund. Taking the remitted funds into account, the local and national figures for 1846 would prove almost identical, at roughly £75,000 each.[118]

Payment of ministers became a serious concern, especially in poorer congregations. The *Free Church Magazine* protested in 1847 that 'the notion that a man's income ought to rise and fall with the wealth or poverty of his people is one of the most perverse fallacies of Voluntaryism'.[119] Across Scotland, congregations struggled to pay their ministers a sufficient wage. Two decades after Chalmers' death, it was noted that the much-vaunted equal dividend of £150 had yet to be achieved nationally, despite

---

117. *AGAFC 1845*, 12; *AGAFC 1850*, 110.
118. *Common Fund versus the Sustentation Fund*, 7.
119. *FCM*, iv (February 1847), 62–4.

the country's wealth doubling in the interim.[120] According to Chalmers, this situation emerged from a combination of 'apathy and selfishness' and an overt reliance on the General Fund to meet the equal dividend. 'Ulterior motives' such as the half-more scheme were deemed necessary to convert this insular ethos into 'larger sacrifices for the Christian good of our general population', but in reality these steered the fund further away from its original principles.[121] While Chalmers had envisioned a great constitutional and centralised General Fund to act as a surrogate state apparatus, by the late 1840s the realities of voluntary religion and human nature had rendered it a mere charitable fund.[122] Writing to James Lenox in April 1847, a month before his death, Chalmers concluded that the difficulty of 'working up' congregations to contribute to the General Fund had convinced him 'more than ever as to the impotency of the voluntary principle' and cemented his attachment to the principle of a national established church.[123]

Beyond the hierarchy of Chalmers and Candlish, who inevitably criticised the inherent feebleness of the voluntary principle, much of the blame was pitted on the actual implementation of the system by the Free Church leadership. Thomas Longcroft Chalmers of Glasgow argued in 1854 that the management of the Sustentation Fund was 'not only unsatisfactory, but alarming', owing to its failure to reach the minimum targets set a decade previously. This was, according to Longcroft and unsurprisingly Begg, not the fault of the people or the fund itself, 'but in the adoption of arrangements which render failure inevitable' and threatened to divide the Free Church.[124] These arrangements included a policy of 'undue' church extension, from which Begg argued 'our difficulties have mainly sprung'. This 'reckless multiplication of weak charges to swell up our ranks', to the detriment of the equal dividend, was viewed by the Newington minister as one of a series of ill-fated decisions by a seemingly untouchable Free Church leadership.[125]

Though initially viewed as a bulwark against the spread of internal and

---

120. The Association for the Maintenance of National Religion, *Dr Chalmers On Voluntaryism versus the present Free Church majority* (n.d.), 3.
121. Chalmers, *On the Economics of the Free Church*, 7, 22, 26, 40.
122. David Thorburn, *The Sustentation Fund of the Free Church of Scotland: being a plea for a return to the principles on which the fund was established* (Edinburgh, 1852), 22–3, 27, 29; Thomas Chalmers of Longcroft, *The Sustentation Fund in danger: its disease and its cure* (Edinburgh, 1854), 4.
123. Thomas Chalmers to James Lenox, 29 April 1847, NYPL, James Lenox Papers, MssCol 1732.
124. Thomas Chalmers of Longcroft, *The Sustentation Fund in danger*, 3.
125. James Begg, *Reform in the Free Church: or the true origin of our recent debates* (Edinburgh, 1855), 10. Begg's position against church extension contrasted sharply with his earlier role as convenor of the Building Committee, in which he espoused the 'national' importance of the erection of new churches. James Begg, *Circular on the late convenor, John Hamilton, and the need to replenish the Building Fund* (Edinburgh, 1848).

overtly local voluntaryism, the centralised character of the General Fund was criticised by Begg as hindering rather than strengthening national cohesion. He argued that this 'idea of centralised power' was 'quite foreign to the genius of a Presbyterian church', and though it was designed to directly replace the British state, embodied its most despised qualities. 'A limited number of men notoriously manage all our affairs in any way they please', Begg claimed, before suggesting that 'the Free Church is as completely managed by an oligarchy at this moment, as ever the British government was'.[126] Discontent over the increasingly centralised structure of the Free Church boiled over during what became known as the Colleges controversy. Though the prospect of at least three Free Church colleges, in Edinburgh, Glasgow and Aberdeen, had been touted at the Disruption Assembly, between 1843 and Chalmers' death in 1847 there was general agreement within the church that the theological halls in the north and west of Scotland would only be developed once Edinburgh's New College had been firmly established. Nevertheless, the Aberdeen ministers pressed ahead: their first professor, James Maclagan, was appointed in 1845 and by 1847 the Aberdeen College was catering for over thirty theological students (although these students were initially required to complete their final year at Edinburgh). At the 1848 General Assembly calls were made to establish the Aberdeen and Glasgow colleges, but these proposals were bitterly opposed by William Cunningham, Chalmers' successor as New College Principal. Cunningham, a formidable yet confrontational leader who fell out with Candlish during this debate, believed that stretching already thin Free Church resources across three theological colleges would curtail efforts to ensure that New College was fully equipped and thriving. The college extensionists on the other hand warned against the overt centralisation of ministerial training in Edinburgh and argued that as a purported national church the Free Church should be offering the same opportunities for aspiring ministers throughout the country, not just in its capital. Despite Cunningham's continued objections, an expanded Aberdeen College moved into a new building at Alford Place in 1849 and a Glasgow College was finally established in 1856, though tensions remained between these new colleges and their Edinburgh counterpart.[127] One anonymous author's assertion that dissatisfaction with the active management of church affairs simply arose from 'a jealousy of our Clergy in the metropolis' did nothing to allay fears that the Free Church was fast becoming a hierarchical and unequal body.[128] Free Church voluntaryism, even in its most centralised and external form, appeared to be ill-equipped to create a truly national church.

---

126. Begg, *Reform in the Free Church*, 4.
127. Brown, 'The Disruption and the Dream', 44–5.
128. [Junius], *The Church in Danger: a letter to the Rev. James Begg D.D.* (1849), 1.

Chalmers' assertion to the 1847 Committee on Sites that 'we of the Free Church are not Voluntaries' echoed his famous speech at Tanfield Hall four years before. While in that period the Free Church had attempted to create a national rival to the Church of Scotland through voluntary means, by 1847 Chalmers appeared resigned to the conclusion that state endowment – but only 'upon right principles' – was the 'most efficient of all machinery for pervading the people with religion'.[129] Though in the immediate aftermath of the Disruption, Chalmers entertained the belief that a voluntary funded Free Church had the potential to Christianise the masses to a greater extent than the 'old' Kirk before 1843, five years into their voluntary experiment, the Free Church, by and large, remained stern defenders of the establishment principle.[130] Any attempts to embrace voluntary ideals on a theoretical level, such as Peter Waddell at Girvan, received the most hostile response. However, in a practical sense, the Free Church did become voluntaries. This turn to practical voluntaryism was nevertheless offset by the struggle to implement it on a national level, thus failing to shape fully the new body as a viable 'true' Church of Scotland. The pitfalls of a full voluntary system, in which the local mattered as much as the national, proved a significant barrier to the Free Church ever being fully national. While the voluntary principle was deemed a failure in itself to create a fully functioning national church, enhanced co-operation with Scotland's other dissenting bodies on the grounds of practical necessity opened another door for achieving this objective: church union. Union within Scottish evangelical dissent, either through the broad-stroke definition of union found in the Evangelical Alliance or actual denominational amalgamation, would become a defining feature of Scottish Presbyterianism in the mid-nineteenth century, as the next section will show.

---

129. *Committee on Sites*, 130.
130. *PGAFC, May 1844*, 252.

PART TWO

Co-operation and Incorporation

CHAPTER THREE

'Co-operation without Incorporation': Dissenting Relations after the Disruption

The history of Scottish Presbyterianism, as we saw in the first chapter, has been dominated by periods of schism and union. After the upheaval and schismatic tendencies of the eighteenth century, the nineteenth century witnessed a slow but increasing inclination towards Presbyterian amalgamation. Though Scottish Presbyterianism's most dramatic split, the 1843 Disruption, dominated the ecclesiastical landscape, the possibility of union and reunion, particularly among the non-established seceding bodies, became increasingly prevalent. In fact, in 1852 the United Presbyterian minister John Brown hailed the Disruption as a path towards greater union. The schism in Scotland's national church, Brown argued, facilitated the emergence of the Evangelical Alliance, a broad worldwide coalition of Protestants formed in 1846, and ever-closer relations between the major Presbyterian dissenting churches, erstwhile rivals during the Voluntary Controversy of the 1830s, but brought together by their common position outside the religious establishment after 1843.[1] However, as the Relief minister Gavin Struthers acknowledged in 1845, party spirit remained rife in Scotland after the Disruption, even as the Scottish dissenting churches formed closer links.[2] Deep-rooted divisions over abstract principle, particularly the role of the civil magistrate in religious affairs, tended to override the practical benefits of potential dissenting co-operation, even as the sectarian animosities of previous decades subsided. This chapter will examine the often fraught nature of ecclesiastical co-operation in Scottish dissent after 1843, by assessing the relationship between Scotland's non-established Presbyterians in the immediate aftermath of the Disruption, and their role in the creation of interdenominational societies such as the Evangelical Alliance between 1845 and 1846. It will question how this formative period for Scottish dissenting relations, dramatically changed by the events of 1843 and characterised by caution on all sides towards a common dissenting purpose, facilitated the period of church union that characterised the decade after the Disruption.

---

1. John Cairns, *Memoir of John Brown* (Edinburgh, 1860), 313.
2. Gavin Struthers, 'Party Spirit: its prevalence and insidiousness', in *Essays on Christian Union* (London, 1845), 387–411.

'Fellow workers'? Free Church and Voluntary Relations in the Immediate Post-Disruption Period

Delivering the concluding address at the bicentenary of the Westminster Assembly in July 1843, Thomas Chalmers claimed that he could 'see no obstacle in the way' of the Free Church and Scotland's voluntary Presbyterians becoming 'fellow-workers . . . for the objects of our common Christianity'.[3] Despite occurring amid the turbulence and sectarianism of the immediate post-Disruption period, the bicentenary commemorations cemented the growing co-operation between Scotland's dissenting churches. John Wolffe has described the event as a Free Church 'demonstration' that asserted the new body's claim to be the 'heirs' of the Westminster divines and thus constituting the true national church.[4] While this was evidently the case, the meeting also adopted a broad dissenting tone. Alongside the Cameronian Reformed Presbyterians, led by Andrew Symington, voluntary ministers from the United Secession and Relief churches engaged in debate throughout the event with their establishmentarian colleagues in the Free and Original Secession churches. The Church of Scotland, on the other hand, was notable for its absence. The variety of the non-established denominations involved, coupled with the celebratory nature of the bicentenary and its general theme of unity on the principles of the Westminster standards, marked the first significant stirrings of a cordial relationship between the new kirk and its voluntary counterparts.[5] Chalmers' speech, a far cry from his now infamous 'no voluntaries' declaration only two months previously, encapsulated the new mood. The Free Church leader directly addressed the 'well-known and oft-repeated aphorism' that had been attributed to him in the months leading up to the Disruption, and which would define dissenting relations for much of the following decade. This motto, 'Co-operation without Incorporation', despite the Free Kirk's hostility to the voluntary principle, had already proven a major feature of the new dissenting framework after the events of May 1843.[6]

Recognising the shared principles and ecclesiology of Scotland's various non-established Presbyterian denominations, 'co-operation without incorporation' suggested a loose and ambiguous dissenting coalition, deemed necessary to tackle Scotland's social and moral ills, while also challenging the apparent hegemony of the Established Church. According to one Free Churchman, the Disruption offered Scotland's dissenters an opportunity

---

3. *Bicentenary of the Assembly of Divines at Westminster, held at Edinburgh, July 12th and 13th, 1843* (Philadelphia, 1845), 172.
4. John Wolffe, 'The Evangelical Alliance in the 1840s: An attempt to institutionalise Christian Unity', *Studies in Church History*, xxiii (1986), 337; *Bicentenary of the Assembly of Divines*, 237–8.
5. *Bicentenary of the Assembly of Divines*, 237–8; Drummond and Bulloch, *The Church in Victorian Scotland*, 312.
6. *Bicentenary of the Assembly of Divines*, 173.

to co-operate on an equal footing, free from the privileged position and exclusivity of the establishment.⁷ At the Disruption Assembly, Thomas Guthrie called for co-operation between Scotland's dissenting churches through a united social mission, though he recognised the apparent barriers to any immediate incorporating union between Scotland's dissenters. Even Chalmers' controversial opening address at that same assembly similarly described Scotland's voluntary churches as 'coadjutors in the great work of evangelising the people of our land'.⁸ Alluding to this address in a letter to the leading voluntary politician Adam Black a week after the Disruption, David Welsh claimed that the Free Church was willing to 'co-operate with all evangelical dissenters' on matters that did not involve a 'compromise of principle', and that they were 'looking forward to some happier period' during which incorporating union could be contemplated.⁹ Robert Smith Candlish, a joint convenor alongside Robert Buchanan on the Free Church's committee on co-operation with other evangelical churches, most neatly defined the new doctrine. He claimed a willingness within the Free Church to 'hold out to the Protestant world the flag of unity . . . based on the recognition of common truths, and the protest against common errors', though he warned against the 'danger of incorporating unions' and any compromise of the new church's principles.¹⁰

However, by the time of the bicentenary commemorations two months later, Chalmers, and to a lesser extent Candlish, had relaxed their opposition to potential dissenting church union. While the Free Church leader claimed to 'have no quarrel with the co-operation' aspect of the maxim, and advocated its extension, he refuted the negative connotation placed on 'incorporation' as 'far too absolute'. 'The truth is', Chalmers argued, 'that whenever incorporation can be effected with advantage, and without violence to the consciences of the parties, it is in itself a most desirable object.' He asserted that there was 'no insuperable bar . . . in the way of an eventual, and, I do hope, of a speedy incorporation' between the Free Church and Scotland's other Presbyterian dissenters. In one speech Chalmers attempted to undo the sectarianism of the previous decade and the harm inflicted by his denunciation of voluntaryism weeks before. Union between Scotland's non-established Presbyterians, on the right principles and at the right time, was now a distinct, if distant, possibility. 'Co-operation without incorporation' had become 'co-operation now, and this with the view, as soon as may be, to incorporation afterwards'.¹¹

Though far from being a direct overture for immediate union between Scotland's dissenting bodies, Chalmers' address was essential to the gradual

---

7. *A Memorial on Education, to the General Assembly of the Free Church, by the son of a clergyman* (Edinburgh, 1844), 15–16.
8. *PGAFC, May 1843* (Edinburgh, 1843), 98–9, 11.
9. David Welsh to Adam Black, 23 May 1843, NLS, Black and Tait Letters, MSS 3713.
10. *AGAFC, May 1843* (Edinburgh, 1843), 40; *PGAFC, May 1843*, 37.
11. *Bicentenary of the Assembly of Divines*, 173–6; *Aberdeen Journal*, 19 July 1843.

thaw in relations between the churches following the bitterness and hostility of the Voluntary Controversy. The Free Church General Assembly in October 1843 saw both Chalmers and Candlish dismiss the significance of the establishment principle as a 'mere theoretical opinion' that 'could be no obstacle to harmonious co-operation ... in promoting great practical objects'. The great yet vague practical objects for dissenting co-operation recommended by Candlish were to be found in politics, social mission, antipopery and the assertion of the church's spiritual independence. According to Chalmers, these 'movements of convergency' would find their 'landing-place' in incorporation.[12] This sentiment was echoed by Chalmers' United Secession counterpart, John Brown, who claimed to 'look forward with an earnest desire and a confident hope, to the period, which we think is not likely to be a distant one, when the two bodies will be closely united'.[13]

Ironically, despite Brown's desire for union and Chalmers' attempts to distance himself from the phrase, 'co-operation without incorporation' became the favoured stance among many voluntary ministers. As part of the United Secession deputation to the Free Church's October General Assembly, James Harper of Leith commended the 'spirit of co-operation' and feeling of Christian brotherhood increasingly prevalent among Scottish dissenters following the 'emancipation' of the Free Kirk, while Thomas Struthers suggested that 'surely they were prepared, if not for a union of incorporation, at least for a union of co-operation'. Hugh Heugh, a prominent opponent of ecclesiastical establishments during the Voluntary Controversy, hoped that the Free and United Secession churches would be able 'to cultivate honesty of purpose with kindness of feeling', though he conceded that 'some jostling' and the 'occasional collision' was inevitable due to the national coverage of both churches. Heugh considered the 'great object' of Christian union not as a 'hasty and ill-considered amalgamation of Churches', but as a 'harmonious co-operation in practice'. He exercised caution towards any premature hopes for incorporative union that would impinge upon the unique characteristics of the respective bodies. He asserted that 'union, whether by co-operation or amalgamation, must include no compromise of principle, no rejection, no concealment, of any portion of the truth of God, no violence to conscientious conviction, no suppression of the utterance of that conviction'.[14] This tension between sectarian principle and latitudinarian forbearance would prove a major feature of the drive for Christian union in the years to come.

Though concerns remained regarding the ultimate result of such a practical alliance, the ideal of co-operation without incorporation gathered momentum after 1843. Candlish, reporting on a Free Church deputation to the United Secession Synod in 1844, professed to be 'deeply

---

12. *PGAFC, October 1843* (Glasgow, 1843), 35; *Caledonian Mercury*, 21 October 1843.
13. *Caledonian Mercury*, 21 October 1843.
14. *PGAFC, October 1843*, 47–52.

impressed with the kindness and cordiality with which they received us', and while allowing for differences of opinion on both sides, rejoiced 'in the prospect of there being increased union and co-operation between them and us'. The Free Kirk's separation from the establishment, Candlish claimed, resulted in the new body forging closer bonds with other evangelical churches. These churches, in Scotland at least, consisted of the United Secession, Relief and Original Secession bodies, which according to the leading Free Church minister Angus MacKellar at the 1844 General Assembly, were 'those of our own brethren who differ from us on some things, but are on the most important agreed'.[15] The moderator of the Relief Synod, Peter Brown, in a letter to a Free Churchman, predicted that Scotland's evangelicals, once they had forgotten their previous quarrels, would 'unite as one great army, and consult with each other, how they may most speedily conquer the kingdoms of this world'.[16] In August 1844, one contributor to the *United Secession Magazine* opined that 'union is impracticable between the two bodies, while the Free Church makes the establishment principle part of her constitution, and while Voluntaries continue honest men'. However, the writer did acknowledge the desire for 'friendly intercourse, and joint usefulness on the principle of co-operation without incorporation'. 'Among us', he emphasised, 'the union of incorporation is never named.'[17]

This was not always the case. In the weeks leading up to the Disruption, the United Secession minister James Robertson recommended that, in the event of a non-intrusionist secession, there ought to be 'a speedy and scriptural union' between the two bodies of 'Free Evangelical Presbyterian Brethren'. Condemning any display of 'jealousy or sectarian spirit', Robertson urged unity at the expense of 'multiplying sects and unnecessary divisions'. The voluntary minister claimed that in such a union 'there will not be a shadow of difference', excluding the establishment principle, which he believed would be held by Free Churchmen 'only in theory' and 'ought not to be a ground of separation'.[18] In essence, Robertson was proposing to make the divisive role of the civil magistrate in any potential union a matter of forbearance. While the issue of ecclesiastical establishments was a term of communion in the Free Kirk, the voluntary principle did not hold the same power in the United Secession or Relief churches. The vision held by some voluntaries of a dissenting national church would make such issues a matter for individuals to decide upon, and not the united body. Later that year, the *United Secession Magazine* elaborated upon Robertson's suggestion by emphasising the shared anti-erastian principles

15. *PGAFC, May 1844* (Edinburgh, 1844), 8, 116–17, 188–9.
16. Peter Brown, Moderator of the Relief Synod; private letter to a Free Church Minister, dated 18 March 1844, in Wallace, *Testimonies in favour*, 33–4.
17. *USM*, i (August 1844), 426–7.
18. James Robertson, *Ought the Non-Intrusionists to join with the United Secession? A letter addressed to the Rev. Dr Candlish, by a minister of the United Secession Church* (Edinburgh, 1843), 1–4.

of Scotland's dissenting factions. According to the writer, the five main non-established Presbyterian bodies – the Free, United Secession, Relief, Reformed Presbyterian and Original Secession churches – were largely if not wholly similar regarding matters of church government, doctrine and discipline. In practical terms, they were also agreed in supporting the 'overthrow' of Scotland's and Britain's existing establishments. The major difference between the various denominations was, according to the magazine, a 'mere matter of speculation' that was 'not likely to be reduced to practice' and therefore insufficient ground for continued separation. A 'United Presbyterian Church' was advocated involving the five denominations, on the basis of the Westminster Confession of Faith, with the establishment principle an article of forbearance left to the 'conscientious convictions' of each party in the union. This general union, the author claimed, would constitute a national dissenting church, concentrating 'the now divided and scattered energies of the Presbyterian churches' in order to exert 'a powerful moral influence upon the country'. However, the writer conceded that the immediate implementation of such a grand scheme was impossible due to the 'unsettled state' of the Free Church. Instead, 'preparatory steps', such as increased co-operation and shared committees on schools and education, pulpit-exchange and joint-church membership, would 'effectually prepare the way' for the eventual amalgamation of Scotland's evangelical dissenting Presbyterians.[19]

Unsurprisingly, these voluntary-led gestures towards union were greeted with dismay within certain sections of the Free Church. In a series of anonymous public letters directed to leading clergymen such as Chalmers, a Free Church elder from Glasgow, James Wright, criticised the policy of co-operation without incorporation. Unlike his United Secession counterparts, Wright questioned the coexistence of the 'hostile and eternally irreconcilable' voluntary and establishment principles within such an arrangement. For ultra-establishmentarians such as Wright, forbearance on this matter was not an option. 'Is it to be understood', he asked, 'that the Co-operators shall henceforth strike their respective flags of church government? Is Voluntaryism to lift its "voice still for war", and is the establishment principle still to respond, "No surrender"?'[20] While voluntaries were quick to dismiss such differences as mere 'theory', Wright argued that the establishment principle 'must of necessity be practical', and comprised an 'integral part' of the constitution of the Reformed Church of Scotland, of which the Free Church claimed to be the successor. He alleged that the policy of forbearance offered Free Churchmen seeking co-operation the opportunity to rid the establishment principle of its practical character and be 'conveniently enough shelved and boxed up'. To the ultra-establishment

19. *USM*, xi (November 1843), 597–9.
20. [James Wright], *Letter to Thomas Chalmers, D.D., L.L.D., on 'Co-operation without Incorporation'. By a Free Church Presbyterian* (Edinburgh, 1845), 38.

wing of the Free Church, this desire for co-operation with Scotland's voluntaries at the expense of its establishmentarian ethos amounted to a refusal to 'acknowledge and testify to her most prominent and leading features'.[21] By doing so, the Free Kirk would abandon the Westminster Standards and the Claim of Right, and 'strip them of any claim to be longer regarded as the True Church of Scotland'.[22] Though Wright and his fellow anti-voluntary polemicists appear out of touch on the issue of co-operation, their establishmentarian opposition to incorporation retained the support of a large proportion of the Free Church's leading clergy, as will be discussed in the next chapter.

With reservations remaining even over the benefits of co-operation, it is no surprise that such a strategy yielded mixed results. In January 1844, the *Fife Journal* reported that 'an extension of friendly intercourse' had emerged between the Free and United Secession churches in Kirkcaldy. Led by the United Secession minister James Law, this correspondence resulted in two Free Churchmen, Henry Laird and David Purves, as well as two ministers from the national church, preaching to Law's congregation at Bethelfield.[23] The catholicity of Law's gesture was not always repeated elsewhere. In the same year, the Free Church was criticised for indiscriminately admitting discontented Secessionists. Prominent cases appeared in Aberdeen and Dundee, where the minister had charged the United Secession Synod with heresy.[24] At a Free Church meeting in Edinburgh, James Begg warned how a general acceptance of this system of loose admission could damage the kirk's relationship with other dissenting bodies. He claimed that 'they could never maintain a friendly and consistent fellowship or proper understanding with other denominations of Christians, if they made the Free Church a refuge' for discontent. Doing so, Begg claimed, would cause the Free Church to 'sink in the estimation and regard of all the churches at home and in other countries'.[25]

The apparent sectarian aloofness of the Free Church, at least in the eyes of voluntaries, in the period after the Disruption proved a significant barrier to co-operation on national, social and political issues, topics which will be discussed in greater detail in subsequent chapters. While the Free Church appeared to play an active role in the co-operative home missions assessed in Chapter Seven, its 'project' to evangelise the nation was heavily criticised by the *United Secession Magazine*.[26] The *Dundee Courier* also criticised attempts by Free Church deputations to excite religious revival across

---

21. [James Wright], *Letter to Thomas Chalmers, D.D., L.L.D., on the present position of the Free Church of Scotland. By a Free Church Presbyterian* (Edinburgh, 1844), 15–16.
22. Anon., *A word to Free Churchmen on union with Voluntaries* (Edinburgh, 1845), 4.
23. *Fife Journal*, 8 January 1844.
24. *Dundee Courier*, 13 August 1844.
25. *The Aberdeen Journal*, 27 November 1844.
26. *The Herald of the Churches; or monthly record of Ecclesiastical and Missionary Intelligence*, i (March 1846), 29; *The Aberdeen Journal*, 18 November 1846; *USM*, ii (May 1845), 234–5.

Scotland 'without the aid or recognition of other Seceders', a movement that was privately conceded by Candlish to be 'offensive'. Highlighting that 'it would have been doubtlessly desirable to enact "co-operation without incorporation" for this very purpose', the newspaper argued that such a tumultuous coalition was 'not creditable to either party' or expected to be of long duration'.[27]

However, it is clear that the Free Church's policy on co-operation was based not on abstract principle, but the practical circumstances of each specific situation. As will be discussed further in Chapter Seven, in December 1846 they declined to join a 'broad and catholic' movement organised to alleviate the effects of the famine which ravaged the Highlands from the mid-1840s, largely due to a desire to continue their own extensive and successful relief effort.[28] Nevertheless, at the same time, numerous Free Church ministers were among the signatories on a pan-denominational protest against the Edinburgh and Glasgow Railway's decision to run Sunday trains.[29] However, as Drummond and Bulloch have pointed out, though the Sunday trains protest cut across the Presbyterian divide, winning 'respectful or reluctant' assent in all of the churches, the real leadership came from within the ranks of the Free Church.[30] It is clear, in this period at least, that while the Free Kirk was content to co-operate in cross-party societies, it was much more at ease in a leadership role or, in some cases, ploughing its own furrow.

While some tensions clearly remained, by the mid-1840s the sectarian animosities of the Voluntary Controversy had dissipated to the extent that practical and durable co-operation between Scotland's dissenting bodies began to grow considerably. Chalmers' death in 1847, for instance, provoked an outpouring of sympathy across Presbyterian evangelicalism. This was most pointedly illustrated by the United Secession minister and poet Robert Wilson's elegy on the Free Church leader, which placed Chalmers alongside Bruce and Wallace as an icon of Scottish national history.[31] The burgeoning practical relationship between Free Churchmen and dissenters was consolidated in the aftermath of the House of Lords' 1849 decision to identify the *quoad sacra* churches of Scotland as property of the Established Kirk.[32] Following the case, the thirteen abandoned Glasgow Free Church congregations were accommodated by the now unified United

---

27. *Dundee Courier*, 13 August 1844; Robert Smith Candlish to Thomas Chalmers, c. 1844, Chalmers Papers, NCL, CHA. 4.312.50.
28. *Caledonian Mercury*, 21 December 1846.
29. *Scottish Guardian*, 21 December 1846.
30. Drummond and Bulloch, *The Church in Victorian Scotland*, 306.
31. Robert Wilson, *Elegy on the death of Thomas Chalmers, D.D.* (Glasgow, 1847), 7.
32. *Legitimacy (Scotland). List of all cases that have been decided in the House of Lords on appeal from the Court of Session, Scotland, from the 1st January 1839 to 7th June 1849, in reference to rights of property in which the legitimacy of any party was raised as a point for decision*, H.C. 1849 (389), vi, 336–9.

Presbyterian Church, with special arrangements organised to facilitate the public worship of both churches. According to the *United Presbyterian Magazine*, 'this is as it ought to be; and we doubt not that, in a spiritual view, the disadvantage sustained will be more than compensated by the kindly Christian feeling it will tend to promote between the two denominations, thus brought into contact and intercourse'.[33] This emergence of 'kindly Christian feeling' would form the basis of the broader and more substantial debate on Christian union that would dominate interdenominational, particularly dissenting, discourse in this period.

A Dissenting Alliance? Christian Union and the Formation of the Evangelical Alliance

By the mid-1840s, the increasing Protestant fear of the zeal of Rome and the development of Tractarianism in the Church of England had resulted in a growing desire among Britain's evangelical churches to 'close ranks' and seek negotiations for some kind of visible unity.[34] The practical effects of co-operation without incorporation ensured Scotland's dissenting Presbyterian churches, and in particular the Free Church, a prominent role in influencing the direction of these debates. Writing a quarter of a century later in his memoir of William Cunningham, the future pro-union leader Robert Rainy claimed that the Free Church had been 'providentially placed' to facilitate a 'practical understanding' between various sections of the Protestant community.[35] This belief in the Free Church's heavenly ordained position at the forefront of the movement for Christian unity would heavily influence its development in Scotland in the post-Disruption period. While Candlish advocated 'Christian union on the basis of Christian principle', it soon became clear that union on the basis of 'Free Church principle' was as equally important.[36]

Unsurprisingly, the Church of Scotland was carefully excluded from the Free Church vision of evangelical unity. At a meeting organised to promote Christian union at Exeter Hall in London less than two weeks after the Disruption, Hugh Miller placed the Established Church firmly alongside the other perceived enemies of Britain's common Protestantism.[37] Miller claimed that the absence of certain denominations and sects from the

---

33. *UPM*, iii (October 1849), 191–2.
34. S. J. Brown, *National Churches*, 378; J. F. Maclear, 'The Evangelical Alliance and the Antislavery Crusade', *Huntington Library Quarterly*, 42 (Spring 1979), 143–4; Daniel Ritchie, 'Abolitionism and Evangelicalism: Isaac Nelson, the Evangelical Alliance, and the transatlantic debate over Christian fellowship with slaveholders', *Historical Journal*, 57 (2014), 427–8.
35. Robert Rainy and James Mackenzie, *Life of William Cunningham* (London, 1871), 252.
36. *PGAFC*, October 1843, 38.
37. *Christian Union. A full report of the proceedings of the great meeting held at Exeter Hall, 1st of June, 1843, to promote and extend Christian Union* (London, 1843).

meeting 'served but to indicate their character' and antagonism to the principles of Christian union espoused by the Free Kirk: 'the Papist was not there, nor the Puseyite, nor the High Churchman, nor the Socinian, nor the Unitarian, nor the *Residuary*'. While Miller was keen to advocate this negative, anti-erastian vision of Christian brotherhood, he also backed the more positive dissenting vision of union increasingly prevalent in the Free Church. The bicentenary commemoration of the Westminster Assembly, Miller argued, was 'well suited' to 'forward and mature the scheme of general co-operation'.[38] This scheme of broad dissenting union germinated at the bicentenary would be advanced during the 1845 visit to Scotland of the Swiss Protestant minister and historian Jean-Henri Merle d'Aubigné. Addressing d'Aubigné and two other guests from France and Germany at the Free Church's General Assembly, Chalmers offered a stirring endorsement of Christian unity, primarily focused on Scottish evangelical dissent. He asserted that 'among the great majority of evangelical Dissenters in this country, I am not aware of any topics of difference which I do not regard as so many men of straw; and shall be exceedingly delighted if these foreign gentlemen get the hearts of the various denominations to meet together, and consult to make a bonfire of them'. While deprecating the latitudinarianism that 'would lay too little stress on what is important', Chalmers also denounced 'the evil of that ultra and exclusive sectarianism which lays too great stress upon what is insignificant'. The 'suppression' of this ethos, an obvious reference to the disagreements over voluntaryism between Scotland's otherwise comparable dissenting churches, 'would remove a mighty obstacle which at present lies in the way of a visible union of Christians'.[39]

This desire to avoid sectarian conflict in order to attain unity would permeate even the most ultra-establishmentarian of Scotland's dissenting sects. Writing to Chalmers, the leading Original Secession minister Thomas McCrie expressed concern that his comments to d'Aubigné on voluntaryism would obstruct the prospect of broad Christian union. According to the *United Secession Magazine*, after corresponding with McCrie, d'Aubigné was 'shocked' to find his 'dear Scotch friend' believed that the voluntary principle stipulated 'that civil governments have nothing to do with God, and that God has nothing to do with civil governments'.[40] McCrie denied to Chalmers that he had 'wrongfully' described the voluntary principle as held by Scotland's dissenters, and claimed that he had merely described the principle 'which we oppose'. Nevertheless, he admitted that he felt anxious that he had done 'injustice to our Voluntary brethren' and that his com-

38. Hugh Miller, *The Headship of Christ, and the rights of the Christian people; a collection of essays, historical and descriptive sketches, and personal portraitures*, ed. Peter Bayne (Boston, 1872), 490–1.
39. J. H. Merle d'Aubigné, *Germany, England, and Scotland; or, recollections of a Swiss minister* (New York, 1848), 139.
40. *USM*, ii (December 1845), 665–6.

ments would 'hinder such a desirable consummation' between Scotland's dissenting churches.[41] McCrie's desire to appease concerns on matters of principle indicated an unwillingness on the part of Scotland's establishmentarian dissenters to offend their voluntary colleagues. While this was certainly true of smaller denominations such as the Original Secession, the Free Church was more intent on claiming a leadership role in any co-operative agenda. Following d'Aubigné's visit, Chalmers and Candlish devised a scheme for the potential publication of an English-language edition of the Swiss minister's account of his trip to Scotland, which was eventually published in 1848. A cross-denominational association to oversee the financial arrangements, subscriptions and publication of the book was proposed, and would include leading dissenting ministers such as McCrie and John Brown. However, Candlish insisted that such a committee should be comprised of 'mostly Free Church' members so 'that we may lead in it'.[42] Candlish's scheme was indicative of the Free Church approach to dissenting and broader Christian union. While it was beneficial for the Free Kirk to be seen to be engaging in an equal and democratic partnership with other evangelical churches, this co-operation was almost wholly reliant on the ability of Candlish and his colleagues to dictate or at least influence the principles and practice of such organisations.

While the Free Church leaders were keen to advocate dissenting union on Free Church grounds, the same could be said of their voluntary counterparts. For new co-operative dissenting societies such as the British Anti-State Church Association, the Disruption represented an opportunity to enact evangelical Christian union on voluntary principles. Formed in 1844 by the radical journalist and politician Edward Miall, the British Anti-State Church Association, known as the Liberation Society from 1853, emerged from the militant voluntary agenda and increased politicisation of nonconformist grievances in England in the mid-1840s.[43] According to Ian Machin, the society was the first 'effectively organised' voluntary movement (though the Scottish Central Board for Dissenters, established a decade earlier in December 1834, may possess a legitimate claim to this title) and it soon became the most popular and forceful nonconformist voice in Britain, placing the disestablishment of the Church of England as its ultimate goal.[44] At the Association's inaugural conference, held in London in 1844, John Burnet, a Congregational preacher born in Perth, called for the Free Church to repudiate the establishment principle and become part of

---

41. Thomas McCrie to Thomas Chalmers, 25 October 1845, NCL, CHA.4.318.71.
42. Thomas Chalmers to Jean-Henri Merle d'Aubigné, 14 April 1845, NCL, CHA.3.17.91; Robert Smith Candlish to Thomas Chalmers, c. 1845, NCL, CHA.4.312.49.
43. Timothy Larsen, *Friends of Religious Equality: Nonconformist Politics in Mid-Victorian England* (Woodbridge, 1999), 31–2.
44. Ian Machin, 'Disestablishment and Democracy, c. 1840–1930', in Eugenio F. Biagini, *Citizenship and Community: Liberals, radicals and collective identities in the British Isles, 1865–1931* (Cambridge, 1996), 123.

the anti-state church movement.[45] Another speaker claimed that the Free Church was a 'child of voluntaryism', and though its members 'repudiated their own parentage, and renounce the honour of being dissenters', the Disruption was nevertheless 'the first fruits' of the voluntary struggle to dissolve the connection between church and state.[46]

The emergence of a unified English voluntary movement coincided, rather ironically, with the stagnation of the Voluntary Controversy in Scotland after 1843. The British Anti-State Church Association therefore proved an effective shield against the Free Church's 'national' and establishmentarian pretensions at a period when Scottish voluntaryism itself was disorganised and ineffective. This was recognised during a March 1846 meeting of the Edinburgh Association for Promoting Voluntary Church Principles, with one speaker praising the exertions of the Anti-State Church Association, while expressing hope that 'its friends in Scotland, who had the honour of taking the lead, will not now sink into apathy and inactivity'.[47] A *United Secession Magazine* article of the same year conceded that the 'active agitation' of voluntaryism in Scotland 'is more frequently suspended now than it was in former years', though the author adamantly denied that the controversy had 'ceased'. The article offered three explanations for this recent lack of voluntary zeal – the 'signal triumph' of the Disruption, the relative weakness of the Church of Scotland, and the development of a 'good understanding' with the Free Church.[48] A fourth reason not offered was the intra-church tension and potential loss of theological unity stemming from the concurrent Atonement Controversy. The controversy, which took place between 1841 and 1845, centred on the suspension of the United Secession minister at Kilmarnock, James Morison, for his views on universal atonement, which challenged the traditional orthodoxy of the church and the Westminster Confession of Faith. The strict Calvinist Andrew Marshall, widely regarded as the instigator of the Scottish voluntary movement, believed that Morison's views were actually those of his professors John Brown and Robert Balmer, and charged them with heresy, even attempting to libel Brown. After a bitter and divisive campaign, Brown was acquitted (Balmer died before his case was heard), and the synod censured Marshall, eventually culminating in his withdrawal from the United Secession fold in October 1846.[49] Despite the inner turmoil surrounding

---

45. British Anti-State Church Association, *Proceedings of the first anti-State Church conference, held in London, April 30, May 1 and 2, 1844* (London, 1844), 129; Herbert Skeats, *A History of the Free Churches of England, from A.D. 1688–A.D. 1851* (London, 1868), 584.
46. British Anti-State Church Association, *Proceedings of the first anti-State Church conference*, 89–90.
47. *USM*, iii (April 1846), 191–2.
48. *USM*, iii (July 1846), 46–7.
49. For the Atonement Controversy, see Andrew Robertson, *History of the Atonement Controversy in connexion with the Secession Church, from its origin to the present time* (Edinburgh, 1846).

the church's voluntary figurehead, the *United Secession Magazine* writer pointed to the recent meeting in Edinburgh as evidence that the voluntary banner in Scotland remained 'unfurled'.[50]

The formation of the Anti-State Church Association, the council of which contained almost a hundred Scottish representatives, acted as a clarion call for the re-emergence of unified voluntary action in Scotland. At the July 1845 meeting of Scottish dissenters in Edinburgh, the Congregational minister Ralph Wardlaw echoed the militant voluntaryism of the previous year's London conference. Wardlaw called on all dissenters 'to occupy our *own* ground – the great, broad, firm, impregnable ground of *no endowments at all.* Here we are one.'[51] After the Disruption, however, this unified and singular brand of voluntary dissent, so evident and influential during the disestablishment debates of the 1830s, had all but disappeared in Scotland. While elements of 'spiritual pride' undoubtedly remained among the varying sections of Scotland's non-established churches, after the hostilities of the Voluntary Controversy Scottish dissent adopted a much more moderate and conciliatory view of co-operation than its counterparts south of the Tweed.[52] Though Wardlaw may have been desperate to stress the 'one ground' of voluntaryism, forbearance on the establishment principle was crucial to any movement for Christian unity among Presbyterian voluntaries at least.

This desire to tackle the schismatic spirit traditionally associated with Scottish Presbyterianism was perhaps most forcefully articulated by John Henderson, a leading United Secession layman. Inspired by the ecumenical nature of the 1843 bicentenary commemorations, Henderson sponsored the publication of a volume of essays on the subject of Christian union. Headed by Chalmers' essay on the means and aims of union, Henderson's volume was very much a Scottish Presbyterian dissenting exercise: with the exception of Wardlaw and the English nonconformist John Angell James, all of its contributors were ministers from the Free, United Secession, Relief and Reformed Presbyterian churches.[53] Though both Chalmers' and the Relief minister Gavin Struthers' essays offered rather downbeat assessments of the current state of Scotland's sectarian divisions, the theme of forbearance would recur throughout the volume.[54] While defending the right of individuals to protect their own 'peculiarities', Chalmers wrote that 'it is truly unfortunate' when 'an undue stress is laid on certain distinctive

---

50. *USM*, iii (July 1846), 47.
51. *Report of the speeches delivered at the great meeting of Scottish Dissenters, held in the music hall, Edinburgh, on Wednesday evening, the 2 July 1845* (Edinburgh, 1845), 11.
52. *Report of the speeches delivered at the great meeting of Scottish Dissenters*, 45; Wright, *On 'Co-operation without Incorporation'*, 2–6.
53. W. B. Sprague to Thomas Chalmers, 19 March 1846, NCL, CHA.4.327.50.
54. Thomas Chalmers, 'How such a union may begin, and to what it may eventually lead', in *Essays on Christian Union*, 10; Gavin Struthers, 'Party Spirit: its prevalence and insidiousness', in *Essays on Christian Union*, 387–411.

peculiarities', and leads churchmen to believe 'that they must stand up for every pin of the tabernacle'.[55]

Robert Balmer, the professor of Systematic Theology to the United Secession Church and one of the professors at the centre of the Atonement Controversy, called for forbearance on issues not 'essential to salvation' and claimed that 'all true Christians ought to walk together in all things in which they are agreed'. He argued that while the likes of Thomas McCrie 'have clung with fond affection or obstinate pertinacity' to the Solemn League and Covenant, such a scheme of absolute uniformity would prove antithetical to 'the scripture plan of unity and concord'.[56] This distrust of elusive uniformity was echoed by Candlish and David King, Balmer's United Secession colleague.[57] Citing the principle of 'unity in variety' championed in 1840 by John Gibson Macvicar, minister of the Scottish Church in Ceylon and former assistant to Candlish, King argued that 'there may be uniformity in religion without unity, and unity without uniformity'. Despite the antagonistic and 'warlike' existence of Scotland's competing sects, King asserted that Scottish Presbyterians were in 'marvellous accordance' on doctrine, discipline and government, and all belonged 'to the one church of Christ in Scotland'.[58] This principle of unity in variety based on mutual forbearance, dominant throughout the essays, would pave the way for the formation of the Evangelical Alliance, the institutional embodiment of the thrust of Henderson's collection.

The momentum generated by Henderson's volume, combined with the emergence of the anti-Maynooth grant campaign (see Chapters Five and Six), made the prospect of a grand Protestant confederation appear almost inevitable by the summer of 1845. However, as John Wolffe has argued, opposition to the Peel government's decision to increase the endowment afforded to the Roman Catholic seminary at Maynooth seemed more important in purely ecclesiastical terms to an English and Anglican perspective than a Scottish and dissenting one, though as the next chapters will show, Maynooth had a profound effect on Scottish dissenting politics.[59] Following the decision by the Anti-Maynooth Committee to decline the offer of organising a Protestant confederation, on the grounds that it would give the movement an unduly political character, the leading Scottish dissenters took up the baton. The honour initially fell to Henderson, who in May 1845 influenced the United Secession Synod to consider what Rainy described as 'the possibility of something like public and declared alli-

55. Chalmers, 'How such a union may begin', 11.
56. Robert Balmer, 'The Scripture Principles of Unity', in *Essays on Christian Union*, 33–9.
57. Robert Smith Candlish, 'Christian Union in connection with the propagation of the Gospel', in *Essays on Christian Union*, 121–2.
58. J. J. G. Macvicar, *The Catholic Spirit of True Religion* (London, 1840); David King, 'Union among Christians viewed in relation to the religious parties of Scotland', in *Essays on Christian Union*, 229–30, 233–7, 257–60.
59. Wolffe, 'The Evangelical Alliance in the 1840s', 338.

ance between ministers and members of different Protestant churches'. Following a public meeting to discuss the subject, the Free Church General Assembly authorised a committee to represent the kirk in any conference concerning Christian union.[60] The following month, a letter was issued to evangelical churches in England, Wales and Ireland bearing the names of fifty-five Scottish ministers and elders, including Chalmers, Candlish, Brown and King, calling for a meeting at Liverpool in October with the expressed aim of forming an 'Evangelical Alliance'.[61] It declared that the 'imperative duty' of Christian union was now 'not a figment but a reality'.[62] The Evangelical Alliance, officially constituted at an international conference in London in August 1846 and remaining in operation today, was a worldwide fellowship of Protestant churches drawn from Britain and America with some participation from continental Europe.[63] Its stated objects were to 'promote a closer intercourse and warmer affection' among Christians, 'exhibit before the world the actual oneness of Christ', and 'adopt measures for the defence and extension of the common Christianity'.[64] These measures included a declaration of common principles on issues such as the divine authority of Scripture, the resurrection and atonement, the right of private judgment and the divine institution of the Christian ministry.[65] In short, the Alliance stood for 'mutual affection, manifested unity, and common measures'.[66]

The statement by the Scottish ministers and elders also epitomised the dissenting nature of the initial movement. Of the fifty-five signatories, twenty-one belonged to the Free Church, while fifteen were members of the United Secession and Relief churches, and ten others belonged to the smaller Presbyterian denominations.[67] At the Liverpool meeting, the demographic was similar. Of the forty-eight Scottish Presbyterians present at the Conference at Mount Pleasant (over two hundred delegates from seventeen denominations attended in total), only two members of the Established Church of Scotland – one minister and one layman resident in

---

60. Rainy and Mackenzie, *Life of William Cunningham*, 252–3; *PGAFC, May 1845* (Edinburgh, 1845), 144.
61. *FCM*, ii (September 1845), 313–14; *Conference on Christian Union. Narrative of the proceedings of the meetings held in Liverpool, October 1845* (London, 1846), 3; David King, 'Historical Sketch of the Evangelical Alliance', in Edward Steane (ed.), *The Religious Condition of Christendom, exhibited in a series of papers, prepared at the instance of the British organisation of the Evangelical Alliance* (London, 1847), 39–40.
62. *Conference on Christian Union*, 72–3.
63. Wolffe, 'The Evangelical Alliance in the 1840s', 333–46.
64. *Proposed Evangelical Alliance. An address on behalf of the London branch of the provisional committee* (London, 1845), 8.
65. Evangelical Alliance, *Report of the proceedings of the conference, held at Freemasons' Hall, London, from August 19th to September 2nd inclusive, 1846* (London, 1847), 77.
66. *Proposed Evangelical Alliance*, 8.
67. *Scottish Congregational Magazine*, v (December 1845), 583.

Liverpool – were present.[68] Though the doctrines of the alliance presented at Liverpool indicated a 'broad basis' of Christian union, steering between what the *Free Church Magazine* described as 'the extremes of bigotry and latitudinarianism', the decision to marginalise the Church of Scotland and exclude the Puseyite faction of the Church of England ensured that the organisation's Protestant catholicity was promptly called into question.[69]

As Wolffe has suggested, the Scots responsible for summoning the October meeting were 'treading on dangerously thin denominational ice' due to their reluctance to invite those belonging to any state church; indeed, only fifteen Church of England and four Church of Ireland members attended.[70] However, David King defended the lack of participation by Britain's and Ireland's established churches in Liverpool due to the preliminary nature of the meeting.[71] Nevertheless, a growing fear among Free Churchmen of Established Kirk involvement became prevalent as the grand international conference in London, scheduled for August 1846, approached. Though Chalmers suggested the creation of a doctrinal committee comprising 'our ablest and wisest men on both sides of the voluntary question', he recognised that any involvement from the Establishment would be firmly opposed by his fellow Free Churchmen.[72] In early 1846, William Maxwell Hetherington argued that 'it would be best for Church of Scotland ministers not to join the Evangelical Alliance, lest it harm the organisation's cause'.[73] The admission of 'decided and avowed Erastians' to the alliance, claimed one Free Church minister, would preclude the body from bearing testimony to Christ's sole Headship of the Church, and its doctrine would 'be stated in so vague and indefinite a manner as to deprive it of all real meaning'.[74] The lengthy debate over the organisation's title also betrayed the Free Church anxiety towards the Church of Scotland's role. While Chalmers preferred 'Protestant Alliance', claiming that the group's 'primary objective' was to defend Protestantism from popery, Robert Buchanan's support of the term 'Evangelical' as a more 'positive' testimonial limited its appeal for the Church of Scotland's moderate churchmen.[75] While the Liverpool meeting may have ended positively, the desire to defend the 'peculiar testimony' of the Free Church from an undesirable coalition ensured that the very basis of the Evangelical Alliance would be scrutinised. As the Alliance expanded beyond the vision of its

---

68. *The Congregational Magazine*, ix (November 1845), 774.
69. *FCM*, ii (October 1845), 337–9.
70. Wolffe, 'The Evangelical Alliance in the 1840s', 338.
71. *Conference on Christian Union*, 72.
72. Thomas Chalmers, *On the Evangelical Alliance: its design, its difficulties, its proceedings and its prospects: with practical suggestions* (Edinburgh, 1846), 65–6.
73. *FCM*, iii (February 1846), 43.
74. *FCM*, iii (March 1846), 67.
75. *FCM*, iii (January 1846), 3; *Christian Observer* (February 1846), 112; Thomas Chalmers, *On the Evangelical Alliance*, 23; Hanna, *Memoirs of Thomas Chalmers*, iv, 386.

Scottish instigators, its initial reputation as a dissenting body significantly weakened.

The ambivalence of the Evangelical Alliance to what the Free Church and Scotland's voluntaries described as the 'Protestant antichrist' of erastianism resulted in a prolonged debate within these churches over the actual composition and aims of the movement.[76] While the invitation to the Liverpool conference was directed to Britain's evangelical 'churches' and Candlish had initially spoken of the alliance as a 'marriage union' of Protestant denominations, it became clear throughout 1846 that the movement was a 'union of individuals', not churches.[77] This significant alteration offered denominations much more space to operate within the admittedly loose doctrinal basis of the Evangelical Alliance. As churches were not required to subscribe to the alliance itself, there would be no 'silencing of particular testimonies'. Individuals were free to join on the merits of what they agreed upon, without any 'surrender of conscientious principle'.[78] According to Candlish, the Evangelical Alliance would be based on the 'footing of recognising not one another's Churchmanship, but one another's Christianity'.[79] At a meeting in Canonmills Hall in December 1845, the United Secession minister James Harper argued that his 'denominational principles' were not a subject of concern while co-operating 'in the accomplishment of common objects' of the Evangelical Alliance. Harper maintained that 'my brother knows that he is just a Congregationalist now as before he heard of this movement, and I am just as much a Voluntary Seceder here as on the floor of the United Synod'.[80]

Despite this caveat, apprehension remained over what many Scottish dissenters viewed as the alliance's 'lax' doctrinal basis. Though John Brown claimed that the object of the Alliance was 'to get such a doctrinal declaration as will bring together the greatest number of the right class', the Alliance's articles of union were criticised by the Free Churchman Andrew King as tending to 'discredit and discard important portions of Christ's truth'.[81] With an obvious reference to the admission of Church of Scotland ministers to the Alliance, King asserted that the movement 'establishes religious fellowship with those from whom a regard to principle, and the authority of scripture, ought to keep us at a distance'. He

76. *FCM*, iii (May 1846), 130–1.
77. *Conference on Christian Union*, 3; *Christian Observer* (April 1846), 244–5; *Objections to the principles of the proposed Evangelical Alliance, stated in the speeches of the Rev. Andrew King, A.M., and Rev. James Gibson, A.M., in the Free Presbytery of Glasgow, February 4, 1846* (Glasgow, 1846), 35; *FCM*, iii (January 1846), 4.
78. *FCM*, ii (December 1845), 407–8.
79. *Objections to the principles of the proposed Evangelical Alliance*, 56; Samuel Hanson Cox to Thomas Chalmers, December 1845, NCL, CHA.4.316.98.
80. *Witness*, 8 December 1845.
81. John Brown, *Discourses and sayings of our Lord Jesus Christ, illustrated in a series of expositions* (3 volumes, New York, 1854), iii, 389; *Objections to the principles of the proposed Evangelical Alliance*, 11.

affirmed that the articles of union 'do not exclude those whose principles and conduct we condemned when we left the Establishment', a sentiment echoed by another prominent opponent of the Alliance, James Gibson.[82] The loose doctrine associated with the Alliance on issues such as Sabbath observance, toleration and free communion was described by the Free Church-supporting New York businessman James Lenox as a 'rope of sand', and came increasingly under fire from Free Churchmen desperate to defend their unique and Calvinist principles.[83] At the 1846 Free Church General Assembly, Angus McGillivray questioned if 'the doctrinal basis adopted by the Evangelical Alliance ought to be the banner which, either as the Free Church, or as ministers of the Free Church, we ought to unfurl in the presence of the world?' McGillivray asked, 'is it by the omission of the doctrine of Christ's Headship over the nations . . . that Popery was to be vanquished?'[84] James Wright went further, claiming that the Alliance was a 'misrepresentation of Christian union' and that the Free Church, by committing itself to 'lax views' on these 'great questions', had 'forfeited her claim of Identification, and even substantial agreement, with the Historical Church of Scotland'.[85]

The impact of the Free Church's shift in attitude towards the Evangelical Alliance was felt even before the official inauguration. Following a meeting in March to discuss the issue, the Free Kirk in May 1846 adopted a position of neutrality on the Alliance, distancing itself as a church from any of the union's decisions while permitting its clergy and laity to remain as members in an individual and private capacity.[86] Furthermore, a report from the church's Standing Committee on Popery and Christian Union washed the Free Church's hands of all responsibility for the organisation of the Liverpool conference. It expressed its regret that this position of individual action had not been made clear from the beginning, and urged such individuals to 'be careful to advert on all occasions to the importance of maintaining this Church's testimony uncompromised'.[87] Candlish, though acknowledging the duty of the Church as 'bound to aim at Christian union in its corporate capacity', implored his colleagues to 'keep ever in view the maintaining of the testimony of this Church inviolate and uncompromised', effectively 'leaving the Church free from all responsibility in the

---

82. *Objections to the principles of the proposed Evangelical Alliance*, 18–20; The Free Church of Scotland, *A report of the proceedings in the General Assembly, on Wednesday, May 27, 1846, on the subject of Christian Union* (Edinburgh, 1846), 4–5.
83. *FCM*, iii (August 1846), 273; iv (July 1847), 237; James Lenox to Thomas Chalmers, 26 January 1847, NCL, CHA.4.329.30.
84. Free Church of Scotland, *On Christian Union*, 43.
85. [James Wright], *The Evangelical Alliance, the embodiment of the spirit of Christendom. Addressed to the moderator of the Free Church* (Edinburgh, 1847), iii–iv, 32.
86. *Presbyterian Review*, lxxii (April 1846), 284; Free Church of Scotland, *On Christian Union*, 75.
87. *AGAFC, May 1846* (Edinburgh, 1846), 74–5; *Presbyterian Review*, lxxii (April 1846), 285–6.

matter'.[88] In the same vein to their approach to co-operation without incorporation, it appeared that Christian union was desirable so long as it was based on Free Church principles.

This new position of neutrality and the criticisms of the Evangelical Alliance from its members were viewed by the movement's proponents as evidence of the Free Kirk's lingering 'pride and obstinacy'.[89] The *Christian Observer*, a Church of England organ, was scathing in its criticism of what it described as the Free Church's backsliding regarding the Alliance. It argued that 'the effective originators of the scheme were the leaders of the Free Church; and their movements must materially affect the proposed institution'. The original proposal for the Alliance was for a 'marriage of churches', though one suited to the Free Church's sectarian vision and excluding the Church of Scotland. The increased English involvement in the movement after Liverpool lessened the Free Kirk's control, leading the 'doctrinal zealots' in their membership 'to turn upon their leaders, and ask "Why have you dragged us into union with Erastians, Residuaries, Prelatists, and Arminians?"' The shift in focus to a 'union of individuals', claimed the *Observer*, offered the Free Church leaders an opportunity to distance themselves from a movement comprising members of the establishment.[90] The *Observer* noted that this was not the first time members of the Free Church had been involved in confrontation with the Established Kirk in a pan-denominational organisation. The same year saw its ministers actively seek to displace Church of Scotland members from holding positions as directors of the Gaelic School Society, an organisation renowned for its catholicity. Under the influence of the Free Church, the society's members voted in favour of an Establishment-free list of new directors, provoking the resignation of the minority of eleven 'on the ground that the decision was at variance with the avowed principles and practice of the Society'.[91] Despite their claims to the contrary, the *Observer* asserted that the inherent sectarianism associated with the Disruption-era Free Kirk remained stubbornly intact three years on.[92]

It was clear that the Free Kirk's stance on the Evangelical Alliance had become noticeably lukewarm by late 1846. In December, Hetherington wrote that 'we look back on its various meetings and aspects with mingled feelings of joy and sorrow – joy that such a truly Christian idea has taken possession of so many minds – sorrow for the little prospect yet afforded of its entering on a course of vigorous life and action'.[93] Though failing to challenge fully the divisions within Scottish Presbyterianism, the Evangelical

88. Free Church of Scotland, *On Christian Union*, 4, 7, 75.
89. John Aldis, *Six Lectures, on the importance and practicability of Christian Union, chiefly in relation to the movements of the Evangelical Alliance* (London, 1846), 80.
90. *Christian Observer* (April 1846), 244–5, 247–9.
91. *Caledonian Mercury*, 23 March 1846.
92. *Christian Observer* (April 1846), 245–6.
93. *FCM*, iii (December 1846), vi.

Alliance did provide at least some semblance of co-operation and mutual affection especially between Scotland's dissenting communions. While Robert Rainy argued that the Alliance was overly concerned with a 'mere demonstration of brotherly love' and failed to fully promote substantial Christian work or oppose 'anti-Christian efforts', he conceded that it had at least turned dissenters' minds to the benefits of co-operation.[94]

In Scotland the Alliance, though highlighting the severe breach between the establishment and the Free Kirk, cemented the growing mutual affection between Scotland's dissenters. By bringing them together as co-instigators of the movement, it helped heal the wounds opened during the Voluntary Controversy. At the Liverpool conference, William Cunningham delivered a speech admonishing denominational hostilities while recognising his own role in the perpetuation of such relations. In doing so, he directed his contrition to the panel's chair, John Brown, Cunningham's erstwhile friend but bitter enemy during the previous decade's disputes. Deeply moved, Brown responded that Cunningham 'was early an object of deep interest to me, and all along he has been an object of deep interest; and at no time, whatever hard words he has used towards me, (and I too have erred in that way) did I cease to admire him. I always esteemed him; and I would have a strange heart, if I did not say that, henceforth, I shall esteem and love him more than ever.'[95] This spirit of cordiality and reconciliation was echoed by even the most ardent of Free Church sectarians. James Begg, calling for eventual 'complete unity' of Christians, admitted that he did not believe that the Free Church 'must be right in all things – very far from it'. He implored his fellow Protestants to 'not merely seek to be united in feeling, and to avoid asperities and alienations; but let us bring our differences to the Word of God, and see if . . . light may not be thrown upon that Word, which may lead to a real and lasting Unity'.[96] Though it provoked a mixed reaction within Scottish dissent, the desire to enact real and lasting union between evangelicals through the Alliance would lay the groundwork for 'the age of unions' within Presbyterian dissent that followed its creation, which will be discussed in the next chapter.

---

94. Rainy and Mackenzie, *Life of William Cunningham*, 255.
95. *Conference on Christian Union*, 53–4; Cairns, *Memoir of John Brown*, 268–9.
96. Evangelical Alliance, *Report of the proceedings of the conference, held at Freemasons' Hall*, 60–1.

CHAPTER FOUR

The Age of Unions?
Dissenting Reunion, 1847–63

While the immediate aftermath of the Disruption witnessed a period of fitful 'co-operation' between Scotland's dissenting churches, the United Presbyterian union of 1847 and the 1852 absorption of the majority of Original Seceders into the Free Church ushered in a brief spell of 'incorporation'. According to Robert Rainy, the Free Kirk leader who spearheaded the drive for dissenting amalgamation in the second half of the nineteenth century, the decade after the Disruption marked an 'era of unions' within Scottish Presbyterian dissent.[1] These incorporative unions epitomised the dual dissenting and national ambitions of non-established Presbyterianism in Scotland in this period. The 1847 amalgamation of the United Secession and Relief churches was largely based on their shared voluntary, or dissenting, values, while the union of 1852 represented a Free Church attempt at recreating the national church, outside of the national establishment.[2] The 1847 and 1852 incorporations were viewed by contemporaries as the inevitable mergers of denominations all but united in theory and practice. However, the potential for a 'national' and 'dissenting' church based on an alliance of the Free and United Presbyterian churches, increasingly touted from the mid-1850s, was regarded as anything but inevitable. In many respects, the two dissenting unions of this period were much more straightforward affairs than the minefield of abstract ideals that often accompanied any attempt at co-operation between the advocates of the establishment and voluntary principles. Nevertheless, difficulties over principle, even within voluntaryism and establishmentarianism, remained strikingly prevalent during the respective union negotiations. The unions of 1847 and 1852 also raise questions over the ultimate aim of dissenting incorporation in this period – was union a means of making voluntary dissent a major force in Scottish Presbyterianism, or a means of recreating Scotland's national kirk? While historians of this period have tended to overlook the decade before 1863, when formal negotiations began between the Free and United Presbyterian churches, this chapter will establish this as a formative period of convergence between Scotland's non-established

1. Norman L. Walker, *Chapters from the History of the Free Church of Scotland* (Edinburgh, 1895), 247.
2. Kidd and Wallace, 'Biblical Criticism and Scots Presbyterian Dissent', 40–1.

bodies and assess the dual 'dissenting' and 'national' character and aims of both churches.

The United Presbyterian Union of 1847

The union of Scotland's two largest voluntary denominations, the United Secession and Relief churches, had appeared inevitable for over two decades prior to 1847. Following the abolition of the controversial Burgess Oath in March 1819, the 'New Licht Burghers' and 'New Licht Antiburghers' united in 1820 to form the United Associate Synod of the Secession Church, or as it was more commonly known, the United Secession Church.[3] By the early 1830s, this new body, numbering roughly 400 congregations, began negotiations for increased 'intercourse' with the smaller but steadily growing Relief Synod, a seceding church formed in 1761 by the anti-patronage minister Thomas Gillespie and comprising over a hundred congregations. The prospect of union between Scotland's two largest dissenting Presbyterian groups accelerated in the 1830s for a variety of reasons – the trend towards a more tolerant form of evangelicalism, the increased co-operation between Scottish dissenters and their Presbyterian and voluntary counterparts in England, Ireland and America, and the growing numerical and political power of voluntaryism in Scotland. The Relief Church was traditionally much less thoroughly Calvinistic than its United Secession counterpart, though following the 1820 union enough convergence had been achieved on both ecclesiastical and theological grounds to make increased co-operation a distinct probability.

Gavin Struthers preached at the opening of the Relief Synod in 1831 on his church's terms of communion, for what he described as 'the purpose of giving the Secession Church a correct notion of what they were'.[4] The response to this statement of intent in the United Secession Church was led by William Mackelvie, a minister in the parish of Portmoak, former home to the father of the First Secession, Ebenezer Erskine.[5] In April 1834, Mackelvie introduced a motion to the Dunfermline Presbytery that steps should be taken 'to begin and maintain a friendly intercourse with the Synod of Relief as a sister Church'. While Mackelvie initially proposed co-operation, his 'ultimate object' was incorporation. Increased co-operation between the churches, he presumed, would remove any lingering prejudices and 'render union both easy and certain'. This vision was advanced three weeks later in the Relief Presbytery of Dysart, which passed a motion for 'friendly intercourse' with the United Secession Church 'with a view

---

3. William Kidston, *Summary of principles of the United Secession Church, agreed upon September 14, 1820* (Edinburgh, 1820), 9–10; McKerrow, *History of the Secession Church*, ii, 410.
4. Gavin Struthers, *History of the Relief Church*, 475.
5. Cairns, *Memoir of John Brown*, 270; *Memorials of the Union of the Secession and Relief Churches, now the United Presbyterian Church, May 1847* (Edinburgh, 1847), 6.

ultimately to union'.[6] The location of the Relief Presbytery meeting was one of the breeding grounds for seceding division a century before, while Mackelvie's motion took place at Queen Anne Street, Dunfermline, an Erskine church located one hundred yards from the building in which Gillespie ministered after his expulsion from the Established Kirk. To its supporters, these reminders of Scotland's dissenting past only served to underscore the historical significance of the movement towards union. The merger of the United Secession and Relief churches, according to its proponents, was not a mere denominational affair; it would serve as the conclusion to a hundred years of dissenting division and acrimony.

While the significance of union was rooted in Scotland's dissenting history, the onset of the Voluntary Controversy after 1829 gave the negotiations a contemporary resonance. In much the same manner as the later debates on the atonement within the United Secession Church, the unified voluntary reaction to the non-intrusionists' church extension agitation highlighted the striking similarities between the two largest dissenting denominations. The controversy, according to Mackelvie, 'brought fully out the views of both denominations on ecclesiastical polity, and not only showed that they entertained the same principles, but that they had common interests to support and defend'. Despite the 'distraction' of the Voluntary and Atonement controversies hindering any full-blown movement for union in the 1830s and early 1840s, the realisation of these common principles and interests did spur sporadic attempts at incorporation. A joint committee met twice in July 1838 and November 1839 and eventually produced a provisional scheme of union in April 1840.[7] Though the onset of the Disruption temporarily halted these talks, the creation of the Free Church only added to the narrative of dissenting union cultivated before 1843. For the future United Presbyterians, the Disruption represented the triumph of dissent in Scotland. 'The little leaven', according to John McKerrow, was 'leavening the whole lump'.[8] Despite what many regarded as the 'cooling' of Scotland's voluntary agitation in this period, the imminent merger of the United Secession and Relief churches was viewed as a culmination of the dissenting success of the Disruption. The formation of a 'new and prosperous dissenting church' in May 1843 fitted this narrative.[9] Following the Disruption, the stage was now set for the confirmation of dissent's victory in Scotland.

In November 1843, the *United Secession Magazine* claimed that the incorporation of the two bodies had 'been all but consummated'.[10] Two years later, David King argued that 'the Secession and Relief denominations

6. *Memorials of the United Presbyterian union*, 7–8.
7. *Scheme of union betwixt the United Associate and Relief Churches* (Edinburgh, 1840); *Memorials of the United Presbyterian union*, 15–16, 28.
8. *USRM*, i (February 1847), 54.
9. *USRM*, i (May 1847), 93.
10. *USM*, xi (November 1843), 593.

have so much in common that they seem almost one church'.[11] The emergence of the Evangelical Alliance, according to one United Secessionist, had proven instrumental in focusing the union question into 'a more practical shape'.[12] Perhaps due to these external influences, the prospect of union had significantly accelerated by the mid-1840s. A joint committee was founded in May 1844 to draw up a scheme of union, while in February and March 1845 John French and John Brown gave addresses in support of union at meetings of the two churches in Edinburgh.[13] The eventual scheme of union, adopted by both synods in October 1846, acted as a statement of the seceding principles of the two bodies. It also emphasised the importance of forbearance on seemingly non-essential matters, which meant the United Secession's maintenance of public covenanting and the Relief's more tolerant interpretation of communion. These points of difference, according to the scheme, would require 'no compromise, no renunciation, no concealment of conscientious conviction'.[14] Article X of the basis of union maintained both churches' 'state of secession and separation from the judicatories of the Established Church', and of the 'lawfulness and obligation of separation from ecclesiastical bodies in which dangerous error is tolerated; or the discipline of the church, or the rights of her ministers, or members, are disregarded'.[15]

Though not a fully fledged avowal of voluntary principles, the United Presbyterian basis of union appeared to the majority of the churches' adherents to be the epitome of dissenting incorporation in this period. However, disputes arose within the churches over the dissenting or voluntary credentials of both denominations as union approached. Despite its early adoption of voluntaryism, the Relief Church was traditionally viewed with suspicion by members of the United Secession as a kind of establishment-lite. Until 1825 the Relief had no distinct theological institution of its own, with its ministers trained at the divinity halls of Scotland's universities under the auspices of the Church of Scotland.[16] The denomination's 'lax' communion policy, according to one secessionist writer, also tended to 'homologate too much with the Established Church'. These apparent connections with the Church of Scotland prior to the Voluntary Controversy had fuelled the United Secession prejudice that the Relief operated as an 'interchangeable commodity with the mother church' or as mere 'Chapels of Ease to the Establishment'.[17] This reinforced the belief that the denomination

---

11. David King, 'Union among Christians viewed in relation to the religious parties of Scotland', in *Essays on Christian Union*, 261.
12. *USM*, iii (October 1846), 443.
13. John French and John Brown, *Reasons for the union of Christian churches, and the love of the brotherhood* (Edinburgh, 1845); *Memorials of the United Presbyterian union*, 52–5.
14. *USM*, iii (October 1846), 444.
15. *UPM*, i (June 1847), 258.
16. Struthers, *History of the Relief Church*, 301–2.
17. *USM*, xi (November 1843), 593–4.

represented only 'relief' from patronage, and did not fully constitute a dissenting church.[18] However, the advent of the Voluntary Controversy witnessed what the *United Secession Magazine* described as a 'great rebound in the opposite direction'.[19] During the controversy, the Relief asserted their dissenting and anti-establishment credentials by joining the United Secession's protests as an 'unexpected ally' against the Church of Scotland's extension programme and the perceived injustice faced by dissenters.[20] By ridding itself of any remaining link to an increasingly alien establishment and participating 'manfully' in the Voluntary Controversy, any lingering doubts from the United Secession Church regarding the Relief's position as genuine dissenters had been quashed from the early 1840s.

Ironically, by the time of the 1847 union the Relief Church had appeared to usurp the United Secession as the bastion of dissenting values. During the debate over the new body's proposed title, one Relief member argued that the term 'Secession' should not be used as it did not fully encapsulate the dissenting and voluntary ideals they wished to project. He argued that his proposal, the 'Associate Relief Church', would 'remove all objections on the part of those who hold strongly the voluntary principle; as the term "Relief"' – unlike 'Seceder' – 'implies no idea of returning to the Establishment, but rather the contrary, for it includes a relief from patronage, from all state control, and all external influences'.[21] This marked a significant reversal of the previous decade's debates. It also paved the way for opposition to union from certain factions of the Relief Church on the grounds of the voluntary principle. John Craig, who along with David Anderson was the most prominent opponent of union within the Relief Church, claimed that the United Presbyterian Synod had 'been constructed upon *Secession*, not *Voluntary* principles'. He claimed that this 'seceding' principle was not a protest against establishments, but merely against the prevailing party in the establishment, to which the seceders may return once the 'real or supposed evil doings by the judicatories of the church' were overturned. According to Craig, this meant that 'Establishment principles lie at the very foundation of the United Presbyterian Church'.[22]

To illustrate this point, he highlighted the Free Church's support for the 'mild' version of voluntaryism proffered by the United Presbyterian Church. According to the *Free Church Magazine*, there was nothing in the basis of union 'which the loudest stickler for the legality of Establishments needs hesitate to describe'.[23] The United Presbyterian Church, Craig claimed, was a church 'into which no consistent Voluntary can enter', to the extent that he would

---

18. *Memorials of the United Presbyterian union*, 16.
19. *USM*, xi (November 1843), 594.
20. *Memorials of the United Presbyterian union*, 17.
21. *USRM*, i (May 1847), 210.
22. John Craig, *Relief Principles: reasons for declining to enter the United Presbyterian Church* (Cupar, 1847), 6–7.
23. *FCM*, iii (November 1846), 478.

no more 'violently outrage his Voluntaryism, by entering the Church of Scotland' than by entering the new denomination. While United Secessionists a decade before may have thought differently, Craig maintained that the Relief Church was 'founded on totally different principles'.[24] Unsurprisingly, Craig and Anderson dissented from the union in May 1847.[25] On the United Secession side there were barely any traces of anti-unionist protest, mostly due to the censure and subsequent withdrawal of another maverick ultra-voluntary, Andrew Marshall, from the church the previous winter following the Atonement Controversy. As a member of the church's committee on union, Marshall had initially appeared receptive to the idea and even invited some Relief ministers to assist him with communion during the summer of 1846. However, his opposition to the Relief Church's more liberal theology and belief that the united church (under John Brown's leadership) would only drift further from Calvinist orthodoxy ultimately cemented his exit from the United Secession Church, clearing the way for union.[26]

The debate within the Relief Church raised questions regarding the precise definitional status of the new church and non-established Presbyterianism in general. In this period Scotland's unendowed Presbyterian denominations who had seceded from the Kirk were comprised of three distinct but overlapping categories (the Reformed Presbyterians, who favoured re-establishment on the grounds of the Covenants, never belonged to the reconstituted Church of Scotland after the Revolution Settlement so existed outside of these categories). The Free Church and the Original Secession were 'seceding' bodies. These Auld Licht denominations had seceded from the national church yet had retained most of its character and values, including support for the establishment principle. On the other side of the scale stood Scotland's 'voluntary' Presbyterians, such as Craig and Anderson, who opposed the establishment principle and any recognition or endowment of religion by the state. In the middle, while containing elements of the establishmentarian and voluntary factions, was 'dissent' – Presbyterians who were actively against and reflected values opposed to the current establishment. In this sense, both the Free and United Presbyterian churches could be described as dissenting bodies, though to a greater or lesser degree they professed an adherence to seceding and voluntary values respectively. The United Presbyterian union was presented as a clear dissenting union, but was not as overtly voluntary as expected by some within the Relief Church. This careful if superficial distinction allowed the new church to retain a broad platform capable of encompassing all shades of Scottish non-established Presbyterianism, including the Free Church. By not advocating a hard-line voluntary ethos, the 1847 union left the door open for the creation of a 'dissenting' and

24. Craig, *Relief Principles*, 11.
25. *USRM*, i (April 1847), 186–7; *Memorials of the United Presbyterian union*, 58.
26. *UPM*, iv (October 1850), 452–4.

'national' church, simply based on not belonging to the current Established Church, if not much else.

Despite the hostile reaction of a small subsection of ultra-voluntaries, the union of the United Secession and Relief churches represented this broad recognition of shared dissenting values and heritage. This was reinforced by the historical dissenting rhetoric that dominated the proceedings. The date of the union, 13 May 1847, was fixed to mark the centenary of the original Secession split over the terms of the Burgess Oath, while its location in Tanfield Hall, packed to a capacity of 3,500, was the site of the Disruption.[27] According to Mackelvie, the two events were intrinsically intertwined; one was the 'bursting of a torrent', the other 'the meeting of the waters'.[28] Though the Free Church featured prominently in this dissenting narrative, the role of Scotland's eighteenth-century dissenters was certainly not ignored. At the soiree to celebrate the union, Struthers and William Anderson argued that the Seceders led by Erskine and Gillespie respectively, 'at the head of the other Dissenting bodies, have been found the palladium of the civil and religious liberties of our fatherland'.[29] In his pastoral address to the congregations of the newly formed church, the synod moderator William Kidston asserted that while 'Secession' and 'Relief' should now be dropped to make way for the single term 'United Presbyterian', the new church nevertheless adopted the historical significance of both: 'Secession from abounding corruption, and Relief from galling oppression.'[30] Though the United Presbyterian Church was technically instituted in May 1847, the historical rhetoric employed by its founders linked it to the churches of Erskine and Gillespie.

While the narrative cultivated for the 1847 union largely focused on Scotland's dissenting past, its future also proved a major theme in the celebrations. After the incorporation, the United Presbyterian Church comprised 518 congregations, with a strong concentration in the thriving business districts of Scotland's major cities, and a youthful and vibrant clergy.[31] This placed the new body in an ideal position to reinforce the numerical supremacy of Scottish dissent over the establishment. Understandably, attention swiftly turned to the potential of union with the Free Church. John Brown claimed that the use of the Free Kirk's Tanfield Hall for the consummation of the United Presbyterian incorporation would 'suggest the idea to some people's minds that they were on the

---

27. Cairns, *Memoir of John Brown*, 270; *Caledonian Mercury*, 13 May 1847, 17 May 1847.
28. *Memorials of the United Presbyterian union*, 57, 60.
29. *UPM*, i (June 1847), 268; *Memorials of the United Presbyterian union*, 174, 209.
30. *Pastoral Address to the congregations of the United Presbyterian Church* (Glasgow, 1847), 5–6, 14.
31. *The Summary of Principles of the United Presbyterian Church (Scotland)* (Toronto, 1856), 6; Robert Wilson, *The Consummation: an ode on the auspicious union of the United Secession and Relief Churches, May 13, 1847* (Edinburgh, 1847), 6; J. R. Fleming, *The Story of Church Union in Scotland: its origins and progress 1560–1929* (London, 1929), 30.

road to wider union yet'.[32] Outside of Scotland, this was certainly the case. The London Congregational newspaper *The Patriot* questioned the 'perplexing phenomenon of two Presbyterian non-established Free Churches, holding precisely the same doctrines and discipline, yet quite distinct in all their institutions'. The combined weight of the Free and United Presbyterian churches, numbering roughly 1,200 congregations in 1847, emphasised the threat such an incorporation could pose to the Church of Scotland, and the church–state connection in general. Therefore it is no surprise that the dissenting newspaper expressed hope that by utilising the 'healing' principle of voluntaryism the two denominations would amalgamate 'before another fifty years shall have run out'.[33] David King highlighted the relative strength of the Scottish dissenting churches compared to the establishment, and indicated the national benefits that could be derived from such a union. He suggested that if the Free and United Presbyterian churches 'were to see their way in this country to such incorporation as two divisions of them have this day effected, there is not a deficiency in the outward means of grace which they might not supply to our neglected fellow country-men'.[34]

However, not all roads led to union. To an enthusiastic reception from the soiree's attendees in Edinburgh's Music Hall, William Anderson called for the United Presbyterians to re-Christianise a Scottish population left in spiritual destitution by the establishment. Anderson claimed that by doing so, the United Presbyterian Church would assert its own claim to the title 'Church of Scotland', with or without union with the Free Kirk.[35] He claimed that 'there is no other party more "the Church of Scotland" than we are', and argued that 'no party holds a superior commission' than the United Presbyterian Church to 'take possession of the waste places throughout the land'. In a thinly veiled appeal to his colleagues to directly challenge the social and moral apathy of the national kirk, he criticised the 'ignominy and unfaithfulness of that cowardice which fears to enter upon an aristocrat's estate, or within shot of the towers of a parish church, for the reclaiming of a field spiritually neglected and uncultivated'. 'That field', claimed Anderson, 'is ours by Divine grant, if we are first there to enter upon it; and let us take possession boldly.'[36]

Anderson's bold assertion highlighted the fact that though many within

32. *Caledonian Mercury*, 13 May 1847. Incidentally, Brown initially preferred the smaller Bristo Street Church as the location of the union, due to its historical resonance with Scottish dissent: it was the site of both the first split among the Presbyterian seceders of Scotland, and the reunion of the Burgher and Antiburgher churches in 1820. However, due to its relatively small size and the anticipated large audience, the Free Church's premises in Canonmills was utilised instead.
33. *The Patriot*, 27 May 1847.
34. *Memorials of the United Presbyterian union*, 211–14.
35. *Caledonian Mercury*, 17 May 1847.
36. *Memorials of the United Presbyterian union*, 207.

Scottish dissent viewed the 1847 union as a step towards greater and broader incorporation, most probably with the Free Church, the creation of a non-established Church of Scotland did not entirely rest on this presupposition. While not necessarily levelling the Presbyterian playing field, the amalgamation of the United Secession and Relief churches offered a new body of considerable size and influence the opportunity to reclaim Scotland's national religious heritage. Though the Disruption and the Free Kirk undoubtedly played a role in the narrative that preceded the events of May 1847, it was clear that the United Presbyterian Church possessed its own distinctively dissenting history, and therefore its own claim to the position of Scotland's national church. While this ideal of the Church of Scotland was grounded in dissenting principles, the merger of the Original Secession into the Free Church in 1852 heralded a different vision of the national kirk, based on establishment values.

The 'True' Church of Scotland? The 1852 Union of the Original Secession and Free Churches

The concept of union between the Free and Original Secession churches emerged almost immediately in the wake of the Disruption. Newly unified in 1842, the United Original Secession Church, or the Auld Licht Antiburghers, formed a small minority of Scotland's non-established Presbyterians who maintained the original establishmentarian principles of the Seceders, while their brethren in the United Secession and Relief churches declared their allegiance to voluntaryism. At the Free Church General Assembly of October 1843, Candlish distinguished the Original Secession's address to the new body, which included a suggestion for future incorporation, from those of the other evangelical denominations who simply viewed the Disruption as a means to furthering the voluntary principle. He praised the Original Seceders for entering 'far more intelligently' and 'far more thoroughly into the movement that has recently taken place' and approving of the 'whole principles' associated with the Free Kirk's separation from the establishment. Unlike Scotland's other dissenting Presbyterians, there was 'perfect practical agreement', according to Candlish, between the Free Church and the Original Secession on the 'fundamental' tenets of the church–state relationship. This adherence to the establishment principle ensured that the Original Secession Church could 'most truly claim to be the representatives of the minds of the Erskines'. Union between the two churches appeared as early as 1843 to represent not only the combination of the historic seceding principles of Scotland's original secession bodies with the 'more recent witness-bearing' of the Free Kirk, but also the creation of a non-established national church based on the ideals of the Disruption.[37]

---

37. *PGAFC, May 1843*, 36, 38–9.

However, one major difference separated the Free Church and the Original Secession, and proved a significant obstacle to their eventual union – the historical obligations of the covenants placed upon church and country. Once again, the debate centred on the duty of churches to hold certain principles as bodies, regardless of the position of individuals within these churches. The descending obligations of the National Covenant (1638) and Solemn League and Covenant (1643) were free to be held by members of the Free Church according to their own individual preference. The disputes that arose within the smaller denomination focused upon how willing they were to merge into a church not prepared to adopt as a body the covenanting principles espoused by the Original Secession Church.[38] Shortly after the Disruption, the Original Seceder James Gray claimed that the two churches were 'of the same mind and the same judgment' concerning the establishment principle. William Hetherington's depiction of the Solemn League and Covenant as 'the wisest, the sublimest, and the most sacred document ever penned by uninspired men' was also hailed by Gray as a 'token for good'.[39] Despite his praise for individual members of the Free Church regarding their covenanting professions, Gray nevertheless cautioned against diminishing the Original Secession's rigid standards for the sake of a larger and looser union. Quoting the seceding historian Thomas McCrie the elder, Gray warned against 'healing one breach at the expense of making another', and acknowledged that only potential union with the Reformed Presbyterian Synod would result in no loosening of principle.[40]

The reticence of some members of the Original Secession Church to engage in union negotiations with the Free Church was primarily due to their historic identification with the Second Reformation. Archibald Brown, a seceding opponent of union, claimed during these 'purer days' of the Solemn League and Covenant, the fathers of the Original Secession 'not only espoused the principles of the Covenanters' but 'were themselves Covenanters'. According to Brown, they were 'the only religious body in the country who renewed the National Covenants in a bond suited to their circumstances, and thus practically recognised their obligation as national deeds on posterity'.[41] In an attempt to appease the strident covenanting allegiance of the Original Seceders, and ultimately to bring about union, Candlish introduced a document on the Free Church's testimony into the

---

38. Rainy and Mackenzie, *Life of William Cunningham*, 256; John Robertson, *Review of the account of the late conference of the members of the Original Secession Synod, given in the March number of the 'Original Secession Magazine'* (Edinburgh, 1852), 1, 5.
39. James Gray, *Day and Duty: the late Disruption of the Church of Scotland, and the present duty of the Free Church and of the Original Seceders* (Edinburgh, 1843), 3–5, 18–20; William Maxwell Hetherington, *History of the Westminster Assembly of Divines* (Edinburgh, 1843), 134.
40. Gray, *Day and Duty*, 23–4; *UPM*, i (May 1847), 240.
41. Archibald Brown, *Free Churchmen and Seceders: or, an examination of plans proposed for union between them* (Edinburgh, 1851), 31.

1847 General Assembly. This testimony aimed to define the Free Kirk's relationship with the historical Church of Scotland, admitting to the 'permanent moral identity' of nations and the descending obligation of the covenants.[42] While the *Original Secession Magazine* denied that Candlish's proposed testimony would remove every ground of difference between the two denominations, it acknowledged that 'every friend of the covenanted cause in Scotland must rejoice in his heart to see such a document brought forward in the General Assembly of the Free Church of Scotland', a body on which 'the future welfare of our country seems so much to depend'. The magazine concluded by claiming that the Free Kirk 'can only become one with the Church of the past, by voluntarily identifying itself with their principles' as proposed by Candlish.[43] In a telling indicator of the prevailing attitude within the Free Church towards covenanting obligations, Candlish's motion was withdrawn due to 'emphatic opposition' to portions of the testimony.[44]

The ambiguity of the Free Church's covenanting position following the rejection of Candlish's testimony resulted in marked division and often hostile exchanges between the Original Secession's unionist and anti-unionist wings. In a series of pamphlets challenging two ardent supporters of union, William McCrie and William White, Matthew Murray claimed that incorporation with either the Free or United Presbyterian churches would rid the Original Secession of the pledge of its seventeenth-century forbears. Any concession on this matter was 'not real union', and would leave Scotland's dissenting bodies 'as much disunited as they were before'. In a similar vein to Chalmers' desire to see a non-erastian Church of Scotland re-established, Murray argued that for union negotiations with the Free Church to proceed, it was perfectly acceptable for Original Seceders to demand a 'perfect' national church based on their own historic principles and grounds of secession.[45] However, McCrie warned against such an overt focus on abstract historical concepts and argued that the Free Kirk's anti-voluntaryism and eulogising of the Covenanters lent itself to the principles of the Original Secession.[46] In 1850 McCrie, along with three fellow elders, motioned to the Original Secession Synod to renew union negotiations with the Free Kirk. During the debate that followed, he acknowledged that though 'the Free Church has failed to identify formally and judicially, as

---

42. *PGAFC, May 1847* (Edinburgh, 1847), 247–52.
43. *OSM*, i (January 1848), 320–1, 326.
44. Rainy and Mackenzie, *Life of William Cunningham*, 257.
45. Matthew Murray, *Remarks on the position and principles, and present duty of Original Seceders in relation to National Covenants, ecclesiastical standards, church communion, &c.* (Edinburgh, 1849), 6–7, 14; Matthew Murray, *Reply to a pamphlet entitled 'Union with the Free Church'* (Edinburgh, 1849), 17.
46. William McCrie, *Union with the Free Church. Observations upon the pamphlet of the Rev. Matthew Murray of Glasgow, on the position, principles, and present duty of Original Seceders* (Edinburgh, 1849), 5–7.

Seceders have done, with the Church of the second Reforming period, it does not follow that therefore she is not sincerely attached to the principles and attainments of that time'.[47] This sentiment would be echoed two years later by the Free Churchman Begg, who argued that Presbyterians should endeavour to aim at the 'real objects' of Scotland's Covenanters, without fixating on the 'mere technicalities' of documents.[48] Though McCrie's motion ultimately failed due to a belief within the Seceders that negotiations at that point were 'not likely to accomplish the end desired', this impasse would be rectified only a year later with the Free Church's 'Act and Declaration'.[49]

The Act and Declaration, accepted by the 1851 General Assembly, affirmed the Free Church's continuity with the Reformers and the Covenanters. The act also asserted the claim of the Free Kirk to be identified as the national church, arguing that 'it is her being Free, and not her being Established, that constitutes the real historical and hereditary identity of the Reformed National Church of Scotland'.[50] This display of unbroken connection with Scotland's covenanting history and the decided claim to nationality paved the way for renewed negotiations between the Free and Original Secession churches. The ideal of the recreation of a perfect national kirk, earlier alluded to by Murray, pervaded the union discussions that followed. William White claimed that after 1843 the Free Church was the 'National Church *de jure*' and had even strengthened its claim to this title by leaving the establishment and sacrificing its endowments in order to 'maintain whatever was good in the old National constitution'.[51] Thomas McCrie Jr, son of the celebrated historian and a leading seceding figure in his own right, called on his colleagues 'to seek reunion with that party which, under the name of the Free Church of Scotland, we regarded as representing the Church from which we had seceded'. 'A return to her communion' was 'the enviable termination of all our contendings in a state of separation'. For McCrie, the Free Church was the 'constitutional' Church of Scotland and the 'genuine representatives of the Church of our fathers, on the table of whose Assembly the protest of our seceding fathers was lying'. McCrie also equated the nationality of the Free Church with the historic principles and national pretensions of his own denomination.

---

47. *Report of speeches delivered by the Rev. Edward A. Thompson, Dundee, and Mr W. M'Crie, Edinburgh, in support of an overture of union with the Free Church, before the Synod of United Original Seceders, Edinburgh, May 1850* (Edinburgh, 1850), 3.
48. *Union of Synod of United Original Seceders with the Free Church of Scotland. Proceedings of the General Assembly in the case* (Edinburgh, 1852), 11.
49. *Report of speeches in support of union*, 3.
50. *The Subordinate Standards, and other authoritative documents of the Free Church of Scotland* (Edinburgh, 1851), v–x.
51. William White, *Reply to a letter from the Rev. Matthew Murray, Glasgow, to the editor of the Original Secession Magazine, on the question of union with the Free Church of Scotland* (Edinburgh, 1852), 11.

He warned that if the Original Secession viewed the Free Kirk as 'nothing more than a larger body of Dissenters' and not as the mother-church, 'all her late noble contendings for truth and freedom, no longer identified with the struggles of our fathers, would lose their elevated and patriotic type as national, and sink into the mere squabblings of a party'. In an effort to lessen the significance of the covenanting question, McCrie denied that by joining the Free Church the Original Secession was 'laying down' its present testimony, or exchanging it for the Act and Declaration. Instead, it was those 'solemn engagements' which tied the Original Secession to the Covenanters that also impelled them to seek union with the Free Church 'on the ground of the Standards of the Covenanted Church of Scotland'.[52] To the members of the Free Church and the Original Secession seeking union, incorporation between the two bodies amounted to the first step to reconstituting this true Church of Scotland – free, non-established but staunchly establishmentarian, and adhering to the principles and values of Scotland's Presbyterian heritage.

However, the anti-union faction of the Original Secession did not accept the Free Kirk's claim to sole nationality. The question of 'where is the Church of Scotland?' dominated debate as union approached. McCrie's claim that the Seceders' protest now solely lay on the table of the Free Church was dismissed by a number of his Original Secession colleagues. According to Murray, until the grounds for secession were removed, the protest lay on the tables of both the Free Kirk and the Established Church, as 'both are historically identified with the pre-Disruption Church of Scotland' and therefore morally obligated to represent the 'Society from which our fathers seceded'.[53] The Established Church, according to the Dundee minister George Jack, 'however corrupt and defective, is still to be regarded as a portion of the true Church of Scotland'.[54] This argument was vehemently opposed by John Sandison, who claimed that the Scottish establishment was 'in violent and confessed antagonism' to the principles of the Second Reformation, the secession testimony and the Free Church. The issue over what body constituted the true Church of Scotland, Sandison argued, was settled in May 1843, when the Original Secession Synod's deputation met with the newly formed Free Assembly and cemented that kirk's position as the church from which their fathers had seceded.[55] However, Jack refuted this assumption, contending that the Free Church had 'little claim' to be solely regarded as the 'true, historical, and constitutional'

52. Thomas McCrie, *Thoughts on union with the Free Church of Scotland, specially addressed to his own congregation* (Edinburgh, 1852), 1–16.
53. Matthew Murray, *Strictures on the Rev. William White's reply to the letter of the Rev. M. Murray, on the question of union with the Free Church of Scotland* (Glasgow, 1852), 10–12.
54. George Jack, *Free Church and Original Secession: Address to the congregation of United Original Seceders, Dundee* (Dundee, 1852), 3.
55. John Sandison, *Review of discussions on union between the Original Secession and Free Church* (Edinburgh, 1852), 24–5.

– and covenanting – Church of Scotland. He ironically stated that 'if a Church with an undefined form of government – a Church that refuses to own the Covenants – a Church that mangles the Westminster Standards to suit the loose notions of her leading members – if such a Church be the true Church of Scotland, I shall no more dispute her claim'.[56] As Jack illustrated, even the claim to historic lineage was not enough for those in the anti-union camp. Archibald Brown claimed that while 'hereditary historical identity with the National Reformed Church of Scotland' was one thing, 'actual nationality is quite another'. He argued that unless the Free Kirk was 'sanctioned and appointed by the nation' and its government, any claim to such a designation was 'groundless'. According to Brown, Free Churchmen, like every other seceding body in Scotland, had 'purchased their freedom at the expense of their nationality'.[57]

Regardless of these concerns, on 1 June 1852 at Tanfield Hall a majority of the Original Secession Church joined the Free Church. The rhetoric surrounding the Free Kirk's position as the 'mother-church' unsurprisingly dominated the union proceedings. The Representation and Appeal of the Original Seceders, presented to the Free Church General Assembly two weeks prior to the consummation of union, sought 're-union with the Church of our Fathers', thus 'redeeming the pledge which they gave to return to the communion of the mother Church'.[58] The General Assembly's response to the Seceders' appeal acknowledged that it was consistent with present Free Church principles as well as the principles for which the national church 'has been honoured to contend in the best and purest periods of her history'. While the Free Church was content to place the Original Secession within its own historical model, concessions were also made to seceding principles, including a full and unreserved acknowledgement of the 'obligation to prosecute the ends of the Covenants'.[59] During the proceedings, Candlish declared that the two bodies 'mutually' claimed 'historical descents and historical identities', and highlighted the intrinsic link between church and nation espoused by the Free Kirk, claiming 'we are of one mind and of one heart in owning the identity of this Church with the Church of the First and Second Reformations; and in owning, moreover, the identity of the nation with the nation in other days, when it was led to make high attainments as a nation in the sight of God'.[60]

Unsurprisingly, a significant proportion of the Original Secession

56. Jack, *Free Church and Original Secession*, 3, 9.
57. Archibald Brown, *Free Church door for the Seceders; or Dr Candlish's altered overture, as passed in the late Free Church Assembly, and lauded in the 'Original Secession Magazine', considered* (Edinburgh, 1852), 17–19.
58. *Union of Original Seceders with the Free Church*, 35.
59. 'Act anent the Representation and Appeal of the Synod of United Original Seceders', *AGAFC, May 1852* (Edinburgh, 1852), 417-8.
60. *Union of Original Seceders with the Free Church*, 18–19.

Church was not 'of one mind' with the Free Church on these issues, and with union came disruption in the seceding ranks. While the United Presbyterian union of 1847 only caused a mild tremor on the fringes of the Relief Church, the debate over covenanting and historical heritage seriously fractured the body of Original Seceders. McCrie's overture for union at the Synod in April was passed by a narrow majority of one – thirty-two members (eighteen ministers and fourteen elders) voted for union, while thirty-one voted against the proposal, of whom thirteen were ministers and eighteen were elders. However, including those ministers not in attendance at the Synod, the ministerial majority was much greater, with twenty-two or twenty-three joining the Free Church. The thirteen who remained were led by John Aitken and were destined for what the *United Presbyterian Magazine* uncharitably termed 'ecclesiastical death'.[61] Following the union, the remaining members of the Original Secession continued to challenge the Free Church's claim to nationality as a 'claim of superiority over seceders'.[62] At the first Synod of the continuing church, Anderson noted that while the Free Church comprised an 'important section of the historical Church of Scotland', its failure 'to identify herself fully and explicitly with the Church of the Second Reformation' meant that 'she neither occupies nor professes to occupy higher ground than the Established Church did previous to the Disruption'.[63] In response to Candlish's claim that 'the Secession is extinguished in Scotland', Archibald Brown claimed that while 'the Free Church takes the latitudinarianism, Seceders take the Covenanted Reformation'. He argued the Free Kirk's 'idea' of being the national church would do little to disguise the failings of 'an uncovenanted latitudinarian union taking place between the Free Church and a party of Seceders', which he affirmed was 'surely not a whit better' than the voluntary United Secession union of 1820.[64]

Despite Brown's claim, the 1852 union to its supporters gained a greater significance than any mere seceding union could muster. According to the Original Secession's Representation and Appeal, it represented the first step to the ultimate aim of rejoining a 'pure' Church of Scotland. Candlish claimed that the amalgamation of the Seceders into the Free Church was pivotal to 'the beginning of a revived testimony for the principle of a National Establishment'.[65] In this sense, the 1852 union marked the true beginning of the Free Church's attempt to recreate the national church outside of the current defective establishment and grounded in

---

61. David Scott, *Annals and Statistics of the Original Secession Church: till its disruption and union with the Free Church of Scotland in 1852* (Edinburgh, 1886), 193–7; *UPM*, vi (June 1852), 284.
62. Archibald Brown, *The Free Church tending to voluntaryism: letter to the Rev. R. S. Candlish, D.D., occasioned by his proclamation, 'The Secession is extinguished in Scotland'* (Edinburgh, 1853), 27.
63. *OSM*, i (September 1852), 12.
64. Brown, *Free Church tending to voluntaryism*, 27–8.
65. *Union of Original Seceders with the Free Church*, 21, 37.

the principles of the Disruption. Incorporation with the Original Secession Church represented the perfect opportunity to launch this ambition. This new national-church-in-waiting would stand between the dual dangers of erastianism and voluntaryism, and represent the true historic and spiritually independent Church of Scotland. However, seceding critics of this scheme argued that the Free Kirk was not offering a new dissenting national church but was in fact drifting towards voluntaryism.[66] It is plain to see why such opinions were becoming increasingly prevalent. Reflecting on the union at the end of 1852, William Hetherington observed that it was merely paving the way for broader union among Scotland's dissenting Presbyterians. Alluding to possible incorporation with the United Presbyterians, which he claimed was 'looming in the future', Hetherington pointed out that 'there are other true-hearted Presbyterians in the country, with whom it would be a pleasure to be united in body, as we already are united in spirit'. 'Let us hope, in these days of rapid movement', he concluded, 'that the consummation may not be a very distant one.'[67] For much of the 1850s, it appeared that Hetherington might have been proven right.

A National Free Church? Attempts at Free Church–United Presbyterian Union

The spirit of union that had emerged in Presbyterian dissent in the decade after the Disruption naturally led to whispers of potential union between the erstwhile adversaries in the Free and United Presbyterian churches. This was understandable, particularly due to the rhetoric employed throughout the proceedings of the 1847 and 1852 unions. Union between the two largest non-established Presbyterian bodies would prove the culmination of the 'dissenting' and 'national' aims of these respective incorporations, in effect creating a dissenting national church. In the period surrounding these unions, increasing co-operation within Scottish dissent provided the context in which incorporation was becoming more of a possibility. A decade after the Disruption, the Free Church's original 'anomalous, Mahomet-coffin-like position of suspension' between the establishment and voluntary factions of Scottish Presbyterianism was slowly moving closer in line with their fellow dissenting churches. While a small minority within the Free Church favoured a return to the Established Church and occasionally called for such a reunion, these appeals were invariably rejected by the kirk's leadership. The empathic rejection of any lingering attachment to the Church of Scotland, combined with the increasing convergence with their voluntary colleagues on issues such as national education and the anti-Maynooth campaign (which will be discussed in later chapters), was indicative of

66. Brown, *Free Church tending to voluntaryism*, 28.
67. *FCM*, i (1852), iii.

this Free Church drift and lent itself to suggestions of possible union within both camps.[68]

However, despite even the earliest voluntary assertions to the contrary, the Free Church's maintenance of the establishment principle remained a significant barrier.[69] In 1852 John Brown argued that while he viewed the Disruption as 'a step towards further union', he nevertheless warned against jumping immediately into an unsafe and insecure incorporation with a Free Church still stubbornly clinging to the principle of ecclesiastical establishments.[70] The 'undue importance' afforded to the establishment principle within the Free Church was, according to the *United Presbyterian Magazine*, one of the great, if not 'insurmountable' obstacles to an otherwise possible and logical amalgamation. One of the solutions offered to this seemingly intractable problem was the policy of forbearance. In this case, the Free Church would not be required to change their views, according to the magazine, 'we only ask them not to force their views upon us'.[71] On the other hand, the situation was much more clear-cut to some Free Churchmen – union with professed voluntaries, and any latitude on their historic principles, would strip their kirk of any right to be regarded as the 'True Church of Scotland'.[72] This adherence to what many voluntaries viewed as the 'idle notion' and 'foolish question' of nationality was pivotal to voluntary objections to union on Free Church grounds. The Free Kirk claim to be the national church and 'something more than other dissenters or seceders from the Establishment' was rejected by voluntaries as an unnecessary and unsubstantiated claim of superiority. 'If we meet at all', wrote one, 'it must be on equal terms and on a common platform.'[73] Nevertheless, by the early 1850s the Free Church's attachment to the establishment principle was perceived to be increasingly weak, while the ideal of a voluntary national church recognised by the state and asserting the national convictions of the population was beginning to gain acceptance as a satisfactory alternative to the question of differing principle within Scottish dissent.[74]

A precedent for incorporation and forbearance on the voluntary principle was set in this period by ongoing talks between England's Presbyterian bodies, the 1861 union of the Free and United Presbyterian churches in Canada, and the negotiations between the various Presbyterian denominations of the Australian colonies, culminating in the 1859 union between

---

68. Sir George Sinclair, *A letter addressed to the non-established Presbyterian communions of Scotland* (Edinburgh, 1854), 11–12; Rainy and Mackenzie, *Life of William Cunningham*, 258–9.
69. Robertson, *Ought the Non-Intrusionists to join with the United Secession?*, 2.
70. Cairns, *Memoir of John Brown*, 313–14.
71. *UPM*, vi (August 1852), 341.
72. Anon., *A word to Free Churchmen on union with Voluntaries* (Edinburgh, 1845), 3.
73. *UPM*, vi (August 1852), 342–3.
74. Archibald Gillies, *Free Churchmen and Voluntaries: may they honourably and consistently seek a union?* (Glasgow, 1853), 5–9.

the Free Church, United Presbyterian Church and Church of Scotland in Victoria.[75] As in Scotland, the role of the civil magistrate, particularly the state's duty to uphold Christianity, was also viewed as the most significant point of contention between the colonial Presbyterian churches, which largely adhered to the same principles and ideology of their Scottish counterparts. In Canada, divisions over the church–state connection, and the prospective ideology of the unified church, ensured that union negotiations were protracted and often difficult. According to an article in the *Canadian United Presbyterian Magazine*, written as union negotiations began in earnest in 1855, 'entire forbearance as to existing differences' was the 'only step to union'; a policy that would prove essential in securing unity six years later.[76]

This spirit of union among Presbyterians in the colonies, combined with increasing co-operation and convergence at home, inspired the Free Church elder and MP Sir George Sinclair to take up the cause of Presbyterian incorporation in Scotland. Sinclair was no stranger to union movements. Praised by one friend for the 'amazing catholicity of his temper', he corresponded with Thomas McCrie Sr in 1820 with the aim of reuniting Scotland's seceding bodies with the national church.[77] During the Ten Years' Conflict he was a consistent voice for peace, and as a member of the Church of Scotland following the Disruption attempted to secure its reunion with the Free Church soon after. However, this proposal was short-lived and he eventually concluded that 'the ecclesiastical policy of the Establishment was characterised by grasping and worldly-minded exclusiveness' that 'enforced the letter of the law, and set at defiance the spirit of the Gospel'. In 1851 he joined the Free Church, believing that 'the affairs of the unendowed communions were conducted on a far sounder and more scriptural basis'.[78]

After playing an active role in union with the Original Secession, Sinclair turned his attention to the unification of all of Scotland's unendowed churches into 'one compact and influential Church'. He engaged in dialogue with Brown and the Reformed Presbyterian Andrew Symington, and over the following three years hosted meetings of representatives of the major dissenting denominations at his Edinburgh home. However, these meetings tended to result in little more than an expression of 'brotherly feeling' and vague concepts of 'confederation'.[79] In 1854 he penned an open letter to Scotland's non-established churches calling for a 'firm

---

75. *Newcastle Courant*, 24 April 1857; Richard Vaudry, *The Free Church in Victorian Canada, 1844–1861* (Waterloo, ON, 1989), 111–26; Valerie Wallace, *Scottish Presbyterianism and Settler Colonial Politics: Empire of Dissent* (London, 2018).
76. *Canadian United Presbyterian Magazine*, ii (April 1855), 97–104.
77. Thomas McCrie, *Life of Thomas M'Crie, D.D.* (Edinburgh, 1840), 291.
78. Sinclair, *Letter to the non-established Presbyterian communions*, 7–8.
79. Cairns, *Memoir of John Brown*, 312; Sinclair, *Letter to the non-established Presbyterian communions*, 7–8; Rainy and Mackenzie, *Life of William Cunningham*, 259–61.

and permanent union' between these dissenting churches. In the letter, Sinclair contrasted the 'make-shift' and 'limited' appeal of the Evangelical Alliance with the 'more palpable and permanent blessings derived from a scriptural incorporation of various sections of the church into one'. Regarding the civil magistrate's role in religion as a 'matter of forbearance', he emphasised the similarities between the 'practical voluntaries' of the Free and United Presbyterian churches and, in doing so, advocated the creation of a 'National Free Church'. This new church, 'emancipated from state coercion, and untrammelled by state endowment', would assume the national history, influence and control pursued by the Free Church, while holding the distinctively dissenting and voluntary tendencies of the United Presbyterians.[80]

Unsurprisingly, the *Original Secession Magazine* criticised Sinclair's latitudinarianism, and argued that though he 'discards the kind of union sought by Protestant alliances and conferences', he nonetheless was attempting to pursue a 'union of parties no more closely united in sentiment'. Sinclair's policy of forbearance and his recent arrival in the Free Kirk were also dismissed. 'With one bound' he had passed 'from the extreme of attachment to the idea of an Established Church, to the extreme of voluntaryism.'[81] The United Presbyterians were of course much more supportive of the politician's aims. The *United Presbyterian Magazine* echoed Sinclair's call for forbearance, in which there would be 'no surrender of principle', and claimed that the convergence of the past decade had resulted in the two churches occupying a 'relatively proximate position'.[82] John Brown was one of Sinclair's most zealous supporters, though he adopted a much more cautious approach towards the immediate likelihood of union. Brown responded to the politician's pamphlet by describing Presbyterian dissenting incorporation as 'one of the most certain of futurities; and such publications as his are fitted to prepare for what assuredly will come'. However, the voluntary stalwart conceded that 'things are not ripe for union'.[83]

Following the brief flurry of discussion that followed the publication of Sinclair's letter, the topic of union drifted out of the mainstream public consciousness. This was largely due to an increasing divergence between the two churches that occurred during the mid-1850s, marked most notably by the collapse of the anti-Maynooth electoral alliance and the public dispute that followed the failure of James Moncrieff's series of national education bills. The antagonism of this period also saw both churches reaffirm their respective denominational principles and positions, eschewing the spirit of co-operation and collective dissenting identity that had steadily emerged

---

80. Sinclair, *Letter to the non-established Presbyterian communions*, 14–30.
81. *OSM*, i (May 1854), 532–4.
82. *UPM*, viii (August 1854), 353–4.
83. Cairns, *Memoir of John Brown*, 314.

after 1843.[84] In May 1856, the *United Presbyterian Magazine* published an article criticising Candlish, a chief animator during the education controversy (see Chapter Eight), for what it regarded as his frequent attacks on both the voluntary principle and the United Presbyterian Church itself. The article lambasted the Free Kirk's self-proclaimed status as the true Church of Scotland, and claimed these national 'pretensions' provoked an 'instinctive apathy' within all United Presbyterian members. According to the writer, the 'repulsive' character of this 'all-grasping ambition' and 'overweening self-complacency', seemingly embodied in Candlish, presented the most 'powerful barrier' to dissenting union. The increasing prevalence of sectarian ambition, to the detriment of interdenominational co-operation, was also evident in the magazine's claim, in response to a similar accusation by Candlish, that the United Presbyterian Church's 'denominational action would be much more unencumbered, if we did not encounter the Free Church at every turn and winding'.[85] By 1856 the dissenting co-operation that had emerged in the decade following the Disruption appeared to be in ruins, and with it any hope of union between the two major non-established churches.[86]

This lack of activity and increasing hostility within Presbyterian dissent explained the general surprise when on 2 May 1857 resolutions for the union of the Free and United Presbyterian churches were published in a number of Scottish newspapers.[87] These resolutions followed William Hanna's aborted attempt a month earlier to appoint the United Presbyterian John Cairns to the chair of Exegesis at New College, and represented an abrupt shift in dissenting relations after the turbulence and antipathy of the mid-1850s.[88] Drawn up by Sinclair and edited by Alexander Murray Dunlop, the author of the Claim of Right, the resolutions were signed by 140 prominent laymen who were evenly divided between members of the two churches. They included Free Church politicians such as Charles Cowan, Henry Dunlop and Francis Brown Douglas, and leading voluntary agitators James Peddie and Duncan McLaren.[89] Following the resolutions' publication, the number of signatories rose to 1,671.[90] The declaration proposed that union between the Free and United Presbyterian churches should be considered by members of both bodies 'in the spirit of Christian brotherhood and love'. The issue of forbearance dominated the resolutions. The fifth resolution asserted that both churches 'maintain, with equal steadfastness and sincerity, the great principles of non-intrusion and spiritual independence'. While this appeared to fit the principles of the Free Church, the

---

84. *HFRFC*, iii (June 1853), 306.
85. *UPM*, x (May 1856), 237–40.
86. Hutchison, *A Political History of Scotland*, 70, 77–80.
87. *Glasgow Herald*, 13 May 1857; Rainy and Mackenzie, *Life of William Cunningham*, 262.
88. *Fife Herald*, 16 April 1857.
89. *Glasgow Herald*, 4 May 1857; *Belfast Newsletter*, 7 May 1857.
90. Drummond and Bulloch, *The Church in Victorian Scotland*, 316.

resolutions adopted a much more voluntary tone concerning state endowments, which were dismissed as a matter of forbearance, 'as any formal deliverance on this subject is of no practical consequence in the case of self-supporting communions'.[91] Though Sinclair did not intend for the resolutions to 'excite any premature discussion', the opposite was the case. The *Scotsman* criticised the unsubstantiated desire for union within certain sections of Scottish dissent, claiming that 'amicable separation' between these competing bodies was better for the future of dissent than any potentially short-lived and hostile union. The newspaper argued that union only appeared viable for those with 'short memories', and that it was impossible for the voluntary question to be dismissed simply by practicalities.[92] Speaking at a meeting of the Congregational Union in Edinburgh the evening the resolutions were published, the liberal politician and voluntary Adam Black likewise criticised the creation of 'such a great ecclesiastical confederacy' and the 'one or two Popes' he believed would emerge from it as 'dangerous to civil liberty'.[93]

While criticism from traditional opponents of the Free Church was to be expected, the extent of opposition to the resolutions among the Free clergy, which amounted in some cases to proposals for formal ecclesiastical censure, highlighted the gulf that had emerged between what seemed to be the voluntary inclinations of the laity and its ministers since the Disruption.[94] For instance, in the days following the publication of the resolutions a motion moved in the Synod of Lothian and Tweeddale called for reunion with the Established Church (it was not seconded and was swiftly withdrawn).[95] At the Glasgow Presbytery, James Gibson claimed that the resolutions, which 'were very much calculated to cause divisions and fractions', were 'founded on a defective exhibition of the truths contained in the standards' of the Free Church and therefore failed to represent the views of those in the church 'who were not prepared to resile from their constitutional principles for the sake of union'. Another member, Robert McNab, ominously warned that Sinclair's proposals were nothing more 'than a suggestion for the formal dissolution of the Free Church, and the adoption of its integrity and whole constitution' by the United Presbyterian Church.[96] While some Glasgow ministers believed that a lack of official response from the Free Church repudiating the resolutions would create the potential for 'two disunions', others such as John Smyth tried to avoid discussing the matter altogether, claiming that any 'premature' discussion on such a delicate topic would 'tend rather to widen branches than to heal them'.[97]

91. *Glasgow Herald*, 4 May 1857; *Daily News*, 6 May 1857.
92. *The Scotsman*, 8 May 1857.
93. *Dundee Courier*, 6 May 1857; *Glasgow Herald*, 11 May 1857.
94. Cairns, *Memoir of John Brown*, 317.
95. *Glasgow Herald*, 11 May 1857; *Caledonian Mercury*, 14 May 1857.
96. *Caledonian Mercury*, 8 May 1857; *Glasgow Herald*, 13 May 1857; *UPM*, i (June 1857), 283.
97. *Glasgow Herald*, 13 May 1857.

A similar incident occurred at that month's Free Church General Assembly where, after an interminably long discussion on the technicalities of the motion, the debate centred not upon the rights and wrongs of union with their fellow Presbyterian dissenters, but the merits of actually discussing such a case. It was clear that union, in the immediate future and on the principles espoused by the resolutions, was unacceptable to most Free Church ministers, though the reasons for supporting and opposing its discussion significantly varied.[98] While Candlish claimed to see 'no peril' in debating the prospects of union, William Hanna expressed concern that any premature discussion would pit the ministers of the Free Kirk against the laity. The seemingly inevitable prospect of a Free Church debate on dissenting union was dramatically halted by one of the resolution's signatories, the Whig politician and Secretary of State for War, Fox Maule. Though he defended his decision to sign the declaration for union, Maule recognised that any 'hasty' debate would only fuel the antagonistic 'spirit' already evident in the Free Church as a result of the resolutions, creating even deeper divisions. In response, Candlish withdrew his motion, in a bid to uphold the 'dignity of the House', prevent division within the church and to avoid the awkward scene of Maule, a distinguished and respected government minister, attempting to vindicate his actions.[99] Maule's intervention and the 'remarkable' manner in which the Free Church Assembly disposed of the issue highlighted both the 'evasion of discussion' surrounding potential dissenting union that permeated the Free Church and the decline of Candlish's position and influence as undisputed leader of his kirk. In a review of the 1857 General Assembly, the *Dundee Courier* argued that Candlish's climbdown was proof that his 'reign was nearly over'. Beyond the union debate, 'scarcely a day passed during which his dictation was not disputed', while in several important matters 'his assumed leadership was unceremoniously repudiated'. Candlish's reputational decline among his fellow ministers and the prospect of church union 'from below' due to the increasing influence of the laity highlighted a trend towards a more democratic structure in dissenting Presbyterianism in the mid-1850s. 'These days', the *Courier* pointedly argued, 'are not favourable to the establishment of a Popedom in Scotland.'[100] Ultimately, this period did not last long – due to the emergence of an equally autocratic but much more subtle Free Kirk pope in Robert Rainy – yet its effects were certainly not marginal.

To the United Presbyterian leader John Brown, the hostile response to the resolutions from the Free Church clergy vindicated his more cautious approach to the union question. His ardent voluntaryism and distrust of the Free Church's lingering establishmentarianism ensured that he 'would not narrow the basis of toleration for the sake of an outward peace'. While

---

98. *Caledonian Mercury*, 14 May 1857.
99. *PGAFC, May 1857*, 174–9.
100. *Dundee Courier*, 3 June 1857.

the United Presbyterian leader 'longed for the downfall of sectarian differences, he could not consent to union on any principles which would only enthrone a numerically larger sectarianism in their place'. In 1857 it was clear to Brown that 'the time of figs was not yet'.[101]

While the reticence of many within the dissenting leadership made the probability of union between the Free Church and the United Presbyterians unlikely in the late 1850s, a loose dissenting identity had nevertheless been forged in the aftermath of the Disruption, creating a space in which future church union could at least be treated as a possibility. Despite the failure of Sinclair's 1857 resolutions, a lingering desire for union, particularly among the laity, led to further attempts to reignite the discussion in the late 1850s and early 1860s. In February 1858, a joint conference was established in Paisley containing members of the town's thirteen Free, United Presbyterian and Reformed Presbyterian churches. These conferences, held every three months, were presided over by ministers of the respective churches on a rotating basis and attended by 180 of the town's dissenters. Largely interested in the potential of union between the major 'unendowed' Presbyterian churches of Scotland, these quarterly conferences were also conducted alongside joint prayer meetings organised every month. The prayer meetings were attended by members of the three denominations and superseded the churches' ordinary weekly devotional exercises. According to the senior secretary of the Paisley conference, the 'special object' of this interdenominational co-operation was to 'promote a spirit of union, with a view to the ultimate incorporation of the three churches'.[102]

This successful attempt at dissenting co-operation in Paisley was invariably supported by Sinclair, who was invited to speak on church union in late 1858. Sinclair viewed these congregational efforts as evidence of the increasing gap between, on the one hand, the establishmentarian and anti-union principles of the leading Free Church clergy and some elders, and on the other, the majority of the laity and more junior ministers, who generally favoured union with the United Presbyterians. According to Sinclair, while the bulk of the Free Kirk had embraced their dissenting status in the two decades after the Disruption, a significant number of the church's leaders, and a group of respected elders in the establishment, were actively contemplating a reunion with a more spiritually independent state church.[103] Their hopes were bolstered by the tentative emergence in 1859 of an 'anti-patronage' movement within the resurgent Established Church, initially led by the prominent Middle party evangelical Norman MacLeod. MacLeod believed that by abolishing patronage,

101. Cairns, *Memoir of John Brown*, 317–18.
102. *Paisley Herald and Renfrewshire Advertiser*, 19 January 1861.
103. *Elgin Courier*, 5 November 1858, 14 January 1859.

Scotland's dissenters could be enticed to return to the national church.[104] At the Kirk's General Assembly in 1859, he argued that it was the 'duty' of the Established Church to actively seek union with the Free Church, and that the 'national' aspirations of both churches were dependent on reunion.[105] One of MacLeod's fellow early supporters of the abolition movement – which would not be fully adopted by the Church of Scotland for another decade – Robert Gillan claimed that the generational shift within Presbyterianism since the Disruption had even rendered a grand reunion of all Scotland's Presbyterians possible, so long as the great obstacle of patronage was removed. According to Gillan, who appeared out of touch with the ever-closer relationship between the bulk of Scotland's dissenters, the new wave of United Presbyterians were more concerned with protesting patronage than advocating voluntary principles, while young Free Church ministers had dropped the violent anti-erastianism of the Disruption era. Of course, the Kirk's anti-patronage movement underestimated the resentment their campaign for legislative abolition would engender in seceders who had sacrificed so much in opposition to patronage. The *United Presbyterian Magazine* unsurprisingly dismissed the movement and claimed that the Kirk's 'only hope' for reunion, however 'impracticable', lay with the ultra-establishmentarian strand of the Free Church.[106]

The increasing gulf between the pro- and anti-union wings of the Free Church was exemplified by the Free Church elders Archibald MacGillivray and James Johnstone, who criticised Sinclair and the various attempts at dissenting union as based on the 'grossest latitudinarianism'.[107] The suspicion of overt latitudinarian ideas in the Free Church was also embodied by the waning Free Church pope Candlish, who, at the opening of the 1862 General Assembly, preached on the importance of 'unity in diversity' in the church.[108] However, despite Candlish's ambiguity regarding incorporating union, his speech opened the door for a dissenting relationship that encompassed the national and voluntary strands of Scottish Presbyterianism. Within a year, the sentiments and increasing weight of the 'religious masses' would result in the opening of negotiations between the Free and United Presbyterian churches.[109] Though these talks would last a decade and ultimately fail, the increasing convergence between Scotland's

---

104. Brown, 'After the Disruption', 103–25; Jones, 'Evangelicalism in the Church of Scotland'.
105. Donald MacLeod, *Memoir of Norman MacLeod, D.D.* (New York, 1876), 261–3.
106. *UPM*, iii (March 1859), 142–3.
107. Archibald MacGillivray, *Letter to Sir George Sinclair, Bart, of Ulbster, on the extensive prevalence of religious error, and the sinfulness and danger of latitudinarian schemes of union* (Glasgow, 1859); James Johnstone, *Church union considered and Presbyterian Church of Victoria case discussed: embracing the subjects Latitudinarianism in the Free Church, and heresy in the United Presbyterian Church* (Edinburgh, 1860); *OSM*, v (September 1860), 33–5.
108. R. S. Candlish, *The Church's Unity in Diversity* (Edinburgh, 1862).
109. John Tyndal, *Free and United Presbyterian union opposed to the principles of the Reformation: review of speeches on union in the Free Church General Assembly of 1863* (Edinburgh, 1864), 5.

two largest non-established Presbyterian denominations in the 1860s would pave the way for the unification that eventually occurred by the turn of the twentieth century.

Despite the seemingly unmovable barriers to incorporation, the Free and United Presbyterian churches had forged strong links in the twenty years after the Disruption.[110] The beginning of the 'age of unions' had moved the voluntaries of the United Presbyterian Church and the establishmentarians of the Free Church closer together. Though the incorporations of this period were based mostly on ideological issues – 1847 was a distinctly 'dissenting' affair, while the Original Secession merger into the Free Kirk in 1852 represented an attempt at recreating a 'national' church – the looser forms of co-operation symbolised by the Evangelical Alliance allowed for a broad association that enveloped Scottish Presbyterian dissent as a whole. Despite the evident convergence between the non-established churches in this period, differences over the establishment and voluntary principles hindered any attempts to create a dissenting national church to rival and perhaps supersede the Established Kirk. Co-operation had become standard practice within Scottish dissent by the late 1850s. On the other hand, the possibility of incorporation, which would have required forbearance from both parties on the divisive issue of voluntary religion, remained elusive, despite Sinclair and others' willingness to encourage further convergence. Nevertheless, as the debate over the 1857 resolutions illustrated, it appeared that these theoretical divisions were mostly limited to sections of the clergy of the respective churches. As the next four chapters will show, alliance on social and political issues, largely detached from the ecclesiological fissures of the period, was able to flourish between Scotland's dissenting churches at a grassroots level.

---

110. Walter Smith, *Recent sermons on the Headship: Reviewed* (Edinburgh, 1860), 8.

PART THREE

Politics and Anti-popery

CHAPTER FIVE

Truth, Error and Principle: Anti-Catholicism in Presbyterian Dissent

The twenty years that followed the Disruption witnessed one of the most intense and prolonged outbreaks of anti-Catholicism in nineteenth-century Britain. In 1845 the Tory Prime Minister Sir Robert Peel proposed a measure to make permanent and increase from £9,000 to £26,000 the annual governmental stipend afforded to the Roman Catholic seminary at Maynooth, County Kildare. This decision followed the Charitable Bequests Act of a year earlier, allowing Roman Catholics to bequeath money to the Catholic Church in Ireland, and unleashed a torrent of public opposition to the endowment, emanating from all Protestant churches and political parties.[1] According to the *Presbyterian*, the ensuing national campaign against the grant instilled a unified 'zeal' hitherto missing in Scottish public life in the aftermath of the Disruption, claiming that 'the country has not, as a whole, been more in earnest upon any political or religious topic for a long time'.[2] This national fervour would be redoubled five years later in the wake of the supposed 'papal aggression'. The restoration of the Roman Catholic hierarchy of bishops in England in 1850, countered by the Protestant chauvinism of Liberal Prime Minister Lord John Russell's Ecclesiastical Titles Act, succeeded in reawakening the 'hope' of the anti-Maynooth lobby and ushered in a new wave of public meetings and petitions against the grant.[3]

The controversy surrounding the Maynooth bill, lasting for much of the following decade, centred upon the slow death of Britain's 'Protestant constitution'.[4] The Maynooth grant, as Jonathan Parry has observed, 'dealt a devastating blow to the idea that the state was a religious force' and prompted Peelites such as William Gladstone to disengage with what voluntaries regarded as the 'untenable' High-Church Tory conception of the

---

1. G. I. T. Machin, 'The Maynooth Grant, the dissenters and disestablishment, 1845–1847', *The English Historical Review*, lxxxii (1967), 61–2; Gilbert Cahill, 'The Protestant Association and the anti-Maynooth agitation of 1845', *The Catholic Historical Review*, xliii (1857), 273–5.
2. *Presbyterian*, 3 May 1845.
3. *Aberdeen Journal*, 17 December 1851.
4. J. C. D. Clark, *English Society 1660–1832: religion, ideology and politics during the ancient regime* (Cambridge, 2000), ch. 6.

state's 'conscience'.⁵ However, as the previous sections have discussed, this belief in the British state's Protestant conscience remained a central tenet to the establishmentarians within the nominally dissenting Free Church. It was this ecclesiastical, social and political context that enabled Scottish Presbyterian dissent to emerge as a strong, unified yet diverse component of the British anti-Catholic movement after 1845.

Due to a combination of the anti-Maynooth campaign, the 'papal aggression' and the rapid rise in Irish immigration following the famine, anti-Catholicism became 'endemic' and dominated British public life throughout the 1840s and 1850s.⁶ In Scotland, this prolonged outbreak of anti-popery shaped – and was shaped by – the relationship between Scotland's Presbyterian churches after 1843. As John Wolffe has argued, the anti-Catholic campaign in Britain reflected the existing theological and institutional divisions within British Protestantism.⁷ This was especially the case in Scotland. Though apparently eager to present a united Protestant front, denominational differences and divergent reasons for opposing Catholicism often threatened to scupper any attempts at long-lasting harmony between the major Presbyterian churches on the common platform of 'no-popery'. Nevertheless, anti-Catholicism, particularly the pan-denominational character of the anti-Maynooth campaign, offered the surest opportunity for Scottish Presbyterians to co-operate during the uncertain period after the Disruption. However, this co-operation was largely limited to the dissenting churches, with a notably less zealous Established Kirk preferring to operate either alone or on the fringes of national anti-Catholic movements. In a similar manner to the tentative attempts at ecclesiastical co-operation examined in the previous two chapters, unity between the Free and United Presbyterian churches on the basis of anti-popery, though ubiquitous in the two decades after 1843, was hindered by familiar divisions over the voluntary principle and the state's role in religion.

Militant Protestants within the Free Church generally viewed the battle against popery as one between 'truth and error', and the Maynooth grant as a dangerous and potentially treacherous endowment of that error by a British government nominally pledged to uphold Protestantism. Free Church establishmentarians argued that the British Protestant ascendancy,

---

5. Parry, *Rise and Fall*, 163; Hilton, *The Age of Atonement*, 341–2; Perry Butler, *Gladstone: church, state and Tractarianism, a study of his religious ideas and attitudes 1809–1859* (Oxford, 1982), 95; *Reasons for declining to vote in favour of Mr Macaulay, as M.P. for the City of Edinburgh, By an Elector* (Edinburgh, 1852), 6.
6. Machin, *Politics and the Churches in Great Britain*, 253; G. F. A. Best, 'Popular Protestantism in Victorian Britain', in Robert Robson (ed.), *Ideas and Institutions of Victorian Britain* (London, 1967), 116.
7. John Wolffe, 'Change and Continuity in British Anti-Catholicism, 1829–1982', in Frank Tallett and Nicholas Atkin (eds), *Catholicism in Britain and France since 1789* (London, 1996), 72–3.

and Scotland's Presbyterian character, should be defended from the errors and malevolence of Roman Catholicism.[8] For the Free Kirk, Romanism was the 'enemy of all classes' which threatened the destruction of Victorian values such as free trade, intellectual endeavour and patriotism.[9] Like their English counterparts, Free Churchmen were concerned with the political loyalty of Catholics in Britain (labelled by one Free Church writer as a 'foreign body'), a factor which influenced the uproar regarding the albeit small number of Scottish conversions to the Roman faith in this period.[10] While Tom Gallagher has argued that Irish immigration did not spur any nationalistic sentiment, the apparent internal and external threat from a foreign power in Rome, evident in the controversies over Maynooth and the papal aggression respectively, allowed the Free Church to draw on a distinctly Scottish and Presbyterian defence of British Protestantism.[11] This Presbyterian Whig interpretation of British history, co-opted by the non-intrusionists at the Disruption to assert their links to the Presbyterian past and to highlight the government's apparent violations of the Treaty of Union, emphasised Scotland and the Kirk's providential role in securing Britain's religious and civil freedoms and the Protestantism of the throne.[12] On the other hand, the voluntaries of the United Presbyterian Church positioned the debate within their broader struggle to secure the disendowment of all religious bodies and the creation of a level religious playing field. While Free Churchmen believed that the maintenance and special position of British Protestantism provided the best defence against Rome's incursions, the United Presbyterians argued the opposite: that the vaunted position of Britain's established churches was to the detriment of the 'true' faith, and that free trade in religion was essential to the triumph of Protestantism.[13]

Though they remained divided along establishmentarian and voluntary lines, the shared anti-Catholicism of Scottish dissenters was largely based on overlapping theological, social, moral, ecclesiastical, national and political factors. As Steve Bruce has noted, the growth of anti-Catholicism after 1830 must be placed in the context of the development of evangelical Protestantism globally in the same period.[14] Evangelicals on both sides of the Atlantic were keen to 'stress the Protestant strand in their religion' against the anti-Christ of Rome and emphasise their continuity with the

8. Bernard Aspinwall, 'Popery in Scotland: Image and Reality, 1820–1920', *RSCHS*, xxii (1986), 239.
9. *HFRFC*, iv (April 1854), 227–8.
10. Edward Norman, *The English Catholic Church in the Nineteenth Century* (Oxford, 1984), 203; Aspinwall, 'Popery in Scotland', 236–7; *HFRFC*, iii (February 1853), 173.
11. Gallagher, *The Uneasy Peace*, 34.
12. Mallon, 'A church for Scotland?', 6.
13. *UPM*, iv (September 1860), 418.
14. Steve Bruce, 'Militants and the Margins: British Political Protestantism', *Sociological Review*, 34 (1986), 797–811.

Reformation.[15] This close relationship between evangelicalism and anti-Catholicism, outlined by Wolffe and Bruce, offers some explanation for the prominent roles played in the anti-Catholic agitation by Scotland's evangelical dissenters compared to their more 'moderate' counterparts in the Established Church. The 'competing denominational and national concerns' associated with the anti-Catholic movement in Britain, and in the United States, also mirrored the contrasting ideologies within global evangelicalism.[16] Philomena Sutherland has argued that within the overarching worldview of evangelicalism existed a variety of religio-political stances, ranging from a theologically and politically liberal outlook to a 'covenantal evangelicalism' which stressed the maintenance of Protestant national identity from the threat of Rome.[17] These contrasting interpretations of evangelical Protestantism loosely reflected the competing ideologies inherent in Scottish dissent and its otherwise shared opposition to anti-popery after 1845.

The most striking example of the varying yet overlapping principles behind the anti-Catholicism of Scottish dissent is found in the opposition to the Maynooth Bill of 1845, which utilised both anti-popery and voluntary rhetoric in its opposition to the endowment of Catholicism, and therefore provided a broad platform on which Scotland's Presbyterian dissenters could unite. This chapter will place the anti-Catholic movement in Scotland after 1845 within this context of shifting Presbyterian dissenting relations. The main weapons for the dissenting crusade against Maynooth, and the later defence against the perceived 'papal aggression', were the pulpit, the presbytery, pamphlets and petitions, and politics.[18] While the relationship between Scotland's dissenting churches and electoral politics will be explored in greater depth in the next chapter, this chapter will assess the role of popular anti-Catholicism in fostering closer bonds within Scottish dissent. First, it will explore the various reasons and motivations behind the surge of anti-Catholicism that engulfed Scotland's non-established churches between the introduction of Peel's bill in 1845 and the tercentenary commemorations of the Scottish Reformation in 1860. Second, it will assess how these different interpretations coexisted in the practical attempts to create a united front against popery in this period, both within Scottish dissent and British Protestantism in general, focusing on the anti-Maynooth agitation, the growth of institutional anti-popery through the proliferation of Protestant societies following the papal

15. Wolffe, 'Change and Continuity', 71.
16. Andrew Holmes, 'Religious Conflict in Ulster, c. 1780–1886', in John Wolffe (ed.), *Protestant-Catholic Conflict from the Reformation to the Twenty-First Century: the dynamics of religious difference* (Basingstoke, 2013), 115.
17. Philomena Sutherland, 'Sectarianism and Evangelicalism in Birmingham and Liverpool, 1850–2010', in Wolffe, *Protestant–Catholic Conflict*, 132, 135–6.
18. *Protestant Magazine*, published under the direction of the committee of the Protestant Association, xvi (April 1854), 113; J. E. Handley, *The Irish in Scotland, 1798–1845* (Cork, 1945), 299.

aggression, and the national and denominational events that marked the 1860 tercentenary. By exploring the apparent unity of the Protestant and evangelical opposition to Catholicism in mid-nineteenth-century Britain, this chapter will illuminate the principles and practical actions that both strengthened and weakened Scottish dissenting relations in the aftermath of the Disruption.

Scottish Presbyterianism and Anti-Catholicism before 1845

The dominance of anti-Catholicism within Scotland's Presbyterian churches in the mid-nineteenth century was by no means a new phenomenon and, in many respects, was a direct descendant of three centuries of anti-Catholic hostility in Scotland. Following the Scottish Reformation of 1560, the defence of 'British' Protestantism from the perceived popish threat was central to the formation of a distinct Scottish Presbyterian identity. The strident anti-popery sentiments of the patriarch of Scottish Presbyterianism, John Knox, who characterised Catholicism as unscriptural and ungodly, and Catholics as servants of Antichrist, created a stark dichotomy that would influence the worldview of generations of Scots and prove integral to their distinctively Presbyterian and Whig conception of British Protestant liberty.[19] The apparent synonymous relationship between anti-Catholicism and the defence of Britain's civil and religious liberties would later find expression in the virulent anti-popery of the seventeenth-century Scots covenanting movement, the opposition to James VII's Catholic policies, and the popular anti-Catholic demonstrations that accompanied the Revolution settlements of 1688–9.[20] The prevailing Catholic attachment to the flagging Jacobite cause for much of the eighteenth century also cemented the albeit qualified and far from monolithic support among Scottish Presbyterians (especially within the Cameronian fringes) for the 1707 Union and the Hanoverian regime against the exiled Stuarts.[21]

While Catholics formed a numerically insignificant portion of Scottish society before 1800, these lingering Presbyterian suspicions of Catholic

19. R. A. Mason, 'Usable Pasts: History and Identity in Reformation Scotland', *Scottish Historical Review*, lxxvi (1997), 58–9; Forsyth, 'Presbyterian historians', 104, 109–10; Coleman, *Remembering the Past*, 130, 133; Andrew Holmes, 'The Scottish Reformations and the origin of religious and civil liberty in Britain and Ireland: Presbyterian interpretations, c. 1800–60', *Bulletin of the John Rylands Library*, xc (2014), 139.
20. Cowan, *Scottish Covenanters*, 26; Robert Paul Barnes, 'Scotland and the Glorious Revolution of 1688', *Albion*, iii (1971), 119; Alasdair Raffe, 'Presbyterianism, Secularisation, and Scottish Politics after the Revolution of 1688–1690', *Historical Journal*, liii (2010), 324; S. A. Burrell, 'The Apocalyptic Vision of the Early Covenanters', *Scottish Historical Review*, xliii (1964), 19.
21. Christopher Whatley, *The Scots and the Union: then and now* (Edinburgh, 2014), ch. 9; Kidd, 'Conditional Britons', 1147–76; Daniel Szechi, 'Defending the True Faith: Kirk, State, and Catholic Missioners in Scotland, 1653–1755', *Catholic Historical Review*, lxxxii (1996), 397–8.

and Jacobite motives ensured the 'No Popery' cry remained entrenched in Scotland, and occasionally incited outbreaks of rioting, such as in Edinburgh in 1779 and Glasgow in 1788.[22] By the turn of the nineteenth century, there were an estimated 30,000 Catholics in Scotland out of a total population of 1.6 million, mostly based in the rural Highlands and Islands and away from the centres of the Kirk and anti-popery in the Lowlands.[23] Nevertheless, according to the mid-nineteenth-century historian 'Senex', while in the 1770s and 1780s all of Glasgow's Catholics, numbering no more than thirty, could fit into a single room of a private dwelling for worship, there were up to eighty-five anti-Catholic societies in the city containing roughly 12,000 members.[24]

The historical tradition of anti-Catholicism in Scotland was compounded by the influx of (largely Catholic) Irish immigrants in the first half of the nineteenth century. The early decades of the century witnessed both a steady increase in Irish settlers into Scotland and a shift in character of these migrants from seasonal rural labourers to a permanent industrial workforce.[25] By the time of the Disruption, nearly 5 per cent of Scotland's population was Irish-born; in addition, second- and third-generation migrants brought the total number of Irish in Scotland to roughly 10 per cent of the total population.[26] As Ben Braber has argued, it was at this point that 'the migratory swell turned into a wave'.[27] The Irish famine from 1845 resulted in the largest sustained period of immigration from Ireland to Scotland in the nineteenth century. It changed the face of Scottish society, anti-popery and the Roman Catholic Church in Scotland, which, for the first time, could attempt to threaten the traditional numerical pre-eminence of Presbyterianism in the cities.[28] By the time of the 1851 census, Scotland's Irish-born population had risen in a decade by 90,000 to over 207,000 (three-quarters of whom were Catholic), accounting for over 7 per cent of Scotland's total, the highest percentage of the nineteenth century; in contrast, the Irish-born percentage in England and Wales was less than 3 per cent.[29] The impact of this upheaval was heightened by the geographical and regional concentration of nearly three-quarters of the new immigrants

22. Gallagher, *The Uneasy Peace*, 9.
23. John F. McCaffrey, 'Roman Catholics in Scotland in the nineteenth and twentieth centuries', *RSCHS*, xxiii (1983), 275.
24. 'Senex' [Robert Reid], *Glasgow: Past and Present* (3 volumes, Glasgow, 1884), ii, 272–3, iii, 253.
25. Bruce, *No Pope of Rome*, 25; Gallagher, *The Uneasy Peace*, 11–12.
26. *Census of Great Britain in 1851; population tables* [Cd. 1632], H.C. 1852, lxxxvi, 103, 218; Handley, *Irish in Scotland*, 89–90, 111.
27. Ben Braber, 'Immigrants', in Devine and Wormald (eds), *Modern Scottish History*, 492–3.
28. Peter Hillis, *The Barony of Glasgow: a window onto Church and people in nineteenth-century Scotland* (Edinburgh, 2007), 46.
29. *Census of Great Britain, 1851. Religious worship, and education. Scotland* [Cd. 1764], H.C. 1854, lix, 75, 103, 218; J. A. Jackson, *The Irish in Britain* (London, 1963), 191; Handley, *Irish in Scotland*, 89–90.

in the industrialised centres of Lanarkshire and Renfrewshire in the west of central Scotland.[30]

This new and unprecedented wave of immigration, and its heightened visibility in the towns and cities, coincided with a famine in the Highlands, the economic depression that gripped Scotland in 1847–8 and localised outbreaks of cholera in 1848.[31] Inevitably, the new Irish settlers, alongside their pre-famine compatriots, became scapegoats for the appalling living and working conditions and social turbulence of this period. As Steve Bruce and Bernard Aspinwall have noted, the native Scots held the perception that the Irish were responsible for the worst effects of industrialisation and its erosion of Scotland's traditional agrarian Presbyterian community simply because they arrived at the same time.[32] These communal tensions would later be stoked by the Presbyterian churches' attempts to evangelise the cities through a renewed urban mission in the 1850s, and the proliferation of notorious 'No-Popery' preachers in the aftermath of the papal aggression.[33] The increasing general hostility towards Irish Catholic immigrants in the mid-nineteenth century, combined with the traditional anti-popery of Presbyterian Scotland, paved the way for the nationwide anti-Catholic fervour that engulfed the country during the 1845 Maynooth controversy.

'Bigotry' or Voluntaryism? The Reaction of Scottish Presbyterian Dissent to the Maynooth Bill of 1845 and the 'Papal Aggression'

The 1829 Roman Catholic Relief Act, which permitted Catholics to sit in parliament, provoked a decidedly mixed response among Scottish Presbyterians; while the western Lowlands witnessed vociferous opposition to the Act, there was considerable support for the measure in the east of Scotland among voluntaries and liberal evangelicals in the Kirk, most notably Thomas Chalmers. By contrast, the furore surrounding the government grant in 1845 to the Roman Catholic seminary at Maynooth created an unprecedented sense of unity within Presbyterianism, particularly the dissenting churches, in opposition to the endowment and Catholicism in

---

30. Brenda Collins, 'The origin of Irish immigration to Scotland in the nineteenth and twentieth centuries', in T. M. Devine (ed.), *Irish Immigrants and Scottish Society in the Nineteenth and Twentieth Centuries* (Edinburgh, 1991), 11; T. M. Devine, *The Scottish Nation: a Modern History* (London, 2012), 291–2.
31. Braber, 'Immigrants', 495.
32. Bruce, *No Pope of Rome*, 28; Mark Doyle, *Fighting like the Devil for the sake of God: Protestants, Catholics and the origins of violence in Victorian Belfast* (Manchester, 2009), 27; Aspinwall, 'Popery in Scotland', 239, 257.
33. Smith, *Memoirs of James Begg*, ii, 133–5, 188; Machin, *Politics and the Churches in Great Britain*, 253–4; Gallagher, *The Uneasy Peace*, 20–2; Best, 'Popular Protestantism in Victorian Britain', 140; Wolffe, 'Change and Continuity', 80; S. J. Brown, 'Thomas Chalmers and the communal ideal in Victorian Scotland', in T. C. Smout (ed.), *Victorian Values* (London, 1992), 70.

general.³⁴ The decision by Peel to increase the annual grant to Maynooth college and place it on the consolidated fund, thus removing it from annual discussion, produced a national movement and hastened the split within a Tory party which had suffered increasing fragmentation since the 1820s. Despite Peel's integral role in fostering British 'No Popery' sentiment while in opposition between 1835 and 1841, the Maynooth controversy marked conservatism's second major fracturing in sixteen years on the grounds of anti-Catholicism and the Irish question, following the Duke of Wellington's support for emancipation in 1829. To the anti-Catholic colleagues who had helped propel him to the premiership, Peel's acquiescence to Irish grievances was a 'betrayal' and, coupled with the repeal of the Corn Laws a year later, would bring down his ministry.³⁵

Beyond this intra-party conflict, the increased annual endowment of £26,000 to Maynooth dominated British religious and political discussion in general for most of the 1840s and 1850s. One observer commented that 'the whole newspaper press' and 'periodical reviews and magazines, all teemed with this one engrossing subject'.³⁶ As Gilbert Cahill has noted, the popular agitation that followed the Maynooth bill was a product of organisational activity and the 'outraged and spontaneous outburst of Protestant, national feeling'.³⁷ According to the *Spectator*, by April 1845 Maynooth was the focal point of political debate in Britain, 'both in and out of Parliament'. Public meetings were held across the country in opposition to Peel's decision and between February and June 1845 ten thousand petitions to the House of Commons calling for the bill's withdrawal collected over one and a quarter million signatures.³⁸ Liberals, Conservatives, High Churchmen and voluntaries united to condemn the bill, often for very different reasons, prompting *The Times* to 'praise' Peel's ability to alienate such a wide range of MPs and extra-parliamentary groups with one proposal.³⁹ This surge of 'extraordinary' popular disapproval incited Morgan O'Connell, son of Daniel O'Connell, to speculate in parliament that should the 'strange coalition' in opposition to the grant continue, he 'should tremble not only for the Legislative Union, but even for the connection between England and Ireland'.⁴⁰

Despite the national and cross-party nature of the opposition, the

---

34. Gallagher, *The Uneasy Peace*, 10; Bruce, *No Pope of Rome*, 29–31.
35. Gilbert Cahill, 'Irish Catholicism and English Toryism', *The Review of Politics*, xix (January 1957), 62–76; Machin, 'The Maynooth Grant, the dissenters and disestablishment', 61–2; Cahill, 'The Protestant Association and the anti-Maynooth agitation', 273–5.
36. *Reasons for declining to vote in favour of Mr Macaulay*, 4.
37. Cahill, 'Irish Catholicism and English Toryism', 73.
38. *Spectator*, 19 April 1845; A. S. Thelwall (ed.), *Proceedings of the Anti-Maynooth Conference of 1845* (London, 1845), clxxxi.
39. Joseph Coohill, *Ideas of the Liberal Party: Perceptions, Agendas and Liberal Politics in the House of Commons, 1832–52* (Chichester, 2011), 154.
40. *Spectator*, 3 May 1845.

Maynooth endowment was justified by the supporters of the bill, in the churches and in parliament, on both religious and political grounds. Politically, the endowment sought to placate Catholic agitation in Ireland, and also offered recognition that the Roman Catholic Church could provide a stabilising influence on Irish society.[41] Religious advocates of the bill, particularly within the Church of England, believed that by placing Catholicism on the same level as Britain and Ireland's endowed Protestant churches, attempts could therefore be made to 'purify' the apparent errors of Romanism. Unlike the anti-popery and voluntary opponents of the measure, these supporters argued that error is 'most surely perpetuated when it is neglected' and that the defeat of Catholicism could only be achieved 'not by a crusade of avowed enemies from without her camp, but by a defection from within'. This goal would be accomplished through a 'generous and common sympathy' for both the Catholic people and their teachers. Otherwise, any attempts to proscribe the priesthood would result in forcing them 'within the fortress of a more relentless bigotry', and drive the 'victims' of Rome's 'tyranny into a closer league with her'.[42]

Despite the concerns of these more moderate churchmen, the 'crusade' that followed Peel's proposal maintained that the disendowment of popery, on its own or as part of a wider policy of disestablishment, represented the only means by which it could be defeated. One voluntary commentator wrote that 'it is a false and sickly taste which does not prefer truth to error, or know how to separate between truth and the unfitting adjuncts sometimes connected with it'. According to the writer for the *British Quarterly Review*, those 'liberal' churchmen in support of the Maynooth grant were acting 'as though recognised and endowed error were to be preferred to unrecognised and unendowed truth'.[43] The Edinburgh United Presbyterian layman Duncan McLaren criticised the exclusivity of the grant, and argued that according to the principle outlined by supporters of the bill, if Maynooth were to be endowed, so should the Free Church college in Edinburgh; a proposal he claimed would be rejected by MPs. McLaren contended that 'if the principle on which that grant was based was right, it ought to be extended to all classes, and not to be confined to one religious denomination, and that the Roman Catholics alone'.[44] These arguments were utilised to varying degrees by both the establishmentarian and voluntary strands of British Protestantism. In Scotland they would form the basis of the coalition of Free Churchmen and United Presbyterians in opposition to the endowment and on the basis of a broader joint anti-Catholicism.

41. Donal Kerr, *Peel, Priests, and Politics: Sir Robert Peel's Administration and the Roman Catholic Church in Ireland, 1841–1846* (Oxford, 1982); Gallagher, *The Uneasy Peace*, 19.
42. *The Maynooth endowment vindicated: on the grounds of religious principle, by a clergyman of the Church of England* (London, 1845), 24, 54–7.
43. *British Quarterly Review*, ii (August 1845), 119, 127.
44. *Caledonian Mercury*, 11 December 1851.

From the outset of the anti-Maynooth agitation, Scotland's non-established churches were at the forefront of popular opposition. The early prominence of evangelical dissent in the anti-Maynooth campaign was noted in April 1845 by the voluntary campaigner Sir Culling Smith, who would chair the following month's national conference against the grant in London. Smith acknowledged the important role of the Free and United Secession churches, alongside their Methodist, Independent and Baptist counterparts in England, in organising and promoting petitions to parliament.[45] Unsurprisingly, the Church of Scotland was absent from Smith's praise. Norman MacLeod, dismayed at the lack of anti-papal zeal in his church, was the only establishment minister actively to protest against the grant in the early months of 1845.[46] The desire for immediate action was most evident among the Free Church leadership. In March 1845, a proposal to raise a petition against the bill was brought by Robert Smith Candlish in the Free Presbytery of Edinburgh.[47] At May's General Assembly, a committee was established to prepare a petition to the Queen and the House of Lords, while a standing committee on popery was also formed. The petition, drafted by ministers such as Robert Buchanan, Patrick Macfarlan and Candlish, alongside the Whig politician Fox Maule and lawyer Alexander Dunlop, emphasised the Free Church's deep reverence for the 'Protestant principles' of the British throne and constitution. The endowment of Ireland's Catholic priesthood, the petition argued, was the most 'direct and effectual way of encouraging any system of religious error' and damaging to the interests of 'this Protestant nation'.[48] However, some Free Church ministers such as William Cunningham expressed reticence about participating in such a politically motivated agitation outside of the church's remit. Nevertheless, though Cunningham doubted that the campaign would change the attitudes of Britain's political elite, he hoped that it would at the very least 'tend to rally and combine the evangelical Dissenters on Protestant ground'.[49]

The dual dissenting and anti-Catholic rhetoric, which focused on common ground against a shared enemy, would permeate Scotland's non-established churches throughout the anti-Maynooth campaign.[50] As discussed in the previous chapter, this desire for united action against the supposed papal threat was grounded in a context of ever-closer relations between Britain's evangelical – and dissenting – Protestants in the mid-1840s. The creation of the Evangelical Alliance the following year, of which Peel's bill was an immediate catalyst, offered an institutional platform for cordial co-operation between Scotland's non-established Presbyterian

45. *Spectator*, 12 April 1845.
46. John Wellwood, *Norman MacLeod* (Edinburgh, 1897), 49.
47. William Wilson, *Memorials of Robert Smith Candlish, D.D.* (Edinburgh, 1880), 353–4.
48. *AGAFC, 1845* (Edinburgh, 1845), 68, 37.
49. Rainy and Mackenzie, *Life of William Cunningham*, 307–8.
50. *UPM*, v (June 1851), 274.

bodies.[51] By appealing to the most basic of Protestant instincts, a shared opposition to the state's endowment of popery provided the simplest instrument for consolidating the closer bonds that had emerged between Scotland's dissenters in the aftermath of the Disruption. The potential for a unified dissenting front based on anti-popery was evident long before the introduction of the Maynooth bill. At the Free Church General Assembly of October 1843, Candlish outlined the two shared principles around which all of Britain's Protestant dissenting churches could unite: 'that the Church, whether established or not, must be wholly free, and that Popery is a system of anti-Christian superstition, to support which is sinful'.[52]

Following the introduction of the Maynooth bill in 1845, these principles, to varying degrees of interpretation, would come to define much of the dissenting opposition to the grant. Commending the Free Church's immediate and zealous reaction to the controversy, the *United Secession Magazine* expressed disappointment at the 'inactivity and apathy' of Scotland's other non-established Presbyterians towards Maynooth, and asked 'why have others not been more prompt at least to imitate such a good example?' Reiterating the Free Church call for united action, the writer argued that it is 'surely desirable that there should be a common understanding' of the principles on which the endowment to Maynooth would be opposed. However, the journal's advocacy of voluntaryism as the 'most tenable ground which can be taken', and on 'which the greatest number of our countrymen will be found heartily to rally', only served to emphasise that while there may have been increasing convergence and common ground among Scotland's Presbyterian dissenters against the Maynooth bill, common principle was noticeably lacking.[53]

While the issue of Maynooth united Protestants of all denominations in opposition to Peel's bill, the reasons for this opposition varied greatly. G. I. T. Machin summarised the major fault lines within the British anti-Maynooth campaign as consisting of 'orthodox' ultra-Protestants, solely opposed to the endowment of a Catholic seminary, and voluntaries, opposed to endowments in general.[54] This dichotomy was most evident in a series of conferences held in May and June 1845 to protest the grant. The largest of these meetings, organised by the Central Anti-Maynooth Committee and held in Exeter Hall, London, from 30 April to 3 May, adopted an 'orthodox' anti-Catholic approach. On the other hand, a conference at Crosby Hall three weeks later, attended by over 300 dissenting ministers and organised by the British Anti-State Church Association, represented the dissenting and

51. Wolffe, 'Evangelical Alliance', 338.
52. *PGAFC, October 1843* (Glasgow, 1843), 40.
53. *USM,* ii (April 1845), 120.
54. Machin, 'The Maynooth Grant, the dissenters and disestablishment', 62.

ultra-voluntary argument against Maynooth.⁵⁵ To some Church of England clergymen, the Crosby Hall meeting and its accompanying 'Address to the Roman Catholics of Ireland', which offered a broad ultra-voluntary critique of all state endowments of religion, was 'proof' that the Anti-Maynooth Committee had failed, 'and that union between the voluntaries and those who held the Establishment principle was impossible'. James Blackwood, the chairman of the Central Anti-Maynooth Committee, refuted these claims and argued that there were members of his group 'who held the voluntary principle as firmly as the delegates of Crosby Hall', but 'whose Christianity being stronger than their voluntaryism, enabled them to sink, for the present, that secondary question altogether'.⁵⁶ The parliamentary petition that emerged from the Anti-Maynooth Conference reinforced this point, and emphasised the petitioners' opposition to the Maynooth grant on 'religious grounds'. Presenting the petition to the House of Lords, John Campbell, the Marquess of Breadalbane, concurred that the bill was 'opposed to the interests of Protestantism'.⁵⁷ The desire to relegate the thorny issue of church–state relations in order to secure unity was echoed by the Leith Congregationalist G. D. Cullen. He stressed that following the Disruption the voluntary principle should not provide a barrier to the 'common ground' of opposition against Maynooth. For Blackwood and many of his colleagues at Exeter Hall, the anti-Maynooth campaign was solely about 'contending for the Truth, and against the endowment of Error'.⁵⁸

The debates over truth, error and principle that emerged during the London conferences of May 1845 would be replicated within the alliance against the Maynooth bill between the Free Church and the United Secession and Relief bodies. Reporting on an Edinburgh meeting of the anti-Catholic Scottish Reformation Society (SRS), founded in the wake of the papal aggression, the *Aberdeen Journal* noted the apparent sectarian and ideological divisions within a group nonetheless 'unanimous in their object'. While the Free Church members of the society condemned the grant 'on the ground that it implicated the nation in the guilt of supporting a false and idolatrous belief', the voluntaries of the United Presbyterian Church 'were as much opposed to the endowment of any of all the forms of Protestantism, or of Roman Catholicism, or any other "ism" in the whole category of religious creeds'.⁵⁹ James Begg, the founder of the SRS and one of the Free Church's most violent critics of voluntaryism as well as popery, was blunter in his assessment, claiming that while the United Presbyterians

55. John Blackburn, *The three conferences held by the opponents of the Maynooth College Endowment Bill, in London and Dublin, during the months of May and June, 1845* (London, 1845), 19–24; *Sheffield and Rotherham Independent*, 31 May 1845; *Quarterly Review*, lxxvi (June 1845) 257.
56. Thelwall, *Anti-Maynooth Conference of 1845*, cxxix.
57. *Hansard's Parliamentary Debates*, 3rd series, vol. lxxx (23 May 1845), 785.
58. Thelwall, *Anti-Maynooth Conference of 1845*, 152.
59. *Aberdeen Journal*, 17 December 1851.

were willing to 'treat truth and falsehood as if they were alike', the establishmentarians of the Free Kirk believed that 'it is wrong to endow error' but 'it is a right thing to endow truth'.[60]

Exemplified in the person of the controversial Begg, the establishmentarian principles of the Disruption and its doctrine of spiritual independence, combined with elements of social activism and Scottish patriotism, defined the character of mid-century militant Protestantism in the Free Kirk. To many of the Free Church establishmentarians in the years after 1843, distrust of voluntaryism and Catholicism went hand in hand.[61] As Karly Kehoe has pointed out, these suspicions were not entirely unfounded. The rise of the voluntary movement between 1830 and 1860 facilitated Catholic ambition by enabling the beginnings of an ecclesiastical system in which non-established churches could flourish.[62] The complete disendowment of Protestantism as propagated by Scotland's voluntaries, Begg argued, would not strengthen the vitality of Christianity in Britain but would drag it 'down to Atheism's level' and offer 'fair play to Romanists' to 'overthrow the Protestantism of the throne'.[63] Despite this scathing criticism of the voluntary approach to the campaign, the primary focus of the 'orthodox' anti-Catholics remained the Roman enemy and its British agent at Maynooth. The seminary, Begg claimed in 1852's controversial and bestselling *Handbook of Popery*, was 'deluging all parts of the Kingdom with determined emissaries of Rome', and formed part of the Vatican's plot to take 'the fullest advantage of liberty conceded to her by Protestant nations, for the very purpose of overthrowing their liberties, and trampling them under her feet'.[64] The 'dominion of the Romish priesthood', funded by the British government, was viewed as 'utterly inconsistent with civil liberty or social progress', while the broader system of Roman Catholicism was depicted as 'entirely subversive of the truth of God and the purity of the gospel'.[65]

This brand of simple anti-popery espoused by Begg, focused on the perceived 'errors' of Rome and its threat to British liberty, permeated much of the Free Church opposition to Maynooth and would be redoubled following the 'papal aggression'. According to the Free Churchman Robert Rainy, the restoration of a national Catholic hierarchy of bishops and dioceses in England and Wales in 1850 'set the country in a blaze'

---

60. Balfour, *Establishment principle defended*, vii; James Begg, *Voluntaryism indefensible; or, a nation's right and duty to profess and practise Christianity* (Edinburgh, 1879), 6; Smith, *Memoirs of James Begg*, ii, 428.
61. Peter Bayne, *The Life and Letters of Hugh Miller* (2 volumes, London, 1871), ii, 191.
62. Kehoe, *Creating a Scottish Church*, 59.
63. Begg, *Voluntaryism indefensible*, 6–7.
64. James Begg, *A Handbook of Popery; or, text-book of missions for the conversion of Romanists* (Edinburgh, 1852), 308, 310–11.
65. Edward Beecher, *The Papal Conspiracy Exposed; or, the Romish Corporation dangerous to the political liberty and social interests of man* (Edinburgh, 1856), v–vi.

and produced 'an anti-Papal ferment, which a year before no one would have believed that any Papal proceeding whatever could produce'.[66] The hostile reaction to the ultramontane policies of Pope Pius IX, viewed by Free Churchmen as 'prejudicial to the Protestant interests of the nation', reawakened the anti-Maynooth agitation, incited communal violence in Dunfermline and Greenock during 1850 and 1851, and resulted in the promulgation of numerous 'militant' Protestant organisations such as the Glasgow Protestant Laymen's Association and the London-based Protestant Alliance.[67]

This apparent attack on British institutions was believed to be a part of Rome's attempt to subject Britain 'to the degrading slavery of the Vatican'.[68] The threat of ultramontanism to British sovereignty yielded a patriotic defence of the state's constitution and institutions. Protestant arguments against Catholicism were often 'couched in a patriotic framework', and were derived from the guarded attitudes of the previous century's 'Francophobia'.[69] In the years following Catholic Emancipation, fear of war with the Catholic European states had segued into a fear of both the Vatican's aggressive political strategy and the threat from within Britain's borders. The progress of popery in Britain was also regarded as synonymous with the increasing degradation of Scotland's national, moral and social character, with Begg claiming that only a 'social Reformation' could reinvigorate Presbyterianism and Scottish patriotism.[70] He argued that while it was easy to rebuke the scriptural arguments of Catholicism, meeting 'the policy of Rome is a very different matter. Rome professes to be a religion, but she is nothing else than a banded conspiracy against the rights of God and the liberties of men.'[71]

By invoking the national and political significance of Catholicism's threat to the United Kingdom, Begg moved the debate beyond its narrow theological implications regarding truth and error, and placed the hostile reaction to the papal aggression within the context of the Maynooth debate. The conferences, pamphlets and public meetings that appeared in the years after 1850 not only lamented the 'stealthy progress of Popery' in Britain, and its attached side effects such as the 'evils' of the increasing number of nunneries in this period, but criticised the 'suicidal policy of our rulers' in sanctioning and endowing this perceived threat. In 1853

---

66. Rainy and Mackenzie, *Life of William Cunningham*, 310.
67. Gallagher, *The Uneasy Peace*, 15; Machin, *Politics and the Churches in Great Britain*, 253–4; Braber, 'Immigrants', 498; Wolffe, *Protestant Crusade*, 249; Smith, *Memoirs of James Begg*, ii, 170.
68. *Caledonian Mercury*, 9 April 1859; *Bulwark, or Reformation Journal*, i (July 1851), 1.
69. Wolffe, *Protestant Crusade*, 308; Linda Colley, *Britons: Forging the Nation 1707–1837* (New Haven, 2009), 23.
70. Aspinwall, 'Popery in Scotland', 239; J. A. Wylie (ed.), *Tercentenary of the Scottish Reformation as commemorated at Edinburgh, August 1860* (Edinburgh, 1860), 204.
71. *Protestant Magazine*, xvi (April 1854), 110.

J. A. Wylie, the Original Secessionist turned Free Churchman and close confidant of Begg, argued that the Maynooth grant was 'viewed religiously, a sin', viewed 'politically, unconstitutional' and 'viewed rationally, a folly'. Wylie linked the endowment to the threat to British sovereignty caused by the aggression, and claimed that 'every penny given to Maynooth expedites the advent of a state of things in which Britain will resemble the Spain of two hundred years ago, and the Tuscany of the present day'.[72]

The Free Church opposition to the state's stance on Maynooth conjured the remnants of anti-government distrust lingering from the Ten Years' Conflict. The Peel government's decision to endow the 'errors' of Catholicism, two years after the Disruption, inevitably provoked the ire of the non-intrusionists. During a debate in the House of Commons in April 1845, Fox Maule contrasted the endowment of Maynooth with the government's conduct during the Ten Years' Conflict and treatment of the non-intrusionist demand for 'spiritual independence', which he argued was enshrined by the entitlements and privileges of the 1707 Acts of Union. Maule recounted the government's stance at the Disruption, 'echoed' by the opposition, that 'the idea of an establishment existing in connection with the State, and over which the State had no control, was monstrous and unconstitutional'. He questioned the grounds upon which the British government could ask Free Churchmen, themselves refused permission only two years previously to 'carry on the spiritual government of their Church without the interference of the State', to 'support them on public grounds in a measure which had for its object the creation of another establishment in the sister country, over which there was to be no state control'.[73] Maule also highlighted what he regarded as the personal hypocrisy of Peel who, as leader of the Opposition between 1835 and 1841, 'virtually encouraged' the Tory 'No Popery' cry initially raised in 1829 in hostility to the Catholic Emancipation Act. He recounted an 1838 meeting on the subject of church extension between Peel and a deputation of the Church of Scotland during which the Tory leader 'inveighed against the progress of "Popery" and urged the necessity of a Protestant combination against it'. Maule questioned the confidence that could be entertained in a statesman who 'now, when in office, gave means and promotion to the extension of that very Popery' he opposed less than five years before.[74] Maule's antagonism towards Peel was criticised by the Unitarian *Christian Reformer*, which noted that while the MP was admonishing the government for failing to heal religious divisions in Scotland, his stance on Maynooth was 'anything but healing and conciliatory'.[75]

Despite this criticism, distrust of the state's motives towards Maynooth

---

72. *HFRFC*, iii (February 1853), 172–4.
73. *Hansard's Parliamentary Debates*, 3rd series, vol. lxxix (14 April 1845), 606–7.
74. *Spectator*, 3 May 1845.
75. *Christian Reformer; or Unitarian magazine and review*, i (June 1845), 439.

became a central feature of the Free Church's opposition to the grant and Catholicism in general. However, unlike their voluntary counterparts, this critique was focused on governmental action, rather than a full-blown denunciation of the state's role in propagating religion. The MPs who voted for the bill were charged by Begg with 'ludicrous deceit' on the subject of Maynooth, and of 'aiding and abetting' the 'suppression of the Bible' and 'liberty of conscience'. In the *Handbook of Popery*, Begg was scathingly critical of the Westminster political elite: 'Prating about liberty, they openly subsidise its greatest enemy . . . what are we, then, to think of the would-be wise men of the present day, who not only defend such a system, but give £30,000 a-year to reconstruct it?'[76] Even more severely, Begg also directly implicated politicians in what he regarded as the papal conspiracy to oppress Britain, lamenting the 'amount of treachery implied on the part of statesmen in conniving at the restoration of the dark dominion of Rome'.[77] For the anti-Catholic zealots within the Free Church, such as the SRS's secretary George Badenoch, the endowment of Maynooth was evidence of the British government acting inconsistently with the constitution.[78] While these statesmen were 'determined to throw aside the great principles of the Reformation and Revolution', the Free Church viewed itself as safeguarding Protestantism as the 'essential' principle of that constitution.[79]

For Scottish Presbyterians, liberty and no-popery were intrinsically linked.[80] By 'fighting for the constitution', Free Church anti-Catholics such as Begg, in a similar manner to the non-intrusionist appropriation of Scotland's covenanting tradition prior to the Disruption, could portray themselves as the historical Protestant defenders of British liberty and sovereignty from Romish tyranny and oppression, and 'worthy of the heroic men from whom we are descended'.[81] This defence of Britain's independence from the 'primary idea of the Papacy' that supreme jurisdiction resides with the Pope, combined with the inherent suspicion of the British government, closely resembled the model of spiritual independence advocated at the Disruption.[82] In this case, however, the spiritual independence of the church was transplanted onto British Protestantism in general, free from the encroachments of both popery and erastian government. While

---

76. Begg, *Handbook of Popery*, 316–17; *Bulwark; or, Reformation Journal*, ii (1852), 278.
77. Beecher, *Papal Conspiracy Exposed*, vi.
78. Wylie, *Tercentenary of the Scottish Reformation*, 193.
79. James Begg, *The proposed disestablishment of Protestantism in Ireland* (Edinburgh, 1868), 29; *Caledonian Mercury*, 9 April 1859.
80. Best, 'Popular Protestantism in Victorian Britain', 120.
81. Begg, *Proposed disestablishment of Protestantism*, 24; *Aberdeen Journal*, 17 December 1851; *Protestant Magazine*, xvi (April 1854), 110; Forsyth, 'Presbyterian historians', 93–4, 98–9; D. W. Bebbington, 'Religion and national feeling in nineteenth century Wales and Scotland', *Studies in Church History*, xviii (1982), 502.
82. *HFRFC*, iii (February 1853), 173.

Anglicans generally viewed the close connection between church and state as central to the fight against popery, Begg linked the erastianism and remoteness of the British government to the papacy, arguing that 'the great despotisms of the world have all been established on the basis of ignorance of the Word of God, and by combining all power, civil and ecclesiastical, in a single human centre'.[83]

Despite their self-appointed roles as the guardians of British Protestantism, the violent conjecture and heavy-handed approach of these 'ultra-Protestants' in the Free Kirk ensured that they were readily dismissed by more moderate critics as bigots. The Liberal MP W. E. Baxter accused Begg of 'spiritual terrorism'. Baxter argued that the Free Church-dominated Scottish Reformation Society was 'doing a great deal of harm to Protestantism, not only in Scotland, but in [England]', while the clench-fisted fanaticism of Begg and other Free Churchmen like Hugh Miller was 'rendering the cause of Protestantism ridiculous, and offending its best friends'.[84] The volatile sectarianism associated with the Free Church after 1843 was also viewed as undermining its Protestant aims. The Church of England clergyman Richard Paul Blakeney believed that Free Kirk leaders such as Candlish and William Maxwell Hetherington were 'doing the work of Popery more effectively than Wisemen, Newman and Cahill' due to their repeated 'attacks' on the Established Church of Scotland.[85] The Cork MP Vincent Scully also claimed that the Free Church members' campaign against Maynooth was simply part of their 'wish to upset all church establishments'.[86] To supporters of the grant, particularly within the Church of England, the violent rhetoric, anti-government hostility and overt anti-popery associated with the Free Kirk's 'crusade against religious error' ensured that the Maynooth debate, at least initially, was viewed as a conflict between common sense and bigotry.[87]

This charge of bigotry was extended to the voluntary opposition to the endowment, particularly as it became more closely aligned with the Free Kirk after 1846. In 1852 newspapers such as the *Scotsman* labelled the 'stupidity' of the voluntaries' refusal to support the Whig government 'because of an abstract opinion' as an 'intolerant bigotry'. However, as one Edinburgh United Presbyterian elector acknowledged, to voluntaries the endowment of the Roman Catholic priesthood in Ireland was deemed

---

83. James Begg, *Free Church Presbyterianism in the United Kingdom: its principles, duties and dangers* (Edinburgh, 1865), 14.
84. *Bulwark*, i, (July 1851), 2; Smith, *Memoirs of James Begg*, ii, 349–50; George Rosie, *Hugh Miller: Outrage and Order* (Edinburgh, 1981), 6.
85. Wolffe, *Protestant Crusade*, 255.
86. *Hansard's Parliamentary Debates*, 3rd series, vol. cxxii (8 June 1852), 227–8.
87. Gallagher, *The Uneasy Peace*, 20. For example, *The Maynooth endowment vindicated: on the grounds of religious principle, by a clergyman of the Church of England* (London, 1845); *Common sense v. bigotry; or, reasons for supporting the parliamentary grant to Maynooth, by a clergyman of the Church of England* (London, 1845).

to be a 'lesser question' than '*the* great question of civil establishments of religion' and the 'idea of endowing all sects'.[88] David Young, the United Presbyterian minister at Perth, reiterated the pre-eminence of the voluntary principle in his colleagues' rejection of the grant over the simple anti-popery associated with the Free Church. 'Ask them', he stated, 'to do away with all Irish endowments and you put an intelligent case, which at least is worthy of their grave attention; but ask them to go and nibble at Maynooth, and you outrage their sense of political justice.'[89]

In this sense, the broader issue of disestablishment and religious endowments in general proved central to the voluntary rhetoric against Maynooth. At Westminster, of the thirty-one Liberal opponents of the original bill only one cited 'exclusively Protestant' reasons, while twenty-three opposed it on voluntary grounds.[90] In 1852 the *United Presbyterian Magazine* compiled a list of voluntary members of Parliament. Most of those detailed, such as Thomas Duncombe of Finsbury, voted against Maynooth 'not from any sectarian motives, but because he was opposed to all religious endowments'.[91] This strict voluntary language dominated the petitions that emerged from the United Secession and Relief churches in 1845. In May the Synod of the United Secession Church petitioned the House of Commons against the endowment. The petitioners, claiming to 'abjure all hostile feeling towards the Roman Catholics of Ireland', opposed the grant on the grounds that they regarded 'every system of ascendancy on the part of religious communities, every measure which contemplates the taxation of one portion of the nation for the support of the religious institutions of another as unscriptural, impolitic, and unjust'. Alongside the retraction of the Maynooth bill, the petition also expressed a desire for the state to disendow the Church of Ireland and withdraw future instalments of the *regium donum*, the annual grant afforded to Irish Presbyterians. However, despite this seemingly ultra-voluntary language, the petition notably considered the 'nature' of the system in question which its signatories, as Protestants, claimed to oppose conscientiously.[92]

Therefore, opposition to Maynooth, anti-Catholicism and disestablishment were intertwined in voluntary rhetoric. While Scotland's voluntaries maintained their opposition to 'Protestant ascendancy', or 'mere political religion', they remained as equally opposed to Roman Catholic ascendancy.[93] Though never reaching the hostility associated with Free Church anti-Catholicism, Scotland's voluntaries often shared similar concerns regarding the perceived progress and threat of popery, at home

---

88. *Reasons for declining to vote in favour of Mr Macaulay*, 6–7.
89. *Dundee, Perth, and Cupar Advertiser*, 29 June 1852.
90. Wolffe, *Protestant Crusade*, 209.
91. *UPM*, vi (October 1852), 473.
92. *Appendix to the reports of the select committee of the House of Commons on public petitions* (1845), 307.
93. *Caledonian Mercury*, 11 December 1851.

and abroad.[94] However, this simple brand of anti-popery was often placed firmly within the context of the voluntary movement. For instance, the United Secession leader John Brown believed that the disendowment of all religion was 'the only safeguard against the endowment of Popery'.[95] The voluntary merchant and politician Duncan McLaren also defended his support for the removal of church establishments, 'not because I hold Popery to be innocent . . . but because I hold, that if these were taken out of the way, she would be tenfold more assailable'.[96]

McLaren's argument was echoed by the Glasgow United Presbyterian minister William Lindsay. Like the Free Church zealots Begg and Wylie, Lindsay agreed that there were 'special reasons' for ending the 'sin and folly' of endowing Catholicism and its threat to religious liberty. However, he maintained that 'all our efforts to effect the disendowment of Popery in this country will prove altogether unavailing, so long as Protestant churches and schools are sustained by the funds of the state'. Lindsay was convinced that 'if the Protestant world could tear itself free from all dependence for support upon national funds, then at once we could compel Popery to stand among us upon her own legs', and, 'in a straight up fight between the two systems, I could have no doubt that Protestants . . . would speedily, with the blessing of Heaven, achieve a complete victory'.[97] For United Presbyterians such as Lindsay and McLaren, the removal of funds for English dissenters and the *regium donum* to Irish Presbyterians was as crucial to the Protestant defeat of popery in Britain as the repeal of the Maynooth Act.[98] This belief that the voluntary principle provided an effective barrier to the encroachments of Rome, and the clearest route to ultimate 'victory', sharply contrasts with the ultra-Protestant view that voluntaryism instead offered an open door to popery, a fear espoused by Free Churchmen such as Begg. With Protestantism seemingly 'at stake' in Britain in 1845, voluntaryism could position itself as its most prominent defender.[99]

For some ultra-voluntaries, such as John Ritchie, the rejection of Maynooth and the advocacy of disestablishment were indivisible. Ritchie, a United Secession minister at Ayr, criticised the Free Church's inconsistent approach to the Maynooth grant and endowments in general. He argued that it was 'the height of absurdity for him who holds the Establishment principle to object to the endowment of any Establishment'. The Free Church, Ritchie claimed, could not oppose the endowment of Maynooth 'because she says she ought to be endowed'. In other words, any church which receives or wishes to receive state funds could not conscientiously

---

94. *Protestant Magazine*, xvi (April 1854), 111.
95. Cairns, *Memoir of John Brown*, 171.
96. Duncan McLaren, *History of the resistance to the Annuity Tax, and of the origin and application of seat rents for payment of ministers' stipends* (Edinburgh, 1836), vii.
97. *UPM*, iv (September 1860), 418.
98. *Caledonian Mercury*, 11 December 1851.
99. *Spectator*, 12 April 1845.

object to grants afforded to any other church, regardless of denomination. According to Ritchie, only voluntaries, 'who themselves have it not, and would not take it, and say themselves ought not to get it', could 'with decency protest against the Maynooth grant'. Despite his fierce criticism of the Free Church, Ritchie nevertheless saw the potential for the Maynooth controversy to bring Scotland's dissenters together in the common cause of voluntaryism. He claimed that Peel's decision to increase the endowment to Maynooth would possibly give the Free Church 'the scunner at Establishments, for all time coming', and called for Candlish to 'redeem his pledge, by instituting a crusade against all Parliament-religion and Parliament-churches'.[100]

Ritchie's prediction that Scotland's dissenters could 'preach from the same text' against Maynooth became an increasing reality after 1845. While never representing a full convergence of principle, the politicisation of the anti-Maynooth campaign in this period saw significant sections of Scotland's non-established churches adopt a much more ambiguous ideological stance. At a public meeting in the Waterloo Rooms, Edinburgh, on 8 April 1845, supporting a resolution brought forward by Begg against the endowment, Candlish admitted 'that sooner than see Popery endowed he would wish there were no endowments whatever'.[101] Candlish's pragmatic recalibration of Free Church principle to suit the anti-Maynooth campaign was repeated throughout the establishmentarian dissenting churches. The Reformed Presbyterian minister William Goold conceded that, while he was 'no voluntary', the theory that state endowment would provide 'error' with a 'power and a perpetuity which it would not otherwise enjoy' was 'one of the strong points of their case'.[102] It appeared that the spectre of Maynooth and the state endowment of popery was enough to force even the most establishmentarian of Scotland's dissenting Presbyterians to declare, albeit pragmatically, 'let justice be done to voluntaryism'.

A Loose Coalition: The Politicisation of the Alliance and the By-elections of 1845 and 1846

The potential for a loose alliance between Scotland's dissenters on the grounds of an ideologically ambiguous anti-Catholicism dominated both the anti-Maynooth agitation and institutional anti-popery in Scotland in the decade after 1845. While the relationship between Scottish dissent and Liberal politics will be explored more fully in the next chapter, this section will assess the beginnings of the dissenting coalition that would later dominate liberalism and Scottish electoral politics for more than a decade. The prospect of a political alliance between Scotland's dissenting

---

100. John Ritchie, *True-Citizen-Christianity* (Edinburgh, 1845), 4–5, 17.
101. Wilson, *Memorials of Robert Smith Candlish*, 354; *Scotsman*, 12 April 1845.
102. Goold, *The Maynooth Endowment*, 6.

churches first came to the fore at the Greenock by-election in April 1845. Following the withdrawal of the Chartist candidate, the election pitted the Free Church lawyer Alexander Dunlop against Walter Baine, a merchant and member of the Church of Scotland.[103] Dunlop, born in Greenock and originally a Conservative but soon siding with the Whigs, framed the Claim of Right at the Disruption and was viewed as a 'trusted advisor of Chalmers and his associates'. Though known as a prominent anti-voluntary during the Ten Years' Conflict, after 1843 Dunlop came to represent the new dissenting character of the Free Church, and would later help produce George Sinclair's 1857 resolutions for union between the Free and United Presbyterian churches. Baine, on the other hand, had remained a member of the Established Church after 1843, though prior to the Disruption he was a staunch opponent of the Patronage Act and petitioned parliament for its abolition.[104] Regardless of these denominational differences, the Maynooth question was the sole political dividing line between two candidates otherwise indistinguishable as Whigs and supporters of free trade.[105] While Baine supported Peel's bill, Dunlop was tasked with 'uniting together in one common cause Christians of various denominations against the common enemy' of Maynooth. This brand of single-issue politics produced by the controversy paved the way for a clear 'dissenting' opposition to the grant. Despite narrowly failing to secure the seat by six votes, the Free Churchman was lauded by his dissenting colleagues 'for the great service he has rendered to the Protestant cause'.[106] Following his defeat, Thomas Guthrie described Dunlop, though in 'one sense, the rejected candidate for Greenock', as 'one who has gained a glorious and triumphant victory' in terms of the broader fight against the Maynooth endowment.[107]

A banquet held in Edinburgh in honour of Dunlop's 'victory', with over 500 in attendance, emphasised the pan-dissenting nature of the anti-Maynooth campaign in Scotland.[108] Citing Dunlop's electoral performance as evidence of the potential political power of Scottish dissent, the United Secession minister George Johnston proposed 'union and co-operation among all evangelical Christians'. Support for a dissenting alliance against Maynooth was aided by a convergence between Scotland's non-established churches on matters of principle. Throughout Dunlop's campaign, the lines that distinguished the respective Free Church and voluntary opposition to Maynooth had become steadily blurred. Prior to the election, Dunlop redefined the Free Church's traditional doctrine on the endowment of truth and error to suit the impending political and ecclesiastical

---

103. *Spectator*, 19 April 1845.
104. *Appendix to the reports of the select committee of the House of Commons on public petitions* (1843), 551.
105. *Spectator*, 19 April 1845.
106. *Christian Reformer*, i (June 1845), 437.
107. Thelwall, *Anti-Maynooth Conference of 1845*, 191.
108. *Inverness Courier*, 7 May 1845.

situation. He claimed that 'if it be the case that Government cannot endow truth without at the same time endowing error, then he would say, by all means endow none'. At the Edinburgh celebration he went further, vowing to 'sacrifice the principle which he held' on church establishments rather than submit to the governmental support of 'error'.[109] Dunlop argued that opposition to the Maynooth grant and support for general disestablishment were intertwined, and provided 'the basis upon which all classes of evangelical dissenters could consistently unite' against the bill.[110] The rising influence of this disendowment rhetoric, if based solely on Maynooth and a pragmatic desire for voluntary votes, also began to be felt within the hierarchy of the Free Church. On the same evening, William Cunningham, 'though favourable to endowing his own religion', stated his desire for 'sweeping away the Established Church of Ireland altogether'.[111] While Cunningham fixed this quasi-voluntary gaze on Ireland, Guthrie, in a speech at the anti-Maynooth conference soon after the Greenock election, claimed to 'believe that every Free Churchman in Scotland, rather than see Popery endowed, would root up every Establishment'.[112] To the *United Secession Magazine*, Guthrie's speech was striking evidence of the Free Kirk's drift towards the voluntary principle. The writer argued that 'it bore closer on voluntaryism than would have been acceptable had it fallen from the lips of an ordinary Nonconformist'.[113] For their voluntary counterparts, the Maynooth controversy was instrumental in steering the Free Church, which by 1845 appeared 'midway' between the voluntary and establishment principles, at least partially towards the doctrine of full disendowment.

The anti-Maynooth campaign was also instrumental in forging a new dissenting framework from the mid-1840s. Illustrated by the Free Kirk's increasingly ambiguous ideological stance on Maynooth, from 1845 Scotland's non-established churchmen could hold their respective principles without professing a complete version of either. Therefore, an identity emerged from the Maynooth debate that was neither fully voluntary nor establishmentarian, but dissenting. This dissenting identity fluctuated depending upon the church – as evidenced by the United Presbyterians' 'dissenting' union of 1847 – but was pivotal in moulding and consolidating the pragmatic political alliance that emerged to combat Maynooth after 1846. Following the perceived 'success' of the Greenock by-election, the politicisation of this ideologically ambiguous alliance gathered pace. In a pastoral address of the General Assembly, the Free Church moderator Patrick Macfarlan echoed the quasi-voluntary rhetoric espoused by Dunlop and Guthrie. Criticising the Peel government's perceived view that

109. *Christian Reformer*, i (June 1845), 437; *Greenock Advertiser*, 15 April 1845.
110. *Inverness Courier*, 7 May 1845.
111. *Christian Reformer*, i (June 1845), 438.
112. Thelwall, *Anti-Maynooth Conference of 1845*, 194.
113. *USM*, ii (July 1845), 359–60.

'truth and error may be equally endowed' as a 'most dangerous infidelity', Macfarlan called upon Britain's political elite, 'if they profess their inability to discern light from darkness, to withdraw from all interference on either side'. 'Rather than endow popery,' he declared, 'let all endowments together cease.' Nevertheless, the Free Church moderator believed that the ultra-voluntary position of 'merely denouncing the establishment principle' was 'not an adequate discharge of present duty, in reference to Protestant union and Popish error'. Macfarlan instead urged forbearance on what he regarded as the irrelevant issue of voluntaryism, fearing that such a debate within Scotland's anti-Maynooth campaign would 'diminish the special and peculiar anxiety' towards the progress of Catholicism, and the subsequent duty of 'evangelical Protestants everywhere uniting in earnest co-operation against it'. To Free Churchmen such as Macfarlan, Maynooth, though an indictment of the government's current policy on establishments, transcended the broader debate over the voluntary principle. Scotland's non-established Presbyterians were to unite, not on a shared voluntaryism or liberalism, but in simple opposition to the Maynooth endowment. Explicitly politicising this opposition, Macfarlan reminded the Free Church electors of 'the duty of sending those only to the legislature who, whatever may be their secular politics and their opinions about establishments, are prepared, for conscience sake, to resist the encroachments of Popery'.[114]

Following its tentative but largely successful first outing at Greenock, the politicisation of the anti-Maynooth alliance, based on Macfarlan's pragmatic policy of forbearance, became fully realised after April 1845. Addressing a meeting of Scottish Presbyterian dissenters opposed to the bill, Candlish declared support for a 'cordial union' between Scotland's non-established churches in order to overturn what he regarded as offensive legislation, while relegating the issue of church–state relations from the debate. He claimed that it was the 'urgent duty of all, whether voluntaries or advocates of church establishments', to 'energetically' oppose the endowment.[115] Writing in the *Witness*, Hugh Miller also called for a 'decided movement on the part of Christians of various denominations' to 'send men of avowed Christian principle to parliament'.[116] The support within the Free Church for some kind of electoral pact among Scotland's dissenters was echoed by the voluntary-led Scottish Board of Dissenters. This body was the successor to the Central Board, the political wing of Scottish dissent and thorn in the side of the Free Kirk during the previous decade's Voluntary Controversy. However, by April 1846 the Scottish Board of Dissenters had notably altered its hitherto ultra-voluntary stance. In a public address, the board noted the necessity for 'amicable co-agency' in

114. Free Church of Scotland, *Pastoral Address of the General Assembly* (Edinburgh, 1845), 5–6.
115. *Scotsman*, 12 April 1845.
116. *Witness*, 11 July 1846.

the 'parliamentary conflict' over Maynooth, and advised that 'where the same measures are approved of, there may be a mutual forbearance as to abstract opinion'. The political expediency and pragmatism of the anti-Maynooth campaign was strikingly evident in the board's realisation that 'unless Dissenters can vote for Free Churchmen and Free Churchmen for Dissenters, union is impossible and defeat certain'.[117]

Despite this broad support for forbearance, the United Secession Church's opposition to Maynooth nevertheless maintained a strong voluntary emphasis. The board urged Scotland's dissenting electors to 'say to every parliamentary candidate' that 'you shall not have our support unless your mind is made up to vote against any proposal to endow the Roman Catholic priesthood, and all proposals for new grants to the ministers of any other denomination'.[118] In some cases, the hostile remnants of the Voluntary Controversy could also not be fully forgotten. At the Edinburgh by-election of 1846, both the voluntary merchant Duncan McLaren and the Free Churchman and former Provost James Forrest did not stand as candidates, due to fears that doing so would reignite the animosities of the previous decade and threaten the alliance.[119] McLaren, like Forrest on the non-intrusionist side, was a prominent and contentious agitator during the Ten Years' Conflict. However, despite his reputation to Free Churchmen as the arch-voluntary, a role that would retain its significance as the political alliance progressed, following the Disruption McLaren recognised the necessity for a broad coalition of non-established Presbyterians in opposition to Maynooth. He alluded to the potential political power of this alliance in a May 1844 speech, claiming that 'Whigs, Tories, or Radicals' would unite in opposition to the impending bill.[120] While the policy of forbearance was instrumental in uniting Free Churchmen and voluntaries, it also succeeded in creating a broad coalition of numerous political stripes.

The loose political character of the dissenting opposition to Maynooth was highlighted by the Free and voluntary churches' disapproval of the Liberals' preferred candidate at the August 1845 by-election in Kirkcudbrightshire. The proposed candidacy of a supporter of the grant, M. C. Maxwell, a Roman Catholic landlord and Whig, forced Scotland's dissenters to throw their weight behind the Tory candidate Colonel McDouall.[121] In the face of such religiously motivated antagonism, described by the *Scotsman* as an 'unjust and bigoted' attempt to repeal the Emancipation Act, Maxwell withdrew his candidacy.[122] His replacement, the moderate Whig and Presbyterian Thomas Maitland, won the seat, though with a significantly

117. *Address by the Scottish Board of Dissenters* (Edinburgh, 1846), 1–7.
118. *USM*, iii (April 1846), 191.
119. *Scotsman*, 11 July 1846.
120. Duncan McLaren, *Substance of a speech delivered at the meeting of the Edinburgh Anti-Corn Law Association, on the 9 May 1844* (Edinburgh, 1844), 13.
121. *Economist*, 2 August 1845.
122. *Scotsman*, 13 August 1845.

reduced majority.¹²³ This episode underlined Scottish dissent's commitment to a political platform based solely in opposition to the Maynooth grant, irrespective of party allegiance. Upon learning of Maxwell's controversial candidature, one Presbyterian advised his co-religionists to 'value religious and Protestant truth, above the mere questions of Whig or Tory interests'. The author urged 'every evangelical dissenter' to 'be in no haste to promise his vote to any party'.¹²⁴ This policy was indicative of the early political opposition to the grant within Scottish dissent, and was criticised as 'narrow-minded bigotry' by the victorious Maitland.¹²⁵ In the immediate aftermath of Peel's bill, broader political concerns and principles were a secondary concern, if they mattered at all, to the great fight against the governmental indulgence of popery. In the eyes of Scotland's dissenters, the ideal parliamentary candidate was 'of the stamp of the good old Scotsman, who, when asked whether he were Whig or Tory, replied – "Sir, I am a Presbyterian"'.¹²⁶

Unsurprisingly, the lack of political principle and the narrow nature of their aims resulted in fierce criticism of the dissenting alliance. Prior to the Edinburgh by-election of July 1846, a committee was established to support the candidacy of Sir Culling Smith, the leader of the Evangelical Alliance, against the newly appointed Paymaster General, Thomas Macaulay. Chaired by Forrest and consisting of over sixty prominent Free Churchmen and voluntaries, the committee marked the first full and direct employment of the political alliance that had slowly emerged during the previous year's by-elections. In accepting the proposal to stand, Smith acknowledged that his political views, centred on liberalism and support for free trade, were of little immediate consequence compared to 'the great subject now forcing itself before the country', the maintenance of Britain's 'Protestant testimony'.¹²⁷ The campaign's politically diverse range of supporters and narrow agenda alarmed the Whig commentator Henry Cockburn, who observed that the typical evangelical elector, when asked of his preferred candidate's views on universal suffrage, would reply, 'These are matters I do not think it worthwhile asking about. I know that he hates every Catholic.' Cockburn described the committee behind Smith as consisting of 'Established Churchmen and wild voluntaries, intense Tories and declamatory Radicals, who agreed in nothing except in holding their peculiar religion as the scriptural and therefore the only safe criterion of fitness for public duty'.¹²⁸ Though in this instance Macaulay comfortably

123. *Dundee Courier*, 30 July 1845; *Spectator*, 23 August 1845; *MacPhail's Edinburgh Ecclesiastical Journal, and Literary Review*, i (February 1846), 79.
124. *Dumfries and Galloway Standard*, 30 July 1845.
125. *Preston Chronicle*, 23 August 1845; *Scotsman*, 27 August 1845.
126. *Dumfries and Galloway Standard*, 30 July 1845.
127. *Caledonian Mercury*, 13 July 1846.
128. Henry Cockburn, *Journal of Henry Cockburn, being a continuation of the memorials of his time, 1831–1854* (2 volumes, Edinburgh, 1874), ii, 160–1.

defeated Smith by 1,735 votes to 832, the political appeal of a fully functioning alliance against Maynooth led by Scotland's Presbyterian dissenters would become the prominent feature of Scottish politics in the decade to come.[129] However, as the next chapter will illustrate, in the build-up to the 1847 general election, the broad pan-political origins of the anti-Maynooth alliance yielded to a more focused electoral approach based on the organisation of the Liberal party. By contrast, institutional anti-popery maintained its appeal to all strands of Scottish Presbyterianism, particularly after the 'papal aggression' of 1850. Nevertheless, these societies, despite their catholic ethos, were driven as much by denominational allegiance and principle as their apparent common Protestantism.

Institutional Anti-popery: Rhetoric and Reality

The crisis within British Protestantism that emerged after the 1850 restoration of the Roman Catholic hierarchy marked the culmination of the 'anti-papal fervour' that dominated this period. The national response to the ultramontane policies of the papacy also reinvigorated hopes for united action among Britain's Protestants of all denominations.[130] At the fifth annual conference of the Evangelical Alliance, the first meeting of the pan-denominational group following the 'aggression', resolutions were passed to challenge the 'revived zeal of the Romish priesthood'.[131] However, amendments calling for specific action were defeated, while the vague nature of the resolutions passed highlighted the generality and lack of commitment to anti-popery within the Evangelical Alliance.[132] This hostile religious climate and desire for unity, and the Alliance's failure to satisfy these hopes, resulted in the creation of numerous 'militant' evangelical Protestant organisations.[133] In the five years after the 'papal aggression', two major and seven minor Protestant societies were formally constituted in Britain. The two most influential, active and zealous were the Protestant Alliance, largely centred on English evangelical anti-Catholicism, and the Edinburgh-based Scottish Reformation Society. Both of these societies were at least nominally interdenominational, and acted as political pressure groups (focused almost exclusively on the Maynooth debate) and commentators on the Catholic persecution of Protestants in mainland Europe. However, their main mutual object was the defence of British Protestantism.[134]

Founded by the 7th Earl of Shaftesbury and John MacGregor (not to be confused with the Glasgow MP of the same name) in late 1851, the

---

129. *Fife Herald*, 23 July 1846.
130. Wolffe, *Protestant Crusade*, 249.
131. *Evangelical Christendom: its state and prospects*, v (November 1851), 433.
132. Wolffe, *Protestant Crusade*, 248.
133. *Bulwark; or, Reformation Journal*, i (July 1851), 2; Wolffe, *Protestant Crusade*, 249.
134. Wolffe, *Protestant Crusade*, 318–19; Machin, *Politics and the Churches in Great Britain*, 55.

Protestant Alliance soon established over forty provincial societies throughout England.[135] MacGregor shared his Scottish colleagues' suspicion of Rome. In an 1852 pamphlet, he envisaged a dystopian future in which Britain was controlled by Rome. MacGregor's nightmarish vision of 1900 included a system of over a thousand district courts of inquisition, the replacement of the English language with Anglo-Latin, and the suppression of the satirical magazine *Punch*.[136] Despite the harsh critique of popery offered by his published works, the relatively conciliatory and subtle character of MacGregor, combined with the prestige associated with Shaftesbury and the society's broad principles, ensured support for the Protestant Alliance from a wide body of notable evangelical churchmen.[137] While the restoration of the Catholic hierarchy only practically affected England, the vociferous Scottish reaction to the measure spawned a number of arguably more militant anti-popery groups than in England itself.

The Alliance's counterpart north of the Tweed, the Scottish Reformation Society was founded by James Begg and supported by fellow Free Churchmen Robert Candlish and James Wylie. The SRS was established on 5 December 1850 as a direct and immediate response to what Begg viewed as the papacy's 'desperate, and to some extent successful, attempt to regain its former supremacy in Britain'.[138] The general objects of the society were to 'resist the aggressions of Popery, to watch over the designs and movements of its promoters and abettors, and to diffuse sound and scriptural information on the distinctive tenets of Protestantism and Popery'.[139] Though never quite constituting a mass movement, the society achieved considerable visibility in a significant number of Scottish towns, except Glasgow, which had its own anti-Catholic organisation, the Glasgow Protestant Laymen's Association. This success was largely due to the seemingly ceaseless activity of its membership. Between November 1853 and November 1854, within the thirty-five branches which supplied details (sixty-four were claimed to be in existence), 249 committee meetings and 211 lectures took place, with nine branches holding committee meetings at least once a month. Branches in Edinburgh, Hamilton and Leith were particularly active, with Leith alone organising twenty-six lectures in that year.[140] The society's organ, the *Bulwark*, edited by Begg and still in existence today, also became the bestselling Protestant periodical in nineteenth-century Scotland. In the journal's first year of publication it claimed to have circulated 30,000 copies, and was published simultaneously in Edinburgh, London and Dublin.[141] Meetings were organised in Edinburgh by the SRS throughout

---

135. Wolffe, *Protestant Crusade*, 158–9.
136. J[ohn] M[acGregor], *Popery in A.D. 1900* (London, 1851).
137. Wolffe, *Protestant Crusade*, 251.
138. Begg, *Handbook of Popery*, 9.
139. *Caledonian Mercury*, 30 December 1850.
140. Wolffe, *Protestant* Crusade, 160–1.
141. Wallis, 'Anti-Maynooth Campaign', 536; Gallagher, *The Uneasy Peace*, 20.

1851 in protest at the 'papal aggression', and it was claimed they had been attended by 'almost every eminent individual of the Protestant persuasion in the Scottish capital'.[142] By the end of the society's first year, 43,700 members in Edinburgh had signed a petition against the aggression (a fifth of the city's population), while over 130,000 signatures had been added to 540 petitions nationwide.[143]

Beyond the immediate fallout of the 'papal aggression', the SRS also reinvigorated opposition to the Maynooth Act by appealing to MPs to vote against the endowment in parliament, while also calling on electors to vote only for candidates openly opposed to the grant.[144] This surge in activity coincided with popular nationwide engagement. In 1852 approximately 325,000 signatures were added to 951 public petitions against the Maynooth grant across Britain, the largest number since the first year of the agitation in 1845.[145] However, this would prove the high-water mark for the anti-Maynooth campaign. Three years later, though the number of petitions had doubled, almost 8,000 fewer signatures were collected, a number that would fluctuate greatly over the next decade before petering out by the mid-1860s.[146] The apparent decline in enthusiasm for anti-Catholicism from the mid-1850s was noted by a disappointed Begg in the seventh volume of the *Bulwark* in 1858, which nevertheless maintained both its crusading zeal and position as Victorian Britain's most influential Protestant periodical.[147] In any case, the success of the SRS and the *Bulwark*, the general fervour of Scottish anti-Catholicism and its importance within the wider British framework facilitated a 'partial shift of gravity' of the movement in the 1850s from London to Edinburgh.[148]

Like the Protestant Alliance, the SRS was founded amid a national desire for united Protestant action. At its inaugural meeting, the society claimed to have the support of 'all classes of the Protestant community'.[149] The first acting committee of the society included members from all of Scotland's major Presbyterian churches, while also featuring Episcopalian, Methodist, Independent and Congregationalist representatives.[150] The committees of both the Scottish Reformation Society and the Glasgow Protestant Laymen's Association were claimed by the *Bulwark* to 'indicate the powerful combina-

---

142. *Belfast Newsletter*, 2 April 1851.
143. *Caledonian Mercury*, 11 December 1851. Despite the apparent success of the SRS, the organisation was £91 in debt following its first year of operation.
144. *Bulwark, or Reformation Journal*, i (January 1852), 162; *Caledonian Mercury*, 11 December 1851; *Protestant Magazine*, xvi (April 1854), 113.
145. *Hansard's Parliamentary Debates*, 3rd series, vol. cxii (8 June 1852), 226–7.
146. Wallis, 'Anti-Maynooth Campaign', 547.
147. *Bulwark, or Reformation Journal*, vii (July 1858), 1–2.
148. Wolffe, *Protestant Crusade*, 160–1; Machin, *Politics and the Churches in Great Britain*, 255.
149. *Caledonian Mercury*, 30 December 1850; Wylie, *Tercentenary of the Scottish Reformation*, viii.
150. *Oliver and Boyd's New Edinburgh Almanac and National Repository for the year 1851* (Edinburgh, 1851), 551.

tion which Popery must contend with in Scotland'.[151] Co-operation among Scottish Protestants was also a major theme among supporters of the SRS in the months following its creation. An editorial for the *Bulwark* in October 1851 argued that 'the organisation of British Protestantism is absolutely necessary', not only because 'we are dealing with an enemy most thoroughly united and disciplined over the three kingdoms', but also 'because we all have one object, and because without union and co-operation we can neither discharge our duty to ourselves nor to the Papists around us'.[152] The *Bulwark*'s enthusiasm for 'facts' and statistical inquiry, a popular phenomenon of Victorian periodicals, was used to great effect to highlight the apparent growth and unity of the Catholic threat, and to frighten Protestants into their own unified response.[153] Promoting the cause of the SRS at the 1852 Free Church General Assembly, Begg described the battle 'against the enemy of our common Protestantism'. This battle, he believed, would return Protestantism to the 'very ground of Reformation, anterior to all the sects into which we are now divided'. He stressed to his fellow Free Churchmen the need for unity against Catholicism and lamented the existing divisions within Protestantism.[154] To the supporters of the SRS, united action from all 'earnest' Protestants across the United Kingdom was crucial to the success of their anti-papal crusade, and the expansion of the Scottish Reformation Society was viewed as pivotal to this endeavour.[155]

While the SRS emphasised its standing as a body representing all of Scottish Protestants, the potential for co-operation within the anti-popery movement was most evident between Scotland's Presbyterian dissenting churches. In May 1851, Begg approached the synods of the United Presbyterian and Reformed Presbyterian churches, as well as the Free Kirk's General Assembly, in an attempt to raise funds for the creation of a Protestant Institute, which would act as an educational wing of the SRS and provide the 'head-quarters of a mission for Roman Catholics'.[156] This emphasis on united Protestant effort offered even the most divisive of Scotland's dissenters such as Begg a common platform on which to unite against the perceived threat posed by Rome. A staunch anti-voluntary, Begg nevertheless admitted to the United Presbyterian Synod at Queen Street, Edinburgh, that it gave him 'pleasure to meet them on a battle-ground where they could all heartily unite together in opposing their old enemy – Popery'. Begg argued that the £6,000 required to establish the Protestant

151. *Bulwark, or Reformation Journal*, i (December 1851), 150.
152. *Bulwark, or Reformation Journal*, i (October 1851), 77.
153. Miriam Elizabeth Burstein, '"In Ten Years There Is an Increase of 450 Priests of Antichrist": Quantification, Anti-Catholicism, and the Bulwark', *Journal of British Studies*, lvi (2017), 580–604.
154. Smith, *Memoirs of James Begg*, ii, 187, 210, 213.
155. *Protestant Magazine*, xvi (April 1854), 111–12.
156. *Appeal in reference to the extension of the Edinburgh Irish Mission and Protestant Institute, addressed to the friends of Protestantism* (Edinburgh, 1851).

Institute could be easily raised if the United Presbyterian Church, the Free Church and Scotland's other dissenting bodies 'would agree to co-operate in the matter'.[157] While the Free Churchman received a nominally positive response from the three largest dissenting churches, it would be another nine years before the Institute was established.[158] The failure of Begg to immediately raise the funds necessary to complete such a project, despite the appearance of support from his fellow Presbyterians, was indicative of John Wolffe's observation that Protestant solidarity in this period was 'more apparent than real'.[159]

According to Karly Kehoe, Begg's enthusiasm regarding his plans for the Protestant Institute after 1851 highlighted not only the conversionist priorities of the Free Kirk, but also deeper insecurities over the ability of Scotland's 'weak and divided' Presbyterians to tackle the threat of Rome.[160] This insecurity was heightened by the lack of a unified Protestant voice throughout Britain. Despite their pretensions towards unity, the creation of multitudes of anti-Catholic societies after 1850 only served to stifle and undermine calls for unified action by promoting competition between the new Protestant groups and pre-existing organisations. Common ground was also noticeably lacking within most Protestant societies. For instance, the failure of the British Reformation Society to establish a committee consisting equally of dissenters and churchmen was indicative of the lack of unity between England's Protestant clergy.[161]

This problem would be repeated in the SRS. While it espoused Protestant unity, the SRS in practical terms operated as an anti-Catholic vehicle for Scottish Presbyterian dissent, and in particular the Free Church and its leading no-popery activists such as Begg and Wylie. While eleven different denominations were represented, of the twenty-two SRS committee members in 1851 nine were Free Churchmen, three were United Presbyterians, and the Reformed Presbyterians and Original Seceders had one member each. Two Free Churchmen, John Gibson and George Lyon, acted as treasurer and secretary respectively.[162] This pattern also appeared on the editorial board of the *Bulwark*; of the eight members of the original committee, half were from the Free and United Presbyterian churches.[163] As Wolffe points out, the dissenting, and Free Kirk, dominance of the Scottish anti-Catholic movement was greater than even the numbers suggest. The

157. *Elgin Courier*, 23 May 1851.
158. *Bulwark, or Reformation Journal*, i (July 1851), 9; Wylie, *Tercentenary of the Scottish Reformation*, xvi.
159. Wolffe, *Protestant Crusade*, 249.
160. Kehoe, *Creating a Scottish Church*, 59.
161. Wolffe, *Protestant Crusade*, 247–8, 253.
162. *Oliver and Boyd's New Edinburgh Almanac*, 551. The Original Seceder on the committee was Thomas McCrie, who would join the Free Kirk after the union between the two churches the following year.
163. *The Bulwark, or Reformation Journal*, i (October 1851), 77.

SRS had close links with the Free Church's General Committee on Popery, and established churchmen were absent from the original meeting that inaugurated the society. The two Church of Scotland ministers on the society's committee in 1851 lacked the clout of Free Church heavyweights such as Robert Candlish and William Cunningham, while William Stevenson, the sole representative of the Auld Kirk on the *Bulwark*'s editorial board, was 'clearly no match' for the domineering personality of Begg.[164] Even members who did not belong to the Free Church such as William Goold, the Reformed Presbyterian minister who would join the Free Kirk at the 1876 union, were in broad agreement with its principles.

The dissenting character and membership of the SRS ensured that support from the Church of Scotland was lukewarm at best, a general ambivalence that prevented the organisation from becoming a truly mass movement. The establishment's answer to Begg, the lawyer and philanthropist John Hope, only joined the committee of the SRS in 1852, though he did assist in the organisation of the society's set-piece conferences in February and March 1854.[165] His caution was largely due to his concerns over its members' attitudes towards establishments, and his resentment at the Free Kirk's usurpation of the anti-Catholic movement in Scotland. Hope had initially sought the support of Free Churchmen for the intended creation of an anti-popery society in Edinburgh in 1845, but proved unsuccessful due to the Free Kirk's unwillingness to engage in an organisation associated with the establishment so soon after the Disruption.[166] He thought that the likes of Begg and Wylie were 'very active and talked much, yet they did not come down with the money, proposing to make everything pay for itself, and to publish tracts at 2d each – a price beyond the working class'. Instead, Hope favoured the distribution of cheap or free anti-papal literature. To Hope, the energies of the SRS were 'mostly spent in talking, and but little work of a practical kind was done'.[167] Like his church, Hope remained in the 'independent' tradition of anti-popery, preferring to work and publish either alone or through his own denomination. Though he played a limited role in the beginnings of the SRS, he was integral to the Church of Scotland's Anti-Popery Committee set up in 1851, and founded and acted as secretary of the Scottish Protestant Society, the establishment's riposte to the SRS founded in 1854. Despite disagreements over the organisational structure and hierarchy within anti-popery, Hope's views echoed those of his dissenting counterparts and combined the philanthropy, social and political reform, and patriotic no-popery associated with Begg.

Though Hope acted as a standard-bearer of anti-popery within the

---

164. Wolffe, *Protestant Crusade*, 249–50; *Caledonian Mercury*, 30 December 1850.
165. David Jamie, *John Hope, philanthropist and reformer* (Edinburgh, 1907), 131; *Protestant Magazine*, xvi (April 1854), 111–12.
166. Wolffe, *Protestant Crusade*, 138.
167. Jamie, *John Hope*, 129, 333.

establishment, he attracted little support from his own denomination. By 1852, a number of churches withdrew their circulation of Hope's monthly tract, *The Banner of Truth,* and seven years later the Church of Scotland General Assembly's committee on Popery merged with the Home Missions Board.[168] This move highlighted the realisation within the Established Kirk by the late 1850s that the fight against popery now formed only part of the broader struggle against the erosion of the church and Scottish Presbyterianism. The general apathy towards anti-Catholicism within the Church of Scotland, with the notable exceptions of Hope and the anti-Maynooth campaigner Norman MacLeod, was indicative of the peripheral role the establishment played in the Scottish anti-Catholic movement. While the Free Church dominated the meetings, committees and pamphlet literature of the SRS, Established Church members showed more interest in the English anti-Catholic movement, participating in the Protestant conferences of the 1850s and fostering close links with the British Reformation Society.[169] In this respect, the overt influence of Scottish dissent, and in particular the Free Church, prevented Scottish anti-popery from becoming a broad, non-sectarian movement encompassing all of Scotland's 'earnest' Protestants.

While Presbyterian institutional anti-popery in Scotland was mostly divided along dissenting and establishment lines, distinctions between the Free and United Presbyterian churches, though initially blurred during the first anti-Maynooth agitation, plagued the movement after 1850. At the annual public meeting of the SRS in December 1851, a disagreement between the society's Free Church treasurer John Gibson and Duncan McLaren, the voluntary politician and chair of the meeting, emphasised the gulf in principle that existed on the common ground of the SRS. Though he acknowledged some reticence from his fellow United Presbyterians towards the group, the newly elected Lord Provost of Edinburgh McLaren argued that as a voluntary 'he saw no inconsistency whatever' in participating in a meeting of the Scottish Reformation Society, 'for the Church Establishment question was not raised'. According to McLaren, the society instead focused on condemning all grants to Roman Catholics and standing up for the Protestant faith in the struggle against Catholic 'error', issues which dissenters 'of all opinions regarding such establishments might cordially co-operate together without sacrifice either of consistency or principle'. However, McLaren also argued that the anti-Maynooth agitation would be strengthened by further opposition to all other religious grants, and that the disestablishment of the Church of Ireland would cause Protestantism to prosper. He predicted that 'when the missionaries would have nothing in their hands but the Bible to meet the Irish peasantry,

---

168. Jamie, *John Hope,* 130; Bruce, *No Pope of Rome,* 38–9.
169. E. W. McFarland, *Protestants First: Orangeism in Nineteenth Century Scotland* (Edinburgh, 1990), 132; Wolffe, *Protestant Crusade,* 310–11.

they would meet with a success which they did not now meet' due to the alienation felt by Ireland's Catholics towards a Protestantism 'so mixed up with questions affecting their civil rights and interests'. Amid a hostile atmosphere and fearing that the Lord Provost's remarks would potentially damage the principle and standing of the society, a worried Gibson stressed that while he supported the interdenominational character of the SRS, 'if the principles on which we are to oppose Popery, and grants to Popery, were those on which we oppose grants to other Protestant sects, I for one would never have had anything to do with it'. McLaren duly responded by suggesting that if Gibson's views were correct, 'consistent voluntaries ought not to give this Society their support'. William Cunningham attempted to defuse the situation by defending the broad platform on which anti-Catholics of all stripes could unite within the SRS, while admonishing the 'unnecessarily squeamish' attitudes to co-operation displayed by McLaren and Gibson. Nevertheless, their hostile encounter on perceived common ground provided a microcosm of Wolffe's assertion that the apparent unity of the anti-Catholic movement in Britain merely provided a reflection of pre-existing denominational differences and disputes.[170]

The Tercentenary of the Scottish Reformation, 1860

The discrepancy between the rhetoric of unity and the reality of denominational distinctions was perhaps most evident during the 1860 tercentenary celebrations of the Scottish Reformation. While the anti-papal fervour of the previous fifteen years had considerably subsided by 1860, the anniversary of Scotland's Reformation from Catholicism offered a 'fresh starting point for renewed and more vigorous efforts against Rome'.[171] It also provided the opportunity for Scottish Presbyterians to display a united front on the grounds of the Reformation. Andrew Holmes has noted three distinct phases of the year-long celebrations, in May, August and December. The annual denominational assemblies held in May, while adopting the traditional Protestant rhetoric of unity, inevitably displayed elements of 'denominational distinctiveness'. While the Church of Scotland emphasised its privileged position as the Established Kirk, the United Presbyterian Synod made particular reference to voluntary and anti-establishment principles. The Free Church General Assembly was also used as a 'vehicle' for the Scottish Reformation Society and the proposed Protestant Institute, though these meetings adopted a more international tone than the other two churches.[172] The international character of the Free Church General Assembly was repeated in the August celebrations organised by the SRS.

---

170. *Caledonian Mercury*, 11 December 1851; Wolffe, 'Change and Continuity', 72–3.
171. *Popery: its progress and position in Great Britain, and the relative duty of Protestants; being the ninth report of the Scottish Reformation Society* (Edinburgh, 1860), 7.
172. Holmes, 'The Scottish Reformations', 150.

These were held at the Free Kirk's New College in Edinburgh between 14 and 17 August to mark the date the Reformation became a national event in Scotland. A number of foreign guests attended, including the Canadian convert, preacher and evangelist Father Charles Chiniquy, praised by Begg as the 'John Knox of the present time' for reportedly converting over six thousand Catholics, Cohen Stuart of Utrecht, the Australian William Miller, and other delegates from Gibraltar, Nova Scotia and India.[173]

The international character of the proceedings was steeped in the broader rhetoric of Protestant unity. According to Begg, unlike the denominational and 'sectional' commemorations in May and December, the SRS's event, organised by a body 'ready-made and representing all classes of earnest Protestants', would be a 'national convention' during which 'men of all parties could meet'.[174] The apparent 'broad and unsectarian basis' on which the commemoration was organised was repeated throughout the event by speakers such as Thomas Guthrie.[175] Calling for the erection of a monument to John Knox in Edinburgh during the commemoration's opening sermon, Guthrie proclaimed that Knox was 'enshrined in the heart of every Scotchman – not Free Churchmen, not Established Churchmen, not Episcopalians, not Independents – but every man who loves human liberty, and loves religious freedom'.[176] According to the *Bulwark*'s report of the event, a 'cordial spirit of union seemed to pervade' the two thousand attendees.[177] Throughout the conference, individuals were allowed freedom of expression and were responsible only for their own opinions; a rule which, according to Begg, 'indicated most strikingly the real unity of true Protestants, although from different lands and of widely different denominations'.[178] The conference's recurring theme of Protestant unity and 'common duties and dangers', outlined by Begg and the United Presbyterian minister Alexander Leitch, was echoed by the Birmingham evangelical John Miller, who acknowledged that 'if there was any platform, any common ground' upon which Protestants could meet, 'it was surely upon the platform of combination against Rome'.[179]

Despite these constant appeals to Protestant unity, the August commemorations remained a distinctly Free Church affair. While Begg described the attendance as 'an ample and worthy representation of the Protestantism of Scotland and the world', he begrudgingly acknowledged the 'callous and unconcerned' responses from many British Protestants to the SRS's call for a 'national' convention. In his introduction to the edited volume of

---

173. *Caledonian Mercury*, 17 August 1860; *Bulwark, or Reformation Journal*, x (September 1860), 57–8; Wylie, *Tercentenary of the Scottish Reformation*, 205; *Popery: its progress and position*, 8.
174. Wylie, *Tercentenary of the Scottish Reformation*, viii–ix.
175. *Popery: its progress and position*, 7.
176. *Dumfries and Galloway Standard*, 15 August 1860.
177. *Bulwark, or Reformation Journal*, x (September 1860), 57.
178. *UPM*, iv (September 1860), 418; Wylie, *Tercentenary of the Scottish Reformation*, ix.
179. Wylie, *Tercentenary of the Scottish Reformation*, iv, xv, 199, 180–2.

proceedings that followed the commemorations, James Wylie asserted that the diversity of the papers reflected the unity inherent in the Protestant movement in Scotland. However, of the fifteen speeches selected for inclusion in Wylie's collection, only three were given by representatives who did not belong to the Free Kirk (two of whom were noted Free Church supporters).[180] Francis Brown-Douglas, the Free Church Lord Provost for Edinburgh, was also selected to chair the conference, while Begg convened a committee to arrange business which included four Free Churchmen, and one member each from the United and Reformed Presbyterian churches, and the Presbyterian churches of Ireland and England.[181] The tension between the rhetoric of Protestant unity and the maintenance of denominational distinctiveness was most evident during a speech by the Glasgow United Presbyterian minister William Lindsay at the inauguration of the Protestant Institute that followed the conference. While Lindsay regarded the new Institute as a 'rallying point to all the Protestants of the land', and believed that the simple anti-popery associated with the Free Kirk and the SRS could combine with the voluntaryism of his own church, he nevertheless proclaimed that anti-popery could only be successful in Scotland if all state endowments of religion were abolished.[182]

The dichotomy between the rhetoric of unity and the practicalities and realities of Presbyterian division were also strikingly apparent at the 'national' tercentenary celebrations, held on 20 December to commemorate the opening of the first General Assembly of the Church of Scotland.[183] The *United Presbyterian Magazine* regarded the December anniversary as a 'high day' for 'all the Protestant communions' and 'nearly the whole population of the land'.[184] Despite these pan-Presbyterian pretensions, the national character of the tercentenary was somewhat overshadowed by the competition among the churches to claim the Reformation. For example, the Kelso minister Henry Renton, speaking as the convenor of the United Presbyterian Church's committee regarding the tercentenary celebrations, argued that his church (and its United Secession and Relief forbears) had the strongest claim to being the true guardians and promoters of the Reformation and its principles. He argued that the Seceders were the first and, with the exception of the Reformed Presbyterians, the only church 'to adopt and formally avow all the principles asserted by our reforming and covenanting ancestors'; in essence, the voluntary spiritual independence of the Kirk. On the other hand, according to Renton, the 'approbation and adherence thus testified by our first founders were omitted and refused by the Established Church ... and have never since been expressed by

---

180. Wylie, *Tercentenary of the Scottish Reformation*, iv.
181. *Bulwark, or Reformation Journal*, x (September 1860), 58.
182. *UPM*, iv (September 1860), 417–18.
183. Holmes, 'The Scottish Reformations', 153; Wylie, *Tercentenary of the Scottish Reformation*, viii.
184. *UPM*, v (January 1861), 48.

it nor declared in any testimony of the Free Church'.[185] The denominational characteristics outlined by Renton and inherent throughout institutional anti-popery in the mid-nineteenth century only served to undermine the irenicism fuelled by a common Protestant opposition and hostility to Roman Catholicism. While many initially viewed the tercentenary celebrations as an opportunity to reinvigorate Scottish anti-Catholicism and rally Scotland's Presbyterians on this common ground, by the end of the year Begg was mourning 'our many divisions and the ominous apathy in regard to distinctive Protestantism which pervades too many of our pulpits'.[186]

Rather than simply a symptom of anti-Irish feeling, mid-nineteenth-century Scottish anti-Catholicism was a complex moral, theological, social and political tapestry that combined competing theories on the role of the church, state and society that cut to the very essence of Scottish Presbyterianism and its differences after 1843. Thus, the anti-Catholic movement in this period must be viewed both in the context of Scotland's historical opposition to popery and these new and shifting Presbyterian relations. The growing ecclesiastical co-operation between Scotland's dissenting churches following the Disruption, and the peripheral national role played by a recovering Church of Scotland during this period, was expressed in the opposition to popery that erupted in Britain in response to the Maynooth Act. The dissenting character of this anti-Catholicism was born from the impulse to anti-erastian and non-established Christian union in both Scotland and England from 1845. While the desire to achieve common ground between the Free and United Presbyterian churches was mirrored in the dissenting alliance that emerged from the anti-Maynooth campaign, the continuing divisions over the state–church question that dogged such advances were reflected in the lack of unity of principle that prevented organisations such as the Scottish Reformation Society from becoming truly national movements.

In essence, the anti-Catholic movement in Scotland during the 1840s and 1850s reflected and often neatly encapsulated the gulf between rhetoric and reality in Scottish dissent. While the policy of 'mutual forbearance' dominated discussions between Free and United Presbyterians on the subjects of increased ecclesiastical co-operation and the combined Protestant opposition to popery, denominational distinctiveness remained a pressing issue and one that prevented full practical agreement on the terms on which church union could be agreed and popery should be opposed. The Free Church distinction between truth and error, and their respective right to state endowment, was grounded in establishmentarian terms, while the United Presbyterian opposition to Maynooth, though containing anti-papal aspects, formed merely one part of their broader volun-

---

185. *Caledonian Mercury*, 20 December 1860.
186. Wylie, *Tercentenary of the Scottish Reformation*, xix.

tary campaign for the complete disendowment of religious institutions in Scotland. Despite these underlying differences, the national tidal wave of anti-popery after 1845 did provide a focal point for Scotland's dissenting churches to assert an identity that maintained their distinctly denominational principles while offering a largely dissenting and anti-erastian vision for Presbyterian Scotland – and Protestant Britain – as a whole. In this sense, the national and zealous anti-Catholicism of this period allowed the Free and United Presbyterian churches to cement the broad dissenting identity that emerged in the aftermath of the Disruption. The intertwined nature of this loose dissenting ideal and anti-Catholicism was also resituated in the context of the electoral growth of the Scottish Liberal party, as the next chapter will illustrate.

CHAPTER SIX

Bigotry or Liberalism?
Dissenting Politics and the Liberal Party

The post-Disruption period coincided with profound political change throughout the United Kingdom. In Scotland this was marked most notably by the development and rapid growth of political liberalism, which would become the dominant party of Victorian Scotland. It is no surprise that in the complex and shifting religious and political landscape of the 1840s and 1850s, Scotland emerged as the citadel of British liberalism. The Liberals' opposition to the elitism and erastianism of the Whigs and Conservatives echoed the secular and religious concerns of Scotland's dissenters who appeared at the forefront of the party's electoral surge. In the decade or so after the Disruption, liberalism was also, as Gordon Pentland has acknowledged, in a crucial formative phase; an 'inchoate creed' reliant upon malleable alliances and local circumstances, and able to be exploited by ambitious new political figures.[1] Therefore it is clear to see how the astonishing growth of the Liberals in Scotland owed much of its success to the emergence of a political alliance within the major Scottish dissenting churches based almost solely on a shared opposition to the further endowment of Maynooth College. The previous chapter charted how the tidal wave of anti-Catholicism that engulfed mid-nineteenth-century Britain in reaction to the Maynooth grant after 1845, and the so-called 'papal aggression' that followed in 1850, offered Scotland's dissenters the opportunity to unite under a common Protestant banner based on 'sound' and 'evangelical' as well as dissenting and anti-erastian principles. The changing nature of Scottish Presbyterianism after 1843 had a dramatic impact on Scottish electoral politics in the 1840s and 1850s. Michael Dyer has argued that the anti-Maynooth agitation enabled voluntaries and Free Churchmen to politically converge through their 'common opposition' to the endowment, which 'offended the voluntaristic sentiments of the former and the anti-Catholicism of both', and a shared support for the newly dominant Scottish Liberal party.[2] This desire for common political purpose and action, manifested most explicitly in the spectacularly successful electoral collaboration

1. Gordon Pentland, 'By-elections and the peculiarities of Scottish politics, 1832–1900', in T. G. Otte and Paul Readman, *By-elections in British Politics, 1832–1914* (Woodbridge, 2014), 282.
2. Dyer, *Men of Property and Intelligence*, 55.

between the Free and voluntary churches after 1846, would arguably draw Scotland's dissenters closer together, for a brief period at least, than any concurrent attempts at purely ecclesiastical co-operation or education and social reform.

The success of this narrowly focused alliance, according to Iain Hutchison, would alter the political complexion of Scotland for over a decade.[3] This chapter will place the complexities and nuances evident in the Free Church–United Presbyterian political alliance within the context of a shifting dissenting landscape in Scotland after 1843. It will assess the politicisation of the anti-Maynooth alliance after 1846, focusing on the general elections of 1847, 1852 and 1857, and the most notable by-election campaigns during this period. While the dissenting anti-Maynooth alliance was widely ridiculed for its narrow focus and loose political composition and principles, it had a profound impact on Presbyterian relations, liberalism and Scottish politics in general. However, this chapter will note that the success of this brand of single-interest politics was firmly rooted in the ecclesiastical context from which it emerged. Once other issues came to the fore by the mid-1850s, such as the divisive education debates and increasing concerns over dissenting union, the strength of the anti-Maynooth campaign as a focal point for cohesion between Scotland's non-established Presbyterians withered, along with the churches' influence on Scottish politics.

Liberalism and Dissent before Maynooth

Though Andrew Drummond and James Bulloch have pointed out that the geographical popularity of the Free Church in the burghs and Highlands often correlated with Liberal electoral success, the organisational structure and ideology of mid-nineteenth-century Scottish liberalism, and in particular its increasingly prominent radical faction, largely lay in its association with the voluntary churches.[4] Organised voluntaryism and radical-liberal electoral politics had emerged almost concurrently in Scotland during the late 1820s and 1830s. Scottish voluntaries, alongside bourgeois progressives, working-class radicals and the reinvigorated Whig party, formed part of a broad coalition of reformers who sought to achieve parliamentary and local government reform, reduce taxes and implement free trade policies, particularly the repeal of the controversial Corn Laws.[5] The Whigs, under the leadership of Prime Minister Earl Grey, had been responsible for the 1832 Reform Acts. The Scottish Reform Act had a much greater impact on the social composition of the electorate than its English counterpart,

---

3. Hutchison, *A Political History of Scotland*, 61.
4. A. L. Drummond and James Bulloch, *The Church in Victorian Scotland 1843-1874* (Edinburgh, 1975), 30.
5. Hutchison, *Industry, Reform and Empire*, 212–36.

passed five weeks earlier. While the English electorate rose by 41 per cent, in Scotland it increased by 1,400 per cent from 4,571 to 63,369 electors, enabling middle-class urban dissenters to claim a greater share of political power and break the Tory dominance of Scottish politics.[6] The failure of the Whigs to enact further institutional change following their resounding success at the 1832 general election (with the exception of the Police and the Municipal Corporations acts of 1833) saw both middle-class dissenters and radicals combine to press for sweeping reform in areas such as public spending, wider suffrage, free trade and the Corn Laws, and, of course, disestablishment of the Church of Scotland.[7]

While the increasing influence of dissent during the Voluntary Controversy and Ten Years' Conflict coincided with, and owed much to, this rise of radical-liberalism as a major political force, the proponents of voluntaryism viewed their religious convictions as the 'most powerful motive in placing Scotland in the vanguard of British Liberalism'. The voluntaries' demand of a 'fair field and no favour' was regarded as 'the foundation of Liberalism', while the concept of 'a free church in a free state' was deemed to constitute an 'essential plank' of the Liberal programme.[8] The ideological link between voluntaryism and liberalism, particularly in their shared resistance to a seemingly 'oppressive' spiritual and temporal establishment, was emphasised by the United Secession minister John Brown. In an 1840 sermon, Brown declared, 'what is right in the enemies of the slave trade and of slavery, and of the corn laws, cannot be wrong in the enemies of other oppressions and monopolies; what was right in Reformers, cannot be wrong in voluntaries'.[9]

To its supporters, voluntaryism provided the 'best security for evangelical teaching on the one hand, and popular rights on the other'.[10] This equation of the political, social and ecclesiastical was formalised with the creation of the Scottish Central Board for Vindicating the Rights of Dissenters in December 1834. The board, which claimed to represent all classes of evangelical dissenters in Scotland, sought to 'vindicate and secure the civil and religious rights' of non-established churchmen and lay members.[11] The Central Board played a pivotal role in organising and harnessing the unified

---

6. Gordon Pentland, 'Scotland and the creation of a National Reform Movement, 1830–1832', *Historical Journal*, xlviii (December 2005), 999; Gordon Pentland, *Radicalism, reform, and national identity in Scotland, 1820–1833* (Woodbridge, 2008); William Ferguson, 'The Reform Act (Scotland) of 1832', 105.
7. Hutchison, *Industry, Reform and Empire*, 253.
8. Mackie, *Duncan McLaren*, i, 167–8.
9. John Brown, *What ought the Dissenters of Scotland to do in the present crisis?* (Edinburgh, 1840), 20.
10. Mackie, *Duncan McLaren*, i, 171.
11. McKerrow, *History of the Secession Church*, ii, 745; *Report from the Select Committee on King's Printers' Patent* (Scotland), H. C. (9), xiii (1837), 37; Scottish Central Board for vindicating the rights of Dissenters, *Statement relative to Church Accommodation in Scotland* (Edinburgh, 1835), 2.

political power of Scottish dissent after the 1832 Reform Act in opposition to an ecclesiastical and secular establishment. The Board also ensured Scotland's dissenting churches, and their bourgeois radical laymen, an 'inflated share' of political attention in the decade before 1843.[12] This was partly achieved through the prolonged and vociferous attack on church establishments and more specifically the 'aggressive' extension policies of the Chalmersite wing of the Church of Scotland during the Voluntary Controversy.[13] The Board also focused on the broader radical touchstone of the anti-Corn Law movement and issues such as the Annuity Tax, a 6 per cent levy imposed often forcibly on Edinburgh householders and shopkeepers partly for the maintenance of the city's established clergy. These campaigns were instrumental in uniting Scotland's voluntaries into a cohesive body through the Central Board and formed part of a wider agenda calling for sweeping religious, political and social change.[14]

The coalescing of radical and dissenting values in the Central Board was essential to its challenge to the tepid Whig policy of reform after 1832. The Whigs' inability to implement the religious, civil and social changes deemed necessary by Scotland's dissenters resulted in a shift within these churches from the traditional anti-toryism of the pre-1832 period to the anti-Whig agenda that would dominate radicalism and create division within the broader liberal movement from the late 1830s.[15] The typically middle-class, radical and dissenting characteristics of the United Secession and Relief churches provided an effective counterpoint to the landed, secular and erastian Whig establishment. As John McCaffrey has pointed out, voluntary leaders such as the United Presbyterian layman and radical politician Duncan McLaren aimed to shift political control away from the Edinburgh aristocracy towards the 'needs of the modern urban Scotland', while the new voting power of dissenters and bodies such as the Central Board placed Whig policies under increasing scrutiny.[16] The Annuity Tax agitation, for example, was often depicted as a conflict between Edinburgh City Council, the dissenting and liberal 'guardians of the public interests', and the city ministers, who the Central Board leader McLaren derided as 'the representatives of privilege and monopoly'.[17] Despite his brief adoption during the Irish Tithes debate of 1834–5 of the 'appropriation clause'

12. Michael Fry, *Patronage and Principle* (Aberdeen, 1987), 38.
13. Mackie, *Duncan McLaren*, i, 173, 178.
14. For example, see Duncan McLaren, *History of the resistance to the Annuity Tax, and of the origin and application of seat rents for payment of ministers' stipends* (Edinburgh, 1836); Duncan McLaren, *Evidence given before the Select Committee of the House of Commons, respecting the Annuity-Tax* (Edinburgh, 1851); John R. Fyfe and William Skeen, *The injustice and immoral tendency of the Corn and Provision Laws* (Edinburgh, 1842); Duncan McLaren, *The Corn Laws Condemned on account of their injustice and immoral tendency* (Edinburgh, 1842).
15. J. C. Williams, 'Edinburgh Politics: 1832–1852', unpublished PhD thesis, University of Edinburgh, 1972, 9–11.
16. McCaffrey, *Scotland in the Nineteenth Century*, 48, 60–1.
17. McLaren, *Evidence given before the Select Committee*, 17; Mackie, *Duncan McLaren*, i, 181–4.

that enabled the use of Church of Ireland endowment funds for other purposes, Whig leaders such as Lord John Russell were also regarded as earnest defenders of the establishment principle, fuelling dissenting suspicion of their policies during the Ten Years' Conflict.[18] This establishmentarian ethos was most evident in Grey, who advised Russell to abandon appropriation in Ireland and once admitted that 'I for one am no admirer of the voluntary system. I believe it to be a bad one.'[19] The Whigs' adherence to a 'manly' Protestant establishment under Russell proved at odds with the voluntary character of their dissenting electorate in Scotland, while the party leader's late conversion to a policy of immediate abolition of the Corn Laws also jarred with the radical sensibilities of these dissenters.[20]

Dissenting mistrust of the Whigs and fear of government submissiveness to the Established Kirk's demands filtered through to the polls. Throughout the 1830s, Whig parliamentary candidates were challenged on their approach to the ecclesiastical controversies of the period. At the 1837 general election, where the Church controversy was a major issue following a botched attempt by the government to rectify religious deficiency in rural parishes by building more established churches, the Whigs received only lukewarm and conditional support from radical dissenters who, though not defecting to the Tories, in some cases actively abstained or threatened to oppose Whig candidates.[21] This partial voluntary and radical support throughout Britain, combined with a Conservative resurgence under Peel, led to substantial Whig losses and left Melbourne with a precarious majority in the House of Commons, unable to satisfy the demands of both Scotland's dissenters and the church extensionists.[22]

Though the Whigs eventually succumbed to voluntary pressure and in 1838 refused to provide further endowments for church extension – a decision that most clearly paved the way to the Disruption – Scottish dissenters remained aggrieved at the party's treatment of their concerns.[23] In a series of letters in 1840 to the leading Whig politician and historian Thomas Macaulay, McLaren complained that the Whig government was 'overriding the legitimate claims of the dissenters on every occasion, and perpetually sacrificing their rights to the necessity, real or assumed, of conciliating the Church and Tory party in order to pass some bill'. According to McLaren, the 'settled policy' of the Whigs towards Scotland's dissenters was to 'sacrifice them to conciliate powerful opponents'.[24] This deep mistrust of Whig

18. Paul Scherer, *Lord John Russell: a biography* (London, 1999), 84.
19. *Spectator*, 7 July 1838; *Reasons for declining to vote in favour of Mr Macaulay*, 4; *Nonconformist*, 11 August 1847.
20. Parry, *Rise and Fall*; John F. McCaffrey, 'Political Issues and Developments', in W. Hamish Fraser and Irene Maver (eds), *Glasgow, Volume II: 1830 to 1912* (Manchester, 1996), 196.
21. *Scotsman*, 20 July 1837.
22. *Perthshire Advertiser*, 27 July 1837.
23. Brown, 'Religion and the Rise of Liberalism', 703.
24. Mackie, *Duncan McLaren*, i, 222.

religious policies and the intensification of the Voluntary Controversy from the mid-1830s saw Scotland's dissenters increasingly neglect the wider radical agenda in favour of a solely ecclesiastical approach. The politicisation of Scottish voluntaryism as a stand-alone interest was further compounded by what the dissenters believed was the effective reintroduction of the Test and Corporation Acts in the late 1830s through the exclusion of anyone outside of the establishment from becoming a prison chaplain, serving on the Bible Board or having a say in the appointment of School Inspectors. The 'spirit of exclusion' brought about by these decisions prompted one dissenting minister to question the legality of the Whigs' conduct towards dissenters.[25]

The ecclesiastical controversies of the late 1830s were instrumental in forging a singular voluntary interest in Scotland, which divided the radical vote and allowed the Whigs to regain some electoral ground (despite dissenting criticism of the Whigs, their deeper disdain for the Tories prevented any defections). Nevertheless, the desire to maintain both dissenting and radical policies and ideals remained intact within Scotland's voluntary churches. The duality of this position was highlighted by an 1841 speech by Duncan McLaren. In an attempt to counter the dual threat of an aggressive Kirk and an apathetic government, the run-up to that year's election was characterised by calls from voluntary groups such as the Central Board to support only dissenting candidates. Deriding the conduct of the Whigs, McLaren asserted that any prospective candidate should 'possess that intimate knowledge of their principles and tried attachment' to the dissenting cause, in order to 'defend our rights'. However, he also stressed that the proposed member should be 'thoroughly liberal on all the great questions of the day' and a 'true friend of the people, and one who would not consent to legislation or carry on the Government of the country for the benefit of any one sect or party whatever'.[26] Despite the concerns they had consistently voiced during the 1830s, many dissenters, such as the leading Central Board member William Alexander, stressed that they were not 'enemies' of the Whig government. Alexander even emphasised that Melbourne's government was the best in British history, and 'if they would only treat us openly and fairly, they should have our cordial and continued support'.[27] The internal wrangling within Edinburgh dissent over what kind of candidate to support at the 1841 election – centred on a choice between the ultra-voluntary Sir Culling Eardley Smith and the leading radical Joseph Hume – eventually resulted in two archetypal Whigs, Thomas Macaulay and William Gibson-Craig, being returned unopposed.

25. Brown, *What ought the Dissenters*, 22–3.
26. Duncan McLaren, *Protecting the civil rights of Dissenters from the unjust encroachments of the High Church party and their abettors in parliament* (Edinburgh, 1841), 3–4, 14; *The Times*, 1 June 1841.
27. Brown, *What ought the Dissenters*, 23.

Throughout Scotland the pattern was similar, with dissenters still tending to vote for the Whigs largely due to fear of the Tory alternative.

While McLaren and Alexander disavowed any sectarian motives, there nonetheless remained the expectation during the Voluntary Controversy that Whig or Radical MPs would uphold the dissenting cause in parliament. At a meeting of the Central Board in 1838, the Kirkintilloch minister Andrew Marshall expressed this expectation, utilising rhetoric that would be repeated by voluntaries during the following decade's elections. Marshall, widely regarded as the initiator of the Voluntary Controversy, claimed that it was 'an act of dishonesty on the part of the Liberal members from Scotland, should they be found voting for a grant' of additional endowments to the Established Kirk. He argued that 'they obtained their seats through the exertions of dissenters, and on the express condition that they should oppose these endowments'.[28] While voluntaries such as Marshall expected Liberals to defend the interests of Scotland's non-established churches in exchange for votes, the prominence of organised voluntaryism throughout Britain in this period marked a significant challenge for a party attempting to juggle competing aims and factional rivalry. As G. I. T. Machin has observed, the sectarian zeal of voluntaryism had the potential to embarrass the Liberals unless restricted to lesser ends that could be supported by Anglican radicals such as Richard Cobden. Thus, Machin concludes, the growth of the voluntary movement posed a major problem for an increasingly fragmented Liberal party.[29] These divisions, between both whigs and radicals, and dissenters and churchmen, would become strikingly apparent by the late 1840s.

Though Scotland's voluntaries viewed liberal and dissenting principles as largely synonymous throughout the 1830s, the immediate period after the Disruption witnessed a decline in voluntary influence over the radical faction of the Liberal party. Perhaps due to an element of temporary complacency following the perceived success of their decade-long campaign, after 1843 Scotland's voluntaries struggled to retain their position as the 'backbone of Liberalism'.[30] The renewed desire in the mid-1840s to maintain this prominent position within the Scottish Liberal party was largely due to increasing dissenting insecurity brought about by a relative decline in the voluntary churches' political and religious power after 1843. In 1845 the defunct Central Board was 'resuscitated' as the Scottish Board of Dissenters in response to the apparent misunderstanding and misrepresentation of voluntary principles during the parliamentary debates over Maynooth. This new organisation was inherently political and immediately focused on both the endowment issue and the registration of electors.[31]

---

28. *Caledonian Mercury*, 6 January 1838.
29. Machin, *Politics and the Churches in Great Britain*, 110.
30. Mackie, *Duncan McLaren*, i, 169–70.
31. *The Scottish Congregational Magazine*, v (August 1845), 403–4.

The crusade against the Maynooth grant after 1845, combined with the revitalised Central Board and the upcoming United Presbyterian union, offered dissenters the opportunity to regain lost political ground within a shifting ecclesiastical landscape.

The traditional voluntary desire to defend liberal and dissenting principles in the face of perceived neglect by both Tory and Whig governments was the major feature of the elections after 1843 and was aided by the emergence of the Free Church as a quasi-dissenting ally.[32] This voluntary opposition to the Whig elite was complemented by the Free Church's mutual and lingering distrust of the party's religious policies stemming from the Ten Years' Conflict and Disruption.[33] From the mid-1820s, the Whigs had been intrinsically linked to the middle-class evangelicals in the Kirk who would go on to form the Free Church, while the Church of Scotland's Moderate wing was associated with the ironclad Tory regime led by Henry Dundas. However, though Scotland's voluntaries believed that the Whig government up to 1841 favoured the church-extension policies of Chalmers' non-intrusionists, by the Disruption the Free Church was of the opinion that the party had not done enough to defend its Established Church. This criticism was extended to Peel's Conservatives following the rejection of the non-intrusionists' Claim of Right in 1842. In a bid to entice the Kirk's liberal evangelicals as part of his plan to remould the Tories as a modern centrist party, between 1835 and 1837 Peel had capitalised on the Whigs' acquiescence to voluntary demands by instigating his 'Church in Danger' electoral platform in Scotland. His eventual refusal to bow to non-intrusionist demands in government, however, culminated in the Disruption and lost the Tories their 'only real card' in Scotland, that of upholding the present constitutional link between church and state.[34] The hostility of virtually all of the Free Church towards the Conservatives, who they blamed for permitting the Disruption, proved a heavy electoral blow for the party, as urban middle-class Tories such as James Forrest, a Lord Provost of Edinburgh, and William Collins became leading lights in Scottish liberalism.[35]

The Free Kirk's combination of conservative theology and liberal social and political values embodied in ministers such as James Begg would also complement the 'ultra-liberal' tendencies of their dissenting colleagues. This would help carve a specific role for Scotland's non-established Presbyterians within the broader structure of the Liberal party. Much like the Central Board in the 1830s, the new body's organ, the *Free Church Magazine*, adopted an anti-aristocratic tone, based on a resentment of the Tory lairds who refused the Free Church sites in the wake of the Disruption, while advocating a wider liberal agenda that included support for free

---

32. Mackie, *Duncan McLaren*, i, 222.
33. *Nonconformist*, 11 August 1847.
34. McCaffrey, 'Political Issues and Developments', 195.
35. Hutchison, *Industry, Reform and Empire*, 247.

trade.³⁶ This broad anti-Tory and anti-Whig agenda and the emergence of the anti-Maynooth campaign proved crucial to the Free and voluntary churches' desire to re-establish their own political constituency and power within the more 'ultra-liberal' and dissenting fringes of Scottish politics after 1843. The impact of the Maynooth controversy on the British political system also brought to a head the decade-long struggle of Scotland's dissenters to unseat the old Whig clique and set a new direction in Scottish politics that was led by men from outside the current establishment who were willing to defend dissenting rights and 'unhackneyed in the ways of existing parties'.³⁷

British Politics and the Maynooth Question

As well as instigating the national anti-Catholic outcry discussed in the previous chapter, the Maynooth controversy after 1845 also upended the traditional Tory–Whig dichotomy in British party politics. In August 1845, the *British Quarterly Review* observed that the grant 'has disturbed nearly all the old landmarks of party. Everywhere, on this question, the men who have been accustomed to do battle side by side have been marshalled against each other.'³⁸ The conduct of the leaders of both major parties was publicly criticised. Peel's decision to increase the endowment led to over half of the Tory MPs voting against their leader and provided the foundations for the definitive split that would occur within the Conservative party a year later in reaction to the Prime Minister's repeal of the Corn Laws.³⁹ The grant would also have a 'disastrous' effect on the Whig leadership and created tension between the Whig mainstream of the Liberal party and its growing radical-dissenting faction.⁴⁰ Due to the splits and hostility within the Tories and the downfall of Peel in 1846, it was the Whigs, under the premiership of Russell, who were charged with implementing the changes to the Maynooth endowment.⁴¹ Despite his establishmentarian reputation, British dissenters criticised Russell's decision to support the grant in opposition and in office as contradicting the liberal voluntaryism of his party's nonconformist voters.⁴² The *British Quarterly Review* claimed that the 'schism' between 'liberal politicians and the great majority of Protestant nonconformists' was the most conspicuous result of the controversy, and portrayed the Maynooth debate as a 'collision' between 'the refined sense of the

36. Allan W. MacColl, *Land, Faith and the Crofting Community: Christianity and Social Criticism in the Highlands of Scotland, 1843–1893* (Edinburgh, 2006), 12–13.
37. Kenneth J. Cameron, 'William Weir and the Origins of the "Manchester League" in Scotland, 1833–39', *Scottish Historical Review*, lviii (April 1979), 85–6.
38. *British Quarterly Review*, ii (August 1845), 104.
39. Cahill, 'Irish Catholicism and English Toryism', 73.
40. Parry, *Rise and Fall*, 171.
41. Doyle, *Fighting like the Devil*, 132.
42. Cahill, 'Irish Catholicism and English Toryism', 73–5.

statesman and the common sense of humbler men'. The *Review*'s criticism of the establishmentarian inclinations of the Whig political elite emphasised the anti-aristocratic character of the new breed of radical dissenters. It criticised the 'irritability' of the tone employed by Liberal MPs in favouring a 'forced system of religion' as a protest against the voluntary principle, and highlighted what it regarded as the 'selfish interests' of upper-class Whigs to uphold ecclesiastical establishments. 'The most cultivated and powerful minds', the article remarked, 'are in the greater part governed by opinions decidedly unchristian', while the conduct of Whig statesmen was derided as 'hostile to self-government in the people'.[43]

This intra-party hostility that defined British politics after 1845 enabled the new generation of bourgeois, urban and radical dissenters to unite under a shared opposition to religious endowments, particularly endowments of the 'errors' of Roman Catholicism. The alliance between Free Churchmen and voluntaries that appeared in the wake of the Maynooth endowment not only organised Scotland's dissenters on a common political platform, but also allowed the radical wing of the Liberal party to unite a significant proportion of the country's population behind them by capitalising on the new post-Disruption ecclesiastical landscape. In essence, Maynooth provided the catalyst for what Scottish liberal-radicals had been trying to achieve since 1832: the replacement of the old landed, elite, establishmentarian Whig clique with 'men of their own kind', urban, newly arrived, dissenting and opposed to the public endowment of popery.[44] This desire to uproot the traditional elite of parliamentary politics was evident throughout British nonconformity and the anti-Maynooth movement after 1845. However, as in Scotland, this new opposition, though nominally united against the Whig and Tory supporters of Maynooth, consisted of varying and often opposing principles and policies. Conservative societies such as the National Club were established to defend the 'Protestant principles of the constitution' and publicly campaigned to return a 'Protestant parliament' in the general election of 1847.[45] British voluntaries, on the other hand, were encouraged to refuse their vote 'to the man who shall hesitate to pledge himself against any extension of government grants for the purposes of religion' with the aim of increasing voluntary representation in parliament.[46]

However, for most of the ten years in which the Free Church–United Presbyterian electoral alliance co-operated successfully, a policy of mutual forbearance, especially regarding the voluntary principle, was utilised in order to prevent disputes in what remained a loose and potentially fractious coalition. For instance, the *United Presbyterian Magazine* advised its

---

43. *The British Quarterly Review*, ii (August 1845), 104, 114–16, 121, 124.
44. McCaffrey, 'Political Issues and Developments', 196; Fry, *Patronage and Principle*, 38.
45. *London Standard*, 14 May 1847; Cahill, 'Irish Catholicism and English Toryism', 74.
46. *British Quarterly Review*, ii (August 1845), 127–8.

readers to avoid the hard-line voluntaryism associated with politicians such as Adam Black so as not to alienate the anti-popery opponents of Maynooth in the Free Kirk. Referring to the respective leaders of the voluntary and militant Protestant factions of the anti-Maynooth campaign at Westminster, the magazine asserted the need for the supporters of both Edward Miall and Richard Spooner to co-operate to abolish the grant. Despite their differing objectives and principles, Free Churchmen and voluntaries were 'agreed upon one thing – the demolition of Maynooth; and until this be accomplished, we can act in entire harmony'.[47] Rather than the full campaign for disestablishment feared by statesmen such as William Gladstone, the alliance's opposition to ecclesiastical endowments focused only upon the Maynooth grant and the Whig and Tory support for it, and thus was able to attract the mass support of Scottish dissenters under the political banner of bourgeois liberal-radicalism.[48] Criticism of the loose principles and narrow focus of the dissenting alliance, which the *Aberdeen Herald* would later describe as an 'utterly unprincipled and disgraceful coalition', was rife throughout its existence.[49] At a meeting of electors in Edinburgh in 1852, it was reported that 'there seemed to be but one opinion upon one point, how many so ever there may have been upon any other point'.[50] The London *Daily News* claimed that 'certain sectarian leaders' in the Free and United Presbyterian churches had aimed in 1847 'to divide the representation of Edinburgh between two ecclesiastical associations . . . irrespective of [the candidate's] political character and principles'.[51] This was dismissed as 'simply untrue' by one United Presbyterian, who argued that selecting candidates from the two major dissenting churches ensured 'the greatest probability of getting men whose "political character and principles" were of the right stamp'.[52] Despite this widespread criticism towards the loose character of the alliance, the relative success of this tentative coalition in the by-elections of 1845 and 1846 (see Chapter Five) cemented Maynooth as a viable electoral issue and paved the way for the national unified opposition to the Tories and Whigs at the general election of 1847.[53] Nevertheless, by 1847 there was a recognition within Scotland's dissenting churches that this purely ecclesiastical platform would not be enough to secure electoral

47. *UPM*, x (March 1856), 264. Black was one of only three Scottish MPs who voted for the continuation of the endowment in 1856, because he believed that the Maynooth grant could not be attacked 'singly', but in company with other religious grants such as the Presbyterian *regium donum* in Ireland. The *United Presbyterian Magazine* challenged his consistency by noting that Black had voted for the abolition of the *regium donum* and the Episcopal Ministers' Fund as separate motions while voting for Maynooth's continuation (262–3).
48. Butler, *Gladstone*, 113.
49. *Aberdeen Herald*, 11 February 1856.
50. *Caledonian Mercury*, 19 April 1852.
51. London *Daily News*, 17 June 1852.
52. *Reasons for declining to vote in favour of Mr Macaulay*, 10.
53. Cahill, 'Irish Catholicism and English Toryism', 74.

success. Perhaps due to the voluntary influence within the alliance, the focus of the coalition shifted to a broader anti-Whig and anti-Tory political agenda, and centred on the increasingly influential radical faction within the Liberal party.[54]

The 1847 General Election

The three-fold electoral approach adopted by Scotland's non-established churches, based on Maynooth, anti-Whiggism and the structure of organised liberalism, flourished at the polls. At the 1847 general election, the nationwide success of the Free Church–United Presbyterian alliance reshaped Scottish politics. Both the Tory party and the Whigs were generally swept aside in the largely urban constituencies in which the Free and voluntary churches formed a substantial portion of the electorate.[55] As a result of the success of the dissenting anti-Maynooth alliance, the Liberal party gained a majority in Scotland, winning thirty-three of the fifty-nine seats.[56] This fastened liberalism's position as a 'national crusade' north of the Tweed and earned the party a single-figure majority in the House of Commons.[57] In the twenty-three seats available in the burghs, the 'best index of public opinion' and the heartland of Presbyterian dissent, only one Tory, Lord Lincoln, was returned, with a narrow win at Falkirk.[58] This phenomenal and largely unpredicted success was due to a number of factors. The impotence of the Tories after the Peelite split in 1846 ensured that the election the following year was fought out within Scottish liberalism.[59] However, despite the new Prime Minister Russell's desire to address the religious crises of this period, the fragmentation of the party system and the lack of unity within his own party made a coherent Liberal response virtually impossible.[60] This situation, and the prominence of the Maynooth grant as a political football, culminated in the general election in Scotland becoming mainly a straight contest between the pro-Maynooth (Whig) and anti-Maynooth (radical) factions of the Scottish Liberal party. The 1847 election sounded the death knell of a Conservative party which had been suffering in Scotland since Peel's rejection of the 1842 Claim of Right and his unwillingness to acquiesce to non-intrusionist demands during the Ten Years' Conflict. His support for the Maynooth endowment, and the inevitable Free Kirk-led hostility to the measure, cemented the electoral demise of the Conservatives in Scotland for well over a decade.[61]

54. Hutchison, *Political History of Scotland*, 66.
55. Hutchison, *Political History of Scotland*, 65; Millar, 'Maynooth and Scottish Politics', 227.
56. *Scotsman*, 28 August 1847.
57. Paterson, *Autonomy of Modern Scotland*, 48; Parry, *Rise and Fall*, 171.
58. *Perthshire Advertiser*, 19 August 1847.
59. Doyle, *Fighting like the Devil*, 210; Hutchison, *Political History of Scotland*, 82.
60. Parry, *Rise and Fall*, 171.
61. McCaffrey, 'Political Issues and Developments', 195.

While the Tories all but capitulated in Scotland's urban areas, it was the defeats of several prominent Maynooth-supporting Whig candidates that underlined the electoral power of the dissenting alliance and sent shockwaves through Scottish politics. Significant results included the Free Churchman Charles Cowan's spectacular and controversial victory over the 'unprincipled latitudinarianism' of Thomas Macaulay, while Alexander Hastie, the first voluntary Lord Provost of Glasgow, alongside the free-trader John MacGregor, defeated the sitting Whig MPs in that city who had refused to oppose Maynooth.[62] In constituencies such as Dundee, Perth and Paisley, the strength of the alliance was such that no Whig or Tory opponent contested the seats.[63] The national success of these dissenting candidates such as Cowan and Hastie, portrayed as 'outsiders' against the established party-political cliques, represented the most striking example of the development of the 'new groups' that had emerged in the aftermath of the 1832 Reform Act and their increasing influence on urban electoral politics.[64] According to one whig newspaper, the 'whole relations of parties' had been 'completely upset and confounded'.[65] The radical alliance's dominance was mirrored throughout Britain and underlined the new-found prominence of this significant new minority within the Liberal Party. As Jonathan Parry has observed, the dissenting, voluntary and militantly Protestant ethos of these radicals presented a major problem for the party's predominantly Whig leadership and ensured Liberal policy on religion after 1847 was 'fraught with danger'.[66]

The pragmatic recalibration of principle and policy of forbearance over the church–state relationship, witnessed during the by-elections of the previous two years and discussed in the previous chapter, was essential to the alliance's national success in 1847. The Free Church candidate at Peebles, Alexander Gibson Carmichael, claimed that while he was 'very determined to resist every encouragement to the Roman Catholic Church', he was 'generally opposed to all ecclesiastical endowments'. Though he acknowledged his affiliation with the Free Kirk, Carmichael asserted that 'I wish nothing for the Free Church which I would not give to every other.'[67] This desire to avoid the partisanship which remained within sections of Scottish dissent, in favour of a broader and more conciliatory platform, was repeated throughout the 1847 campaign. In Aberdeen, Dingwall Fordyce defeated the Whig candidate W. H. Sykes thanks to what the whiggish *Aberdeen Herald* described as an 'unholy' alliance of 'Free Churchmen, Dissenters, Do-nothings, and Macphersonites [Chartists]'.[68] In a similar

---

62. *Edinburgh News*, 15 May 1852; *Scottish Guardian*, 25 July 1847.
63. Hutchison, *Political History of Scotland*, 65.
64. McCaffrey, 'Political Issues and Developments', 196–7.
65. *Perthshire Advertiser*, 19 August 1847.
66. Parry, *Rise and Fall*, 171, 201.
67. *Scotsman*, 31 July 1847.
68. *Aberdeen Herald*, 7 August 1847.

manner to Alexander Dunlop at Greenock in 1845, Fordyce tactfully redefined the strict establishmentarian ethos associated with the Free Church, and announced his opposition to 'any further extension by the State, of the system of Religious Endowments, in any quarter of the Empire'.[69] This policy ensured the backing of the Religious Freedom Society, an Aberdeen-based voluntary organisation, which believed his opinions to be 'nearly approximate to the principles of this Association'.[70] The *Herald* noted the pragmatism evident in the voluntary support for the Free Churchman, claiming the society 'contrived to bore a hole in Capt. Fordyce's endowment principle, and then shrunk their own voluntaryism into such dimensions as would fit it'.[71] Combined with a common opposition to Whig or Tory supporters of the grant, this policy of appeasement ensured the alliance's ability to function effectively, with very few exceptions, on a national level at the polls.

The success of this loosely bound coalition was most evident in Charles Cowan's stunning electoral victory over the Whig Thomas Macaulay in Edinburgh. This tactical coup, overturning the sitting Paymaster General, was masterminded by the Scottish Board of Dissenters led by Duncan McLaren.[72] Styling itself as the Independent Liberal Committee, the dissenting alliance deliberately and determinedly pursued Macaulay's defeat. Macaulay's opinion on the endowment of the Roman Catholic Church inevitably attracted the brunt of the alliance's attacks. In an 1825 letter to Thomas Chalmers, Macaulay had stated his opposition to any state payment afforded to 'the popish priests' owing to his 'very strong impression of the evils of their religious system'.[73] However, this stance noticeably shifted in the following years, to the extent that by 1860 Macaulay supported the belief that the Church of Ireland had forcefully usurped the property of the Catholic Church in that country.[74] To dissenters, this inconsistency was a glaring indictment of Macaulay's principles and political character. As one voluntary commentator observed, not only did the MP support the Maynooth bill in 1845, 'so strong and decided were his convictions of the rightness and justice of the measure that he spoke most earnestly and eloquently in its favour'.[75] Though critical of the Peel government's handling of the issue, Macaulay was scathing in his attitude towards the anti-Maynooth campaign, which he infamously condemned as the 'bray of Exeter Hall'.[76] Macaulay's denunciation of the dissenting opposition to Maynooth was

---

69. *Aberdeen Journal*, 28 July 1847.
70. *Aberdeen Journal*, 4 August 1847.
71. *Aberdeen Herald*, 7 August 1847.
72. Hutchison, *Political History of Scotland*, 68.
73. Thomas Babington Macaulay to Thomas Chalmers, 26 April 1825, NCL, CHA.4.41.17.
74. Macaulay to Chalmers, 15 June 1835, NCL, CHA.4.231.57; Wylie, *Tercentenary of the Scottish Reformation*, 201.
75. *Reasons for declining to vote in favour of Mr Macaulay*, 5.
76. *Macaulay; the historian, statesman, and essayist* (London, 1860), 81–3.

echoed throughout the recently appointed Whig ministry. Prime Minister Russell argued that though 'those who were exerting themselves to create fear and to excite religious intolerance might be Protestants, they certainly were not Christians'.[77] This policy of tolerance was central to Macaulay and the Whigs' position on Maynooth, and anathema to the dissenting alliance. By becoming a 'political sacrifice to the truth and justice of the cause he espoused', Macaulay earned the votes of Edinburgh's Roman Catholic electors but effectively alienated his former supporters within the dissenting churches.[78]

Though Macaulay's position on endowments offered Free Churchmen and voluntaries a 'common platform' on which to unite, the dissenting opposition to Macaulay in 1847 was not limited to the single-issue politics of Maynooth.[79] Due to the uncertainty surrounding public approval of a campaign based purely on Maynooth, a broader anti-Whig agenda was deemed necessary for electoral success. To a radical voluntary such as McLaren, Macaulay was the arch-Whig. His brand of liberalism was everything the alliance's was not – 'undogmatic, tolerant, erastian'.[80] Through a series of correspondence in the early 1840s, McLaren expressed disappointment at Macaulay's apparent lack of empathy for dissenting grievances, which the Whig MP dismissed as 'little slights' on 'some trifling matters of punctilio'.[81] The seemingly 'haughty, supercilious, and almost disdainful' manner increasingly adopted by Macaulay during the 1847 election campaign was viewed by radicals and dissenters as indicative of the broader Whig indifference to their concerns.[82] The united opposition to Macaulay in 1847, one voluntary observer argued, demonstrated the necessity for the Whigs to finally yield to radical demands and prove 'that they are reformers in deed and reality'.[83] This 'many-headed' attack on Macaulay and the Whigs played into the hands of McLaren in his bid to create an Independent Liberal party in Edinburgh that mirrored his own radical ideals. While Maynooth may have been the focal point of this electoral surge, McLaren's aim to recruit ultra-liberals from across Scotland's dissenting churches was grounded in a shared opposition to the Whigs' political, educational and religious policies.[84]

Ultimately, Macaulay's 'unprincipled latitudinarianism' and hostility to the anti-Maynooth campaign proved equally abhorrent to both the 'earnest voluntary' and the 'zealous Free Churchman'.[85] This ensured he was the

77. *Inverness Courier*, 3 August 1847.
78. *Reasons for declining to vote in favour of Mr Macaulay*, 5; *John O'Groat Journal*, 13 August 1847.
79. Mackie, *Duncan McLaren*, ii, 30.
80. Butler, *Gladstone*, 86; Mackie, *Duncan McLaren*, ii, 30.
81. Mackie, *Duncan McLaren*, i, 215–18.
82. *John O'Groat Journal*, 13 August 1847; *The Eclectic Review*, xxii (September 1847), 377.
83. *John O'Groat Journal*, 13 August 1847.
84. *Scotsman*, 31 July 1847; Millar, 'Maynooth and Scottish Politics', 241.
85. *Edinburgh Evening News*, 15 May 1852.

prime target for a tactical coup, and so it proved as Cowan's electors, the majority of whom plumped for the Free Churchman, were instructed by the Independent Liberal Committee to give their second votes to anyone but Macaulay.[86] While political scheming undoubtedly played a major role in the Free Churchman's success, to his supporters Cowan's victory was the 'result of a deep conviction on the part of the voters that a great principle was at stake'. According to one voluntary elector, the Edinburgh election was 'such a general expression of the fixed determination of the public mind, not to submit to further endowments of any religious body whatever'.[87] While most of this celebratory rhetoric centred on Maynooth, the election of both Cowan and Fordyce in Aberdeen over prominent Whig opponents represented to the alliance 'a cheering indication of the rapid progress of truly liberal opinions'.[88]

Personality also proved a factor in Cowan's victory. If Macaulay seemed the archetypal adversary, Cowan was the perfect unifier between Free Churchman and voluntary. A relative of Chalmers and a highly successful paper manufacturer, he was deemed to meet the wants of the alliance in 'every way'. The *Nonconformist* described Cowan as a highly respected 'liberal and active member' of the Free Church, 'yet going further than most Free Churchmen in his opposition to church establishments'.[89] While he may not have been the 'out-and-out voluntary' as depicted by the United Presbyterian minister at Stonehaven, David Todd – which led some to declare his election a 'triumph' for voluntaryism – Cowan nevertheless displayed an affection for Scotland's older seceding churches often lacking in his Free Church colleagues.[90] A future advocate for union between the two churches in the 1860s, this catholicity included Cowan contributing to remove a large portion of a local United Secession congregation's debt. Gestures such as this ensured that while Cowan was 'nominally a Free Churchman' he was 'no sectary', and led voluntaries such as Todd to regard the candidate and his family as 'true liberals in religion' as well as politics. Cowan's affection for his voluntary counterparts and prominent position within the Free Kirk laity helped ease any remaining fears over the harmoniousness of the alliance and contributed to his resounding victory, defeating Macaulay by almost 600 votes.[91] Of the 1,441 votes cast for Cowan, 563 were from Free Churchmen and 493 were cast by United Presbyterians.[92]

Though the dissenting alliance lauded Cowan's 'honesty and independence' free from partisan 'cliquery', his election was inevitably criticised by

86. *Nonconformist*, 11 August 1847; Hutchison, *Political History of Scotland*, 65.
87. *Reasons for declining to vote in favour of Mr Macaulay*, 4, 6.
88. *John O'Groat Journal*, 13 August 1847.
89. *Nonconformist*, 11 August 1847.
90. *John O'Groat Journal*, 13 August 1847; *Eclectic Review*, xxii (September 1847), 377.
91. *John O'Groat Journal*, 13 August 1847.
92. Morton, *Ourselves and Others*, 220.

the Whig press as an example of those very characteristics.[93] The London *Daily News* described the coalition behind Cowan as 'one of the most dishonest and shabby' in electoral history, while the *Spectator* claimed that it was 'not liberalism' which had ousted Macaulay from his seat in parliament 'but sectarianism'.[94] The Edinburgh electorate's preference for Cowan, a 'plain, unlettered' trader, over 'the most brilliant orator and writer of the present day' also provoked considerable dissension among Macaulay's backers. The *Inverness Courier* argued that in choosing Cowan, the 'eloquence' and 'learning' traditionally associated with Edinburgh and embodied by Macaulay had been 'cast away' and replaced by 'commonplace utility, strong pledges, and sectarian zeal'.[95] This claim was dismissed by the radical Todd, who argued that 'considerations of such momentous importance', primarily Maynooth, were more significant than 'admiration for literary prowess'.[96] Nevertheless, to their Whig opponents the 'Edinburgh disgrace' ensured that the dissenting alliance were viewed as 'among the worst enemies religion could have'.[97] The alliance's overt focus on the Maynooth endowment prompted the *Glasgow Argus*, the leading Whig organ on the Clyde, to suggest that Scotland's non-established churchmen, hitherto the fiercest opponents of ecclesiastical restriction, were intent on effectively restoring a system of tests on Britain and Ireland's Catholic population. The *Argus* accused the dissenters of the anti-Maynooth alliance, formerly 'synonymous with liberality and toleration', of making Scotland 'one of the most intolerant countries in Europe'.[98]

However, while the anti-Maynooth aspect of the 1847 general election provoked the fiercest criticism from ousted Whigs, it was not the sole defining issue of the campaign. In fact, one observer commented that the success of the Liberals across Britain was partly due to the fact that 'no great question' arose during the campaign to act as a 'watchword' for one of the parties.[99] Though Maynooth certainly provided a focal point for the dissenting alliance in 1847, their proposed candidates often adopted other, more secular policies. As we have seen in Edinburgh, Cowan's campaign also drew on the anti-Whig and anti-Macaulay sentiment building among the city's dissenters. As Henry Cockburn acknowledged at the time of the election, Macaulay, 'with all his admitted knowledge, talent, eloquence, and worth, is not popular'.[100] The personal nature of the Independent Liberal Committee's attack on Macaulay was highlighted by the London *Daily News*. The newspaper pointed out that while Macaulay's

93. *Nonconformist*, 11 August 1847.
94. London *Daily News*, 17 June 1852; *Spectator*, 7 August 1847.
95. *Inverness Courier*, 3 August 1847.
96. *John O'Groat Journal*, 13 August 1847.
97. *Perthshire Advertiser*, 19 August 1847.
98. *Glasgow Argus*, 18 August 1847.
99. *Perthshire Advertiser*, 19 August 1847.
100. Cockburn, *Journal of Henry Cockburn*, ii, 158–9.

support for the Maynooth grant was presented as the primary focus of the rejection of his candidature, no such opposition was targeted against his fellow Whig and supporter of the endowment, William Gibson Craig, who secured the second of Edinburgh's seats at Westminster alongside Cowan. To the Whigs, Maynooth was nothing more than a 'poor and paltry reason' for insulting 'such an ornament of the liberal cause'.[101] Combined with a broader political platform, Cowan's victory also owed much to the influence and support of external secular organisations such as the Excise Reform Association, though the *Nonconformist* rightfully acknowledged that even without that society's votes, Cowan would still have won.[102] Similarly in Glasgow, MacGregor's campaign tended to focus more on his expertise in free trade and foreign affairs than the future of state endowments.[103]

Yet a broader platform that utilised but which was not wholly reliant upon Maynooth did not always indicate success. At Greenock, Alexander Dunlop, the harbinger of dissenting co-operation only two years before, was defeated by the Whig Lord Melgund due to the voluntaries' refusal to support the Free Churchman. Despite Dunlop's expression of quasi-voluntary views regarding Maynooth, he believed that an 'old grudge' concerning his status as a militant anti-voluntary throughout the 1830s ultimately cost him his seat.[104] It is clear that while Maynooth served as an effective common ground on which Scotland's dissenting churches could unite as a cohesive electoral force, in constituencies where the grant failed to dominate political discourse the lingering tensions between Free Churchmen and voluntaries were present just below the surface. Though Greenock represented the only significant failure of the pragmatic dissenting coalition, it was obvious to its leaders that a broad anti-Whig agenda could not consistently hold together Scotland's dissenters in stable political union without the pull of Maynooth. In any case, the national success of 1847 proved that these wider political gestures were not necessary to secure sufficient support from the dissenting electorate.

The 1852 General Election

At the following general election of 1852, the increasingly narrow political agenda adopted by the dissenting alliance, focusing almost solely on their shared opposition to Maynooth, was influenced and aided by the perceived threat to British Protestantism posed by the so-called 'papal aggression'. As discussed in the previous chapter, the aggression reignited anti-Catholic zeal in Britain and refocused militant evangelical opposition to the Maynooth endowment. Delivering a speech at the annual meeting of

---

101. London *Daily News*, 17 June 1852.
102. *Inverness Courier*, 3 August 1847; *Nonconformist*, 11 August 1847.
103. *Inverness Courier*, 3 August 1847.
104. *Greenock Advertiser*, 3 August 1847.

the Scottish Reformation Society in December 1851, William Goold warned that the Vatican's new ultramontane policies multiplied the 'dangers' of 1845. In a pointed address aimed at Britain's statesmen, Goold directly linked the passing of the Maynooth Act to the abortive Young Ireland rebellion of 1848 – 'in which many of the priesthood were implicated' – and the 'insult' of the papal aggression. According to Goold, popery was the 'unrelenting enemy of light and freedom', and 'all the education you give its priests at Maynooth, only serves to render them the more able to undermine the fabric of your civil and religious liberties'.[105] This evangelical fear of the enemy within, an endowed and energetic Catholic priesthood, underpinned and strengthened the anxiety surrounding the papal aggression, the external danger to Britain's Protestant state and society. If Rome housed the imperial Antichrist, Maynooth was the centre of rebellion.[106] In Scotland, this sense of fear once again led to inevitable suspicion of the politicians at Westminster. The Whig government's claim that 'the country may now feel at rest' thanks to their purported resistance to the papacy's ultramontane policies was unsurprisingly rejected by the dissenting alliance. According to one voluntary commentator, despite the mildly punitive Ecclesiastical Titles Bill of 1851, the Whigs' politico-religious views were 'unchanged'.[107] Russell's response to the restoration of the Catholic hierarchy failed to win over discontented liberal dissenters as he had hoped and antagonised both the Peelites and Irish MPs who had hitherto propped up his government. Russell's Whig government would collapse in February 1852, to be replaced by a minority Conservative government under Edward Smith-Stanley (the Earl of Derby), which would make marginal gains at the July election by playing the Protestant card.[108]

The papal aggression also sparked widespread popular protest that was instrumental in facilitating the single-issue politics pursued by the dissenting alliance during the 1852 general election campaign.[109] Reporting on concurrent meetings in Glasgow and Edinburgh in protest against the Maynooth grant, the *Aberdeen Journal* remarked that the papal aggression's supposed affront to British sovereignty had given rise to renewed vigour and opposition to the endowment. Though the *Journal* 'thought that the much-vexed matter of the Maynooth Grant had been set at rest' by 1851, the aggression 'had stirred up the anti-papal spirit in some quarters too deeply for it to settle down again'.[110] As the elections of 1852 approached, Maynooth once again proved the most prominent talking point of the political campaign. The anti-Catholic hostility and anxiety stemming from the

105. W. H. Goold, *The Maynooth Endowment, a sin and a blunder* (Edinburgh, 1852), 3–4.
106. Wallis, 'Anti-Maynooth Campaign', 527.
107. *Reasons for declining to vote in favour of Mr Macaulay*, 8.
108. Parry, *Rise and Fall*, 174–5; Alan Sykes, *The Rise and Fall of British Liberalism, 1776–1988* (London, 1997), 39.
109. D. G. Paz, *Popular Anti-Catholicism in Mid-Victorian England* (Stanford, 1992), 8–12.
110. *Aberdeen Journal*, 17 December 1851.

papal aggression ensured that, in contrast to 1847, 'one opinion upon one point' was all that was required to unite the disparate parties of the dissenting alliance.[111] The Scottish Reformation Society's organ the *Bulwark* urged Scotland's electors to 'set all considerations of ordinary politics aside' and to vote only for candidates who opposed the endowment of Maynooth, such as the Free Churchman Cowan.[112] Commenting on the results of the election, one English newspaper noted the dominance of the Maynooth issue over all other political matters, observing that in Scotland 'religious tests have been applied to, and religious pledges exacted from, candidates from whom no single pledge upon political questions was required'.[113] To a large extent, this narrower policy was extremely successful at the polls, and built upon the momentum established in 1847.[114] The national dominance of the alliance led many radical commentators to describe it as the 'death blow' of the old Whig party against which dissenters had been struggling since 1832.[115] In the face of a considerable but ultimately humiliated Whig counteroffensive, every seat won by the dissenting alliance five years before was retained, including Aberdeen, Paisley and Wick, while Alexander Dunlop finally secured Greenock following Lord Melgund's withdrawal to Glasgow.[116]

Learning from the mistakes of the previous campaign, Dunlop made great pains to emphasise his opposition to the Maynooth endowment and popery in general. He argued that the papal aggression exposed the papacy as the 'avowed enemy' of liberty, 'stalking over the continent of Europe'. 'The urgent cry of freedom' voiced by the Free Church lawyer added 'new stimulus to all the considerations which should impel earnest efforts to secure the withdrawal of the support now given by us to its deadliest foe'.[117] Despite some ultra-voluntary objections, Dunlop received a requisition totalling 474 signatures, which according to the *Greenock Advertiser* was one of the most numerously signed in the constituency's electoral history. This prompted Melgund to stand down from the contest, citing a desire to avoid divisions within the Liberal party and risk losing the seat to a Tory candidate.[118] However, in private Melgund confessed that the overbearing presence of the Maynooth debate during the campaign was the primary reason for his withdrawal and accused the 'untiring efforts' of the dissenting alliance of producing and cultivating the public hostility to the grant. Criticising the one-dimensional nature of the alliance's tactics,

111. *Caledonian Mercury*, 19 April 1852.
112. *Bulwark, or Reformation Journal*, i (January 1852), 162–3.
113. *Huddersfield and Holmfirth Examiner*, 21 August 1852.
114. London *Daily News*, 17 June 1852.
115. *Glasgow Herald*, 9 July 1852.
116. Hutchison, *Political History of Scotland*, 66–7; *Fife Herald*, 15 July 1852; *John O'Groat Journal*, 23 July 1852; *Glasgow Gazette*, 10 July 1852.
117. *Greenock Advertiser*, 10 July 1852.
118. *Greenock Advertiser*, 28 May, 8 June, 10 July 1852.

Melgund conceded that 'Maynooth is the great point of opposition. What the nature of the opposition will be upon points other than that of Popery is not very plain.'[119] To Dunlop's opponents, Maynooth was the 'stalking horse' that ensured the Free Churchman's victory over Melgund, an otherwise identical candidate on every other issue.[120] Following Melgund's withdrawal, Dunlop defeated the Tory James Elphinstone, ironically a fellow opponent of Maynooth but much more ambivalent in his denunciation of the grant.[121] Melgund retreated to Glasgow, only to find a similar singular emphasis on the Maynooth question, and finished last in the polls behind the dissenting alliance's sitting MPs, MacGregor and Hastie.[122] This resounding defeat was due to a curious combination of the strength of the anti-Maynooth alliance and the unwillingness of the Catholic electorate to vote for an adherent, and brother-in-law, of Lord John Russell, author of the Ecclesiastical Titles Bill.[123] Despite the evidence of the 1847 general election, Melgund and the Whigs had underestimated the strength of anti-Maynooth sentiment as a viable electoral strategy throughout Scotland.[124]

Unsurprisingly, the dissenting alliance's successful ambition to place Maynooth as the defining issue and 'watchword' of the 1852 elections, particularly at Greenock and Glasgow, was viewed by their humbled Whig opponents as cementing the religious bigotry prevalent in an increasingly fractious Liberal party in Scotland.[125] The *Scotsman* warned that the national success of the anti-Maynooth faction, 'Liberal in nothing but name', would render the Liberal cause 'a nonentity and a sham not worth fighting for', while Scotland would become 'a Presbyterian Rome scarcely fit for living in'.[126] To the Whigs, the Maynooth question was steeped in sectarian conflict beyond the anti-popery traditionally associated with evangelical Presbyterianism. In this interpretation, the issue over the endowment was 'swelled by intolerance and vote-hunting immeasurably beyond its real importance', and was cultivated by the alliance to 'keep out men of ability, honesty, and experience, and to get in men destitute of any qualification save the willingness to swallow anything that is placed before them'.[127] This depiction of Maynooth as the stalking horse concealing the sectarian ambitions of Scotland's dissenting electors was particularly evident at Wick. Samuel Laing's victory over the incumbent MP James Loch exhibited, according to the *Scotsman*, the workings of a political 'engine', not actuated by 'religious fanaticism' but 'by political factiousness and personal spites or

---

119. Hutchison, *Political History of Scotland*, 67.
120. *Greenock Advertiser*, 23 April 1852; *Falkirk Herald*, 24 June 1852.
121. *Greenock Advertiser*, 4 May 1852.
122. *Glasgow Citizen*, 6 July 1852; *Glasgow Gazette*, 10 July 1852.
123. *Edinburgh Evening Courant*, 10 July 1852; *Scotsman*, 7 July 1852.
124. *Greenock Advertiser*, 9 July 1852; Hutchison, *Political History of Scotland*, 67.
125. *Scottish Press*, 7 May 1852.
126. *Scotsman*, 15 June 1852.
127. *Dundee, Perth, and Cupar Advertiser*, 7 May 1852.

ambition'. Though Loch attempted to make concessions to the strength of the dissenting alliance and its 'Maynooth mania' by vowing to vote against the grant in parliament, the Free Churchman Laing was backed instead and took the seat by a narrow margin. This episode led the *Scotsman* to conclude that 'it is not enough that, on the subject of bigotry or prescription, you happen to agree with them, or consent to do whatever they shall bid – you must also be one of their own clique or of their own selection'.[128] In Edinburgh, Henry Cockburn similarly recoiled at the 'bitterness of religious hostility' evident during the city's election, and what he regarded as the 'prevalence and intensity of our bigotry'.[129] However, unlike in the rest of Scotland, the overwhelming sectarianism of the Edinburgh campaign, though once again revolving around the Maynooth issue, was played out between the two dissenting churches.

While in 1847 Edinburgh showcased how efficiently and effectively the dissenting alliance could function, the 1852 election in Scotland's capital highlighted both its fundamental weaknesses and the fault lines that remained between Free Churchmen and voluntaries almost a decade after the Disruption. The overt hostility of this campaign focused on the refusal of the Free Church faction of the Independent Liberal Committee to support the voluntary Lord Provost Duncan McLaren's candidacy. A member of Edinburgh's Bristo Street United Presbyterian Church, McLaren was regarded by fellow radicals such as James Aytoun as the 'life and soul' of the anti-Maynooth campaign in the city.[130] Like much of the voluntary antagonism to the grant, McLaren opposed Maynooth on the basis that he was 'opposed to all grants of that kind'.[131] The anti-Maynooth zeal exhibited by McLaren ensured his role as one of the masterminds within the Central Board of the 1847 electoral coup that unseated Macaulay, a long-standing public adversary of the Edinburgh draper.[132] However, by 1852 McLaren was intent to move Edinburgh Liberalism beyond the confines of the alliance and what he regarded as the Free Church's overt anti-Catholic hostility. Believing that a party 'could not be built on bigotry alone', he aimed to pursue a more orthodox radical agenda and build the 'nucleus' of a new 'Independent' Liberal party with a broader political platform that included electoral reform.[133]

In this period, McLaren was becoming increasingly influenced by leading Manchester Radicals such as his now brother-in-law John Bright. Led by Bright and Richard Cobden and including several prominent Scots

128. *Scotsman*, 28 July 1852.
129. Cockburn, *Journal of Henry Cockburn*, ii, 284.
130. *Standard*, 18 May 1869.
131. Duncan McLaren, *Evidence given before the Select Committee*, 22.
132. For example, Duncan McLaren, *Who has 'perverted' and 'distorted' Mr Macaulay's letter? A letter to the editor of the Scotsman* (Edinburgh, 1844); McLaren, *Substance of a speech delivered at the meeting of the Edinburgh Anti-Corn Law Association*, 3.
133. *Standard*, 16 April 1852; Millar, 'Maynooth and Scottish Politics', 239–40.

such as McLaren, William Ewart and Samuel Laing, this group of 'entrepreneurial radicals' launched a campaign in the early 1850s to build upon the success of the anti-Corn Law movement by pursuing further business-friendly policies, such as wider free trade arrangements, and the reduction of unnecessary government expenditure (particularly militarily and in the Empire) and therefore direct taxation.[134] A typically middle-class dissenter, McLaren's voluntaryism, political liberalism and business acumen (as baillie and treasurer of Edinburgh town council in the 1830s he was credited with steadying the city's struggling finances) allowed him a foot in both entrepreneurial and religious radical camps, and ensured that according to his supporters his views on the 'important points', including voluntaryism, are 'sound, enlarged, and comprehensive'.[135] However, to his political opponents and even former benefactors such as James Robie (the proprietor of the *Caledonian Mercury* and *Weekly Herald*), McLaren was synonymous with the 'selfishness, meanness, and ingratitude' inherent in the typical Tory and Whig depiction of Radicalism.[136]

Months prior to the 1852 election, McLaren and his pretensions for moulding an Edinburgh ultra-liberal party under his guidance were ridiculed by the *Dundee Courier*. According to the newspaper, McLaren was part of the 'Edinburgh shopocracy', a clique of twenty to thirty 'officious busy-bodies . . . who take it upon them to speak and act in all political movements for the citizens of the Modern Athens'. The *Courier* argued that McLaren's radical faction claimed to speak 'not only in the name of the citizens of Edinburgh, but of the entire people of Scotland', while 'their modesty was not a whit behind that of John Bright and his colleagues in the Manchester coterie'.[137] Derisively known as the 'Rose Street cabal', a reference to the Edinburgh United Presbyterian Church in which McLaren's dissenting Central Board was founded, this 'ultra' wing of the Liberal party was accused of pulling the wires of their Independent 'puppets'.[138] To his critics, McLaren appeared to be attempting to assert the dominance of a small band of voluntary radicals over the entire Independent Liberal movement. According to the *Standard*, this 'clique' sought the 'exclusion of all Whigs' and every other candidate 'who is not both radical and voluntary', a policy which would 'exactly suit the views of the "Gracious Duncan" and his Bright associates'.[139]

This desire to move Edinburgh Liberalism beyond the narrow sectarian confines of the anti-Maynooth alliance towards a more broadly radical political agenda, combined with the ultra-voluntary reputation of McLaren's Rose Street faction, inevitably placed a strain on Free Church relations

134. Hutchison, *Industry, Reform and Empire*, 258.
135. *Reasons for declining to vote in favour of Mr Macaulay*, 23.
136. James Robie to Andrew Fyfe, Edinburgh, 10 June 1867, NLS, McLaren Papers, MS 24782.
137. *Dundee Courier*, 14 January 1852.
138. *Dundee Courier*, 21 April 1852; *Standard*, 16 April 1852.
139. *Standard*, 16 April 1852.

with their fellow dissenters in the city. While there appeared to be an initial understanding between the two churches that they 'mutually aid each other in procuring candidates to represent their respective parties', this rapidly fell apart following the decision of the United Presbyterian portion of the Independent Liberal Committee to nominate McLaren as their candidate alongside the Free Kirk's sitting MP Cowan.[140] Although reticent to accept the nomination to begin with, McLaren threw himself into the campaign 'with so much ardour', according to Cobden, 'that he seems bent upon winning both seats'.[141] The debate over the establishment principle, hitherto largely obscured within the alliance by political pragmatism, came to the fore following McLaren's nomination. Hugh Miller reminded readers of the *Witness* of the Lord Provost's history as the 'lay leader of voluntaryism' and the staunch and 'not very scrupulous' enemy of non-intrusionism during the Ten Years' Conflict.[142] Significantly, suspicion over McLaren's reputation as an ardent voluntary clouded his support for the anti-Maynooth campaign, the one remaining unifying feature of the alliance, as the Free Kirk faction forced him to affirm that his opposition to the Maynooth grant was based on both 'sound' Protestant as well as voluntary principles. In a clear attempt to appease, somewhat vainly, this groundswell of Free Church opposition, McLaren declared 'without hesitation or qualification' the 'decided Protestant principles' of both himself and the United Presbyterian Church.[143]

Free Church concerns about McLaren's 'Protestant' stance were not unfounded. In 1855 he claimed that voluntaryism was the 'only ground really defensible' in opposition to Maynooth, and in 1869 he even voted in favour of the grant, in order to maintain his brother-in-law John Bright in a Liberal government dependent on Irish votes.[144] Perhaps unsurprisingly then, as one Free Church elector acknowledged at a meeting of the Independent Liberal Committee, opposition to the Lord Provost was largely based on personal reasons, alongside these ecclesiastical and ideological concerns. In the months leading up to the 1852 election, McLaren was on the receiving end of a litany of personal attacks from both the Whigs and the Free Church. The *Scotsman* pointed out what they believed to be the United Presbyterian's 'personal bitterness and malignity', while Sir William Johnston, McLaren's Free Church predecessor as Lord Provost of Edinburgh, disparaged him as a 'cold little snake'.[145] The London *Standard* was perhaps most scathing in its assessment of the 'rampant' radical voluntary, noting 'as when the pot boils the scum rises to the top, so in

140. *Standard*, 16 April 1852; *Scotsman*, 16 June 1852.
141. Anthony Howe (ed.), *The Letters of Richard Cobden, vol. ii, 1848–1853* (Oxford, 2010), 404.
142. *Witness*, 10 July 1852; Mackie, *Duncan McLaren*, i, 295.
143. *Scotsman*, 16 June 1852; Mackie, *Duncan McLaren*, ii, 32–3.
144. Mackie, *Duncan McLaren*, ii, 33–4; *Hansard's Parliamentary Debates*, 3rd series, vol. cxcvi (6 May 1869), 277.
145. *Scotsman*, 12 May 1852.

popular agitation, persons are brought into notice who would otherwise have remained in the obscurity to which they were doomed by birth and position'.[146]

The personal, ideological and sectarian gulf that had opened within the dissenting alliance in Edinburgh resulted in a split within the Independent Liberal Committee into two distinct sections of 'Independents' and 'Ultras', each containing fifteen members and broadly representing the Free and United Presbyterian churches respectively. A preliminary meeting was arranged in April at Queen Street Hall to discuss a potential resolution. While opposition to the Maynooth endowment was reiterated as a prerequisite for any Liberal candidate to stand for parliament, it was proving to be the only unifying issue. The Original Seceder and soon-to-be Free Churchman William McCrie acknowledged at the meeting that 'there was far more difference' on the 'question of voluntaryism and the connection between the Church and the State . . . than there was on the subject of Maynooth'.[147] Resistance to the endowment may have offered an increasingly narrow common platform for the dissenting alliance, but the growing emphasis on the nature of the church–state relationship provided the most significant obstacle to its ability to function effectively. This would be exacerbated by McLaren's insistence on publicly maintaining a voluntary-infused opposition to Maynooth throughout the election campaign.

Despite the perceived need to uphold his Protestant credentials in the face of Free Church anti-papal hostility, and his active participation in Begg's Reformation Society, McLaren nevertheless remained vocal in his voluntary objections to the endowment. As early as 1843, he urged Edinburgh dissenters to give the Whigs 'no encouragement . . . to play fast and loose with their principles' regarding Maynooth.[148] Campaigning for election, he emphasised his religious identity as a United Presbyterian to legitimise his opposition to Maynooth and all other religious endowments, arguing that 'the body to which I belong has no grant. It desires none. It would take none. I am prepared to put other bodies having grants in the same position.' McLaren stressed the equal importance of opposing all such grants, without the sectarian significance bestowed upon Maynooth by the Free Church. Abolishing the Maynooth grant, according to McLaren, was no more critical to the voluntary cause than the *regium donum* or the funding of the Episcopal clergy in the West Indies. Addressing Edinburgh's electors, the Lord Provost vowed to 'let [these grants] come in whatever form or shape they please, I will vote against them all'.[149] McLaren eschewed the 'bigotry' associated with the Free Kirk's opposition to Maynooth to such an

---

146. *Standard*, 16 April 1852.
147. *Edinburgh Evening Courant*, 15 April 1852; *Morning Post*, 17 April 1852.
148. Mackie, *Duncan McLaren*, i, 304–5.
149. *Scotsman*, 16 June 1852.

extent that he actively pursued Roman Catholic votes during the election campaign, despite his outspoken objection to the endowment.[150]

McLaren's staunch refusal to make his voluntary ideals a simple matter of forbearance was indicative of his desire to assert a 'will of my own' in Edinburgh politics, rather than any allegiance to his dissenting background. By pursuing a more orthodox radical agenda, free from what he perceived to be the fanatical shackles of Free Church support, McLaren affirmed that he would 'not be an instrument in their hands for any purposes whatever'.[151] While the Lord Provost and the Central Board had utilised the fervour and single-mindedness of the anti-Maynooth campaign in 1847 to great effect in their bid to create an Independent Liberal party in Edinburgh, by 1852 he deemed its dissolution pivotal to that very goal. As was the case at Greenock five years before, without the singular pull of Maynooth the dissenting alliance collapsed under its own weight. Following the 'Ultra' wing's nomination of McLaren alongside Cowan, their Free Church counterparts 'decidedly refused to have anything to do with him'. For the remainder of the campaign, both factions acted 'in perfect independence of each other'.[152] By splitting the 'winning alliance' of 1847, according to the London *Daily News*, McLaren and the Ultras were 'playing a bolder and more extensive game'. However, while British Liberals at this time were focused on 're-uniting and extending' their party in the face of the Earl of Derby's new 'unworthy' and 'unscrupulous ministry', the voluntaries in Edinburgh were 'sowing discord and dissension broadcast among reformers'.[153] This discord extended to a fraught relationship between the two Independent Liberal candidates. Cowan expressed his disappointment at what he believed to be McLaren's friendly overtures towards Macaulay, the old Whig foe from 1847, in the hope of an electoral pact. The Free Church MP claimed that 'it must be a miserable cause surely which requires to be propped up by such expedients as these', though McLaren strongly denied any rumours of a possible voluntary–Whig alliance as a 'mere trick by the enemy'. Nevertheless, in a thinly veiled attack on his opponent and former supporter's personal and public character, Cowan declared that a potential political reunion between the competing Free Church and voluntary factions was 'impossible'.[154]

In the end, McLaren and the Rose Street Session were deemed 'too radical', and a deliberate late surge of votes for Cowan, viewed as 'less objectionable' in his political creed by conservatives, proved just enough to push the Lord Provost into third place behind the Free Churchman and Macaulay, ironically this time the profiteer of a less than principled

---

150. Alexander Nicholson (ed.), *Memoirs of Adam Black* (Edinburgh, 1885), 164–5.
151. *Dundee Courier*, 21 April 1852; Millar, 'Maynooth and Scottish Politics', 239, 247–51.
152. *Dundee Courier*, 21 April 1852.
153. London *Daily News*, 17 June 1852.
154. *Caledonian Mercury*, 15 July 1852.

political coup.¹⁵⁵ The 'winning alliance' of Free Churchman and voluntary appeared to be in tatters. The hostile atmosphere surrounding McLaren and the dissenting alliance continued after the election. The *Dundee Courier* described the results as a redemption for the Whigs after the manner in which Macaulay was 'scurvily treated' in 1847, and hoped that McLaren would 'henceforth confine himself to his own humble and appropriate vocation'. The newspaper claimed that the radical leader's return 'would have reflected no credit on Edinburgh, and would have added no dignity to the House of Commons'.¹⁵⁶

The failure of the dissenting alliance in Edinburgh brought to the foreground underlying tensions between the leading members of the two churches beyond the world of electoral politics. These included the dispute over the future of national education in Scotland (see Chapter Eight), a contentious subject that dominated public debate after 1850 and increasingly overshadowed both Maynooth and the political and ecclesiastical cooperation enjoyed by Scotland's dissenters. The education controversy, and in particular the disputes over the role of religious instruction in the proposed national state-run schools system (a reimagining of the traditional debate over the state's influence on the church) would, in a similar manner to the Edinburgh election, pit the voluntaries against the Whigs and the Candlish-led section of the Free Kirk. The divisive nature of this issue was most keenly felt during the Stirling burghs election of that year. While the combined strength of anti-Maynooth sentiment at Stirling was enough to hasten the incumbent MP and Manchester Radical J. B. Smith's retirement to Stockport (only for the Unitarian to be greeted with similar anti-papal hostility there), his replacement James Anderson proved a major source of discontent among the Free Church electorate due to his 'long-held' and 'earnestly expressed' voluntary views on national education.¹⁵⁷ Though Anderson eventually secured a narrow majority to take the seat thanks to strong radical support in Dunfermline, the Free Kirk's backing of the Whig John Miller highlighted the potential threat of issues such as the education controversy to the dissenting political alliance.¹⁵⁸

A lingering suspicion of increased ecclesiastical co-operation had also emerged in this period within certain sections of Scottish dissent, which as discussed in the fourth chapter led to direct hostility following George Sinclair's 1857 resolutions for union between the Free and United Presbyterian churches. Politically, the Edinburgh split sowed the seeds for the eventual collapse of the anti-Maynooth alliance across Scotland by the time of the following general election. To Scotland's dissenters, ecclesiasti-

---

155. Charles Cowan, *Reminiscences* (privately, 1878), 256; Nicholson, *Memoirs of Adam Black*, 164–5.
156. *Dundee Courier*, 14 July 1852.
157. *Lloyd's Weekly Newspaper*, 11 July 1852; *Fife Herald*, 25 March 1852.
158. Millar, 'Maynooth and Scottish Politics', 254–5.

cal and political co-operation and union were intrinsically linked. Following McLaren's defeat, the *Free Church Magazine* noted the deteriorating relations between the two denominations at both the pulpit and the polling booth. The writer claimed that his United Presbyterian 'friends' were 'angry' at the Free Kirk's claim to be the 'Historical Church of Scotland' following the Original Secession union of the same year, and its subsequent assertion that the secession in Scotland 'was now extinct'. 'Last, but certainly not least', the United Presbyterians, according to the Free Church writer, were 'angry beyond all example at our not choosing to support, as member of Parliament for the metropolis, a man whose questionable conduct has deservedly deprived him of the great confidence of the great majority of the electors'.[159]

This 'spirit' of anger, suspicion and hostility alluded to by the *Free Church Magazine*, in both an ecclesiastical and political context, was notably evident in the seemingly 'violent and reckless abuse' that appeared in a series of publications in the aftermath of the Edinburgh election.[160] According to a *United Presbyterian Magazine* editorial entitled 'Union with the Free Church – Why Not?', McLaren's defeat and the fracturing of the anti-Maynooth alliance were a result of the 'crooked policy' of Free Churchmen who 'could not forget their ancient grudge against the Lord Provost'. The magazine criticised what it regarded as the hypocritical actions of the Free Church electors who, with all their 'talk about Protestantism and Maynooth', preferred Macaulay, a determined supporter of the endowment, over the voluntary candidate. The Free Church opposition to McLaren, according to the writer, was based solely on his voluntaryism, and with a direct attack on the co-operation that had emerged within Scottish dissent since the Disruption, he advised his fellow United Presbyterians to 'learn to support no candidate who is a Free Churchman'.[161] This antagonistic sentiment was repeated elsewhere, with the *Nonconformist* expressing hope that 'Scottish voluntaries will break up in good earnest the long truce which they have observed with Free Churchmen'.[162] The *Scottish Press*, an influential United Presbyterian organ, in an article ominously entitled 'Beware of Free Church Co-operation', railed against their dissenting colleagues as a 'domineering sect'. By rejecting McLaren, Edinburgh's Free Churchmen had 'cast every indignity upon their fellow Dissenters' and proved that 'the alliance they offer is hollow'. According to the *Scottish Press*, the common Protestantism advanced by co-operation between Scotland's dissenters was a 'bastard' which the Free Kirk had 'baptized with a Christian name'. In a scathing indictment of the co-operative measures of the previous decade, the newspaper advised its readers to 'work for your own ends by your

159. *FCM*, i (September 1852), 423.
160. *FCM*, i (October 1852), 434.
161. *UPM*, vi (August 1852), 383.
162. *FCM*, i (October 1852), 433.

own means; but when you are invited to take part in the work of our common Protestantism', including the opposition to Maynooth, 'remember Edinburgh and its last election!'[163]

Unsurprisingly, the Free Church rebutted the notion that the refusal to elect McLaren amounted to the hollowness or rejection of any future dissenting co-operation. The *Free Church Magazine* strongly dismissed the accusation from the *Scottish Press* that Edinburgh's Free Churchmen had 'voted against a thorough Dissenter, whose chief, perhaps only, sin consisted in his being a voluntary Dissenter'.[164] 'We are quite certain', the magazine argued, 'that the Lord Provost was *not* rejected by Free Churchmen because he was a "voluntary Dissenter", and especially that the circumstance of his being a member of the United Presbyterian Church had nothing whatever to do with his rejection.' Instead, the Free Kirk believed that McLaren had stood, not as the representative of one or more of Scotland's dissenting bodies, but 'for himself and by himself' and was 'rejected on his own personal merits or demerits alone'. The writer insisted that this personal animosity towards McLaren, instigated by the Lord Provost's determination to oust Cowan in 'an unmanly and insidious way', was not indicative of 'the slightest desire on the part of the Free Churchmen of Edinburgh to cast *any*, far less *every*, indignity' upon their United Presbyterian counterparts.[165] This desire to depict the dismissal of McLaren as the result of personal rather than sectarian grievances was symptomatic of the Free Kirk's attempt to prevent 'paltry electioneering differences' being 'allowed to disturb and destroy the kindly feeling' between Scotland's dissenters. Pondering what Chalmers would have thought of the overt sectarianism of the Edinburgh election, the magazine maintained that the United Presbyterian and Free churches had a 'mutual claim upon each other for sympathy and support in the time of need', and that co-operation should be continued 'for the attainment of common objects', particularly concerning Maynooth, education, and mission work in Scotland's cities and large towns.[166]

Despite the apparent optimism of this call for united action, the Edinburgh election had left scars among certain sections within the two churches. The Free Church's appeal for brotherly reunion was emphatically dismissed by the *Scottish Press* as a blatant act of opportunistic hypocrisy: 'the men who last week were all swords and daggers are this week bespattering us with otto of roses. But it won't do. A thing, even more offensive than ill usage, is to be slavered upon after the deed is done, and in the hope that soft words will atone for hard kicks.'[167] While the *Free Church Magazine* believed that the hostility of the *Scottish Press* did not represent the

---

163. *Scottish Press*, 21 July 1852.
164. *Scottish Press*, 21 July 1852.
165. *FCM*, i (October 1852), 435–6.
166. *FCM*, i (October 1852), 436–8.
167. *Scottish Press*, 21 July 1852.

'precise and prevalent views' of the United Presbyterian Church as a whole, the periodical conceded that 'to some extent it does', and was spreading even among some of the denomination's 'respectable constituents'.[168] To the Free Church, the promulgation of these views among the United Presbyterian Church was an 'evil omen for the Protestant cause' and dissenting co-operation. 'Much though we long for union with all good and true Protestants', the magazine concluded, 'we would shrink from union with men of such a spirit as this paper breathes.'[169] This premonition would be confirmed by the following general election, as political and ecclesiastical fissures steadily increased and the overarching influence of Maynooth upon Scottish public life significantly waned.

The Fall of the Alliance, 1856–7

In an editorial comment for the *Bulwark* in 1858, James Begg bemoaned that Scotland had succumbed to 'popular melancholy' on the subject of Maynooth.[170] During the general election campaign of the previous year, the *Scotsman* noted that the Maynooth 'nuisance' had been 'considerably abated' and was 'not emitting so much smoke as on some former occasions'.[171] This apathy extended to those politicians who for the previous decade had utilised the debate to secure the votes of their Free Church and voluntary supporters. At a House of Commons vote on an amendment to the grant in April 1856, viewed by Machin as the last realistic chance for the campaign to succeed in parliament, two major beneficiaries of the anti-Maynooth campaign's electoral strength, the voluntaries James Anderson and Alexander Hastie, voted against 'their own opinions' and the principle that state endowments of religion should be abolished in general. This decision was repeated by other British voluntary luminaries such as Edward Miall and ensured, according to the *Scotsman*, that voluntaryism, 'especially in Scotland, seems no longer to be a principle or even a policy advocated in earnest by any organised or recognisable section of the community, or even by any ecclesiastical body – it is becoming a mere cry, beginning in faction and ending in betrayal'.[172]

The general lack of united action and organisation between and within Scotland's dissenting bodies was evident in the Edinburgh by-election of the same year. Following Macaulay's resignation due to ill health, the voluntary Whig Adam Black was elected ahead of the radical Free Churchman Francis Brown-Douglas, thanks in part to the increasingly strained relationship between the two churches. In the aftermath of the

---

168. *FCM*, i (October 1852), 434–5.
169. *FCM*, i (September 1852), 423.
170. *Bulwark, or Reformation Journal*, vii (January 1858), 1–2.
171. *Scotsman*, 28 March 1857.
172. *Scotsman*, 19 April 1856; Machin, *Politics and the Churches in Great Britain*, 255.

split of 1852, the dissenting alliance and Independent Liberal Committee now consisted of three main elements, according to Hugh Miller — the Anti-Maynooth party, the 'Modified Ecclesiastico-Political Free Church party' and the Duncan McLaren party.[173] The 'McLaren party', consisting of the 'most heterogeneous elements of Edinburgh politics', threw its weight behind the relatively unknown Brown-Douglas, and bitterly opposed Black, the 'conspicuous champion' of dissenting principles and McLaren's old friend and political ally.[174] By the mid-1850s, support for the entrepreneurial radical movement, associated with McLaren, was on the wane due to Lord Palmerston's successful prosecution of the Crimean War and widespread support for his aggressive foreign policy towards China. McLaren's personal influence was also hurt by his leading role in the Edinburgh Peace Conference of 1853, which was denounced by even his most ardent radical supporters in the press.[175] The by-election of 1856 therefore offered McLaren an opportunity to regain lost ground and rebuild his radical agenda in Edinburgh. While McLaren was able to rally the support of his former adversaries from 1852, including remarkably Cowan and William Johnston (the former Lord Provost who branded the draper a 'snake' at the previous election), the United Presbyterians were notably reluctant to choose a second Free Church and, in Brown-Douglas' case, establishmentarian representative in favour of the out-and-out voluntaryism of Black.[176] Though Black, like his predecessor Macaulay, was deemed by United Presbyterians to be 'too much a mere Whig to satisfy our idea of a liberal', they did not expect him (unlike Brown-Douglas) to 'belie the professions of a long life, by proving recreant to the cause of civil and religious liberty' and supported his candidature.[177] Later that year, Black would alienate his United Presbyterian supporters by voting for the Maynooth grant in parliament, a decision contrary to the church's interpretation of civil and religious liberty.[178]

Though McLaren's ability to garner Free Church backing in 1856 appears to provide some evidence of a healing of the wounds within the anti-Maynooth alliance, the lack of voluntary support for Brown-Douglas, an opponent of the grant, proved that Maynooth was no longer the deciding issue and that the factional hostility of 1852 had not been entirely dampened. While the United Presbyterian minister John Cairns voted for Brown-Douglas due to his desire for a closer political and ecclesiastical alliance with the Free Church, along with his opposition to both Maynooth and the 'old party Whigs', he recognised that this view was 'unpopular

173. Nicholson, *Memoirs of Adam Black*, 169–70.
174. Nicholson, *Memoirs of Adam Black*, 170; *Scotsman*, 6 February 1856, 28 March 1857.
175. Hutchison, *Industry, Reform and Empire*, 258.
176. *The Spectator*, 9 August 1856.
177. *UPM*, x (March 1856), 140.
178. *UPM*, x (June 1856), 262–5.

with multitudes of dissenters'.[179] The by-election campaign was also characterised by a succession of stunning tirades from both McLaren and his opponents, which resulted in the voluntary leader suing the *Scotsman* for attempting to 'lacerate' his public and private character by holding him up to 'public hatred, contempt and ridicule' through their 'false and calumnious attacks'.[180] According to the newspaper, McLaren was 'deserting principles and traducing friends and deceiving enemies, and acting only for his own purposes, and especially his own malignities'.[181]

This lack of principle within Edinburgh Liberalism, and in particular its McLaren-ite faction, was evident in the group's failed attempt at the following year's general election to persuade Lord John Russell, who remained an influential advocate of the Maynooth grant, to stand in opposition to Cowan, a committed opponent of the endowment.[182] Weakening Free Kirk support for an increasingly impotent Independent Liberal Committee in this period, combined with the voluntary refusal to vote for Brown-Douglas, ensured that Cowan and Black were returned unopposed.[183] The desire to move Scottish politics beyond the Maynooth debate and away from what was regarded as the self-servitude of McLaren's radical voluntary junto was encapsulated by Black's speech at the Edinburgh hustings. Black warned the city's electorate to steer clear of those, 'either from a real bigoted or from a hypocritical cry', that were willing to swallow the 'phantom' of Maynooth, an issue that he argued 'would not in the smallest degree affect the interests or the condition of the people of this country'. Instead, he stressed the influence of the education question, an issue which he acknowledged was 'of such infinite importance' to Scotland's dissenters, and one that proved pivotal to lessening the bonds of the anti-Maynooth agitation that had previously held the non-established churches together in united action.[184]

By 1857 it was clear that the anti-Maynooth campaign was losing its position as a viable electoral platform, and that public opposition to the endowment was no longer crucial to success at the polls. Across Scotland, the old Whig clique regained the position they had ceded a decade before, as the former dissenting alliance lost the majority of its seats after succumbing to division over the Lord Advocate James Moncrieff's education bills of the mid-1850s and the role of religious instruction in the proposed national schools. This pattern was repeated throughout Britain, with the leading Radicals Cobden and Bright losing their seats while the Whig Prime Minister Lord Palmerston earned an impressive majority over

179. Alexander R. MacEwen, *Life and Letters of John Cairns, D.D., LL.D* (London, 1895), 420.
180. *The Times*, 21 August 1856; *Sheffield and Rotherham Independent*, 5 April 1856; *Bradford Observer*, 7 August 1856.
181. *Scotsman*, 6 February 1856.
182. *Scotsman*, 28 March 1857.
183. Hutchison, *Political History of Scotland*, 80–1.
184. *Caledonian Mercury*, 28 March 1857.

Derby's Conservatives.[185] At Glasgow, Alexander Hastie, the profiteer of the original dissenting coup of 1847, was defeated by the Whig Robert Dalglish, a consistent critic of the anti-Maynooth camp, after the MP's former supporters within the Free Church deserted him in protest against his strict voluntary views on the education controversy.[186] A similar rupture within the old alliance occurred in Paisley. Following the retirement of the incumbent Free Church MP Archibald Hastie, the ultra-voluntary Humphrey Crum Ewing was proposed as his replacement.[187] However, less than a week later, over 600 Free Kirk electors, incensed at Crum Ewing's public opposition to the education bills, signed a requisition urging Hastie to reconsider his decision.[188] A firm supporter of Moncrieff's proposed reforms, Hastie would ultimately return to defeat the voluntary candidate, who less than ten days before 'had every reason to believe that he would walk into Parliament without encountering any serious opposition'.[189]

It appeared that the Lord Advocate's bills, and not the Maynooth grant, had become 'the testing-point' of the 1857 election.[190] The failure of Scotland's dissenters to unite to achieve educational reform in the mid-1850s, and the re-entrenchment of sectarian positions that accompanied these debates, resulted in a general disengagement in both the Free and United Presbyterian churches with any attempt at a political alliance based on a shared opposition to Maynooth.[191] Those still 'pandering' to the 'religious intolerance' of the anti-Maynooth crusade, in the eyes of the *Dundee Advertiser*, were taught by Scotland's electors that 'they were behind the times, and have misunderstood the spirit of the people'.[192] According to the *Scotsman*, the 1857 general election offered 'compendious proof' that the 'Maynooth clamour' was 'no longer even a bigotry, but has become a mere cloak of hypocrisy and a weapon of malignity'.[193] The withering of the anti-Maynooth campaign's importance in the late 1850s was indicative of the recalibration of political alliances that occurred during this period, which overturned the radical–dissenting – and Free Church–United Presbyterian – dominance of the previous decade. While radicals began to turn away from appeasing the 'No Popery' cry of groups such as the Scottish Reformation Society, divisions over school subsidies drove the Free Church into the arms of the Whigs. The 1857 campaign also highlighted

---

185. Anthony Taylor, 'Palmerston and Radicalism, 1847–1865', *Journal of British Studies*, xxxiii (1994), 170–3; Anthony Howe and Simon Morgan (eds), *The Letters of Richard Cobden, vol. iii, 1854–1859* (Oxford, 2012), xxxiv.
186. Hutchison, *Political History of Scotland*, 82; *Dundee, Perth, and Cupar Advertiser*, 3 April 1857.
187. *Paisley Herald*, 21 March 1857.
188. *Paisley Herald*, 28 March 1857.
189. *Paisley Herald*, 4 April 1857.
190. *Caledonian Mercury*, 20 March 1857; *Paisley Herald*, 4 April 1857.
191. Hutchison, *Political History of Scotland*, 80–2.
192. *Dundee, Perth, and Cupar Advertiser*, 3 April 1857.
193. *Scotsman*, 28 March 1857.

the fact that, even within the respective churches, opposition to the endowment was no longer enough to hold together Scotland's dissenters in political alliance.

This was particularly the case at Leith, where the United Presbyterian principal James Harper and the Free Kirk's prominent anti-popery activist James Begg led the opposition to the Free Church Lord Advocate Moncrieff.[194] The united front between Begg and Harper, both prominent antagonists of their opponent's desire to retain governmental control over religious education, arose due to Moncrieff's suggestion that he would not vote against the Maynooth grant in order to preserve peace in Ireland.[195] Harper, having not received a reply from the Lord Advocate on the matter, issued an address to the Leith electors, alerting them to Moncrieff's contentious speech and suggesting that 'the friends of religious liberty ought to withhold their suffrages from any candidate who held such views' on Maynooth.[196] The Begg–Harper faction proceeded to cover Leith's walls with placards calling on all Protestants 'as they value anything sacred, to vote against the Lord Advocate'. The *Scotsman* was quick to note the irony in the evangelical opposition to Moncrieff, a Free Church elder who had devoted his life to Protestantism, in favour of William Miller, who had just returned to Scotland after over two decades working as a merchant in St Petersburg 'among the worse than Papistical natives'. According to the newspaper, Miller failed to express the slightest hint of missionary zeal and on the rare occasions he publicly campaigned 'did not conceal that he neither knew nor cared anything about Maynooth and other such matters'.[197] While Begg's opposition to Moncrieff's candidacy represented an abrupt division within the traditionally unified Free Church vote, Harper's forceful outspokenness – he was accused of clerical dictation by certain sections of the Whig press – also caused a breach within the United Presbyterian body, culminating in members of his own congregation issuing a protest against their minister's actions.[198] Though the *United Presbyterian Magazine* sided with Harper and Begg, the Leith campaign nevertheless provoked a split not only between Scotland's dissenting churches but within them, and emphasised the waning power of Maynooth as a common platform on which all of Scotland's evangelicals could unite.[199] According to a gleeful *Scotsman*, the most vociferous opponent of the anti-Maynooth alliance for over a decade, the Leith and Edinburgh elections of 1857 offered 'the very strongest proofs of the hollowness of this now collapsing humbug'.[200]

194. *Caledonian Mercury*, 28 March 1857.
195. *Roman Catholic Endowment: a correspondence between the Right Hon. The Lord Advocate and James Harper, D.D., Leith* (Edinburgh, 1857).
196. Andrew Thomson, *Life of Principal Harper, D.D.* (Edinburgh, 1882), 175–7.
197. *Scotsman*, 28 March 1857; *Spectator*, 28 March 1857.
198. *UPM*, i (June 1857), 252; Thomson, *Life of Principal Harper*, 177–9.
199. *UPM*, i (May 1857), 240; *UPM*, i (June 1857), 255–6.
200. *Scotsman*, 28 March 1857.

However, despite the breakdown of the anti-Maynooth alliance in the late 1850s, the same period witnessed a fruitful partnership between Begg and McLaren – bastions of the establishmentarian and ultra-voluntary elements of the Free and United Presbyterian churches respectively – concerning issues of political and national reform. Within the Scottish Social Reform Association (SSRA), founded by Begg in 1850, the pair were instrumental in the campaign for franchise reform and the extension of the forty shilling freehold to Scotland. While the introduction of the forty shilling freehold formed part of the SSRA's agenda from 1850, it was only following a Christmas Day meeting in 1856 at the Queen Street Hall in Edinburgh that the question began to receive national attention.[201] Begg and McLaren were the chief speakers and attendees included prominent dissenters Adam Black, Charles Cowan and Patrick Dove. Following the Edinburgh meeting, the movement grew in popularity, and Begg and McLaren were invited to speak on the issue across Scotland in the early months of 1857.[202] The two men also led a deputation to London later that year, and met with the Prime Minister Lord Palmerston to discuss the issue, though an attempt by McLaren at framing a bill to extend the franchise in Scotland was rejected in parliament.[203]

Scottish rights, and Scotland's place within the union, also formed a major part of the rhetoric employed by the Scottish Freehold Movement.[204] Begg and McLaren highlighted the lack of electoral reform in Scotland compared to England as a symbol of national inequality and claimed that the disproportionate power of the aristocracy in Scottish county elections invested them 'with the power of arresting all measures of social progress for Scotland in the British parliament'. This demand for political, social and national 'justice' was most forcefully expressed by McLaren, who would subsequently establish his reputation as the 'member for Scotland' after finally being elected to parliament in 1865. Outlining what he believed to be Scotland's inadequate representation in the House of Commons, the former Lord Provost of Edinburgh asserted his desire for the rights and privileges apparently offered to England and Ireland 'to be common also to Scotland'.[205] Begg drew on his experience of the Disruption and its anti-English sentiment to conclude that Scottish inequality within the United Kingdom, as underscored by the forty shilling freehold campaign, was due to fraud, ignorance and design.[206] In a lecture delivered at the United

---

201. *Edinburgh Evening Courant*, 25 February 1851; *Scotsman*, 26 February 1851; *Caledonian Mercury*, 26 December 1856.
202. Mackie, *Duncan McLaren*, ii, 142–5; *Ayr Advertiser*, 7 May 1857; *Daily Express* (Edinburgh), 21 May 1857; *Falkirk Herald*, 21 May 1857; *Caledonian Mercury*, 21 April 1857, 19 May 1857.
203. *Dumfries and Galloway Standard*, 4 February 1857; *Falkirk Herald*, 12 February 1857, 4 March 1857.
204. Smith, *Memoirs of James Begg*, ii, 323–4.
205. *Caledonian Mercury*, 26 December 1856.
206. James Begg, *Scotland's Demand for Electoral Justice; or, the forty shilling freehold question explained* (Edinburgh, 1857), 4–5.

Presbyterian minister John French's Edinburgh church in January 1850, this perception of inequality even led Begg, a quarter of a century before the rise of Charles Stuart Parnell in Ireland, to call for potential home rule for Scotland if their grievances were not met.[207] The nationalistic sentiment expounded by Begg and associated with the forty shilling freehold movement was perhaps most evident in the short-lived National Association for the Vindication of Scottish Rights (NAVSR), a group that included Begg and McLaren. Offering a constructionist critique of the Treaty of Union, the NAVSR's increasing shift away from its romantic Tory beginnings towards a more radical agenda in its later years attracted other leading dissenters such as Cowan, Hugh Miller and James Peddie. However, like similar attempts to foster a positive political agenda beyond the narrow boundaries of the anti-Maynooth movement, the NAVSR's proto-nationalism failed to attract widespread dissenting support and was criticised by some Free Churchmen for lacking 'Presbyterian fibre'.[208]

Though eventually dismissed as a hollow humbug by the Whigs, the anti-Maynooth campaign was nevertheless instrumental in reshaping Scottish electoral politics after the Disruption, and also proved a useful indicator of the strength of dissenting Presbyterian relations in this period. As this and the previous chapter have illustrated, between 1845 and 1860 the Free and United Presbyterian churches formed a tentative yet functioning alliance, both institutionally and politically, that for the most part succeeded in creating a loose dissenting identity on the grounds of anti-Catholicism. The pragmatic, ideologically ambiguous and expedient nature of the anti-Maynooth coalition offered a platform for Scotland's non-established Presbyterians to challenge what they regarded as the apathy of a Whig and state church establishment, while also tackling the perceived 'errors of Popery' and defending Britain's Protestant constitution. However, while the nationwide success of the alliance at the 1847 and 1852 general elections fundamentally altered the shape of Scottish liberalism in this period, the underlying tensions over the church–state relationship only served, on occasion, to blight an already narrow political platform. Though Maynooth acted as an effective rallying call for both establishmentarians and voluntaries within Scottish dissent, usually for entirely conflicting reasons, these differences threatened to diminish the broader political significance of the alliance beyond the confines of one piece of legislation.

Even during the staggeringly successful campaigns of 1847 and 1852, during which the formerly dominant Whigs were swept aside in most of Scotland's cities and burghs, the rejection of Dunlop at Greenock in 1847 and in particular McLaren's highly contentious Edinburgh defeat five years

---

207. *Caledonian Mercury*, 14 January 1850.
208. Hanham, 'Mid-Century Scottish Nationalism', 156; Mallon, 'A church for Scotland?', 1–24; *North British Review*, xxi (1854), 82, 93.

later emphasised the shortcomings of a dissenting coalition based almost solely on Maynooth. While the difficulties over these candidacies can be dismissed as the result of mere personal antagonisms, their political and most importantly sectarian justifications exposed the lingering significance of voluntaryism, particularly its more radical element, and establishmentarianism in the respective churches' approach to the Maynooth debate. However, while at least some recognition and acceptance of the voluntary-based opposition to the endowment became widespread among the alliance's politicians from both churches, the ubiquity of anti-popery and the furore within Scotland over Maynooth and the purported papal aggression must not be ignored. A strong unified Protestantism was viewed as necessary to combat the organised internal and external threat of Rome, and it is clear from the campaigns that the popular sentiment of 'bigotry' prevailed over disagreements on church–state relations, at least among Scotland's electors. Up to 1852 at least, the ambiguity of principle in the movement and the urgency and obsession with which it fixated on both the Whig and Catholic 'other' ensured that the major ruptures in Free Church–United Presbyterian relations were often pragmatically ignored in the anti-Maynooth alliance, if not completely hidden. However, as these issues became evermore pressing by the mid-1850s, they exposed the fragility of any kind of co-operation between Scotland's dissenting bodies.

PART FOUR

Reforming Scotland: Social Reform and National Education

CHAPTER SEVEN

Recreating the Godly Commonwealth: Urban Mission and Social Reform

While the character of Scottish Presbyterianism was fundamentally altered by the Disruption, Scotland's society was also undergoing significant change. Perhaps most significantly, the 1845 Poor Law Amendment Act removed yet another element of the Established Church's traditional control over Scottish society and brought poor relief under state management.[1] This weakening of the Church of Scotland's position on social issues was compounded by the increasing prospect of a national, state-run education system that would also take the religious and secular instruction of Scotland's children out of the hands of the parishes. These fundamental changes to the social role of the churches afforded dissenters the opportunity for the first time to tackle Scotland's major social issues on equal ground with the national church. The following two chapters will assess the kind of Scotland these dissenters wanted to create after 1843. While the final chapter will focus on the dissenting response to the education debates, this chapter will provide an overview of the reaction to Scotland's changing social context within the Free and United Presbyterian churches. It will question whether a distinct dissenting social outlook was formed in this period, and the extent to which the ideal of the 'godly commonwealth' was reimagined and recreated in its new dissenting context after 1843.

For Thomas Chalmers, the Disruption represented not only the demise of his hopes for a renewed and spiritually independent Established Church, it also appeared to end his ambitions for a godly commonwealth in Scotland. This social ideal, through which Chalmers attempted to import the communal values of the rural parish into Scotland's cities, formed an integral part of his broader aim to reform the state Kirk before 1843. However, as S. J. Brown, T. C. Smout, Stewart Mechie and others have argued, the Disruption proved the 'final failure' of Chalmers' godly commonwealth.[2] According to Brown, any hope of reviving a spirit of 'Christian community' throughout Scotland was thwarted by the competing sectarian aims of the various Presbyterian churches and the denominational competition that

---

1. Hutchison, *A Political History of Scotland*, 73.
2. Brown, *Thomas Chalmers and the Godly Commonwealth*, xiii; Smout, *A Century of the Scottish People*, 182; Stewart Mechie, *The Church and Scottish Social Development, 1780–1870* (London, 1960), 78; Boyd, *Scottish Church Attitudes*, 15.

characterised Scottish religious life after 1843.³ Nevertheless, the burgeoning co-operation between Scotland's dissenters in this period appeared to offer Chalmers a final opportunity in which his godly commonwealth ideal could be realised. While his ambition for social reform prior to the Disruption was intertwined with the ecclesiastical objective of reviving and extending the Church of Scotland, Chalmers' territorial mission schemes after 1843 attempted to capitalise on the changing character of Scottish Presbyterianism in this period and centred on interdenominational co-operation, especially within the major dissenting churches.⁴

This chapter will examine the extent to which the dissenting churches attempted to reinvigorate Chalmers' ideal of the godly commonwealth outside of the Established Church following the Disruption. First, it will assess whether a distinctive dissenting vision of Scottish society appeared after 1843 and how Chalmers and his dissenting supporters, such as the leading United Presbyterian minister John Brown, tried to recreate this social vision through a comprehensive and pan-denominational network of urban territorial congregations in the poorest districts of Scotland's cities. While Brown and Keith Campbell have noted the lingering denominational interests apparent in these urban missions, particularly regarding the Free Church's claim to be the true national church, Donald Withrington emphasised the increasing desire for co-operation between Scotland's dissenters on matters of social reform, along with a growing impatience with the sectarian divisions that prevented the churches from adequately dealing with pressing issues such as poverty and crime.⁵ The chapter will also examine the legacy of Chalmers' interdenominational mission schemes in the period after his death in 1847, and question the extent to which a dissenting 'happy rivalry' was created within both urban mission and other areas of social reform, such as the campaign for working-class housing provision. While not representing as clear an opposition to the Established Kirk's social position as the later campaign for national education, the reform policies of the Free and United Presbyterian churches offered a distinctly pluralist social vision for Scotland, and represented perhaps most visibly the ideal of 'co-operation without incorporation' within non-established Presbyterianism.

The Disruption, the Poor Law and the Changing Face of Scottish Society

The ideal of the godly commonwealth, revived and reimagined by Chalmers, dominated Scottish social thought in the middle decades of the nineteenth

3. Brown, *Thomas Chalmers and the Godly Commonwealth*, 373–4.
4. D. J. Withrington, 'Non-Church-Going, c. 1750–c. 1850: a preliminary study', *RSCHS*, xvii (1972), 107.
5. Brown, 'Thomas Chalmers and the communal ideal', 73–4; Keith A. Campbell, 'The Free Church of Scotland and the Territorial Ideal, 1843–1900' (unpublished PhD thesis, University of Edinburgh, 1999), 18; Withrington, 'Non-Church-Going', 113.

century. As S. J. Brown has summarised, the godly commonwealth formed an integral component of Calvinist plans in the sixteenth and seventeenth centuries to permeate every aspect of social, economic and political life. According to the Calvinist reformers, it represented the shared Presbyterian communal values of benevolence, unity and spirituality, and embodied the rule of God in a covenanted nation. However, the failure of a full-scale Presbyterian social revolution in the seventeenth century and the subsequent eighteenth-century 'age of improvement' rendered such an ideal outdated, intolerant and uncivilised, with the principles of the commonwealth left only to survive in rural areas neglected by the apparent advances of Union, capitalism and the Enlightenment. In these rural areas the commonwealth ideal was preserved by the old orthodox Calvinist preachers and a popular attachment to Scotland's traditional communal values.[6] This communal ideal was embraced by Chalmers while parish minister in the small rural Fife community of Kilmany between 1803 and 1815. He combined this ideal with his new-found evangelicalism and the nineteenth-century middle-class trait of self-reliance as a means of reforming Scottish and British urban society.[7] After his appointment to the Tron Church in Glasgow in 1815, Chalmers sought to import the communal bonds of rural Scotland into urban areas, in which the rapid population growth facilitated by industrialisation and migration from Ireland and the Highlands had resulted in a dislocated and increasingly polarised society that left its poor isolated and vulnerable to the whims of the post-Napoleonic war market economy.[8]

This 'experiment' in urban ministry, most famously employed in Chalmers' St John's parish after his move there in 1819, involved an emphasis on locality, with the larger city parish broken down into small manageable districts in an attempt to revive among the industrialised working class the pastoral care, parish institutions and communal belonging associated with the countryside.[9] Through lay visitations, reform of local education, regular worship services and the severing of ties with voluntary philanthropic societies (which he believed patronised the poor with charity), Chalmers also aimed to instil individual responsibility within these Christian communities and enable the urban working class to help themselves.[10]

6. Brown, *Thomas Chalmers and the Godly Commonwealth*, xv–xviii.
7. Olive Checkland, 'Chalmers and William Pulteney Alison: a conflict of views on Scottish social policy', in A. C. Cheyne (ed.), *The Practical and the Pious: Essays on Thomas Chalmers* (Edinburgh, 1985), 132; Donald MacLeod, 'Chalmers and Pauperism', in Stewart J. Brown and Michael Fry (eds), *Scotland in the Age of Disruption* (Edinburgh, 1993), 70; Mary T. Furgol, 'Chalmers and Poor Relief: an incidental sideline?', in Cheyne, *Practical and Pious*, 120–8; Enright, 'Urbanisation and the Evangelical Pulpit', 405.
8. Brown, *Thomas Chalmers and the Godly Commonwealth*, 96–7; James Obelkevich, *Religion and Rural Society: South Lindsey 1825–1875* (Oxford, 1976), 313.
9. Charles W. J. Withers, *Geography, Science and National Identity: Scotland since 1520* (Cambridge, 2001), 168–9; Checkland, 'Chalmers and Alison', 137.
10. Brown, *Thomas Chalmers and the Godly Commonwealth*, 99–104.

This Victorian method of self-reliance was rooted in Chalmers' campaign against the legal assessment of poor relief. Influenced by the economic theories of Thomas Robert Malthus and Adam Smith, Chalmers believed that the 'English' compulsory system of poor relief was detrimental to both working-class independence and communal benevolence.[11] In his seminal lectures between 1821 and 1826 on the *Christian and Civic Economy of Large Towns*, Chalmers distinguished between poverty and pauperism. Poverty was an inevitable result of industrialised society, and one that could foster neighbourly assistance and self-improvement; legal pauperism – and the perceived 'right' of the poor to public relief – was dangerous to the moral fabric of society, as it broke the bonds of community, eradicated individual responsibility and institutionalised social conflict.[12]

Through his social experiment at St John's, Chalmers aimed to demonstrate that legally assessed poor relief should be abolished and replaced by a parish-based structure that fostered a community centred on the church and neighbourly compassion. While the communal spirit of the St John's operation has been questioned, its successful reduction of pauperism in the parish allowed Chalmers to portray it as a perfect example of his godly commonwealth ideal and a 'proved' plan for social reform for the rest of Britain.[13] However, Chalmers' social policies and his opposition to legal poor relief drew criticism both from within the evangelical wing of his own church and from dissenters unwilling to pay for the enlargement of the Kirk. To these dissenters, the godly commonwealth model was merely a front for the rejuvenation and reinforcement of the Established Church.[14] In many respects this was the case: the 'national regeneration' aimed for by Chalmers for a quarter of a century centred on both society in general and the Church of Scotland, with the Established Kirk presented as the only means through which the godly commonwealth could be achieved.[15]

Of course, the impact of the Disruption upended this relationship between Scottish society and the national church, and forced Chalmers to resituate the godly commonwealth in a religiously pluralist context. The events of May 1843 also coincided with a severe economic downturn and widespread unemployment in Scotland.[16] Mortality rates peaked, worsening social conditions in the major cities resulted in a typhus out-

---

11. Brown, *Thomas Chalmers and the Godly Commonwealth*, 116–17; Furgol, 'Chalmers and Poor Relief', 116–17; Checkland, 'Chalmers and Alison', 130–7.
12. Thomas Chalmers, *The Christian and Civic Economy of Large Towns* (3 volumes, Glasgow, 1823), ii, 50–2.
13. Brown, *Thomas Chalmers and the Godly Commonwealth*, 123–4, 135, 144, 151; Checkland, 'Chalmers and Alison', 130.
14. A. C. Cheyne, *The Transforming of the Kirk: Victorian Scotland's Religious Revolution* (Edinburgh, 1983), 19; Brown, *Thomas Chalmers and the Godly Commonwealth*, 121, 124.
15. A. C. Cheyne, *Studies in Scottish Church History* (Edinburgh, 1999), 88; Brown, 'Christian Socialist movement', 61–3; James Begg, *Pauperism and the Poor Laws; or, Our sinking population and rapidly increasing public burdens practically considered* (Edinburgh, 1849), 14.
16. Brown, *National Churches*, 358.

break in Glasgow among the unemployed poor in 1843, and a cholera epidemic swept Edinburgh and Glasgow later in the decade.[17] A rise in alcohol consumption led to concerns among missionaries and churchmen about drunkenness and increasing immorality and vice.[18] The effects of the depression of the early 1840s led to the popularisation of William Alison's view that the old Scottish Poor Law needed to be reformed.[19] Though Chalmers' views on poor relief had traditionally been acceptable to the middle and upper classes, the Disruption had 'finally torn down the illusory curtain' that adequate relief could be provided within the parish structure.[20]

The realisation that the Church of Scotland, despite Chalmers' insistence, could no longer address the growing social problems solely through voluntary effort also hastened the conclusion of the report of the Royal Commission on the Poor Laws, originally established in January 1843. This report, published in 1844, laid bare the scale of the task, and called into question the extent to which the godly commonwealth ideal could solve Scotland's social ills.[21] It argued that the funds raised through voluntary means by the kirk session for the relief of the poor were in many parishes 'insufficient' to 'provide the commonest necessaries of life' and that the administration of the current system was 'defective'.[22] The opposition of Church of Scotland ministers to any kind of reform that included compulsory relief was criticised in the report, while one later commentator described the eventual amendment of the Poor Law in 1845 as a 'revolt' against the influence of the Church and its responsibility for the care of the poor.[23] The position of the St John's experiment as an apparent illustration of the benefits of the parochial system was also questioned. The *Ayr Advertiser* argued that its success owed more to Chalmers' popularity

17. George Nicholls, *A History of the Scotch Poor Law, in connection with the condition of the people* (London, 1856), 225–6; Michael Flinn (ed.), *Scottish population history from the seventeenth century to the 1930s* (Cambridge, 1977), 377; Peter Hillis, 'Education and Evangelisation: Presbyterian missions in mid-nineteenth century Glasgow', *Scottish Historical Review*, lxvi (1987), 51–2; Ian Shaw, 'John Paton and Urban Mission in Nineteenth-Century Glasgow', *RSCHS*, xxxv (2005), 168–9.
18. Shaw, 'John Paton and Urban Mission', 177–8; Handley, *Irish in Scotland*, 255.
19. Checkland, 'Chalmers and Alison', 134–5.
20. Brown, *Social History of Religion*, 144; M. T. Furgol, 'Thomas Chalmers' Poor Relief theories and their implementation in the early nineteenth century' (PhD thesis, University of Edinburgh, 1987), 346–7.
21. Brown, *Thomas Chalmers and the Godly Commonwealth*, 350; Cheyne, *Studies in Scottish Church History*, 94; S. J. Brown, 'The Disruption and Urban Poverty: Thomas Chalmers and the West Port Operation in Edinburgh, 1844–7', *RSCHS*, xx (1978), 66.
22. *Report from Her Majesty's Commissioners for inquiring into the administration and practical operation of the Poor Laws in Scotland* [Cd. 557], H.C. 1844, xx, 15–16, 53; William Pulteney Alison, *Remarks on the Report of Her Majesty's Commissioners on the Poor Laws of Scotland* (Edinburgh, 1844), 2.
23. *Report on the Poor Laws*, v; *The Poor Law Magazine and Parochial Journal*, iv (October 1876), 507, (November 1876), 614–16.

and ability for self-promotion than any indication of its practical worth as a model for comprehensive reform.[24] However, despite the hostile attitude to Chalmers from advocates of the commission's report, the subsequent 1845 Poor Law Amendment Act arguably retained some of the Free Church leader's views. These included the refusal of relief for the able-bodied when unemployed, and while it also took responsibility for the care of the poor out of the hands of the church, it maintained an ecclesiastical presence in the parochial boards.[25] Nevertheless, the creation of a partly centralised relief system flew directly in the face of the small, parish-based units of the godly commonwealth ideal.[26]

Unsurprisingly, Chalmers was scathing of the report's conclusions, and rejected the introduction of a legal provision 'under which the poor of our land will become more worthless and wretched than before'. He criticised the advocates of such a provision as 'the enemies of their country, and the cruellest enemies of the poor'.[27] However, though the likes of Adam Black called for unity among Scotland's dissenters, Chalmers' hostile stance on reform was not even supported by many of his colleagues in the Free Church.[28] Despite a church-led petition in June 1845 against the bill, claiming that the proposed measure was 'very far short of the remedy required', the Free Church was in general in favour of the new law.[29] At the 1844 General Assembly, it was clear that a significant number of Free Church leaders believed that the parish administration of poor relief was no longer sufficient and that governmental intervention was required.[30] Speaking to the commissioners in the same year, Thomas Guthrie criticised the old Poor Law system and its provision as 'miserably deficient', producing an 'immoral effect' on the habits of the people, and leading to 'temporal misery' from which a minister 'cannot relieve'. Contrary to Chalmers' long-held beliefs, Guthrie argued for a greatly increased provision by the state to address the needs of the poor, and claimed that the old parochial system did not produce the working-class independence sought by the Free Church but instead compelled the poor to beg and pawn their possessions. Rather than foster a Christian community, the lack of suitable poor relief extinguished 'the very feelings of human nature' in the urban poor.[31] Guthrie was supported by William Maxwell Hetherington, who claimed that the Disruption, by 'emptying the plates' of the churches, had exposed

---

24. *Ayr Advertiser*, 4 July 1844.
25. Nicholls, *History of the Scotch Poor Law*, 168.
26. Furgol, 'Thomas Chalmers' Poor Relief theories', 347.
27. *North British Review*, ii (February 1845), 497.
28. *Scottish Herald*, 15 June 1844.
29. *Appendix to the Reports of the Select Committee of the House of Commons on public petitions, session 1845*, 381–2; Begg, *Pauperism and the Poor Laws*, 14.
30. *Scottish Herald*, 1 June 1844.
31. *Poor Law Inquiry (Scotland), Analytical Index to the report and evidence contained in appendices parts I, II, and III. Part VII* [Cd. 544], H.C. 1844, xxvi, 239–40.

the hypocrisy of the Scottish aristocracy who had favoured Chalmers' policies to 'save their own pockets'. Calling on his fellow Free Churchmen to support reform, Hetherington emphasised what he regarded as a class struggle against the landed elite who had robbed the people of their spiritual rights at the Disruption and were now seeking to rid them of their temporal rights also. Reform was necessary to alleviate the condition of the poor as the Disruption had rendered Chalmers' social ideal, for the time being at least, 'impracticable'.[32]

Despite the obvious concern for the poor evident in Guthrie and Hetherington's accounts, the general support for the new poor law in the Free Church was indicative of a move away from the godly commonwealth ideal after 1843. This embrace of government intervention can also be viewed as part of a broader sectarian shift in the new church's social ideals, towards both a middle-class and 'gathered church' mentality.[33] While its 'church of the people' moniker proved relevant in the Highlands, in the Lowland towns and cities, from which the majority of its leadership was derived, the Free Church quickly exemplified the prosperous, industrious and upwardly mobile character traditionally associated with the older dissenting denominations, particularly the United Presbyterians.[34] As Chapter Two illustrated, this association with affluent middle-class society ensured that the Free Church was prosperous enough to sustain the lengthy and expensive building projects undertaken in the first decade after the Disruption, but it also resulted in a financial burden and subsequent alienation of its poorer members due to the demand for funds. This prompted criticism from opponents of the new body, who condemned the Free Kirk's self-proclaimed status as the 'Poor Man's Church' while its middle-class deacons appeared to be arrogantly placing such economic pressure on their working-class congregations.[35]

The increasingly middle-class character of the Free Church, combined with the bitter sectarianism of the Disruption, also had a profound effect on its social outlook. While Chalmers viewed the Free Church as a potential vehicle for the revival of his godly commonwealth ideal, the new body increasingly began to perceive itself as a 'gathered church' of true believers, and as a bastion of Christianity amid the sins of society.[36] The sectarian ambitions associated with the rapid Free Church building campaigns of this period also saw an erosion of communal and national responsibility within the church. By the mid-1840s, the social focus within the Free Church appeared to shift from that of a de facto national church, with its

32. *FCM*, ii (January 1845), 24.
33. Brown, 'Disruption and Urban Poverty', 69–70.
34. Smout, *A Century of the Scottish People*, 189; MacLaren, *Religion and Social Class*, 133–4; Peter Hillis, 'Presbyterianism and Social Class in mid-nineteenth century Glasgow: a study of nine churches', *Journal of Ecclesiastical History*, xxxii (1981), 51, 55.
35. *Edinburgh Advertiser*, 2 January 1844.
36. Brown, *Thomas Chalmers and the Godly Commonwealth*, 344.

emphasis on the poor and irreligious, to a denominational agenda centred solely on adherents to the Free Kirk and neglecting the broader community and 'socially destitute' beyond its walls.[37] The successful consolidation of the Free Church after 1843 as a gathered church of believers appeared to represent an acceptance of increasing secular authority over society and the narrower social grounds on which the denomination would view itself. It also signified the waning influence of the hitherto dominant Chalmers, whose stubborn desire to preserve the godly commonwealth idea saw him lose ground within the Free Kirk to younger, opportunistic leaders such as Robert Candlish who were more in tune with the changing ecclesiastical, social and political climate.

Territorial Missions, the West Port and 'Co-operation through Competition'

It was in this context of the shifting relationship between the church and the poor, and the publication of the 1844 Poor Law report, that Chalmers launched his last great attempt to revive the godly commonwealth ideal.[38] The renewal of his urban social experiment, modified to suit the altered circumstances of the post-Disruption era and the lack of a national parish-based structure, centred on its two founding principles of 'locality' and 'aggression'. Without the parochial framework of the Established Church, Chalmers envisioned a series of territorial home missions based on 'sufficiently small' localities – poor urban districts of roughly two thousand people or four hundred families – in which local congregations, ministers and philanthropists could thoroughly engage with the spiritual and temporal welfare of their inhabitants.[39] In this scheme, a congregation would select a nearby district, in which a minister would superintend twenty agents who would each be allocated twenty families, while a specially built territorial church would be erected in the locality.[40] Chalmers criticised the city mission schemes, which he argued only provided a superficial and 'inefficient' operation over a large area, and claimed to prefer the 'thickest to the broadest husbandry'.[41] However, simply setting up a church in a poor area, and thereby passively attracting those likely to attend anyway,

---

37. Furgol, 'Thomas Chalmers' Poor Relief theories', 348; Brown, *Thomas Chalmers and the Godly Commonwealth*, 346–9; MacLaren, *Religion and Social Class*, 201; Campbell, 'The Free Church and the Territorial Ideal', 33.
38. Brown, *Thomas Chalmers and the Godly Commonwealth*, 350–1.
39. *North British Review*, ii (February 1845), 497; Thomas Chalmers, *Churches and Schools for the Working Classes* (Edinburgh, 1846), 4; Thomas Chalmers to James Lenox, 21 March 1846, NYPL, James Lenox Papers, MssCol 1732; *Perthshire Advertiser*, 6 February 1845.
40. *Perthshire Advertiser*, 20 June 1844; *Northern Warder and General Advertiser for the counties of Fife, Perth and Forfar*, 25 June 1844.
41. Chalmers to Lenox, 24 February 1847, NYPL, James Lenox Papers, MssCol 1732; Chalmers, *Churches and Schools*, 4.

would not be enough. Chalmers urged potential missionaries to adopt the 'aggressive' principle and 'go forth to the people' in a bid to return them to churchgoing habits. According to Chalmers, only through such an aggressive visitation scheme could missionaries attract the irreligious to local churches and schools.[42] This desire to attract 'new customers' to the church was a deliberate attempt to quell the increasing 'gathered church' mentality of the Free Kirk. He insisted that any potential territorial mission church would not be a threat to existing congregations but would reclaim the 'outfield population' in the most destitute areas of Scotland's cities.[43]

Chalmers also viewed the territorial scheme as a viable alternative, and potential replacement, to legal poor relief. Ministers in charge of each mission would not be viewed as a 'general dispenser of temporal bounty', but would instead be tasked with the primary aim of improving the 'Christian good' of the area's inhabitants.[44] He proposed that local administrators investigate the merits of each applicant for relief, and only utilise the local and voluntary fund after the resources of their family, neighbours and the applicant had been exhausted. According to Chalmers, the communal conscience and 'feelings of nature' evoked by such a system would ensure that 'by the time the old pauperism has disappeared, the new pauperism, if indeed any at all has been formed, can be amply sustained on the basis of the gratuitous system'. By extolling the virtues of voluntary relief within a small Christian community, Chalmers hoped that his territorial scheme, and its subsequent spread throughout Scotland, would 'displace the compulsory provision altogether'.[45]

In a series of four lectures delivered in June and July 1844, Chalmers pitched his territorial scheme to both his fellow Free Churchmen and ministers of other dissenting denominations. Though he claimed that Free Churchmen were now in a better position to carry out his territorial aims than when they were in the establishment, it was nevertheless clear to Chalmers that the Free Church lacked the resources to carry out such an ambitious project alone.[46] While the godly commonwealth had been intrinsically linked to the Established Church before 1843, the newly pluralist religious landscape allowed Chalmers to 'repudiate all sectarian aims' and

---

42. Chalmers, *Churches and Schools*, 4–5; *Fife Herald*, 22 October 1846; *Perthshire Advertiser*, 20 June 1844.
43. *Scotsman*, 27 July 1844; Chalmers to Lenox, 24 February 1847, NYPL, James Lenox Papers, MssCol 1732; Chalmers, *Churches and Schools*, 13–14; *Fife Herald*, 22 October 1846; Chalmers to Lenox, 24 February 1847, NYPL, James Lenox Papers, MssCol 1732; *The Scotsman*, 27 July 1844.
44. *Northern Warder*, 25 June 1844; *John O'Groat Journal*, 5 July 1844; *Caledonian Mercury*, 24 June 1844.
45. *North British Review*, ii (February 1845), 497, 513.
46. *Northern Warder*, 25 June 1844; *A Letter to Dr Chalmers, on the organisation of a Free Presbyterian Church, by the son of a clergyman* (Edinburgh, 1843), 14; *A Memorial on Education, to the General Assembly of the Free Church, by the son of a clergyman* (Edinburgh, 1844), 7–10; *Northern Warder*, 4 June 1844.

pitch his scheme to the dissenting churches, in the hope of eventual co-operation and a fully fledged interdenominational scheme.[47] In the fourth lecture, attended by leading United Secession ministers John Brown, James Harper and John Ritchie, and the Congregationalist politician Adam Black, Chalmers called for co-operation in this home mission work through competition.[48] By urging ministers to set up territorial congregations attached to their own church, Chalmers proposed to 'strive to outrun each other in this good work'. He also called on dissenters to assist missionaries of other denominations in their localities, with the sole 'common object' of reaching the outcast population and not the success of any particular church. This policy of 'intermingling co-operation', alongside its social benefits, would efface the 'lines of demarcation' between Scotland's dissenting denominations and offer the 'likeliest stepping-stone to incorporation'. He believed that a 'great Home Mission', in the same vein as its foreign missionary counterparts who suspended their denominational allegiances, would 'merge our sectarian differences' and prove more effective than any articles or committees on church union.[49]

A year later, Chalmers turned his attentions to the Evangelical Alliance, and in *Essays on Christian Union* proposed a co-operative territorial system throughout Britain that he claimed would place the differences between the country's Protestants in 'juster proportion' and 'smooth the way' to eventual incorporation.[50] While Chalmers' essay was commended by the *United Secession Magazine*, the journal criticised the rest of the Free Church. It claimed that their church extension plan was a 'needless application of resources to sectarian objects', which led to 'over-churching' in wealthier districts. Condemning the 'gathered church' ethos of this section of the Free Kirk, the magazine called on Chalmers' policy of co-operation to 'be employed in the diffusion of the Gospel where it really is required'.[51] In effect, Chalmers' territorial scheme, and its experimental implementation in the West Port, was a practical illustration of this kind of co-operation.

The West Port area of Edinburgh was chosen by Chalmers in 1844 as the model for his territorial experiment. Situated just off the Grassmarket and in the shadow of Edinburgh Castle, the West Port was one of the capital's most crime-ridden and impoverished districts, and was the location of the infamous Burke and Hare murders only sixteen years before.[52] According to Chalmers, its roughly two thousand inhabitants were 'in the lowest grade both of comfort and character', often living in squalid conditions in the dark

---

47. Hanna, *Memoirs of Thomas Chalmers*, ii, 681; *Perthshire Advertiser*, 20 June 1844; *Northern Warder*, 25 June 1844; *Witness*, 27 July 1844.
48. *Northern Warder*, 30 July 1844.
49. *Scotsman*, 27 July 1844.
50. *Essays on Christian Union*, 12–16.
51. *USM*, ii (May 1845), 229–34.
52. Brown, *Thomas Chalmers and the Godly Commonwealth*, 353.

lanes and closes of the area.⁵³ Chalmers' biographer and son-in-law William Hanna claimed that a quarter of the population were either paupers on the poor-roll, or thieves, beggars and prostitutes, while almost three-quarters of the children of school age were without any form of education. Seventy-five per cent of the entire population also did not receive any religious instruction, despite living in relatively close proximity to a church. Of the 115 families, of a total of 411, who did attend church, forty-five were Protestant and seventy Roman Catholic.⁵⁴ For Chalmers, the apparent moral depravity and spiritual destitution ensured that the West Port could act as a perfect example of his territorial system in action and help inspire others.⁵⁵ By reclaiming the West Port from 'this vast and desolate wilderness', Chalmers aimed to stimulate a national and interdenominational scheme that would eventually overtake the 'great and growing evil' of Scotland's social ills.⁵⁶

The personal significance of the West Port experiment and his increasingly failing health led Chalmers to step away from his day-to-day ministerial duties and to devote his remaining strength to the territorial campaign and his position as Principal and Professor of Divinity at New College. This involved relinquishing his duties as a member of the Free Church General Assembly and resigning from his position as convenor of the Sustentation Fund Committee.⁵⁷ Chalmers then set about building his utopian social project and 'reclaiming' the West Port poor. He was assisted by his secretary Finlay MacPherson and James Ewan, a salaried agent from the dissent-dominated Edinburgh City Mission, and aided by anonymous donations from wealthy benefactors such as the New York philanthropist James Lenox.⁵⁸ First, he concentrated his efforts on the educational deficiencies within the area. A school was opened in November 1844, with sixty-four day scholars and fifty-seven evening scholars in attendance. Within a year this would increase to 250 students, mostly from the West Port.⁵⁹ Chalmers insisted that school fees were mandatory, in order to instil individual and communal responsibility and teach the poor that education was 'worthy of its price', though non-paying students were not excluded.⁶⁰ By late 1845,

53. Chalmers to Lenox, 9 August 1844, NYPL, James Lenox Papers, MssCol 1732.
54. Hanna, *Memoirs of Thomas Chalmers*, ii, 682; Chalmers to Lenox, 9 August 1844, NYPL, James Lenox Papers, MssCol 1732.
55. Chalmers to Lenox, 30 December 1844, NYPL, James Lenox Papers, MssCol 1732.
56. Chalmers to Lenox, 9 August 1844, NYPL, James Lenox Papers, MssCol 1732.
57. Chalmers to Lenox, 7 August 1844, 17 February 1845, 21 April 1845, NYPL, James Lenox Papers, MssCol 1732; Chalmers to Adam Black, 23 May 1846, NCL, CHA.3.17.110.
58. Finlay MacPherson to James Lenox, 9 October 1844, NYPL, James Lenox Papers, MssCol 1732; Thomas Chalmers to James Lenox, 21 November 1846, NYPL, James Lenox Papers, MssCol 1732; James Lenox to Thomas Chalmers, 14 September 1844, NCL, Chalmers Papers, CHA.4.314.19.
59. Hanna, *Memoirs of Thomas Chalmers*, ii, 688; Finlay MacPherson to James Lenox, c. October 1845, NYPL, James Lenox Papers, MssCol 1732.
60. Chalmers, *Churches and Schools*, 6–8; Chalmers to Lenox, 21 November 1846, NYPL, James Lenox Papers, MssCol 1732.

Chalmers claimed that the school's total fees amounted to £240, with each scholar paying 2*d* a week. He also noted that children from the nearby Grassmarket were turned away from the West Port day school, in order to avoid 'superficialising' its numbers with children from neighbouring areas.[61] Following the establishment of the school, attention turned to religious instruction and to building the 'nucleus of a good congregation' under the ministry of the missionary William Tasker, appointed to the West Port charge in April 1845. While only ten conversions were officially noted in its first year of operation, Chalmers insisted that the 'elevating' moral effect these conversions had on the wider neighbourhood far outweighed their limited number. Other welfare initiatives such as a library, a savings bank, a laundry room and a female industrial school were also established in the first year of the operation.[62]

Within a year and a half of its foundation the apparent success of the West Port operation allowed Chalmers to present it to Scotland as a model for an expanded territorial system. Chalmers had not made any overt public appeal in favour of the territorial system until he could appear to prove the veracity of his own West Port model.[63] On 27 December 1845, he delivered a public lecture in Edinburgh, published as *Churches and Schools for the Working Classes*, which characterised the West Port as a successful '*experimentum crucis*' and called for the expansion of his interdenominational territorial project throughout Scotland. Proposing a series of West Port replicas in Edinburgh, Chalmers challenged the ministers of all evangelical denominations to create 'a chain of forts all the way from the South Bridge to the Main Point'. However, some critics pointed out the Free Church-accentuated nature of the scheme. Of the seven originally proposed missions, only one – organised by James Robertson's United Secession Church – was not affiliated with the Free Church. Nevertheless, Chalmers insisted that his territorial plan was not a sectarian exercise. Referring to those critics who suggested that he was proposing a Free Church scheme, Chalmers rebutted,

> Who cares about the Free Church compared with the Christian good of the people of Scotland? Who cares for any church, but as an instrument for Christian good? For, be assured, that the moral and religious well-being of the population is infinitely of higher importance than the advancement of any sect.[64]

While Chalmers' dismissal of his own church's denominational objects

---

61. Chalmers, *Churches and Schools*, 7–10.
62. Hanna, *Memoirs of Thomas Chalmers*, ii, 688–9; Chalmers to Lenox, 21 November 1846, NYPL, James Lenox Papers, MssCol 1732; Chalmers, *Churches and Schools*, 16.
63. Chalmers' letter on West Port, c. 1846, NCL, CHA.3.17.116; Chalmers to Lenox, 17 December 1845, NYPL, James Lenox Papers, MssCol 1732; Chalmers, *Churches and Schools*, 3.
64. Chalmers, *Churches and Schools*, 3, 21.

signified a clear expression of disappointment at the Free Church's shift away from the godly commonwealth ideal, it also cemented the interdenominational character of his territorial scheme. He called on 'ministers of every evangelical denomination' to replicate his West Port model, and claimed that 'there would be a far greater likelihood of our coming to closer union, if we were engaged together in such missionary work, than by meeting in committees, and drawing up articles which give rise to interminable controversies'.[65] From the outset of his operation at the West Port, he was assisted by dissenters from the local United Secession, Baptist and Independent congregations. These dissenters, Chalmers claimed, understood that West Port represented a 'far more catholic and generous object' than the mere colonisation of a part of Edinburgh for the Free Church.[66] In January 1846, a month after his lecture, the Edinburgh City Mission attempted to institutionalise the interdenominational character of Chalmers' scheme by establishing a general committee. Under the chairmanship of Adam Black, the committee would oversee and support the implementation of the various territorial schemes in Edinburgh.[67] This support from the Edinburgh City Mission, along with private backing from dissenting leaders such as the United Secession minister John Brown, raised hopes for the success of both the West Port operation and the wider interdenominational system.

The achievements of Chalmers' territorial scheme between 1844 and his death in 1847 can be assessed by examining the success of the West Port mission itself, the territorial scheme's popularity within the Free Church and its ability to foster interdenominational co-operation. Though its suitability as a model for a wider, national scheme is questionable, West Port itself proved a relative success for Chalmers and his agents. Despite encountering serious financial difficulties in its first year of operation, Chalmers and his missionary Tasker were able to foster a substantial Christian community in the West Port centred on a local church and school.[68] The success of the day, evening and Sabbath schools – by March 1846, roughly three hundred children, or three-quarters of the total, were receiving daily schooling and undertaking examinations – created a need for expansion and better accommodation.[69] Chalmers claimed that both the growth and scholarly achievements of his school in the West Port ensured that it was 'a ragged school no longer'.[70] Following Tasker's appointment in April

---

65. Chalmers, *Churches and Schools*, 21; Brown, *Thomas Chalmers and the Godly Commonwealth*, 365–6.
66. *Scotsman*, 27 July 1844.
67. Chalmers to Adam Black, 23 May 1846, NCL, CHA.3.17.110
68. Hanna, *Memoirs of Thomas Chalmers*, ii, 691–2.
69. Chalmers to Lenox, 20 February 1845, 21 March 1846, Finlay MacPherson to Lenox, c. October 1845, NYPL, James Lenox Papers, MssCol 1732; Hanna, *Memoirs of Thomas Chalmers*, ii, 695.
70. *Fife Herald*, 22 October 1846.

1845, the foundations for a functioning congregation were established with 'visible success'. Land was purchased for a larger schoolroom and church more suitable for its expanding membership, while in 1846 Chalmers refurbished a tenement of low-rent 'model houses' for working men.[71]

The growth of the West Port's Sabbath congregation ultimately resulted in the opening of the West Port territorial church in February 1847.[72] In letters to James Lenox, Chalmers described the church's opening as the completion of his thirty-year territorial experiment and 'the most joyful event of my life'. Of the 132 communicants at the church's first sacrament, presided over by Chalmers, one hundred were from the West Port, the majority of whom had never communicated before. The high percentage of churchgoers who lived in the West Port was a particular source of pride for Chalmers, underscoring the ability of the territorial system to foster Christian bonds in 'a locality which, two years ago, had not one in ten church-goers from the whole population'.[73] Following Chalmers' death in May 1847, the Free Presbytery of Edinburgh moved to erect the West port into a regular charge with Tasker as minister.[74] In November 1847, the *Witness* praised the 'manifest progress' of the West Port Church, and claimed that the 'well-filled' church of nearly two hundred communicants offered 'every encouragement' for the success of Chalmers' experiment.[75] The success of the educational and ecclesiastical aspects of Chalmers' scheme continued after his death under Tasker's impressive superintendence. By the early 1850s, the vast majority of the West Port's children attended school, while Hanna argued that the churchgoing habits of the population were 'as general and regular' as the most well-heeled areas of Edinburgh.[76]

Despite this success, the West Port's status as a 'model specimen' for a broader programme was less impressive. The complete collapse of the visitation effort and the West Port Local Society in September 1846 was a major blow to Chalmers' aims to ease class tensions and foster communal bonds. The failure of middle-class missionaries to engage fully with the urban poor in the cramped and squalid closes also exposed the frailties of a purely voluntary relief effort in this period.[77] The experiment also fell short in creating a self-sustaining working-class community emancipated from reliance on the upper and middle classes, as mounting hidden costs far exceeded Chalmers' claimed total expenditure on the project. Chalmers' heavy reli-

---

71. Hanna, *Memoirs of Thomas Chalmers*, ii, 689, 693–4; Chalmers to Lenox, 20 October 1845, 21 March 1846, NYPL, James Lenox Papers, MssCol 1732.
72. Chalmers to Lenox, 18 April 1846, 21 November 1846, NYPL, James Lenox Papers, MssCol 1732.
73. Hanna, *Memoirs of Thomas Chalmers*, ii, 694–5.
74. *Dundee, Perth, and Cupar Advertiser*, 11 June 1847.
75. *Witness*, 10 November 1847.
76. Hanna, *Memoirs of Thomas Chalmers*, ii, 696–7.
77. Brown, *Thomas Chalmers and the Godly Commonwealth*, 361; Brown, 'Disruption and Urban Poverty', 76.

ance on external donations from wealthy benefactors such as Lenox highlighted the difficulties of replicating similar operations throughout the country without the pulling power of the Free Church leader.[78] Pre-existing social issues were also not entirely eradicated. Drunkenness remained a pressing problem, while brothels continued to function in many of the alleys and closes. This prompted Chalmers to urge the Sanitary and Health boards to 'remove these physical nuisances and discomforts' from a 'territory so full of misery and vice at present, yet so full of promise for the future'.[79]

While Chalmers hoped that the apparent achievements of the West Port would act as a catalyst and guide for other evangelicals to create a 'sound and enduring parochial economy' throughout Scotland, the extent to which this was achieved, or even attempted, is highly questionable.[80] Even within the Free Church, tensions remained over the interdenominational direction of Chalmers' territorial campaign. In 1845 Chalmers clashed with the Free Church moderator Patrick Macfarlan over the appointment of Tasker to the West Port, as Macfarlan and other church leaders had intended him for the rural parish of Kilmalcolm, Renfrewshire. Macfarlan complained that Chalmers' interdenominational scheme should not be allowed to deprive existing Free Church parishes in need of ministers.[81] Though Macfarlan and his successor Robert Brown appeared willing to support Chalmers' aims in theory, and called on their fellow Free Churchmen to emulate his ambitions, the cool attitude displayed in practice proved a significant obstacle to the achievement of the territorial ideal.[82] Most notably, at the 1846 General Assembly the Home Missions Committee was amalgamated with the Church Extension Committee.[83] Despite Chalmers' wishes, the West Port scheme, initially at least, was not replicated elsewhere. The attempt to institutionalise Chalmers' national plan through the Edinburgh City Mission, without the personality and fame of Chalmers to draw upon, collapsed in late 1846, with only three similar schemes in operation in Glasgow and Edinburgh.[84]

Faced with such indifference in his own denomination, Chalmers turned

---

78. Chalmers to Lenox, 15 July 1845, 21 March 1846, c. September 1846, NYPL, James Lenox Papers, MssCol 1732; Lenox to Chalmers, 25 September 1845, NCL, CHA.4.318.530, 15 December 1846, NCL, CHA.4.324.78.
79. Hanna, *Memoirs of Thomas Chalmers*, ii, 695–6.
80. Chalmers to Lenox, 21 March 1846, c. September 1846, 28 October 1846, 21 November 1846, NYPL, James Lenox Papers, MssCol 1732.
81. Brown, *Thomas Chalmers and the Godly Commonwealth*, 359.
82. Free Church of Scotland, *Pastoral Address of the General Assembly, met at Edinburgh, in the year 1845, to the people under their charge* (Edinburgh, 1845), 8; *Herald of the Churches*, i (March 1846), 29; *AGAFC 1846* (Edinburgh, 1846), 92–3.
83. *Acts of the Free Church General Assembly, 1846*, 35; Campbell, 'The Free Church of Scotland and the Territorial Ideal', 48–9.
84. Brown, *Thomas Chalmers and the Godly Commonwealth*, 365–6; Campbell, 'The Free Church and the Territorial Ideal', 47–8.

to the newly formed Evangelical Alliance for assistance in his interdenominational campaign, only to find the same self-preservation evident in its membership as in the Free Church. He criticised the opposition within certain sections of the Alliance, most resolutely the clergy of the Church of England, that any implementation of his territorial scheme would 'diminish or distract their existing congregations', and potentially 'let in a list of sectarian ministers to cut and carve open their parishes'. In a letter to Lenox, Chalmers noted that, according to the Evangelical Alliance, 'the Christian interests of the community at large must be sacrificed to the parochial honour and importance of the Established clergy on the one hand, and to the congregational interests of all [dissenting] ministers ... on the other'. This contest between 'the pecuniary or patrimonial good of the clergy and the Christian good of the general population', Chalmers argued, proved the largest barrier to his home mission projects throughout his career, and ironically prevented his plan for interdenominational cooperation being accepted by a society established for the sole purpose of furthering Christian union.[85]

Despite this inability to win over the Evangelical Alliance and his colleagues in the Free Church, the influence of Chalmers' territorial urban mission policies, and his hopes for interdenominational co-operation, were perhaps most keenly felt in the socially energetic circles of dissent, particularly within the urban, middle-class United Secession Church.[86] For instance, the missions organised by the Edinburgh congregations of United Secession ministers John Brown and William Peddie at Broughton Place and Bristo Street respectively, though both predating the West Port experiment, mirrored its territorial and aggressive structure and ambitions. Peddie's mission, based in the East Crosscauseway area of Edinburgh, was established in July 1839 with the opening of a Sunday school. In 1845 the operation was extended, and a year later a home missionary, Alexander Chisholm, was appointed to undertake visitation efforts and organise religious meetings in the locality. Evening classes for adults were organised after 1849, and an infant day school was established in 1853. A Female Benevolent Society was also set up to aid the poor with fuel and clothing during the winter.[87]

Located in the north-side of the Canongate, John Brown's mission was established in April 1835 under the superintendence of David Forrest and utilised the same policies of visitation and missionary activity outlined by Chalmers. Galvanised by the renewal of the Free Church leader's territorial ideal after 1843, by the mid-1840s it had fostered a congregation of two hundred locals and established a day school where 180 children were taught

---

85. Chalmers to Lenox, 24 February 1847, NYPL, James Lenox Papers, MssCol 1732.
86. Withrington, 'Towards a New Social Conscience?', 159; *Aberdeen Journal*, 18 November 1846.
87. James Thin, *Memorials of Bristo United Presbyterian Church* (Edinburgh, 1879), 73–4, 208.

by Alexander Anderson, a future Free Church minister. In 1846 the success of the school led to its relocation to a larger venue in Old High School Close. Afternoon and evening classes for religious instruction were also arranged in the new accommodation, while the old school remained as a preaching station.[88] In a letter to James Lenox in April 1846, Chalmers praised the Canongate mission's 'marvellous progress', citing it as an illustration of his 'co-operation through competition' agenda and the success of his interdenominational campaign.[89] Writing to Brown, Chalmers emphasised the role of urban mission work in fostering the growing co-operation within Scottish dissent, and argued that the 'common work' of missions would eventually lead to a 'common understanding' between the two churches.[90]

In September of that year, Brown invited Chalmers to mark the opening of the new school building by delivering a lecture in support of the Broughton Place congregation's territorial scheme.[91] Despite his failing health that restricted him from attending large meetings or assemblies beyond the West Port, Chalmers agreed, and a month later addressed many of Edinburgh's leading dissenting ministers gathered in Brown's church. After commending both the missionary achievements of the Broughton Place congregation and the 'catholic and pervading charity' of their minister, Chalmers called on the dissenters present to emulate Brown's scheme. Alluding to the recent London meeting of the Evangelical Alliance, Chalmers claimed that the pursuit of Christian union would be better effected by a 'joint operation' in urban mission, rather than set-piece gatherings that would become merely 'one of the theatricals of London'. Despite the indifference of the Evangelical Alliance, Chalmers remained optimistic. Noting the example of Brown and the United Secession Church, he concluded that dissenting co-operation in the 'common work' of urban mission would 'speed on the course of Christian union, as well as Christianising the neglected population' of Edinburgh and Scotland.[92]

Despite this optimism and hopes for dissenting co-operation, the onset of the Highland famine towards the end of 1846 put a halt to Chalmers' national territorial plan, and even called into question his commitment to the godly commonwealth ideal. Following the initial failure of the potato crop in late summer 1846, the Free Church was the first public body in Scotland to react to the crisis and was instrumental in tackling the problems

---

88. John Brown to Thomas Chalmers, 16 September 1846, NCL, CHA.4.321.97; Alexander White, *History of Broughton Place United Presbyterian Church, with sketches of its missionary operations* (Edinburgh, 1872), 283, 287.
89. Chalmers to Lenox, 18 April 1846, NYPL, James Lenox Papers, MssCol 1732.
90. Thomas Chalmers to John Brown, 10 September 1846, NLS, Brown Papers, Acc. 6134.
91. John Brown to Chalmers, 16 September 1846, NCL, CHA.4.321.97; Brown to Chalmers, 17 September 1846, NCL, CHA.4.321.98; Brown to Chalmers, 7 October 1846, NCL, CHA.4.321.99.
92. *Fife Herald*, 22 October 1846.

evident during the formative period of the famine.[93] The Free Church opted, initially at least, to respond to the crisis alone. This was due to exasperation with what it regarded as widespread public naivety and even indifference to the potential scale of the crisis.[94] They were also inspired by loyalty to their significant Highland membership and the memory of its sacrifice at the Disruption. In September 1846, the Free Synod of Argyll was the first group within the church to respond, raising funds, distributing food and petitioning the government for intervention.[95] A detailed survey into the scale of the destitution was also conducted by the Free Church through the autumn, and resulted in the formation on 18 November 1846 of the Committee on the Destitution in the Highlands and Islands. From the first week of December, collections were made in all of the Free Church's congregations and mission-stations, and in the three months of the committee's existence £15,608 was raised for the relief of the Highlanders.[96]

While the Free Church acted alone in its initial relief effort in the Highlands, it stressed that it was not a sectarian effort.[97] Relief was indiscriminately provided by the church to members of all denominations, while the committee acknowledged from the outset that 'the existing distress was too extensive and general to be met successfully by the utmost exertions or efforts which the Free Church, alone, could make'. A proposal for joint effort in early December was even deferred by the Lord Provost of Edinburgh until further information could be gathered.[98] Nevertheless, the Free Church's rapid response to the crisis was perceived by Scotland's dissenters to be indicative of the body's desire to continue 'aloof' from external assistance, and symbolic of their apparent broader mission to solve single-handedly Scotland's social ills. For those outside the Free Church, there was a general suspicion that their effort in the Highlands appeared to have 'party ends in view'.[99] A public meeting was organised in Edinburgh in

93. *Correspondence from July, 1846, to February, 1847, relating to the measures adopted for the relief of the distress in Scotland* [Cd. 788], H.C. 1847, liii, 286; MacColl, *Land, Faith, and the Crofting Community*, 13, 32–3.
94. Thomas Chalmers to John Mackenzie and others, 9 December 1846, NCL, CHA.3.26.26.
95. *Report by the Committee on the Destitution in the Highlands and Islands, appointed by the Commission of the General Assembly of the Free Church of Scotland, November 1846, to the General Assembly, May 1847* (Edinburgh, 1847), 5–6; *Correspondence on the distress in Scotland*, 24; Douglas Ansdell, *The People of the Great Faith: the Highland Church, 1690–1900* (Stornoway, 1998), 63; E. M. MacArthur, *Iona: the living memory of a crofting community, 1750–1914* (Edinburgh, 1990), 3; MacColl, *Land, Faith, and the Crofting Community*, 31; T. M. Devine, *The Great Highland Famine: Hunger, Emigration and the Scottish Highlands in the Nineteenth Century* (Edinburgh, 1988), 116–17, 158–9.
96. *Report by the Committee on the Destitution in the Highlands*, 3; John Rothney Stephen, 'The Presbyterian response to the famine years 1845 to 1855 within Ireland and in the Highlands of Scotland' (MLitt(R) thesis, University of Glasgow, 2011), 143–5.
97. *Report by the Committee on the Destitution in the Highlands*, 6.
98. *Correspondence on the distress in Scotland*, 218–19; *Report by the Committee on the Destitution in the Highlands*, 5; *Witness*, 10 October 1846, 2 December 1846.
99. *Caledonian Mercury*, 21 December 1846; *Dumfries and Galloway Standard*, 23 December 1846.

late December, with the aim to censure the Free Kirk's decision to pursue famine relief independently, and to establish a 'broad and catholic' movement that would exclude the Free Church. Speaking from the audience, Candlish defended the Free Church's position and criticised the meeting's intentions to undermine the church's work. While he acknowledged that the Free Church's 'haste' to aid the Highlands may have been 'an error in judgment', Candlish claimed that this was due to an unwillingness to delay action until the public was fully informed of the scale of the destitution, and stressed that the Free Kirk had 'not the slightest inclination' to 'occupy the field alone'. Arguing against the creation of 'two rival agencies' for famine relief, Candlish refused 'to contemplate for a moment the sad and miserable spectacle of our poor Highland countrymen being made the occasion of division and disaffection among us'.[100] Candlish's proposal to pledge the full support of his church behind the creation of a comprehensive interdenominational agency eventually culminated in the creation of the cross-party Central Board of Management for Highland Relief in February 1847.[101]

Rather than provide the catalyst for a renewed interdenominational social mission, the outbreak of the famine effectively ended Chalmers' hopes for a truly national territorial mission in his lifetime. The outpouring of national sympathy for the Highlands diverted money and energy away from urban missions in the Lowlands, as the public interest in the godly commonwealth ideal slowly began to fade. As Brown has noted, the public outcry over the 'Send Back the Money' controversy in the Free Church, rising to a crescendo in 1846, also presented another barrier to interdenominational co-operation.[102] The Free Kirk's acceptance of donations from American slaveholders provoked an outpouring of opposition across Scotland and the United States, and led to calls by the United Secession and Relief churches to return the money and renounce their fellowship with slaveholding churches.[103] Perhaps most significantly, the sheer scale of the destitution caused by the famine and the failure of purely voluntary benevolence to deal fully with the situation helped produce a dramatic shift in Chalmers' social thinking as he softened his stance on state intervention.[104] In March 1847, Chalmers criticised the government's decision to 'so economise as to put human life in jeopardy' and called on it to launch 'a social lifeboat' for those in the Highlands.[105] According to Brown,

---

100. *Dumfries and Galloway Standard*, 23 December 1846.
101. *Correspondence on the distress in Scotland*, 315.
102. Brown, 'Disruption and Urban Poverty', 86; George Thompson and Henry C. Wright, *The Free Church of Scotland and American Slavery* (Edinburgh, 1846).
103. Iain Whyte, *Send back the money: the Free Church of Scotland and American slavery* (Cambridge, 2012); *Covenanter*, ii (August 1846), 29.
104. Brown, *Thomas Chalmers and the Godly Commonwealth*, 366–9; MacLeod, 'Chalmers and Pauperism', 72–3.
105. *Witness*, 6 March 1847.

the famine underlined Chalmers' reluctant belief that voluntary philanthropy could no longer sustain the godly commonwealth.[106]

The failure of Chalmers' renewed territorial ideal to capture the national imagination was evident in the lack of West Port replicas across Scotland. James Begg, the convenor of the Home Missions Committee of the Free Church, complained that apart from the successful missions at the West Port and Holyrood, little was being done within the church for the purpose of expanding Chalmers' ideal and reclaiming the urban poor.[107] Begg also condemned the 'gathered church' mentality of the Free Church, and criticised ministers in Glasgow for not building churches in poorer areas.[108] However, Begg did note that 'our brethren of other denominations are taking up the matter in earnest, and that a successful effort, on the West Port plan, for reclaiming one of the worst districts of Aberdeen, has been made by our Independent brethren there'.[109] He praised the 'catholic-spirited' Congregational minister James Hall Wilson, who utilised the theories of Chalmers and John Wesley to inspire his own city mission in Aberdeen. Begg argued that 'were this spirit' of co-operation 'to spread amongst the dissenters of Scotland, the axe would be laid to the root of many of our social evils'.[110] Though a relative failure in his lifetime, this spirit of interdenominational co-operation longed for by Chalmers would be revived following his death in May 1847.

A 'Happy Rivalry'? Chalmers' Posthumous Contribution to Territorial Missions and Social Reform

The events of 1848, a year after Chalmers' death, marked a significant transformation in the fortunes of his territorial ideal. Revolution in continental Europe, combined with riots in Glasgow, provided the context for renewed social action among Scotland's dissenters.[111] John Robson, the United Presbyterian minister at Wellington Street, Glasgow, responded to these disturbances by calling for renewed missionary activity by Scotland's dissenters, and claiming that the Gospel is 'the grand [and] efficient remedy for social disorder and individual wretchedness'.[112] Though the Free Church largely failed to take up Chalmers' initiative before 1847, following his death a new generation of social reformers emerged within the church to implement his territorial vision. A series of Free Church-attached

---

106. Brown, *Thomas Chalmers and the Godly Commonwealth*, 367.
107. Begg, *Pauperism and the Poor Laws*, 15.
108. *Scottish Guardian*, 8 October 1850.
109. Begg, *Pauperism and the Poor Laws*, 15–16.
110. James Hall Wilson, *City Missions and how to work them* (London, 1849); Begg, *Pauperism and the Poor Laws*, 16.
111. Robert Buchanan, *The Schoolmaster in the Wynds; or, how to educate the masses* (Glasgow, 1850), 4; *Spectator*, 11 March 1848.
112. Hillis, 'Education and Evangelisation', 52.

territorial missions, modelled on the West Port, sprang up in the late 1840s and early 1850s. Inspired by Chalmers' scheme as carried on by Tasker, Candlish's St George's congregation in 1848 established a mission in the Fountainbridge area of Edinburgh, with the aim of erecting a territorial church and school. A visitation structure was immediately set up, while two day schools and a Sabbath school were also established. According to Candlish, his congregation was taking up 'the work of Chalmers'.[113] Under the supervision of the missionary James Hood Wilson, arguably one of Chalmers' most earnest successors, the day and Sabbath schools were instructing almost 250 children by 1853, and a year later a territorial church was established.[114] Within two years, the number of communicants had risen from twenty-nine to 210, while the overall attendance of the church was over four hundred.[115] Thomas Guthrie's Free St John's congregation, with the aid of Chalmers' son-in-law William Hanna, established in 1850 a similarly successful mission church in the Pleasance, the original kirk-session of which included Begg and Candlish.[116]

In Glasgow, Robert Buchanan's Tron Church set up an urban mission in the deprived Wynds district in 1847. Like Chalmers, Buchanan focused on the role of the church and school in poor areas, the elimination of pauperism through a Christian communal ethos, and the implementation of the 'aggressive' principle in urban ministry. He called for a 'reformation of the masses', to eliminate the 'next door neighbours' of ignorance and pauperism, and to use the aggressive principle to fill the school with locals.[117] The success of the Wynds mission – it was self-sustaining by 1858 – prompted its minister Dugald MacColl to pursue Chalmers' goal of a comprehensive communal system by expanding to neighbouring districts. Aided by the widespread religious revivals of 1859–62, which once again reignited mission work in Glasgow and Edinburgh, MacColl opened a new territorial mission church in Bridgegate in 1860 funded by members of numerous denominations, which soon expanded to four additional areas during the 1860s.[118]

Buchanan's Wynds mission proved the catalyst for the Free Church General Assembly's decision in 1851 to create a special Committee on Glasgow Evangelisation convened by Andrew Gray. Charged with over-

---

113. Robert S. Candlish, *Past Memories and Present Duties; or, Chalmers' Territorial Church, Fountainbridge, opened, on Sabbath, January 8, 1854* (Edinburgh, 1854), 6–11, 23.
114. Brown, 'Christian Socialist movement', 64; Candlish, *Past Memories and Present Duties*, 3, 17–28.
115. *Scottish Guardian*, 31 May 1856.
116. David K. Guthrie and Charles J. Guthrie, *Autobiography of Thomas Guthrie, D.D., and memoir by his sons* (2 volumes, New York, 1875) ii, 186–8.
117. Buchanan, *Schoolmaster in the Wynds*, 4–20, 29; *PGAFC, May 1851* (Edinburgh, 1851), 304, 309–10, 319.
118. Dugald MacColl, *Among the Masses; or Work in the Wynds* (London, 1867), 197, 358–62; Campbell, 'The Free Church and the Territorial Ideal', 88–9; Brown, *Social History of Religion*, 159.

seeing and extending territorial missions in the city, within a year of its founding four of these schemes were operating under the supervision of the committee.[119] The stated object of the Glasgow Evangelisation committee was to support and prosecute the expansion of the territorial scheme 'as projected by Dr Chalmers, and exemplified in the West Port'.[120] In November 1852, Gray argued that the evangelisation of Glasgow was a matter of 'national importance' for all of Scotland's churches. In order to support the work of his committee, and to fulfil Chalmers' vision of a national territorial system, Gray proposed the creation of a 'Chalmers Endowments' scheme, in memory of the churchman who 'first proclaimed the necessity of church extension in Glasgow, and who was the best friend of handicraft and hard labour'. These endowments, sanctioned by the following year's General Assembly and placed under the supervision of the Sustentation Fund committee, were used to support ministers engaged in territorial mission work in the poorest districts of Glasgow, with the aim of sustaining twenty such missions across the city.[121] Within a matter of months almost £6,000 had been raised for the endowments to support four missions; a year later, ten operations were in place under the Chalmers Endowments scheme.[122] By the 1853 General Assembly, fifty-seven mission stations were in operation, including six fully fledged territorial churches, two of which in Holyrood and Tasker's West Port were self-sustaining.[123] In the mid-1860s, the Free Church was supporting thirty-three urban territorial churches, including twenty in Glasgow.[124] Chalmers' vision of independent working-class communities also became a reality, as members of mission stations such as Bridgegate began a process of 'self-extension' by establishing similar projects in neighbouring districts.[125]

While the excitement and fervour of the Free Church home mission in this movement generally embodied the spirit, and fulfilled the ambitions, of Chalmers' territorial agenda, it lacked the interdenominational character he pursued after 1843. In essence, many Free Churchmen viewed mission work as part of their drive to assert their denomination's status as the true national church. Speaking forty years on, during his speech as moderator of the 1895 General Assembly, James Hood Wilson praised Chalmers' continuing legacy in home missions. Wilson argued that Chalmers 'had given a new impulse to aggressive Christian work all over the land, and under that impulse the Free Church had ... become aggressive as no other church

119. Brown, 'Thomas Chalmers and the communal ideal', 69–70.
120. *HFRFC*, iii (August 1852), 11
121. *HFRFC*, iii (November 1852), 97–8, (March 1853), 206; Henry Wellwood Moncreiff, *The Practice of the Free Church of Scotland in her several courts* (Edinburgh, 1877), 175.
122. *Fife Herald*, 2 June 1853.
123. *Caledonian Mercury*, 2 June 1853; *Fife Herald*, 2 June 1853.
124. Brown, 'Thomas Chalmers and the communal ideal', 71.
125. *PGAFC, 1853* (Edinburgh, 1853), 261–2.

then was'. Citing Tasker and MacColl's work, among others, in moulding the West Port and the Wynds as 'models and centres of evangelistic power', Wilson concluded that it was the Free Kirk's home mission work 'which, as much as anything else, gave us a claim to be regarded as in the best sense a national church'.[126] This emphasis on the role of home missions in cementing the national position of the Free Church was a major theme of missionaries in the 1850s. While Candlish nominally called on Christians 'of every name' to join in the territorial effort, he referred to 'especially, all who glory in belonging to the Church of our fathers, the Free Church, the people's Church'. Candlish argued that the Free Church was 'solemnly consecrated' to undertake such 'noble work', which would help it become the 'mother of other churches'.[127]

The triumphalism, inadvertently or otherwise, of this Free Church rhetoric was even echoed in calls for co-operation with other churches. Buchanan's desire for a 'united and vigorous' home mission effort in his pamphlet *The Schoolmaster in the Wynds* was ridiculed by the *United Presbyterian Magazine*, who claimed that the Free Church minister had ignored the ongoing work of other churches in this field.[128] The magazine pointed out that the 'aggressive system' outlined by Buchanan had in fact 'been in operation for many years in the closes and lanes of Glasgow'. It noted the work of David King's congregation near Regent Place, 'inhabited by the poorest and most neglected classes of the community', where a day school, evening class and sewing school were established, together instructing over three hundred pupils. Seven schools, accounting for over a thousand children, at Dovehill and Dempster Street were also supported by the congregations of William Lindsay, John Robson and William Anderson. The journal pointedly argued that Buchanan had to be acquainted with such efforts hundreds of yards from his own congregation, and that he should have paid them sufficient credit in his pamphlet, 'more especially as some of his brethren would seem to be really ignorant that dissenters are doing anything to supply the educational wants of the destitute districts of our country'.[129]

It is clear that the Free Church was not the only body in which Chalmers' posthumous territorial legacy was felt. In 1851 and 1852, a series of articles, written by what the *Greenock Advertiser* described as an author 'unhampered by sectarian prejudices', appeared in the United Presbyterian *Christian Journal* in praise of Chalmers' territorial church at the West Port, and highlighted both the catholicity of Chalmers' scheme and its influence on United Presbyterian missions in Edinburgh and Glasgow.[130]

---

126. *Scotsman*, 24 May 1895.
127. Candlish, *Past Memories and Present Duties*, 11, 54–6.
128. Buchanan, *Schoolmaster in the Wynds*, 32; *UPM*, iv (April 1850), 169.
129. *UPM*, iv (April 1850), 169–70.
130. *Greenock Advertiser*, 7 November 1851; *Christian Journal of the United Presbyterian Church* (November 1851), 493; (January 1852), 3–9, (February 1852), 55–60.

Other similar articles praised Chalmers' impact on dissenting social activism, with the *United Presbyterian Magazine* noting in 1859 that 'it is to Dr Chalmers ... that we owe the idea of a territorial or mission church'. Chalmers' influence ultimately paid dividends for the United Presbyterian Church, whose social impact rivalled that of the Free Kirk. In the second half of the 1850s, of the nineteen mission churches formed in Glasgow, the Free and United Presbyterian churches were responsible for nine each, and the other one was formed by an Independent congregation. All nine of the United Presbyterian missions had become fully fledged churches with over 1,500 members, a thousand of whom had no prior experience of religion. Donald McRae's self-supporting church in the Gorbals also had 345 members in full communion, of whom 262 had no previous church connection.[131] The success of these United Presbyterian missions, particularly within Glasgow, where many of the church's best ministers were moving to work, led to some degree of sectarian envy and animosity from the Free Church. In 1857 the by-then convenor of the Glasgow Evangelisation committee John Roxburgh argued that for the Free Church 'to evangelise Glasgow is a work not only of duty, but of self-interest' and 'self-preservation'.[132]

Despite these rare outbreaks of overt sectarian antagonism, the home missions of the Free and United Presbyterian churches in the 1850s largely resembled, in a muted sense, the 'co-operation through competition' ideal expounded by Chalmers. Echoing Chalmers, Guthrie called for a 'real working Evangelical Alliance' of denominations labouring together in the cities to cover the 'nakedness of the land' by cultivating their own individual areas.[133] The success of this policy was praised by James Hall Wilson in 1859, who commended the number of missions connected with the Free and United Presbyterian churches in Edinburgh. Alluding to Chalmers' policy of co-operation through competition, Wilson concluded that through the proliferation of these territorial schemes, 'there is a happy rivalry in the field of Christian benevolence, and an abundant promise of much future good'.[134] This 'happy rivalry' extended beyond competing mission stations. As well as galvanising their pre-existing urban missions, the religious revival of 1859 also saw members of the dissenting churches meet together for prayer meetings and revival services.[135] Throughout the 1850s, the Free and United Presbyterian churches co-operated together in general missionary societies such as the Glasgow City Mission, as well as in the Sabbath School Union and in Thomas Guthrie's Ragged School com-

---

131. *UPM*, iii (May 1859), 216–17.
132. *HFRFC*, vii (March 1857), 181.
133. Guthrie and Guthrie, *Autobiography of Thomas Guthrie*, i, 386.
134. James Hall Wilson, *Our Moral Wastes, and how to reclaim them* (London, 1859), 70–1.
135. *HFRFC*, iv (July 1860), 287–8; C. J. Marrs, 'The 1859 religious revival in Scotland' (PhD thesis, University of Glasgow, 1995), 193–9.

mittees.[136] Members of other denominations also co-operated in mission stations connected with one particular church, in a similar vein to the large dissenting presence at the West Port under Chalmers. For instance, at the United Presbyterian minister John Henderson's preaching station at the foot of the Saltmarket in Glasgow, ministers of numerous denominations took turns preaching there every Sunday, illustrating in the eyes of the *United Presbyterian Magazine* 'the spirit of the Evangelical Alliance'.[137] In 1858 Hamilton MacGill, the Home Mission secretary of the United Presbyterian Church, wrote to his colleague William Clark calling for a 'union' of Scotland's evangelical churches on the grounds of a common urban mission.[138]

This spirit of co-operation was carried into other areas of social reform. The Free Kirk minister James Begg and the United Presbyterian and radical politician Duncan McLaren's partnership on the issue of working-class housing represented one of the most significant and durable examples of collaboration between the dissenting churches in social reform. As discussed in Chapter Six, though the pair were worlds apart ecclesiastically – McLaren was one of the chief agitators of the Voluntary Controversy of the 1830s while Begg was a staunch anti-voluntary who vehemently opposed union with the United Presbyterians after 1863 – they often aligned, and actively co-operated, in the major social, political and national questions of the period.[139] Following his stint as convenor of the Home Missions Committee between 1847 and 1849, Begg, unlike many of his fellow ministers, turned his attention to the more secular matter of the housing question, an issue in which he became the dominant voice in Scotland for the following fifteen years.[140] Like Chalmers, Begg pursued the creation of an independent, self-sustaining working class. For Begg, ownership of property or, as he put it, a system in which 'every man can become his own landlord', was the key to achieving working-class elevation and independence, and provided a secular counterbalance to Chalmers' Christian communal vision.[141] He argued that 'whilst the grand cure for the woes of society is only to be found in the gospel of the grace of God . . . the most important physical remedy for the woes of man is

---

136. *UPM*, iii (May 1859), 215, 217; Thomas Guthrie, *A Plea for Ragged Schools; or, Prevention better than cure* (Edinburgh, 1849), 14–15.
137. *UPM*, iii (May 1859), 217–18.
138. Hamilton MacGill to William Clark, 7 August 1858, NLS, Letter-books of the Home Mission Secretary and of the clerks in the Foreign Mission Office of the United Presbyterian Church, MSS 7734.
139. Smith, *Memoirs of James Begg*, ii, 148–50; Mackie, *Duncan McLaren*, ii, 141.
140. Smith, *Memoirs of James Begg*, ii, 129–36; James Begg, *Happy Homes for Working Men, and how to get them* (London, 1866), 19.
141. James Begg, *How Every Man May Become His Own Landlord; or, a way by which to elevate the condition of the masses of Britain, and develop the resources of the country* (Edinburgh, 1851), 5–15.

a comfortable and wholesome dwelling'.[142] As convenor of the housing committee from the late 1850s, and as the driving force of the Edinburgh Co-operative Building Society after 1861, Begg aimed to combat what he regarded as the physical and spiritual deficiencies of Scotland's working classes.[143]

From the outset, Begg was supported in his aims by McLaren and other key members of the United Presbyterian Church. His lecture on 10 January 1850, during which he proposed a series of 'reformations' in areas such as housing, sanitation, education and land reform, took place in John French's United Presbyterian Church in South College Street, Edinburgh. In addition, a number of meetings and lectures associated with the Scottish Social Reform Association, founded by Begg a week later, were organised in William Peddie's Bristo Street United Presbyterian Church and attended by numerous dissenting ministers and businessmen.[144] The SSRA, in which Begg was 'powerfully supported' by McLaren, William Lindsay and the Church of Scotland Lord Provost William Chambers, aimed to both elevate the working classes and diminish public burdens by building cheap, new houses in the more spacious suburbs of the cities, reforming the land-laws, including the abolition of entails to enable the poor to purchase their own homes, and creating an industrious working-class community.[145]

While Begg repudiated party interests and stressed that neither he nor his movement belonged to any political party, his agenda for social reform was intrinsically linked to wider political and national issues.[146] For instance, he argued that 'the state of Scotland could never be materially improved until some better plan were fallen upon by which to govern it'.[147] This connection between the spiritual, social and political welfare of Scotland, Begg claimed, was founded in his experience of the Disruption and his subsequent fundraising trip to America. He argued that his attempts to reform the Established Church before 1843 were inseparable to his 'broader platform' of rejuvenating Scotland as a whole. He asserted, 'I am still in connection with true-hearted Scotchmen, both in and out of the Establishment, seeking the accomplishment of the same objects.'[148] As we saw in the previous chapter, Begg's vision of a property-owning Christian democracy led him, alongside McLaren, to campaign for the

---

142. Begg, *Happy Homes for Working Men*, 9.
143. *PGAFC, 1858* (Edinburgh, 1858), 237; Begg, *Happy Homes for Working Men*, 20, 23, 28.
144. *Caledonian Mercury*, 14 January 1850; *Scotsman*, 23 March 1850; *Scotsman*, 26 February 1851; *Dundee, Perth, and Cupar Advertiser*, 19 April 1850.
145. *Scotsman*, 18 December 1850; Begg, *How Every Man May Become His Own Landlord*, 20–2; Begg, *Happy Homes for Working Men*, 20, 50.
146. Smith, *Memoirs of James Begg*, ii, 148–50.
147. *Caledonian Mercury*, 14 January 1850.
148. *Stirling Observer*, 19 February 1857.

extension of the forty shilling freehold to Scotland.[149] According to Begg, the introduction of this expansion of the franchise would help inspire the elevation and independence of the self-improving working class, and in doing so stabilise Britain's class and social structure by creating 'safer' and more responsible citizens.[150]

In many respects, these movements for social and political reform were intertwined with both a secular quasi-nationalist vision of Scotland (evident in Begg and McLaren's prominent roles in the Scottish Rights movement) and the new post-Disruption and religiously pluralist context. The trauma of the Disruption had not only opened up a rift between the state and the church, it also created a blank canvas on which new or reimagined versions of Scotland as a godly nation could be depicted. For Begg, a Free Church minister intrinsically linked with secular concerns, Scotland's national, social and political well-being was bound together with its religious strength. Though interested in distinctly nineteenth-century problems such as urban living standards, Begg's social activism was based on the romanticised memory of Scotland's covenanting history. While Scotland's fragmented churches were losing their grip on an increasingly godless society, Begg, like his mentor Chalmers, longed for a return to an almost certainly imagined past in which Presbyterianism was key to Scotland's social, political and national position. He believed in the 'heavenly power of the Gospel to heal a nation's woes, and convert a land of bleak mountains and inauspicious climate into a garden of the Lord'.[151] As the Church of Scotland, and Presbyterianism in general, could no longer be viewed as the mirror in which to view Scotland's society, the likes of Begg and McLaren utilised the rhetoric and social aims of Chalmers' godly commonwealth ideal, and placed them within a new secular context.

The aftermath of the Disruption offered Scotland's dissenters an opportunity to reshape their own vision of Scottish society. While Chalmers' territorial scheme was nothing new, it nevertheless was reimagined in a new pluralist and dissenting context. Of course, though Chalmers' wish to return to the communal bonds of the eighteenth-century parish was impossible within industrialised cities, his renewed territorial, national and interdenominational vision allowed space for the creation of an energetic and co-operative social identity. However, the creation of this 'happy rivalry' in urban missions and social reform was often offset, as we will see in the next chapter, by intra-church apathy, sectarian jealousies and the Free Kirk's lingering 'national church' agenda. Nevertheless, it did at least shape a society in which the dissenting churches had an increasingly prominent role. This dissenting social vision did not usher in the

---

149. Mechie, *Church and Scottish Social Development*, 135
150. Begg, *How Every Man May Become His Own Landlord*, 19; *Scotsman*, 26 February 1851.
151. Wylie, *Tercentenary of the Scottish Reformation*, xvii.

godly nation as hoped, but instead laid the foundations for increased state interference in the lives of the poor. This prospect of state intervention in traditionally religious affairs and the lack of dissenting unity in the face of Scotland's changing social context was exemplified in the national education debates of this period.

CHAPTER EIGHT

Scottish Education and Dissenting Division

The previous chapters have shown that the period after 1843 was largely one of convergence and co-operation between Scotland's two major dissenting churches. Collaboration in formal and informal groups and initiatives such as the Evangelical Alliance, territorial home mission work and the anti-Maynooth political alliance saw the Free and United Presbyterian churches working together under the loose umbrella of dissent. The relatively organic formation of this dissenting identity even led to calls for union between the two denominations. The increasing prominence of the national education debates, particularly after 1850, offered Scottish dissenters another chance to act in tandem against the religious and political establishment. These debates focused on reform of Scotland's traditional and seemingly defective parochial school system under the control of the Church of Scotland in favour of a national and non-sectarian scheme, and by the mid-1850s the subject had surpassed the Maynooth controversy as the dominant Scottish politico-religious issue of this period.[1]

Despite the anti-establishment appeal of the national education movement, the alliance it created within Scottish dissent was extremely loose, and exposed the shortcomings and fragility of the co-operation employed in other ecclesiastical, political and social matters. Donald J. Withrington has noted that the difficulties encountered in the education debates ensured that, a decade after the Disruption, the Free Church was a 'house deeply, even irrevocably, divided against itself'.[2] This argument could be extended to incorporate both of Scotland's major non-established churches. Both the Free and United Presbyterian churches, to greater or lesser degrees, bickered between and among themselves over the future direction and principles of any proposed national system. While the Free Church, busy with its own educational programme after 1843, argued internally over the merits of national education and split into two distinct camps on the issue, Scottish Presbyterian dissent in general was divided over the role of religious education in such a system. This often bitter debate on the 'religious element' obstructed the passing of an acceptable scheme for over twenty years and underpinned the historiographical tendency to depict the Scottish

---

1. John Stevenson, *Fulfilling a Vision: the contribution of the Church of Scotland to school education, 1772–1872* (Eugene, 2012), 90.
2. Withrington, 'Adrift among the reefs of conflicting ideals? Education and the Free Church, 1843–55', in Brown and Fry, *Scotland in the age of the Disruption*, 92.

education debates as a period of hostility within Scottish Presbyterianism.[3] Nevertheless, the numerous attempts at unity by Scottish dissenters, particularly within the organisation of the National Education Association of Scotland (NEA), ensure that the education debates must be viewed within the context of increasing dissenting co-operation after 1843. While exposing the limits of such convergence, the education question provided one albeit rocky path to union between Scotland's dissenting Presbyterians. This chapter will assess the national education debates in the context of dissenting relations and the various appeals for unity that emanated from this period. First, it will examine how both the Free Church's educational scheme and the national education movement originated and the reasons for their creation. Second, it will examine the divisions within Scottish dissent over education, both within the Free Kirk surrounding its commitment to its own scheme, and the disagreements between the churches over the future direction of any national system. Finally, the chapter will give a detailed overview of the various national education bills of the 1850s, and will assess how the debates surrounding these offer an insight into both the grounds for unity and separation within Scottish dissent in this period, as well as the differing and fluid aspects of dissenting 'identity' adopted by these Presbyterians in the decades after 1843.

The Parochial System and the Free Church Educational Scheme

The Disruption of the Church of Scotland completely changed the face of the Scottish education system. During the 1830s and 1840s, the Established Churches' traditional control over educational provision for children throughout the United Kingdom was coming under threat from the increasing pressures of industrialisation, urbanisation and the growing influence of organised nonconformity. In 1831 a state-run multi-denominational education system was introduced in Ireland, a move which effectively paved the way for the partial disestablishment of the Church of Ireland two years later following the Irish Church Temporalities Act. Despite a brief yet significant revival of church schools in the late 1830s, the Whig government's attempts at reform from 1839 and the spectacularly successful nonconformist opposition to Sir James Graham's 1843 Factory Bill proved a major coup for the dissenting challenge to the national churches' statutory supremacy over education and British society in general.[4] Nevertheless, prior to the events of May 1843 Scottish education, and particularly the country's parish school system, remained seemingly integral to Scotland's national character. At the onset of the Ten Years' Conflict in 1834, the secretary to the Glasgow Education

---

3. Mechie, *Church and Scottish Social Development*, 148–9; Drummond and Bulloch, *Church in Victorian Scotland*, 94; Parry, *Democracy and Religion*, 339–40.
4. Ryan Mallon, 'Scottish Presbyterianism and the National Education Debates', *Studies in Church History*, 55 (2019), 363–4.

Society and future Free Churchman George Lewis linked the maintenance of Scotland's schools with that of the Kirk itself. He wrote that 'in all but our parochial churches and parochial schools we have lost our nationality. In these alone we survive as a nation – stand apart from and are superior to England.'[5] The national parochial system, dating back to the Reformation and John Knox's First Book of Discipline in 1560, aimed to supply religious and secular education to every child in Scotland, with a school planted in every parish and placed under the ecclesiastical superintendence of the Church of Scotland and the heritors. Its heritage and status was central to both Scotland's national pride after the union of 1707 and the mythologising of Scottish education as truly national, democratic and superior to their neighbour south of the Tweed. According to the *North British Review* in 1850, 'if you move but one inch towards the sacred precincts of education, on all sides arouses a loud laudation of the Parochial School System, as perfect and unimprovable'. Before the Disruption, the majority of Scotland's Presbyterians readily viewed these parish schools as 'the glory of Scotland, the nursery of sages, the wonder of the earth, the *ne plus ultra* of wisdom . . . to touch which is profanation and treason against the best interests of the land'.[6]

However, this rose-tinted view of Scotland's national educational heritage only served to mask the realities of the situation, even before 1843. By the time of the Disruption, the parish schools were generally deficient in both quantity and quality, prompting many middle-class Scots to send their children to more attractive private schools.[7] The much-vaunted Scottish education system, though achieving one of the highest literacy rates in early nineteenth-century Europe, appeared to have fallen behind, especially in urban areas as industrialisation changed the face of British society.[8] Despite the idealised tradition of a 'school in every parish', the Church of Scotland's grip on the education of the country's children was slipping. In 1834 just over a fifth of Scotland's schools were part of the parish system.[9] By the end of the 1840s, the educational provision of roughly 200,000 children between the ages of six and fifteen was unaccounted for, and over a third of those who did attend belonged to schools maintained by groups or private individuals with no formal attachment to any religious denomination.[10] Dissenting schools began to proliferate from the 1820s

---

5. Lewis, *Scotland a Half Educated Nation*, 75.
6. *North British Review*, xii (February 1850), 260.
7. D. J. Withrington, 'The Free Church Educational Scheme 1843–50', *RSCHS*, xv (1964), 104.
8. S. J. Brown, 'Religion in Scotland', in H. T. Dickinson (ed.), *A Companion to Eighteenth-Century Britain* (Oxford, 2002), 263.
9. Stevenson, 'Scottish Schooling in the Denominational Era', in Anderson, Freeman and Paterson, *The Edinburgh History of Education in Scotland*, 137.
10. *Report of the Education Committee of the Free Church of Scotland* (Edinburgh, 1849), 25; *UPM*, iv (April 1850), 164; Thomas Gordon, *Education in Scotland: its actual amount, embracing the results of the census* (Edinburgh, 1854), iv–vii.

and a vast network of charity schools was also provided in the Highlands by the Scottish Society for the Propagation of Christian Knowledge (which largely fell under the control of the Kirk) and the Edinburgh Society for the Support of Gaelic Schools.[11]

The Free Church minister William Maxwell Hetherington linked the lack of sufficient quantity of Kirk-led teaching, especially in the cities, to the 'rapidly advancing tide' of crime, intemperance and immorality, especially among young people.[12] The growth of the population, combined with the ecclesiastical and social change of the nineteenth century, ensured that the parochial school system of John Knox had 'long failed to overtake the needs of the country'.[13] According to the Free Church *North British Review*, while the parochial system suited eighteenth-century Scottish society, the changing circumstances emphasised the 'folly' of allowing it to remain in its current state.[14] Those who had left the establishment in 1843 were also quick to point out the deficiencies in quality of the parish system. The Church was viewed as powerless to dispense with bad teachers, while the system of supervision and examination of the schools by the presbyteries was condemned by Thomas Guthrie as a 'decent sham'.[15]

The inadequate state of education in Scotland, and in particular that of the parish schools, was highlighted by the Disruption, which instigated a period of confusion and dispute concerning the future of the parochial system.[16] In a similar manner to the nonconformist opposition to state church schools in England, Wales and Ireland in this period, most of the criticism directed at the parish schools centred on the vice-like grip retained by the Established Church after 1843. As Callum Brown has argued, education traditionally formed an integral part of the Kirk's attempt to control Scottish society. Schoolmasters were paid by the heritors and supervised by the presbytery, and were often key members of the local parish.[17] Despite constituting a minority of the Scottish population following the Disruption, the Church of Scotland nevertheless maintained this privileged position and its adherence to the 'formula', which stipulated that all parochial teachers must belong to the Established Kirk (though the schools were open to all children regardless of denominational background). Guthrie criticised the exclusion of all other Presbyterian teachers as part of the establishment's

---

11. Elizabeth Ritchie, '"Alive to the advantages of education". Problems in using the *New Statistical Account* to research Education: a Case Study of the Isle of Skye', *Northern Scotland*, vii (2016), 85–92.
12. William Maxwell Hetherington, *National Education in Scotland, viewed in its present condition, its principles and its possibilities* (Edinburgh, 1850), 5.
13. Guthrie and Guthrie, *Autobiography of Thomas Guthrie*, ii, 285.
14. *North British Review*, xii (February 1850), 260.
15. Guthrie and Guthrie, *Autobiography of Thomas Guthrie*, ii, 297.
16. D. J. Withrington, 'The 1851 Census of Religious Worship and Education: with a note on church accommodation in mid-nineteenth century Scotland', *Records of the Scottish Church History*, xviii (1974), 138.
17. Brown, *Social History of Religion*, 98–9.

attempt to continue its 'supremacy' over both the schools and Scottish society in general. According to Guthrie, as the Church of Scotland no longer represented the majority of the Scottish people, it could also no longer claim special national and political rights, including over education.[18] James Begg echoed this point and asserted that, because the 'spirit of Knox' had left the establishment at the Disruption, the state church should now end its 'unnatural alliance' with Knox's schools.[19] Guthrie and Begg's colleague William Gunn argued that while 'the parochial schools were designed to be a national institution for the godly upbringing of the whole youth of the country ... their present constitution limits the choice of the teachers to a mere fraction of the community, and regulates the important matters of election and superintendence on principles which are prejudicial to the best interests of education'.[20] The Established Kirk's attitude to its continuing control of the national schools was dismissed by the Free Church as 'the reverse of national – narrow, exclusive, and sectarian'.[21]

In a bid to end what they regarded as a sectarian hold on what should have been national education, and to strike a blow at their former colleagues in the Established Kirk, the solution commonly offered by the Free Church was to abolish the tests and open the position of parochial teacher to all candidates, or at least those Presbyterian dissenters adhering to the Bible and Shorter Catechism.[22] The exclusivity of the current system, and the need for some kind of reform, was emphasised by the furore that surrounded the dismissal of teachers professing allegiance to the Free Church after the Disruption. At the October 1843 Free Church General Assembly, it was noted that 164 Church of Scotland teachers and 198 privately endowed and adventure school teachers had been dismissed for holding Free Church principles. It was claimed that five months after the Disruption, over 20,000 children were receiving daily instruction from teachers adhering to the Free Church.[23] Within a year, the total number of dismissed teachers had risen to 408, including over two hundred former parish school teachers. The entire staff of the two Normal Schools, or teacher-training academies, in Edinburgh and Glasgow were also ejected for seceding to the Free Church. 'Indignation meetings' were held across

18. Guthrie and Guthrie, *Autobiography of Thomas Guthrie*, 291, 295.
19. James Begg, *National Education for Scotland practically considered; with notices of certain recent proposals on that subject* (Edinburgh, 1850), 9.
20. *Fife Herald*, 12 April 1849.
21. *North British Review*, xii (February 1850), 267; Joseph Fletcher, *Education: National, Voluntary, and Free* (London, 1851), 74.
22. Guthrie and Guthrie, *Autobiography of Thomas Guthrie*, 287.
23. *PGAFC, October 1843* (Glasgow, 1843), 78–9. Of the 164 teachers formerly affiliated with the Church of Scotland before the Disruption, eighty were parochial schoolmasters, fifty-seven taught at the Assembly Schools and twenty-seven belonged to the Society for the Propagation of Christian Knowledge.

the country in protest at the treatment of these teachers at the hands of a 'remorseless' establishment.[24] According to Donald Withrington, these dismissals, combined with the aggressive militancy of a large section of the new church, provided the immediate occasion for the establishment of the Free Kirk's own education scheme, with the intention of rivalling the parish schools on a national scale.[25]

At the May General Assembly that followed the Disruption, Thomas Chalmers and David Welsh emphasised the Free Church's moral responsibility and duty to provide jobs for the 'cruelly injured' parochial and private teachers. Robert Candlish went further, expanding the Free Church's duty beyond the teachers, and onto the education of the children of all those who joined the new body at the Disruption. Like many of the more zealous advocates of the Free Church, Candlish was keen 'not to throw the education of our youth', and in essence Scottish education in general, 'into the hands of those whose principles we have condemned'.[26] In order to provide for both the teachers and children of the Free Church, and to protect the values of the new denomination, the creation of a new Free Church education programme parallel and in competition with the old parochial system was deemed necessary by Candlish and his allies.[27] A distinct education scheme, 'equivalent' but separate from the parish schools and ranging from the village school to university, would also prove integral to the Free Church's claim to be the true national church of Scotland. Welsh argued that 'the functions of any Church, and especially of a Church that aspires to the character of national, cannot be considered as completely fulfilled till provision is made for the religious training of the children and young persons connected with it'.[28] The national pretensions of the Free Church education scheme were such that the *Free Church Magazine* called on parents to withdraw their children from the parochial schools. According to the magazine, the Disruption had dissolved the Established Kirk's standing as 'moral police' of the parish, with the Free Kirk now positioning itself as the true guardian of Scottish education.[29] To many within the Free Church, the education scheme represented not only denominational ambition, but the chance to re-energise Scottish religion and society.[30] It also represented the regeneration of Scotland's failing parochial system, in both its national and religious character. Echoing the utopian ideals of John Knox's original system, one Free Church minister 'hoped the Assembly would never rest

24. Brown, *Annals of the Disruption*, 312–13.
25. Withrington, 'Free Church Educational Scheme', 105.
26. *PGAFC, May 1843*, 49, 54, 125.
27. For a detailed account of the early years of the Free Church's education scheme, see Withrington, 'Free Church Educational Scheme', 103–15.
28. *PGAFC, May 1843*, 115, 146.
29. *FCM*, i (February 1844), 38–9.
30. Withrington, 'Education and the Free Church', 83.

from their labours till by the side of every Free Church there was planted a Free school'.[31]

Despite the idealism of supporters of the new scheme, some opposition from a significant minority arose almost immediately. This group, containing the likes of Thomas Guthrie and Hugh Miller, felt that the Free Church should not cut itself off from Scotland's national educational heritage. Instead, they believed that they should attempt to loosen the Church of Scotland's hold on the parish schools, which were already established on an agreeable theological footing that incorporated the Bible and Shorter Catechism. They also pointed out the difficulty of raising funds for an extended school system during a period in which much of the church's attention was drawn to the arguably more important building and sustentation programmes.[32] Nevertheless, Candlish argued that the education scheme was 'one of the most vital and important of the Free Church's undertakings'.[33] At the October General Assembly, John MacDonald, a young minister at the rural parish of Blairgowrie, supported by Candlish, proposed a subscription scheme with the aim of raising £50,000 to build five hundred schools connected with the Free Church.[34] The success of the scheme was immediate. £52,000 was raised within six months before rising to £60,000 by the end of 1844, prompting the General Assembly to make the fund a permanent part of the church's financial constitution, and to consider extending the scheme to the Highlands.[35] By 1847, 513 Free Church masters were teaching roughly 44,000 children.[36] Within a decade of the scheme's establishment, it provided for over seven hundred schools (430 of which were connected to Free Church congregations) and roughly 70,000 pupils, proving an effective rival to the parish schools of the Church of Scotland.[37] Despite the overtly sectarian attitudes of some of its own ministers, who wanted schools set up 'for the exclusive benefit of our own people', the Free Church education scheme did not, unlike its establishment counterpart, place restrictions on the denominational adherence of its teachers.[38] In a report conducted in 1857, of the almost 32,000 scholars in the 568 Free Church schools which supplied information, 10,054 belonged to the establishment, 614 were Roman Catholics and

31. *PGAFC*, October 1843, 82.
32. Withrington, 'Free Church Educational Scheme', 106–7; Withrington, 'Education and the Free Church', 83; Brown, *Annals of the Disruption*, 314; *PGAFC*, October 1843, 82.
33. Guthrie and Guthrie, *Autobiography of Thomas Guthrie*, 286.
34. *PGAFC*, October 1843, 81; *Education Commission (Scotland). First Report by Her Majesty's Commissioners appointed to inquire into the schools in Scotland* [Cd. 3483], H.C. 1865, xvii, 95.
35. Brown, *Thomas Chalmers and the Godly Commonwealth*, 342; Withrington, 'Free Church Educational Scheme', 107.
36. Brown, *National Churches*, 360.
37. *Fife Herald*, 2 June 1853; Mechie, *Church and Scottish Social Development*, 147; Brown, *National Churches*, 407.
38. *A Letter to Dr Chalmers, on the organisation of a Free Presbyterian Church* (Edinburgh, 1843), 12–13; Education Commission (Scotland), *First Report . . . schools in Scotland*, 122.

9,223 were affiliated with the other denominations.[39] According to Stewart J. Brown, the 'national' character of the scheme was a source of pride to the Free Church and reaffirmed its self-proclaimed status as the guardian of Scotland's educational heritage.[40]

However, difficulties had become increasingly apparent in the scheme by the mid-1840s, which threatened to derail Free Church hopes of creating a truly national education system that would usurp the establishment. Funding had dried up and certain projects such as the Normal Training schools in Edinburgh and Glasgow drained increasingly limited resources; in addition, promises for the school-building fund went unfulfilled. The salaries of teachers who had seceded from the establishment were lower than before the Disruption, with only fifty ejected schoolmasters receiving a wage from the Free Church. The education scheme, it appeared, was on the verge of 'inevitable and disastrous bankruptcy'.[41] While the number of children receiving education from the Free Church was undoubtedly impressive, the rise of the education scheme was not as meteoric as was often presented. Withrington has pointed out that at least 124 of the Free Church schools had been in existence before 1843 and were in essence 'ready-made' for the post-Disruption period.[42] Though the Free Church succeeded in ably tending to its own flock, it failed to make any substantial national impact on the educational provision of the poor living in the towns and cities.[43] The emergence of a rejuvenated Established Church in this period also led to desperate attempts by the Free Church to expand their education scheme in the interests of 'self-preservation'. This perceived threat prompted Candlish, hitherto the spokesman for the denominational interests of the Free Church in education, to call on Scotland's voluntaries in the hope that 'all evangelical dissenters should unite and set up an efficient system of schools over the whole kingdom, withdrawing their children from the parochial schools'.[44] Unsurprisingly, this approach fell on deaf ears. In a bid to re-energise the scheme, Candlish replaced William Cunningham as convenor of the Free Church Education Committee in 1846.[45]

In December of that year, the Privy Council Committee on Education opted to extend the system of grants to facilitate the building of schools by all Protestant and Roman Catholic churches operating outside of the estab-

---

39. William Fraser, *The State of our Educational Enterprises: a report of an examination into the working, results, and tendencies of the chief public educational experiments in Great Britain and Ireland* (Glasgow, 1858), 143–4.
40. Brown, *Thomas Chalmers and the Godly Commonwealth*, 342.
41. Hugh Miller, 'Thoughts on the Educational Question', in John Davidson (ed.), *Leading Articles on Various Subjects* (Edinburgh, 1872), 57–61.
42. Withrington, 'Education and the Free Church', 79.
43. Education Commission (Scotland), *First Report . . . schools in Scotland*, 96, 102.
44. Withrington, 'Education and the Free Church', 84.
45. Withrington, 'Free Church Educational Scheme', 107.

lishment. The introduction of these grants prompted a debate that divided the Free Church and offered an indication of the future direction and identity of the education scheme. In the wake of both the Disruption and the controversy over the Maynooth grant, Chalmers and other members of the Free Kirk Education Committee expressed concern about the government's motives and the potential for the 'indiscriminate' endowment of truth and error.[46] The grants also provoked a resurgence of the opposition to the Free Church scheme led by the likes of Guthrie and James Begg. Along with Lord Melgund in parliament, they noted that the Privy Council would offer these grants to the Free Church as a sect, a situation that would highlight and exacerbate sectarianism and denominational disputes in Scottish education, contrary to both the country's traditions and the pretensions of the Free Church to represent the nation.[47] Such was the sectarian pull of the new system that by 1849 even the United Presbyterian Church were considering the grants. Though these voluntaries were historically opposed to making education the subject of denominational rivalry by establishing their own distinct schools, they believed that the new system of grants led to the prospect of otherwise being 'excluded from any reasonable influence over existing institutions'.[48] Candlish's decision to accept the grants at the 1847 General Assembly both shocked his critics – he had previously been one of the most vociferous opponents of state grants – and offered an early sign that the Free Church, at least in education, was beginning to place party over nation.[49] The Free Kirk minister Alexander Moody Stuart claimed that Candlish's acceptance of the grants represented both a deviation in the church's founding principles and a 'dangerous' union with 'unbelievers', therefore 'sinking' the Disruption's protest against the sins of the state.[50]

Rather than provide the much-anticipated solution to Scotland's educational ills, the Disruption, and the growth of the Free Church's own education scheme, only served to complicate further its existing problems. As Stewart Mechie noted, instead of overtaking the outmoded parish schools of the establishment as the true national schools of Scotland, the Free Church scheme and its notable success made the denominational pattern of Scottish education more complex and competitive than ever.[51] The

---

46. Hanna, *Memoirs of Thomas Chalmers*, ii, 756–8; Fletcher, *Education: National, Voluntary, and Free*, 73; Begg, *National Education for Scotland practically considered*, 13.
47. *Ecclesiastical Gazette*, xi (September 1848), 58.
48. *Greenock Advertiser*, 15 May 1849; *Caledonian Mercury*, 5 November 1849. Ultimately, the United Presbyterians largely ignored the Privy Council Grants system, with only three of their schools receiving state funds in 1859 (William Fraser, *The Educational Condition of Scotland: a national disgrace* (Paisley, 1859), 11).
49. *Scotsman*, 5 May 1847.
50. Alexander Moody Stuart, *An inquiry into the character of the present educational connexion between the Free Church and the government* (Edinburgh, 1848), 28–33, 49.
51. Mechie, *Church and Scottish Social Development*, 147.

existence of nine or ten different types of schools belonging to a range of denominations and secular initiatives ushered in an increasingly denominational complexion to Scottish education.[52] The introduction of the Privy Council Grants underlined this new situation – by the late 1850s, over four hundred Free Church and five hundred establishment schools were receiving parliamentary grants, almost a third of the entire number of day schools in Scotland.[53] According to the educationist and Free Church minister at Paisley, William Fraser, this denominational system of education, aided by the Privy Council Grants, was partially responsible for the continuing 'unsatisfactory' position of Scottish education.[54] Regardless of the national or sectarian pretensions of the denominational schools, by the late 1840s it was becoming increasingly apparent that the various churches acting alone could not fully tackle Scotland's education problem, particularly among the lower classes.[55] Though an ambitious attempt to establish their own national system, the denominational nature and shortcomings of the Free Church scheme highlighted the need for a comprehensive national scheme endorsed by the state that encompassed all of Presbyterian Scotland, if not Scotland in general.

The National Education Association and Free Church Tension

The failure of both the established parochial schools and the new Free Church scheme to impart anything close to a fully realised national system suited to the educational needs of Scotland led many Scots to conclude that only the involvement of the state, and the creation of a national compulsory scheme under its control, could unify and adequately provide Scottish education.[56] To opponents of Candlish's denominational scheme such as Thomas Guthrie and James Begg, state intervention provided the only possibility of education reaching the lowest classes. According to his sons, Guthrie's interest in the education and welfare of the poor, illustrated by his central role in the Edinburgh Ragged School movement, 'deepened his conviction that out and beyond all the efforts which Churches and private benevolence can make, the necessities of the case never could or would be met until the State addressed itself to the question'.[57] In an 1850 pamphlet extolling the virtues of national education, Begg went further, and claimed that the inadequacy of Scotland's education system was one of the reasons the country, 'heretofore stood in the first rank of nations',

---

52. Drummond and Bulloch, *Church in Victorian Scotland*, 91.
53. Fraser, *Educational Condition of Scotland*, 11.
54. *Paisley Herald and Renfrewshire Advertiser*, 22 January 1859.
55. Education Commission (Scotland), *First Report . . . schools in Scotland*, 97, 102; Hanna, *Memoir of Thomas Chalmers*, i, 756; *Report of the proceedings of the public meeting of the friends of National Education* (Edinburgh, 1854), 74.
56. Mechie, *Church and Scottish Social Development*, 147; *Caledonian Mercury*, 5 November 1849.
57. Guthrie and Guthrie, *Autobiography of Thomas Guthrie*, 285.

had 'greatly sunk'. For Begg, a 'well-directed' national system of education could provide the 'greatest boon to the poor, the stability of the Church, the best hope of government'. He pointed out that the Free Church education scheme was never intended to be a national system, and lacked the resources to extend beyond its 'narrow and sectarian' aims. Claiming that less than two-thirds of Free Church congregations were supplied with schools, Begg argued that 'our scheme, important and eminently creditable as it is, does not promise to educate the Free Church, far less the nation'.[58] By the middle of the century, the apparent necessity for national education outlined by Begg and Guthrie was beginning to occupy the minds of both church and statesmen, and the attention of the general public, and offered a platform on which Scotland's disparate Presbyterian dissenters could meet.[59]

This increased attention and demand was met by the formation of the National Education Association (NEA) of Scotland in April 1850. This group, led by the Free Church MP for Perthshire Fox Maule (Lord Panmure after his succession to the peerage in 1852), consisted of members of most of Scotland's dissenting denominations, and called for the creation of a comprehensive, state-funded national system of education, freely available but not compulsory, based on the extension of the existing parochial schools.[60] It criticised the exclusivity and sectarianism associated with the establishment's control and management of the parish schools. The society also called for the abolition of religious tests for teachers, raising the pay and status of schoolmasters, and advocated the creation of local boards elected by the parents and ratepayers and consisting of members of all sects and denominations. Taking over from the Church of Scotland ministers and heritors, these boards would manage the schools, appoint teachers, determine the curriculum and would be supervised by a national central board.[61]

The association, while emphasising the importance of an extended religious education, also argued that the government and any proposed bill for national education should focus solely on secular education and not interfere with religious instruction in the schools. As a result of the difficulties that would be perceived automatically to follow any attempt by the government to impose unilaterally a particular kind of religious instruction, responsibility for religion in the schools would be left to the parents and local boards. The association argued that placing the power in the hands of the heads of

---

58. Begg, *National Education for Scotland practically considered*, 3–4, 9–12.
59. *Caledonian Mercury*, 5 November 1849; *Christian Witness and Church Members' Magazine*, vii (March 1850), 187.
60. *National Education Association of Scotland* (Edinburgh, 1850), 1–2; *Friends of National Education*, 13, 26; *Caledonian Mercury*, 15 November 1849. There was some opposition from otherwise staunch supporters of the NEA, such as Guthrie, who believed that education should be compulsory in a national system, in order to reach the lowest classes (Guthrie and Guthrie, *Autobiography of Thomas Guthrie*, 297–8).
61. *NEA*, 2; *Friends of National Education*, 16; *UPM*, viii (March 1854), 142.

families on a case-by-case basis would 'afford not only a basis of union for the great mass of the people of this country, but a far better security than any at present exists both for a good secular and a good Christian education'. According to Maule, by achieving these projected reforms, 'we change the name of parochial into national, and sweep the whole of that mighty institution reinvigorated and revived into the scheme which we are this day assembled to advocate and advance'. The principles advocated by the association promised to form the basis on which practical legislation would be passed, and unity among Scotland's Presbyterians could be achieved.[62]

To a certain degree, this assertion proved correct. By providing a viable alternative to the institutionalised sectarianism of the parish schools and the Privy Council Grants, Scotland's dissenters were able to unite within the National Education Association based on a shared opposition to the current system, if not on an agreed path forward. At a public meeting of the association in Edinburgh in 1854, the Congregationalist W. L. Alexander criticised the government's system of grants, claiming it fostered the 'hostility of sects' and created 'sectarian schools' in which bigotry was 'imbibed as a very part of education'.[63] This need for reform from an overtly sectarian system, and a shared opposition to the Established Church's educational monopoly, pushed sections of the Free and United Presbyterian churches closer together.[64] In October 1849, two presbyteries of the United Presbyterian Church called for co-operation within Presbyterian dissent to reform the 'highly questionable constitution' of the parish schools system, by transferring the national schools from the control of the Church Courts to a 'properly derived local management'.[65]

However, defenders of the Established schools criticised attempts at dissenting co-operation on this basis as simply an excuse to attack the Church of Scotland.[66] This charge was refuted by Fox Maule, who nevertheless maintained that the Established Kirk no longer represented the 'true' Church of Scotland after the Disruption and therefore could not hold exclusive domination over the parish schools.[67] Despite Maule's protestations, it was apparent that one of the major features of the emerging national education movement was its challenge to the Kirk's monopoly over the parish schools. Therefore it is not surprising that the group's core support lay in the dissenting churches. However, according to the *Caledonian Mercury* in late 1849, when it came to deciding which course of action these reformers should take, 'serious differences among those beyond the pale of the Establishment . . . for the time threaten to preclude

62. *NEA*, 1–3; *Friends of National Education*, 16.
63. *Friends of National Education*, 25.
64. *Caledonian Mercury*, 15 November 1849.
65. *Scotsman*, 6 October 1849.
66. *The Education Question in Scotland* (Cupar-Fife, 1853), 5–6.
67. *Friends of National Education*, 14–15.

any co-operation'.⁶⁸ While 'conflicting' views on a potential national education scheme divided Scotland's dissenting bodies, the Free Church itself was at odds over whether to pursue such a system.⁶⁹

The growth of the national education movement brought to a head the factional conflict that had been developing within the Free Church from the advent of its education scheme in October 1843. As noted previously, an influential minority within the Education Committee openly opposed the establishment of the education scheme and the later acceptance of the Privy Council Grants. Led by Thomas Guthrie, Hugh Miller, James Begg and William Gunn, this group believed that the Free Church scheme promoted sectarian interests and would turn attention within the church away from the promotion of a truly national system of education based on the opening up and extension of the parochial schools. Candlish's affirmation of the denominational character of the scheme, and his view that the maintenance of these schools was integral to the future prosperity of the Free Church itself, provoked fierce criticism from Guthrie and his supporters.⁷⁰ In a letter to Fox Maule in September 1846, Guthrie wrote that after speaking with Candlish, 'I am confident his scheme won't succeed, and convinced, moreover, that it should not.' Guthrie's claim that 'I love my Church as well as anyone, but I love my country more than I love my denomination' also earned him sympathy in United Presbyterian circles.⁷¹ For Guthrie, a 'proper' national education act would be 'the most important and blessed measure passed in Parliament since the Reformation'.⁷² The existence of a partisan Free Church scheme receiving denominational grants from the state only served as a barrier to the achievement of such a measure. At a meeting of the Edinburgh Free Church Presbytery in August 1849, Gunn called on the Free Church to take up its own definitive stance on the education question. He argued that unless the Free Church joined Scotland's other dissenters in support of reform, Scottish education would succumb to sectarian divisions. Ironically, according to Gunn, the Free Church's success in prosecuting their own scheme would offer them leverage in any talks on a new measure. With the 'Establishment moving in one way, and the voluntary dissenters moving in another way', the Free Church had the power to act as 'umpire' in the negotiations and to 'virtually decide what the system of national education pursued in this country hereafter should be'.⁷³

68. *Caledonian Mercury*, 12 November 1849.
69. *UPM*, iv (April 1850), 164–5.
70. Robert S. Candlish, *Educational Scheme of the Free Church* (Edinburgh, 1846); Candlish, 'Education in the Free Church of Scotland', in C. Van Rensselaer (ed.), *Home, the school, and the church; or, the Presbyterian education repository* (4 volumes, Philadelphia, 1852), ii, 78–85.
71. Guthrie and Guthrie, *Autobiography of Thomas Guthrie*, 287, 290; Education Commission (Scotland), *First Report . . . schools in Scotland*, 125, 135.
72. Guthrie and Guthrie, *Autobiography of Thomas Guthrie*, 284.
73. *Elgin Courier*, 10 August 1849.

However, the potential for the Free Church to play the umpire in any upcoming debate was hindered by their own deep-rooted divisions on the matter. That same year, Candlish contended that 'no national system of education is worth contending for' unless it swallowed up the established schools into 'one great institute'.[74] This otherwise moderate opinion highlighted, according to opponents from both established and voluntary sides, that Candlish only favoured reforming Scotland's national schools if it directly favoured his own sect. The United Presbyterian *Scottish Press* claimed that Candlish and the Free Church 'would be content were the parochial schools simply detached from the control of the Erastian Establishment, and opened up to themselves'.[75] Nevertheless, amid opposition from the Begg and Guthrie group, Candlish asserted that the Free Church's primary aim was to provide education 'to their own adhering people and to all who would receive it at their hands'.[76] Candlish's decision to defend the existence of the Free Church scheme, based on his preference for the distinctive religious character of the schools, saw him distance himself from the minority in favour of national education, which opened up an increasing chasm within the Free Church on the issue. Essentially, Candlish was in favour of extending and promoting the Free Church's own educational agenda while the education question was 'unsettled' and until agreement could be found among Scotland's dissenters on a suitable national alternative.[77] Unlike his opponents, Candlish was not prepared to risk the success and benefits of the Free Church scheme for the prospect of an improved national system. He also speculated that by building such a strong educational machinery, if a change in the parochial schools did eventually occur, 'the whole education of the country might ultimately fall into their hands'.[78]

This approach was viewed as misconceived by the likes of Begg and Guthrie, who believed that any potential national system would be delayed or even blocked by the existence of a strong, sectarian school establishment running parallel with the parochial system. Instead, Begg proposed that the current Free Church schools should be proactively offered to the government as part of any prospective national system and handed over to the control of the local boards, a suggestion opposed by Candlish who sought to uphold the schools' religious character. Candlish's desire to maintain the church–school connection ensured he was determined to oppose any otherwise acceptable system of national education that threatened to sever this link, driving him to a 'convinced sectarianism' that was arguably redundant in post-Disruption Scotland.[79] The dominance of Candlish's

74. *Fife Herald*, 3 May 1849.
75. *Scotsman*, 21 April 1849; *Scottish Press*, 3 May 1849.
76. Withrington, 'Free Church Educational Scheme', 111–12.
77. Education Commission (Scotland), *First Report . . . schools in Scotland*, 99.
78. *Greenock Advertiser*, 15 May 1849.
79. Withrington, 'Free Church Educational Scheme', 111–15.

elite group on the education issue deepened the ideological animosities evident in this period, and led Begg to criticise the oligarchical structure of the Free Church, which he felt led to the dictatorial supremacy of a 'few' in the General Assembly, with Candlish, the Free Church Pope, at its head.[80]

These divisions came to a head at the 1850 Free Church General Assembly. In a heated debate on the subject, Begg proposed a series of resolutions that called on the Free Church to make their own scheme 'subservient' to the 'great end' of pursuing a 'sound and comprehensive scheme of national education'. He argued that the Free Church 'would never, by the contributions of their members, be able to educate the people belonging to the Free Church – far less the whole people of Scotland' and 'neither was it their duty to attempt it', instead emphasising the duty of the government to educate the masses. Begg's resolutions were supported by John Fleming, the professor of Natural Science at New College, who claimed that the Free Church should never have established their own network of schools, and supported full reform of the parochial system instead. However, these arguments were rejected by the Candlish-led majority within the General Assembly. In a rousing speech defending the success of the Free Church schools, Candlish argued that Begg's resolutions to actively pursue a national system would only serve to 'embarrass' the Free Kirk, by forcing them to dissolve their own education scheme. Instead, while leaving the door open for any future agreement on a national education programme, Candlish claimed that the church 'would be much better employed in continuing to prosecute their own scheme' and called on its members to show that the Free Kirk schools had not yet reached its limits by increasing their contributions. The vote that followed ended in embarrassment for Begg, who lost by 256 votes to sixteen.[81]

The heavy nature of this defeat proved a bitter blow to the reformers within the Free Church, and instilled the impression that the Free Kirk as a whole opposed the burgeoning national education movement. However, Withrington has suggested that Candlish's support owed more to his superior oratorical powers and popularity over the blunter Begg than the actual reasoned opinion of the church on the matter, an argument supported by Guthrie's assertion that the bulk of the laity favoured his proposals.[82] Nevertheless, it certainly deepened divisions within an already fractured Free Church. In the wake of the General Assembly, Guthrie and Gunn both resigned from their positions on the Education Committee, claiming that Candlish's actions were 'rather hindering than facilitating a catholic and comprehensive plan'.[83] In his resignation letter to Candlish, Gunn

---

80. Smith, *James Begg*, ii, 220–9.
81. *Elgin Courier*, 7 June 1850; *AGAFC, 1848–1852* (Edinburgh, 1852), 228.
82. Withrington, 'Free Church Educational Scheme', 113–14; Guthrie and Guthrie, *Autobiography of Thomas Guthrie*, 287.
83. Guthrie and Guthrie, *Autobiography of Thomas Guthrie*, 288.

criticised the Free Church's 'feeble' approach to the issue and the apparent preference for a 'sectarian' system that 'now presents, and is actually intended by many of its most active supporters to present, a barrier to the supply of this country's greatest want'.[84]

These tensions were exacerbated by Candlish and the Education Committee's decision later that year to veto the Privy Council's appointment of Gunn to one of the government inspectorships associated with the Free Church schools. This decision, to which Candlish would later admit his regret, was deemed to have been solely based on Gunn's avowed hostility to the Free Church scheme, and was heavily criticised in the Scottish press.[85] Gunn's friend and ally Guthrie, though hesitant to engage in a public spat with Candlish, expressed his disgust in a letter to Fox Maule, lamenting the 'sickening' nature of the 'jealousies and bigotry and narrow-mindedness' of many within the Education Committee. He joked that 'these men are never without a pair of Free Church spectacles. I suppose they sleep with them on!'[86] Though Guthrie and Candlish aimed to steer clear of any public controversy on the issue which would expose the risk of 'quarrels' within the Free Church, the hostility emboldened supporters of both factions and emphasised the divisions deeply ingrained in the Free Church by 1850. While Hugh Miller painted Guthrie and Gunn in the *Witness* as sufferers in a 'righteous cause' against a Free Church scheme designed as an obstacle to a national system, a supporter of Candlish ridiculed the national movement as a 'phantom of the brain'.[87]

Despite the open hostility of the previous year, 1851 witnessed a rather remarkable attempt at reconciliation between the Free Church's warring camps. Faced with the prospect of an increasingly powerful movement and potential success in parliament, Candlish, a tactical, shrewd and often opportunistic operator, began to pursue his own vision of what a system of national education should entail. Supported by colleagues such as William Maxwell Hetherington, Cunningham and the Sheriff of Fife, Alexander Monteith, Candlish sent a document outlining proposals for a 'cut-and-dry national plan' (which will be outlined later in this chapter) to the Privy Council Committee on Education. In this document, the Free Churchmen expressed their conviction that a comprehensive national system of education, based on 'sound principles of religion', was both 'practicable and highly desirable'.[88] Though still in favour of operating their own scheme in concurrence with pursuing a national plan, this group now concluded that

---

84. *Montrose, Arbroath and Brechin Review*, 5 July 1850.
85. William Henry Oliphant Smeaton, *Thomas Guthrie* (Edinburgh, 1900), 107–8; *Scotsman*, 7 December 1850; *Caledonian Mercury*, 9 December 1850.
86. Guthrie and Guthrie, *Autobiography of Thomas Guthrie*, 288–9.
87. *Witness*, 29 April 1854; *Caledonian Mercury*, 9 December 1850.
88. Education Commission (Scotland), *First Report . . . schools in Scotland*, 107; William Cunningham, Robert S. Candlish, A. E. Monteith and Alexander Wood, *Proposal for a system of National Education in Scotland* (Edinburgh, 1851), 3.

the 'gigantic work of elevating the sunken masses of Scotland' and overtaking the 'educational destitution which prevails' was 'far too formidable for the energies of any mere section of the community'. At a meeting of the Edinburgh presbytery, William Cunningham acknowledged that a full education for Scotland's youth could only be conducted 'not in sections and denominations, but in a general scheme applicable to the whole community'. In a marked turnaround from his position at the 1850 General Assembly, Candlish emphasised the church's duty to obtain from the legislature a 'comprehensive measure for the reform and extension of the parish-school system in Scotland', commensurate with the educational needs of the people and based on 'truly national and unsectarian' principles.[89]

Though Guthrie expressed his approval at Candlish's 'step in advance' on the issue of education, demarcating him from the more staunch Free Church opponents of a national system such as James Gibson, these new proposals failed to bring about reconciliation between the conflicting parties.[90] Begg and Candlish continued to clash over the Free Church's enthusiasm (or lack thereof) for pursuing a comprehensive scheme alongside Scotland's dissenters. During a heated exchange between the pair at the 1853 General Assembly, Candlish claimed that 'if the government waited till the different churches could agree on the subject, Scotland would never get a national system of education'. While old fissures clearly endured, certain sections of the Free Church remained openly opposed to a national scheme. One member stated that a national system was unlikely, and that 'the best way to advance the education of the people was just to go on as they were doing'.[91] While the Free Church remained deeply divided over the education issue, by the early 1850s it was apparent that for the first time the majority of Scotland's Presbyterian dissenters were, to varying degrees, in favour of some scheme of national education. However, divisions remained as to the details of any potential reform, and these would intensify as the issue became a central feature of parliamentary debates throughout the 1850s.

What Kind of National Education? The Problem of Religious Instruction

Most of the divisions surrounding the implementation of a national system of education centred on the role of religion and religious instruction in the national schools. These debates focused on whether the national schools should assume a specific religious identity or character, including the imposition of religious tests. Most significantly, the relationship between religious and secular education proved the greatest source of contention. The various advocates of national education were at odds over what role, if

---

89. *Proposal for a system of National Education*, 3; *FCM*, ii (December 1853), 529–33.
90. Guthrie and Guthrie, *Autobiography of Thomas Guthrie*, 298.
91. *Fife Herald*, 2 June 1853.

any, religious instruction should play in the national schools, and whether the government should interfere by providing legislation on the matter. The variety of opinion across Scotland on these issues inevitably caused division within the national education movement and delayed the passage of any kind of legislation for over a decade. The Established Church and the secular lobby naturally stood on the opposite ends of this spectrum, with the secularists asserting that religion should have no place in the school curriculum, and the Church of Scotland maintaining that the teaching of the Bible and Shorter Catechism should be secured by law. However, between these two extreme opinions, non-established Presbyterianism was loosely divided into three main groups on this issue – the Candlish-led majority of the Free Church, the Guthrie-Begg-Miller faction of the Free Church and the United Presbyterians.

Unsurprisingly, it was Candlish's portion of the Free Kirk which advocated the most openly religious of the proposed schemes. His 1851 letters to the Privy Council Committee and the Marquis of Lansdowne, in which he first openly espoused his preference for a full national system, proposed that religious instruction in the national schools be required by law, and that all teachers and schools profess to Presbyterian standards and additional inspection by the Presbyterian churches.[92] In this system, teachers would be appointed by householders and heads of families, while a central board would oversee the management by the Presbyterian churches.[93] Candlish and his colleagues aimed to reunite the three great divisions of Presbyterianism in Scotland by reconstituting a general system of Presbyterian education under the management and control of the ministers of the three denominations – in essence replacing the Church of Scotland test with a Presbyterian one. Both Candlish and William Cunningham defended this proposal to install an effectively Presbyterian national system by arguing it took advantage of Scotland's overwhelmingly Presbyterian population. Cunningham claimed that the Free Church was not trying to force a particular type of religious instruction on the country, but was aiming to secure 'the general prevalence, and pervading influence of the religious element'.[94] Unsurprisingly, it was heavily criticised by Scotland's other dissenting bodies. One dissenting commentator argued that while such a scheme contained 'liberal' and 'catholic' touches, it directly ostracised non-Presbyterian dissenters who had 'neither part nor lot in this grand national scheme'. According to the dissenting correspondent, while Candlish and Cunningham's proposal 'may be an excellent Presbyterian scheme, and may advance the

---

92. *Proposal for a system of National Education*, 5–6, 17; Robert Smith Candlish, *Letter to the Marquis of Lansdowne, on the reform and extension of the Parish School System of Scotland* (Edinburgh, 1851).
93. Stevenson, *Fulfilling a Vision*, 96–7.
94. *Proposal for a system of National Education*, 5; *Friends of National Education*, 46, 83.

cause of education in Scotland . . . it can have no pretension to the title of a national scheme'.[95]

Nevertheless, the Free Church's desire to create a Presbyterian national system was based on its belief, rooted in its continuing adherence to the establishment principle, that the state was bound to provide for the education of every child by placing it on a 'Christian basis'.[96] This intrinsic relationship between the church, state and education espoused by the Candlish faction of the Free Kirk ensured that it refused to consent to any bill which excluded religion from the curriculum of the national schools.[97] The emphasis on an inherently religious form of education was evident in the Free Church schools from the Disruption, and was central to their plans to tackle Scotland's social ills.[98] 'Mere secular education', argued the social reformer and minister Robert Buchanan, 'will not reform society.'[99] This desire to base the Free Church schools on what Hetherington termed the 'theocratic principle' was carried over to their plans for a national education scheme.[100] While the Free Church acknowledged that it was the duty of the state to provide secular education, and the responsibility of the church and parents to administer religious instruction, they argued that this could only be fully achieved by the direct and distinct recognition of religion, and in particular Presbyterianism, in any national education act.[101] At a Glasgow meeting of the NEA, Buchanan demanded that the Bible and Shorter Catechism be imposed upon the national system as one of its 'legal, fundamental conditions', a stipulation also stressed by Candlish as a minimum requirement of any proposed scheme.[102] In essence, the Free Church were in favour of a legal clause in the bill that would secure the same Presbyterian education in operation in the parish schools, but opened up to other denominations, with the actual management of such a system left to the local boards.[103]

This attempt to impose Calvinist doctrine by law into the core of the national schools was criticised as 'sectarian', and provided a significant barrier to co-operation with Scottish voluntaries who opposed the use of government funds for religious purposes.[104] However, while in favour of such a directly religious clause, the Free Church found common ground

95. *Elgin Courier*, 14 March 1851.
96. *FCM*, ii (December 1853), 530–1.
97. Guthrie and Guthrie, *Autobiography of Thomas Guthrie*, 292; Education Commission (Scotland), *First Report . . . schools in Scotland*, 99.
98. *A Memorial on Education, to the General Assembly of the Free Church, by the son of a clergyman* (Edinburgh, 1844), 17–18.
99. Buchanan, *Schoolmaster in the Wynds*, 16.
100. Hetherington, *National Education in Scotland*.
101. *Caledonian Mercury*, 12 November 1849; *UPM*, iv (April 1850), 165–7; *Friends of National Education*, 41.
102. *Dundee Courier*, 15 February 1854; *Fife Herald*, 3 May 1849.
103. *Friends of National Education*, 80–1.
104. *Scottish Press*, 3 May 1849; *Greenock Advertiser*, 15 May 1849.

with their fellow dissenters in their belief that it was the role of the parents, and the strength of their Presbyterian values, that provided the surest security for religious teaching in the national schools, with or without a legal clause.[105] However, unlike the United Presbyterians, the Candlish-led section of the Free Church believed that a combination of the national piety of Scottish parents and state control would provide the most effective security for the inherent role of religious instruction in the national schools.[106]

The faction on the other side of the Free Church divide, led by Guthrie and Begg, also argued for a religious element to the proposed national schools. However, in their view, the extent to which religious education would permeate the national scheme would be decided by the people, not the state. Guthrie for instance expressed 'no sympathy' with what he regarded as the outmoded connection between church and school held by the majority of Free Church ministers, and emphasised that religious and secular education should be separated.[107] In a letter to Gunn, Guthrie argued that the churches should 'have nothing to do with secular education, beyond giving it, as to the various schemes of patriotism and philanthropy, all due encouragement'. He opposed any attempt at bringing both secular and religious education under the control of the clergy and the church courts, believing that the church should 'keep within her own province' to avoid any aggression or undue interference from external bodies.[108] This argument was echoed by Fox Maule, who warned against overt church control over secular education due to the potential for sectarian conflict.[109] This distinction between the state's duty to administer secular education and the role of the church and parents in religious instruction formed a major part of the Guthrie group's approach to the national education question.[110] However, this did not mean that they agreed with the secularists that the government should actively legislate for the exclusion of religion from the national schools. Guthrie and Begg were of the firm belief that religion, based on the Bible and Shorter Catechism and delivered by the different denominations in co-operation, should form a fundamental part of the national education system, though they did not insist on religion featuring in the government's bill.[111]

The decision to pursue a scheme that would incorporate religion without legislating for it echoed Chalmers' belief that Scotland's current denominational divisions prohibited the government from adopting any

---

105. *AGAFC, 1848–1852*, 228; *UPM*, viii (March 1854), 142.
106. *Friends of National Education*, 90–1.
107. Withrington, 'Free Church Educational Scheme', 115; Withrington, 'Education and the Free Church', 93–4.
108. Guthrie and Guthrie, *Autobiography of Thomas Guthrie*, 285–6.
109. *Friends of National Education*, 14.
110. Stevenson, *Fulfilling a Vision*, 96.
111. *Friends of National Education*, 61.

clear religious agenda, and that religious education in any case should be the result of zeal, not legislation.[112] To the likes of Maule and Guthrie, any government interference in the religion of the national schools was 'unnecessary and inadvisable', and would render the state in the eyes of most Scots 'as going beyond their province'.[113] Leaving the religious question out of any new bill also appeared to provide the most likely hope of achieving some degree of unity among Scottish dissent on the issue. For instance, some members of Guthrie's cohort such as Begg agreed in principle with Candlish's assertion that the state should introduce the Bible and Shorter Catechism into the national schools. However, the perceived necessity to comprehensively reform Scotland's education system, and the dissenting unity that such a measure appeared to require, saw Begg agree to 'waive this principle'.[114] The aversion, or at least indifference, to a religious clause demonstrated this group's adherence to the Disruption principle of the kirk's spiritual independence in religious matters, and its faith in Presbyterian Scotland to deliver an effective system of religious instruction.

This Free Church faction, in agreement with much of the leadership of the NEA, believed that it was the state's duty to provide secular education and that religious instruction should be devolved to the denominations with the consent of the parents and placed under the supervision and management of the various local boards.[115] Therefore, religious instruction would be left to the control of those with the most vested interest in it, the parents.[116] According to Guthrie, this proposal offered the surest security for a sound Presbyterian education in Scotland, and would enable members of all denominations to co-operate under a common banner. Pointing to the interdenominational quality of the Ragged School committees, he declared his confidence 'in the religious feelings of my countrymen as to believe that in a board chosen by their votes, and therefore representing their sentiments, the religious interests of these schools will find as faithful guardians as they have ever enjoyed'.[117] Begg also argued that no statute for religion was required, as historically it had always been upheld by the Scottish people, not the state.[118] However, Candlish dismissed the proposals of Guthrie, Begg and Gunn as equivalent to 'avowedly flinging away all security for the religious character of the schools'.[119] This view was echoed by the Perth minister Andrew Gray, who criticised Guthrie and Gunn's faith in the parents of Scotland to uphold the religious character of education by

112. Hanna, *Memoirs of Thomas Chalmers*, 758–9.
113. *UPM*, viii (March 1854), 143.
114. *Caledonian Mercury*, 12 November 1849.
115. *Friends of National Education*, 46.
116. *Caledonian Mercury*, 12 November 1849; *Friends of National Education*, 64–5; Guthrie and Guthrie, *Autobiography of Thomas Guthrie*, 297.
117. Guthrie and Guthrie, *Autobiography of Thomas Guthrie*, 293.
118. Smith, *James Begg*, ii, 228–9.
119. *Caledonian Mercury*, 12 November 1849.

calling into question the 'sound-minded' nature of the poor.[120] According to one Tory establishment journal, Begg and Guthrie had passed over to the 'secular camp' and were condemned as holding the principles of 'atheists, deists, and infidels'.[121]

Another group that was lumbered with the 'secular' tag by establishmentarian critics was the United Presbyterian Church. Unlike the Free Church, the United Presbyterians were almost 'universally' in favour of a system of national education.[122] While the impact of the Disruption directly shaped the Free Church's stance on education and the parish schools, the voluntary campaign in Scotland for national education preceded 1843 and formed a major feature of their organised opposition to the state Kirk in the late 1830s.[123] The leading United Presbyterian minister John Brown argued that the parochial schools should be completely reformed (but not abolished) in favour of a comprehensive national scheme open to all, with no reference to religious creed and without religious tests.[124] In line with the majority opinion of the NEA, the United Presbyterians were also in favour of relinquishing control of the schools from the church courts and placing them in the hands of popularly elected local boards.[125] While some voluntaries wished to exclude religion actively from any legislation, the majority of United Presbyterians did not adopt this stance.[126] Instead, they simply argued that the state should refrain from actively supporting religious instruction in the schools, and that the issue belonged to the parents and churches to decide in the various districts.[127] In a similar manner to the likes of Guthrie in the Free Church, the United Presbyterians could not consent to a religious clause in the bill, but remained as equally 'anxious' as their dissenting counterparts that 'the Bible should be in the schools'.[128] In a speech dismissed as an 'enunciation of pure secularism' by a Church of Scotland pamphleteer, the United Presbyterian minister John Cairns argued that while propositions regarding religion should remain vague, the results would prove the opposite.[129] Cairns' rather optimistic confidence in the 'general harmony' of Scotland's Presbyterians led him to believe that disputes regarding the management of religious education

---

120. Andrew Gray, *National Education* (Perth, 1850), 4.
121. *MacPhail's Edinburgh Ecclesiastical Journal and Literary Review*, xi (May 1851), 225.
122. Education Commission (Scotland), *First Report . . . schools in Scotland*, 135; Fraser, *Educational Condition of Scotland*, 20. One small section of hardcore voluntaries within the church favoured an entirely voluntary system of education devoid of any state aid, yet still viewed a national system as a 'great improvement' on the existing parochial structure.
123. 'Note on the subject of National Education', 4 October 1838, Letters and papers chiefly addressed to Duncan McLaren, Lord Provost of Edinburgh, NLS, MSS 15911.251.
124. *Friends of National Education*, 30.
125. *Scotsman*, 6 October 1849.
126. *North British Review*, xii (February 1850), 268.
127. Stevenson, *Fulfilling a Vision*, 97.
128. *UPM*, viii (March 1854), 142–3.
129. *A Voice from the Church* (Edinburgh, 1854), 4.

would be 'so few and so exceptional' as to render premeditated legislation unnecessary. In a thinly veiled attack on the views of Free Churchmen such as Candlish and Cunningham, Cairns claimed that 'to raise the outcry of irreligion against the inevitable reform, what is it but to charge the people of Scotland with being a godless, graceless nation'. Cairns was supported by the voluntary politician Adam Black, who noted that 'less evil would arise from free discussion than from dumb despotism'.[130]

Though against the legislative interference of the government in religion, the United Presbyterians proposed that religious instruction, paid for by a small fee, should be given within certain stated hours during which parents could voluntarily withdraw their children.[131] While not simply suggesting that religious and secular education should be completely separated, as some critics of the voluntary proposals claimed, these proposals marked the United Presbyterians out from both factions of the Free Kirk who called for a more overtly religious character in the schools. While this attitude was praised by Lord Melgund as a laudable effort to 'save the country from a sectarian education', it was attacked by establishmentarian Free Churchmen such as Hetherington as an attempt to 'render National Education anti-theocratic, and to place all national teachers in an avowedly anti-theocratic position'. This 'thoroughly unscriptural and un-Presbyterian' approach to education, according to Hetherington, was 'like systematically teaching youth to commit the first sin – to seek knowledge apart from, or without recognition of, the law of God'.[132]

In many respects, the United Presbyterian Church's approach towards education – in particular the de facto separation of the secular and voluntary religious elements – was essentially an attempt to apply the voluntary principle to schools.[133] For instance, they called on the Free Church to 'waive their right' regarding the direct provision of religious education from the state. As both churches agreed that religion would make its way into the schools with or without a specific clause in the bill, the *United Presbyterian Magazine* argued that it was up to the Free Kirk to make the 'required concession', as anything else would require the 'abandonment of principle' on the part of the voluntaries.[134] The need to ensure that their approach to national education – a state-funded and -directed project, after all – was compatible with their voluntaryism proved a prominent feature of the United Presbyterian campaign. One Church of Scotland commentator criticised the apparent hypocrisy of the United Presbyterians in relation to education, and argued that according to their voluntary principles it would be impossible for them to take part in a scheme where religious education

130. *Friends of National Education*, 88–90, 93.
131. *UPM*, iv (April 1850), 166.
132. *Caledonian Mercury*, 15 November 1849; Hetherington, *National Education in Scotland*.
133. *Caledonian Mercury*, 12 November 1849.
134. *UPM*, iv (April 1850), 143.

was endorsed and funded by the state. The *Scottish Guardian* countered this claim and suggested that it was an issue for the United Presbyterians themselves, many of whom had previously availed of the parochial school system and had 'made a marked distinction between the Church and the School, and do not feel that there is any compromise of principle in doing so'.[135] The United Presbyterian minister James Harper made the case that the accession of control of religious instruction to the local boards was completely compatible with voluntaryism, as in that situation the government only had a direct role in the secular education of dissenting children. According to Harper, membership of the heterogeneous NEA did not contradict the United Presbyterian Church's adherence to the voluntary principle, which they would carry 'intact and unfettered to the local boards'. He asserted that 'we do not give up a principle, when we place that principle in a more favourable position than it at present holds' with the 'promise of something more'.[136] This policy of forbearance in order to ensure united action, and therefore more likely success, would prove essential as Scotland's dissenters attempted to form an uneasy coalition to ensure the passing of a national education act during the 1850s.

The National Education Bills and Dissenting Co-operation, 1850–62

Between 1850 and 1862, seven major bills were introduced into parliament with the intention of reforming the Scottish education system.[137] With the exception of the successful 1861 Act, which simply abolished the religious tests imposed on parochial teachers, these bills generally aimed to supplement and extend the existing parish and church schools by bringing them under the control and inspection of a central, national board. Smaller local committees composed of heritors, ministers and householders would take responsibility for the management and supervision of existing schools and the establishment of new ones, which would be paid for partly from local taxation and partly by the Treasury. The chief areas of distinction between the four reform bills of the 1850s concerned the proposed constituency of the central board and, most significantly, the role of religious instruction in the national scheme. Concessions on religion were made by the respective architects of the bills, Lord Melgund and James Moncrieff, at different times throughout the decade to the various Presbyterian churches, but almost invariably came to grief due to the obstinate refusal of their opponents to acquiesce to such compromises. As we will see, it became common for the opponents of one aspect of the bill, in both the establishment and

---

135. *Scottish Guardian*, 13 January 1854.
136. *Friends of National Education*, 54–5.
137. Mechie, *Church and Scottish Social Development*, 148; Stevenson, *Fulfilling a Vision*, 90, 98. A further four bills were introduced in the decade after 1862, culminating in the 1872 Education (Scotland) Act, which overhauled the old parochial system in favour of a national and comprehensive scheme.

dissenting camps, to dismiss the entire measure as one that intrinsically and entirely favoured the opposite side. While the majority of Scots favoured maintaining the religious element to varying degrees within the national schools, the failure of Scotland's churches to reach agreement on religious education ultimately resulted in the demise of the bills and the immediate prospect of educational reform. Despite the often confrontational character associated with the education debates, attempts at co-operation, especially among the non-established Presbyterians, proved a central feature of the effort to achieve a national system in the 1850s. These attempts to create a single dissenting voice with which to approach the British state must be viewed in the context of the ever-closer, if occasionally volatile, relationship between the Free and United Presbyterian churches in this period. The national education debates, therefore, offer an insight into the advantages and pitfalls associated with the bid to create an increasingly unified dissenting body after the Disruption.

In a similar manner to the concurrent anti-Maynooth electoral coalition between the Free and United Presbyterians, the decade of debates after 1850 saw the emergence of an arguably more complex and combustible alliance formed within Scottish dissent to secure the passing of a suitable national education act. However, unlike the anti-Maynooth campaign and its national success in 1847 and 1852, the tensions between Scotland's dissenters over the issue of religious instruction threatened to overshadow any convergence from the outset, and would ultimately put paid to their electoral cohabitation within the Liberal party. Nevertheless, advocates for a national education scheme such as Thomas Guthrie emphasised the 'duty' of Scottish dissenters to co-operate to achieve reform, with 'each party retaining their principles and each agreeing to bury their points and prejudices'. The emergence of a distinctly dissenting Presbyterian identity in the late 1840s, forged by the increasing ecclesiastical, political and social co-operation noted in previous chapters, emboldened the likes of Guthrie to 'hope very soon to see at least the Free Church and dissenting community at one on this subject of education'. Though Guthrie acknowledged that his first instinct was to turn to his former colleagues in the Church of Scotland, in order to 'bury in the grave of our country's welfare the animosity and irritation that may have sprung from the past', the establishment's self-professed 'supremacy' over the national schools presented an insurmountable 'barrier' to any attempt at co-operation. Instead, writing in the *Witness* in January 1850, Guthrie believed that the voluntaries of the United Presbyterian Church, claiming no exclusive power over the schools, offered the surest opportunity for a working Presbyterian alliance. According to Guthrie, the Free and United Presbyterians – both, in his view, against the inclusion or exclusion of religion in any bill – were on a 'common path' on which they could approach the British government.[138]

138. Guthrie and Guthrie, *Autobiography of Thomas Guthrie*, 288–93.

The introduction of Lord Melgund's first national education bill in 1850 quickly thrust this apparent desire for dissenting co-operation into the spotlight. As early as 1848, Melgund, or William Elliot (1814–91), the Whig MP for Greenock and a victim of the anti-Maynooth alliance in 1852, decided to capitalise on the public interest in educational reform in Scotland by openly advocating a national system to replace the parish schools.[139] In the House of Commons, Melgund criticised the Privy Council Grants system as fostering and stimulating the 'evil' of sectarian animosity. According to Melgund, unlike in England an effectively national system of education already existed in Scotland in the form of the parish schools, and only needed to be opened up to all denominations in order for it to be truly considered 'national'. He believed that it was more advantageous to adapt existing systems to suit the altered circumstances of mid-nineteenth-century Scotland rather than introduce a potentially problematic new scheme. Calling for the extension and integration of the parochial system, Melgund argued that the 'old system, altered and extended, would be more beneficial to the cause of education, and less calculated to excite religious disputes'.[140]

In May 1849, Melgund publicly announced his desire to introduce a bill to implement such a measure.[141] This bill, though including no religious requirement for schoolmasters, left considerable power in the hands of the parish ministers and heritors. In districts where a local committee was not established, the ministers and heritors would continue with their previously held task of appointing teachers and superintending the national schools.[142] Despite this concession to the Established Church, the United Presbyterian Church expressed its 'strenuous' support for the measure and praised Melgund, a cabinet minister and brother-in-law of the Prime Minister Lord John Russell, for his 'zealous and powerful advocacy of our cause'.[143] A number of United Presbyterian presbyteries such as Cupar and Kelso also called for unified dissenting support for Melgund's bill, through the organisation of 'public and unsectarian meetings'.[144] This desire for co-operation was soon echoed by the leading advocates of national education within the Free Church.[145] The *North British Review*, a Free Church organ, claimed that the 'government will not stir in the matter without a union on the part of the great dissenting bodies of Scotland' and that such a union could be based on a universally extended national education, with a 'sound religious' element left to the control of the locals. However, it also noted

139. Withrington, 'Free Church Educational Scheme', 115; Stevenson, 'Scottish Schooling in the Denominational Era', 143.
140. *Ecclesiastical Gazette*, xi (September 1848), 58.
141. *Greenock Advertiser*, 15 May 1849.
142. Stevenson, *Fulfilling a Vision*, 98.
143. *UPM*, iii (January 1849), 20–2.
144. *Scotsman*, 6 October 1849.
145. *Caledonian Mercury*, 5 November 1849.

that the only difference between the Free and United Presbyterian churches was to the means in which this common object could be achieved, and the likelihood of 'controversy', particularly on the issue of religious instruction.[146] Melgund reiterated this belief, claiming that religious instruction and its place or otherwise in the bill presented the 'only difficulty in the way of a complete union betwixt the United Presbyterian Church and the Free Church' regarding education.[147]

The failure of Scotland's dissenters to find a 'practical solution' to their differences, despite general agreement on a common goal, proved a recurring theme throughout the national education debates of the 1850s. According to the *Caledonian Mercury*, Candlish's insistence on 'a distinct and direct recognition of religious instruction by the state' ensured that he and the majority within the Free Kirk were 'rowing in the same boat' as members of the Established Church, and 'on a tack the very opposite to the United Presbyterian Synod'. While the disputes within the Free Church and the stubbornness of the Candlish faction highlighted the serious threats to dissenting co-operation, the more conciliatory stance adopted by Begg and Gunn offered an alternative route to union between the two churches. While Begg professed to prefer Candlish's stance, he did not 'hold it to be a matter of conscience' and was willing to 'waive this principle' in favour of unified dissenting action. The *Mercury* claimed that Begg's sentiments, based on a policy of forbearance similar to that employed by advocates of ecclesiastical union and the Evangelical Alliance, offered hope that 'the difficulties may be removed, and co-operation secured for this benevolent end, of course without any compromise on either side'.[148]

Nevertheless, the general hostility of the debates and lack of cohesion within the dissenting churches, encapsulated by the dispute between Begg and Candlish at the 1850 Free Church General Assembly, served as an 'embarrassment' to Melgund and his supporters, and contributed to the bill's narrow defeat by six votes in the House of Commons.[149] The following year, Melgund returned with a similar proposal for reform. Once again, it was defeated by a slim margin of thirteen, and greeted in Scotland with the same curious combination of conciliation and partisanship reserved for the previous year's measure.[150] For instance, one dissenting commentator called for the 'co-operation of all parties' and claimed that neither of the two major Presbyterian dissenting churches were 'of sufficient weight to secure a national system without the co-operation of the other'. According to the writer, any national scheme that would exclude even the 'fag-end of Episcopacy' deserves 'no better designation than liberalised

---

146. *North British Review*, xii (February 1850), 268.
147. *Caledonian Mercury*, 15 November 1849.
148. *Caledonian Mercury*, 12 November 1849.
149. *FCM*, vii (September 1850), 285.
150. Stevenson, 'Scottish Schooling in the Denominational Era', 144.

sectarianism'. The same article, however, lambasted Candlish and his colleagues' attitudes to Melgund's proposals, and dismissed the Free Church as the 'self-elected patron and dictator of the education and religion of the youth of Scotland'.[151] The voluntary suspicion of Candlish's motives was ultimately vindicated as the Free Church leader skilfully undermined the NEA throughout the debates and persuaded the influential Lansdowne to oppose Melgund's 'secular' measure in favour of an overtly religious system.[152] Guthrie, the most prominent advocate of forbearance alongside Gunn and Begg, lamented the partisanship associated with the debates, which he claimed saw the 'best interests' of the country and the churches 'sacrificed to extreme Establishment views on the one hand, and extreme Voluntaryism on the other'. In Guthrie's eyes, the failure of the dissenting churches to unite behind the common goal of reform ensured the failure of a bill which, if carried to the second reading, had the potential to frighten some of the establishment 'into their senses'.[153] The defeat of Melgund's final bill in 1851 coincided with a loss of momentum for the national education movement in Scotland in the early part of the decade. This was compounded by the ambivalent stance of the Candlish-dominated Free Church, which heightened doubts within the British government over the veracity of public support for reform within Scotland.[154]

This cooling of the reform movement did not last long – within two years of Melgund's failure, proposals for a reformed national system of education were being introduced under the leadership of the Lord Advocate and Free Churchman James Moncrieff. Buoyed by the success of his Universities (Scotland) Act in 1853, which abolished university tests for professors, Moncrieff turned his attention to a more comprehensive and national plan for educational reform in Scotland, an obsession that would occupy him for the next decade.[155] Moncrieff's zeal for a national education system also galvanised renewed calls for dissenting co-operation, even from unlikely corners. At the Edinburgh Free Presbytery in late 1853, William Cunningham argued that 'a national system of education, based on right principles, would afford a very wholesome opportunity of bringing together the different evangelical denominations of the community in a manner in which they could carry out, in friendly co-operation, and without compromise of their principles, some most important and useful national object'.[156] However, critics within the Church of Scotland dismissed Cunningham's apparent olive branch to the voluntaries as a mere façade for denominational interests. In a series of columns for the *Fifeshire Journal*, one establishmentarian critic of reform, Norman MacLeod, argued

151. *Elgin Courier*, 14 March 1851.
152. Hutchison, *Political History of Scotland*, 74.
153. Guthrie and Guthrie, *Autobiography of Thomas Guthrie*, 298.
154. Withrington, 'Free Church Educational Scheme', 115.
155. Stevenson, *Fulfilling a Vision*, 99.
156. *FCM*, ii (December 1853), 533.

that the 'present agitation' initiated by Moncrieff was not intended to benefit Scotland's population but was 'merely the cloak with which party would cover its cloven foot'. According to MacLeod, dissenters were 'willing to sacrifice the welfare of millions of their countrymen' so long as 'a Free Church can annoy an Established Church, or a voluntary procure a momentary triumph of his crotchety principle'.[157] Unsurprisingly, these claims were dismissed by the *Scottish Guardian* as 'idle' attempts by the establishment and MacLeod – an advocate for Protestant union in the Evangelical Alliance – to sow the 'seeds of discord' among Scottish dissenters. According to the rather optimistic *Guardian*, there was 'no difficulty as to co-operation' among the Free and United Presbyterian churches regarding education, and any reports suggesting such were simply a 'fancy' dreamt up by the opponents of dissenting union.[158]

The strength or otherwise of this newly galvanised dissenting alliance in support of Moncrieff became fully evident at two major public meetings organised by the NEA in Edinburgh and Glasgow in January and February 1854. Attended largely by members of the Free and United Presbyterian churches, the Edinburgh event represented an opportunity for Scotland's dissenting advocates of reform, despite their differences, to present a unified front based on the shared platform of the NEA.[159] The Free Church politician Alexander Murray Dunlop and the United Presbyterian minister James Harper both stressed the need for forbearance in the name of united action, and argued that such co-operation was necessary to achieve reform. Harper admitted that while the principles espoused by the NEA 'go too far for some', and that voluntaries such as himself 'would carry them a point farther', 'as they are, they form a basis on which many are willing to co-operate'. Harper's belief that Scotland's dissenters had a duty to set aside their smaller, seemingly surmountable differences for the common good of an improved education system was repeated throughout the meeting, including by Fox Maule and the Congregationalist George Wilson. In a letter apologising for his non-attendance, the leading United Presbyterian minister John Brown argued that though 'some may have umbrage over certain principles, they cannot stand in the way of majority opinion' or act as a 'barrier' to reform.[160]

The NEA's policy of concession and conciliation did not entirely prevent conflict within the movement. Late in the Edinburgh meeting, the United Presbyterian John Cairns clashed with William Cunningham over the proposed role of religion in the scheme. Cunningham, the only leading representative of the establishmentarian Free Church faction present at Edinburgh (at the Glasgow meeting Robert Buchanan played this role),

---

157. *Education Question in Scotland*, 5.
158. *Scottish Guardian*, 13 January 1854.
159. *UPM*, viii (March 1854), 141.
160. *Friends of National Education*, 16–18, 30–2, 39, 41, 52, 56.

also admitted that he did not agree with many of the principles embodied in the constitution of the NEA. However, both Guthrie and the United Presbyterians defended this 'honest' difference of opinion as justifying the NEA's status as a 'national' movement. According to the *United Presbyterian Magazine*, a merely voluntary platform could not profess to be national. Referencing Cunningham's 'antagonistic' speech, the journal argued that 'this very diversity of sentiment was the glory of the meeting; and we should have had less confidence in united action, had there been less free expression of opinion'. In concurrence with the meeting's key motif, Cunningham did agree that 'we are thoroughly and cordially at one in respect to the great and most important question of present duty . . . in supporting a truly national and comprehensive system of education'.[161]

Despite the occasional confrontational moment between Free Churchman and voluntary, the perceived success of the reinvigorated dissenting alliance was so much so that Guthrie described the Edinburgh meeting as an 'auspicious omen' for the future union of Scotland's evangelical dissenting churches. For Guthrie, the establishment of a truly national system of education, devoid of denominational disputes and animosity, represented the 'shortest road to that union'. In essence, Guthrie believed that the national schools envisioned by the NEA would act as a prelude to Scotland attaining 'in the true sense of the expression, a National Church'.[162] The prospect of a national education scheme acting as a catalyst for ecclesiastical union in Scotland was also raised, in a slightly more cautious manner, by the bill's architect Moncrieff. In a letter to Guthrie in April 1854, Moncrieff referred to that year's private conferences on ecclesiastical union organised by George Sinclair and John Brown, claiming that these initiatives appeared to be 'preparing the way for union' between the Free and United Presbyterian churches. While the education question and its various disputes appeared to many as an 'obstruction' to such attempts to unite Scotland's dissenters, Moncrieff believed that it instead 'proves most forcibly the need for union, and demonstrates the injury which the country and religion suffer from our divisions'.[163]

The portrayal of the national education movement as a unified dissenting body, or even as a pathway to dissenting union, was once again heavily criticised by the Established Church as a mere façade which concealed deeply held divisions between churchmen who agreed on little but their opposition to the parish schools. Reporting on the smaller NEA meeting held in Glasgow's Merchants Hall, one Church of Scotland commentator noted the 'limited attendance' of Free Churchmen, especially on the speakers' platform, and inferred that a 'serious division exists in the Free Church phalanx' in both Glasgow and Edinburgh. According to the writer,

---

161. *Friends of National Education*, 56, 72, 83–91; *UPM*, viii (March 1854), 142.
162. *UPM*, viii (March 1854), 142; *Friends of National Education*, 56, 65–7.
163. Guthrie and Guthrie, *Autobiography of Thomas Guthrie*, 300.

Buchanan's admission that the Glasgow meeting had been organised by the United Presbyterian Church seemingly proved that 'something in the shape of sectarian animus exists among the party in Glasgow', while Candlish's 'careful' decision to avoid the Edinburgh event appeared to illustrate that 'the clerical Pope of the Free Church does not exactly agree' with the movement.[164]

At one of the numerous rival public and private gatherings organised by the Established Church in the wake of the NEA's meetings, held at the City Hall in Perth and attended by over eight thousand, the Church of Scotland minister at St Madoes, John MacDuff, questioned the support of the Free Kirk for the national education movement. MacDuff expressed surprise at the timing of the renewed aggression upon the parish schools and claimed that many Free Churchmen were in favour of ever-closer union with the establishment and 'if they were to speak out, would confess that their leaders were causing them to err' regarding education.[165] The seemingly homogeneous support of the United Presbyterian Church for national education was also queried by the establishment, with one writer claiming that the United Presbyterian ministers who called the two meetings represented 'only a fraction' of the denomination. According to one Church of Scotland commentator, the NEA was 'an incongruous, dislocated mass, animated only by a common zeal to dissever the parochial schools from the Established Church, but neither agreeing with each other, or harmonising with the rest of their brethren, on the principles of that educational system with which they would erect upon the ruins of the parish school'.[166]

The apparent lack of principle within the movement was a common critique employed by the opponents of national education on both sides of the establishment–voluntary divide. A pamphlet entitled *A Voice from the Church* claimed that there was 'no union' on the NEA platform on 'Bible Protestant principles', while any co-operation was limited to secularism. Pointing out the chasm between the 'Bible speech' of Cunningham and the 'unmitigated secularism' of Harper, Cairns and Adam Black, the pamphlet concluded that the 'union and co-operation of that platform was therefore unprincipled', as points on which there was disagreement were flippantly dismissed as 'non-essential'. The writer criticised Guthrie and Cunningham's attempts to include religious instruction indirectly in the bill, 'stuffed in an almost unnoticeable corner', as evidence of the Free Church's 'unprincipled' approach to the matter. Noting the apparent hypocrisy of the movement, the writer argued that 'the Free Church, as a body, repudiates the voluntary principle in church and school, and yet she will rather side with the voluntaries, who are secularists, against the church which provides by law for the Bible', and declared that Guthrie and

---

164. *Dundee Courier*, 15 February 1854.
165. *Aberdeen Press and Journal*, 15 February 1854; *UPM*, viii (March 1854), 141.
166. *Dundee Courier*, 15 February 1854.

Cunningham 'ought to avow themselves voluntaries'. The charge of 'utter dereliction of principle' was also levelled at the voluntaries by Andrew Marshall, the former United Secession minister and instigator of the voluntary campaign of the 1830s. In a dig at the ministers who ousted him following the Atonement Controversy almost a decade before, Marshall claimed that the United Presbyterians, by engaging in compromise with the Free Church over education, were 'showing themselves in their true colours – they have never been men of principle, and they are not so now'.[167] These criticisms were readily dismissed as attempts to sow division among Scotland's dissenters by both the establishment and the secularists. However, the fear particularly within the United Presbyterian Church that Moncrieff's bill would be altered and 'watered down' reinforced suspicions by the opponents of national education that the 'friendly and cordial' dissenting alliance against the Church of Scotland would be exposed as hollow once the bill was formally introduced.[168]

These suspicions would largely be proven correct as Moncrieff brought forward his first national education bill to the House of Commons in late February 1854. This bill generally built upon Melgund's earlier proposals, including the abolition of the confessional test for teachers and the creation of a system of local and national boards to replace the management and control of the establishment. However, some significant alterations were made in an attempt to achieve consensus among the main Presbyterian churches. Introducing the bill into the House of Commons, Moncrieff reminded his fellow MPs that 'there is no question on which so much difference of opinion exists; and none in which difference of opinion, even on points the most abstract and theoretical, creates so many practical obstacles'. However, he maintained that Scotland's Presbyterians, and their schools, were only separated on the grounds of organisation, not doctrine, adding that 'however important the questions of church government may be that divide us, I see no reason why we should have contending schools established by contending sects'.[169]

Despite this appeal for unity based on a national system, the most important and divisive change concerned the role of religion. Unlike the ambiguity of Melgund's bills, Moncrieff was determined to secure the place of religious instruction in the national school curriculum.[170] Emphasising the centrality of religion to the country's history and liberty, and the cross-party opposition to an exclusion clause, Moncrieff argued that it would 'be a very great mistake to propose a system of secular education in Scotland'. He believed that the state should both acknowledge and pay for religious teaching in the schools, and dismissed voluntary concerns by claiming that

---

167. *Voice from the Church*, 3–5, 7, 12.
168. *UPM*, viii (March 1854), 143–4; *Dundee Courier*, 15 February 1854.
169. *Hansard's Parliamentary Debates*, 3rd series, vol. cxxx (23 February 1854), 151, 1159–60.
170. Stevenson, *Fulfilling a Vision*, 99.

'whatever is beneficial to the community there is no injustice in requiring the community to pay for'.[171] However, while this clause twenty-seven of the bill, legalising religious instruction in the schools, appeared to betray Moncrieff's Free Church allegiance, concessions were made to the other Presbyterian churches. For example, Moncrieff proposed that the day-to-day management of the existing parish schools remained in the hands of the minister and heritors, who would also retain control of the election of schoolmasters declared fit by the local inspector. To appease the United Presbyterian and secular lobby, the bill also stipulated that while religion was part of the schools' ordinary teaching, it would be offered at certain stated hours during which dissenting or Roman Catholic parents could choose to opt out. However, Moncrieff's realisation that concession was required to achieve success led to a disjointed and inconsistent bill that pleased no one. The Manchester Radical Richard Cobden criticised the 'absurdity' of a bill that professed religious values yet abolished religious tests, and failed to provide for any particular doctrinal character. According to Cobden, the bill 'went too far for the voluntaries and not far enough for the state religionists'.[172]

Most crucially, however, the bill also hardened sectarian attitudes and led to a division in the formerly unified national education movement. This retreat to sectarianism was most neatly encapsulated by the United Presbyterian Church's vociferous opposition to the bill. By mid-March, this had grown to a national protest, dominating the church courts and the voluntary press, and resulting in a series of public meetings. According to the *Glasgow Chronicle*, the entire national education movement now appeared to be in 'the direction of Free Church interests and Free Church principles'.[173] While the run-up to the bill had witnessed Scotland's evangelical dissenters converging on a unified platform, an exclusive meeting of United Presbyterians, held in Queen Street Hall, Edinburgh on 10 April, was organised to defend and reassert the church's denominational interests in the face of what they regarded as an unsuitable and Free Church-oriented blueprint for national education. According to one of the primary agitators during the Voluntary Controversy, James Peddie, clause twenty-seven of Moncrieff's bill 'does violence to the religious convictions' of his fellow United Presbyterians and was 'at variance with the voluntary principle'. According to John Brown, the bill would require United Presbyterians to support through a specific tax an 'unscriptural' system that would 'make it impossible for dissenters, with a safe conscience, to take any part in the management and superintendence of such schools' or even to 'avail themselves of their use for the education of their children'.[174]

---

171. *Hansard's Parliamentary Debates*, 3rd series, vol. cxxx (23 February 1854), 1167.
172. Howe and Morgan, *The Letters of Richard Cobden, vol. iii*, 16.
173. *Glasgow Chronicle*, 15 March 1854.
174. *Scotsman*, 12 April 1854.

The apparent disregard of voluntary principles by Moncrieff was blamed on the NEA's failure to assert clearly its 'fundamental' principle that secular education should be met by the state and religious instruction by the parents, due to the infiltration of the society's platform by establishmentarian Free Churchmen such as Candlish, Buchanan and Cunningham. The United Presbyterian minister George Johnston lamented that instead of the NEA and the United Presbyterian Church providing a 'united, clear, and distinct utterance' of their views, the interference of the Free Church leaders resulted in 'only a feeble, hesitating, whispering voice, which had produced no effect upon the country or the government', and led to a bill 'in which not only was the principle which he was advocating not recognised, but it had been directly contradicted and trampled in the dust'.[175] The need to counter this apparent misrepresentation of United Presbyterian principles was emphasised by Henry Renton, the minister at Kelso and chief organiser of the United Presbyterian opposition to the bill. While Renton argued that Scotland's dissenters needed to meet as a united group, and not dissolve into the sectarian strife associated with the Voluntary Controversy, he did concede that the United Presbyterians must defend their own position and principles if they were to retain any influence over the direction of Scottish education.[176]

The Queen Street Hall meeting, along with another organised by the Anti-State Church Association, provided the first indication that even those within Scottish dissent most favourable towards united action were beginning to turn inwards and defend their own sectarian interests. The voluntary opposition to Moncrieff's bill was criticised by Fox Maule at a hostile meeting of the NEA in Edinburgh two weeks after the United Presbyterian gathering. Maule claimed that the United Presbyterians had overlooked the 'great merits' of a bill that they 'ought to have been grateful for', and stressed the need for compromise to achieve reform. He argued that if the voluntaries 'suppose that they can still fall back on the old and rotten ways, and patiently wait till they crumble under their feet . . . they will find themselves in great error'. The need for concessions from all sides was also emphasised at the meeting by Adam Black, who criticised the 'determined stand' all parties appeared to be making for their seemingly 'vital' principles. Black lamented what he saw as 'a good deal of jealousy among a number of the dissenters, who supposed that some of the clauses of the bill had been got up by some parties connected with the Free Church, or to please the Free Church' (a claim he refuted). Though Black recognised the bill's twenty-seventh clause on religious instruction as the 'great bone of contention', he dismissed its impact on the voluntary principle, and called on his fellow dissenters to 'pause and consider whether there might not be something pretty good in a bill which was so decidedly opposed by

---

175. *Paisley Herald and Renfrewshire Advertiser*, 15 April 1854.
176. *Scotsman*, 12 April 1854; *Paisley Herald and Renfrewshire Advertiser*, 15 April 1854.

the Church of Scotland'. However, the United Presbyterian minister James Harper countered Black by asserting that the bill did indeed violate the voluntary principle, and also failed to answer the NEA's call to place religious instruction in the hands of local boards representing the parents.[177]

The hostility and lack of co-operation associated with the bill was condemned by Moncrieff himself, who wrote to Guthrie that he was 'thoroughly disgusted and sickened with the violence of the Established Church on the one hand, and of the extreme section of the voluntaries on the other', and warned that if an alliance of the non-established Presbyterians could not be formed to secure the bill, he would turn to the establishment and 'give them all they ask' regarding the parish schools. Alongside Adam Black, Moncrieff noted that he had approached Harper and David Duncan regarding the 'violence of their voluntary friends' on the education question. He 'told them distinctly that unless, in some way or other, they presented voluntaryism in a less offensive light than as an obstruction in the way of saving our perishing masses', it would 'put an end to all hope of union'.[178]

The desire to overlook 'petty details' was reiterated by the chief conciliator of the national education movement, Guthrie. At the April meeting of the NEA, amid the mud-slinging of the competing sects, the Free Churchman praised Moncrieff's bill, always destined to be opposed by at least one party, as 'so near perfection'. Agreeing with Lord Aberdeen's remark that the bill was a matter of concession, Guthrie argued that in a country so equally and strongly divided along denominational lines as Scotland this policy of forbearance was the only way forward, and failure to achieve this would result in 'one of the greatest national calamities that have befallen Scotland in my day'. According to Guthrie, the divisions caused by the bill were evidence of the necessity of a national, non-sectarian system of education in Scotland, and he called on the country's dissenters to reconcile their differences and act together in common cause, so that the British government would not view the situation 'through the coloured spectacles of extreme men'. While he professed not to sympathise with Harper's objections to the bill, he praised the 'reasonable' nature of the United Presbyterian minister's position, which looked 'above the prejudices and interests of party'. Quoting George Sinclair's desire to 'take the bill as we can get it . . . till we get mair if need be', Guthrie called on Scotland's dissenters to make the necessary sacrifices to save a bill that he claimed would not only secure an improved educational system but place religion in an even safer position than before. He urged the supporters of national education to lay temporarily aside the voluntary principle or the Claim of Right in favour of supporting a bill consistent with the Word of God and for the good of Scotland.[179] Despite

177. *Witness*, 29 April 1854.
178. Guthrie and Guthrie, *Autobiography of Thomas Guthrie*, 299–300.
179. *Witness*, 29 April 1854.

Guthrie's best efforts, the open hostility within Presbyterian dissent, combined with the surprisingly optimistic returns of the 1851 census on Scottish schooling and the opposition of English Tory MPs to any encroachment on the Established Kirk, ensured that Moncrieff's bill was defeated by only nine votes in the House of Commons.[180]

However, this defeat did not spell the end of the Lord Advocate's attempt to reform the Scottish education system, and he returned the following year with a bill chiefly aimed at conciliating the warring divisions of Scottish Presbyterian dissent and placating the hostile voluntaries by amending the offensive clause twenty-seven.[181] Like the previous year's attempt, the initial response was one of unity and compromise. At a public meeting in Edinburgh in April 1855 to support Moncrieff's bill and oppose a rival pro-establishment measure, George Johnston declared that while the maintenance of a place for religious instruction was at odds with his stance as a 'decided voluntary' and ensured 'he did not think the measure was faultless', it was nonetheless an improvement on the 1854 bill. Johnston believed that the bill's clause for separate optional hours for religious instruction could coexist with the voluntary principle, and 'rejoiced' that the denominational clause of 1854 which offered grants to 'deserving' and 'open' church schools was scrapped. Guthrie concurred with Johnston's conciliatory stance, and declared that he viewed Moncrieff's new bill as 'far more adapted to meet the views of different parties, than he had believed it possible to have done'.[182]

Of course, the proposals were not without their opposition among dissenting groups. The dissenting campaigner and founder of the British Anti-State Church Association Edward Miall criticised the measure as a Free Church bill purely designed to give the body its share of educational control alongside the establishment, while hard-line voluntaries within the United Presbyterian body lobbied MPs to oppose the measure.[183] Nevertheless, supporters of the bill believed that the vast majority of Scots, and most of the United Presbyterian Church, were in favour of Moncrieff's amended proposals.[184] The Lord Advocate defended the bill from the aspersions of Miall, and claimed that the 'religious difficulty was no difficulty at all', as religion would be provided for by the people of Scotland regardless of the contents of the bill. Moncrieff criticised the constant 'squabbling about mere theories' that characterised the debates in both the Commons and the churches and led to numerous amendments to the original measure. Nevertheless, he hoped his decision to amend the twenty-seventh clause

180. *Glasgow Constitutional*, 28 March 1855; Withrington, '1851 Census', 139; Stevenson, *Fulfilling a Vision*, 99–100.
181. Hutchison, *Political History of Scotland*, 78.
182. *Caledonian Mercury*, 26 April 1855.
183. *Hansard's Parliamentary Debates*, 3rd series, vol. cxxxix (9 July 1855), 627–9; *Montrose, Arbroath and Brechin Review*, 27 July 1855.
184. *Montrose, Arbroath and Brechin Review*, 27 July 1855.

on religious instruction to appease his voluntary opponents would prove unnecessary 'because all the religious difficulty would vanish the moment the Bill passed'.[185]

Though initially supported by two-thirds of the United Presbyterian Synod, increasing grassroots unease at the prospect of government control of religious education, paid for by rates, culminated in a repeat of the previous year's voluntary opposition. The amendments made to the bill in the House of Commons, deemed necessary by Moncrieff to secure its passage but which severely weakened the scheme's voluntary credentials, ultimately fastened the United Presbyterians' rejection of the Lord Advocate's proposals for a second consecutive year.[186] Despite eventually making it through the Commons, Moncrieff's latitudinarian attempt to appease all sides in the hope of success, dismissed as 'clumsy' doctoring by *The Times*, was rejected unanimously by the House of Lords.[187] The *Morning Herald* was particularly scathing of the bill, arguing that Moncrieff 'defied public sentiment, in order to carry through a measure which had no principle, which defied all consistency, and from first to last was patched and pared and adjusted to each onslaught, entirely for the one absorbing end of being passed'. The *Herald* also labelled Moncrieff a Free Church 'puppet' and claimed that the bill was a 'sectarian attempt' to 'sacrifice the education of a country to the ambition of a politico-ecclesiastical party'.[188] The voluntary *Edinburgh News* agreed, labelling the bill 'a monster job on behalf of the Free Church', a claim refuted by the Free Church-supporting *Scottish Guardian*, which maintained that the Free Kirk 'had nothing more to do with [the bill] than any other party in the country approving of its general scope and spirit, excepting that no religious body was prepared to sacrifice so much as the Free Church in supporting the bill'. While the Free Kirk claimed to be willing to relinquish their own scheme in the event of a successful national bill, the voluntaries, 'who have done nothing themselves for the education of the people', were ridiculed for persisting 'in obtruding their preposterous crotchets in the way of a Government desirous of supplying its deficiencies'. The *Guardian* also dismissed criticisms of the latitudinarianism of Moncrieff's bill and argued that such compromise on all sides was necessary for the passing of any future bill.[189]

Despite this belated and somewhat hollow call for compromise by the Free Church, the failure of the 1855 bill underscored the increasing cynicism surrounding the national education movement and its calls for dissenting unity. In the wake of the bill, Fox Maule lamented the 'defective' state of education in both the parochial and voluntary schools of Scotland,

---

185. *Hansard's Parliamentary Debates*, 3rd series, vol. cxxxix (9 July 1855), 628–9.
186. Hutchison, *Political History of Scotland*, 78–9.
187. *The Times*, 27 July 1855.
188. *Morning Herald*, 27 July 1855.
189. *Edinburgh News*, 7 July 1855; *Scottish Guardian*, 27 July 1855.

exacerbated by the failure to install an effective national system.[190] In a similar manner to the United Presbyterian reaction to the 1854 bill, the demise of Moncrieff's national project swiftly saw a return to pre-existing denominational interests, with an increasingly aloof Candlish calling on his fellow Free Churchmen to fall back on their own education scheme with 'fresh ardour and success'.[191]

A third less extensive attempt at reform by Moncrieff in 1856, though receiving nominal backing from the major dissenting leaders, was criticised by the *United Presbyterian Magazine* as a 'paltry instalment of a large debt'.[192] With little support from an increasingly ambivalent Free Church, the voluntaries and a hostile Tory contingent in the House of Commons, the bill was also withdrawn.[193] Amid widespread apathy concerning a unified national movement, the desire to batten down the sectarian hatches became commonplace in the years following Moncrieff's second bill. At the Free Church General Assembly in May 1857, Candlish dismissed an overture calling for the kirk to pursue a system of national education, arguing that the question was not currently on the agenda at parliament and that Free Churchmen should not be distracted by such a 'phantom'. Instead, he reasserted the General Assembly's commitment to its own education scheme. He claimed that involvement in the recent national education debates had 'contributed very materially to slacken the exertions of our people' towards the Free Church scheme. With a pointed reference to Guthrie's faction of the kirk, Candlish criticised those who 'have been waiting and watching, as if they were entitled to hold their hands and button up their pockets, and to stand gazing until this panacea of a national education bill comes down from the parliamentary heavens'. This criticism of Guthrie, Begg and Gunn as 'mere waiters' was echoed by another Free Church member, who questioned how these 'sanguine expectants' of a national scheme could reconcile their duty to it with the 'destitution under their own eyes'. While rather obliquely maintaining his preference for an eventual national scheme, Candlish recognised the failure of Moncrieff's bills as evidence that 'we ought to prosecute our efforts as a Church without any respect whatever to the prospect of a national system of education'. According to Candlish, the Free Church had for 'far too long' held back its own efforts in favour of a national system, and he vowed not to let the kirk be 'paralysed' by its 'shadowy and vague' prospect, and instead argued that the entire debates should be viewed as if they were 'indefinitely postponed'. Demonstrating his usual shrewdness by attempting to keep a foot in both camps, Candlish stressed that without a strong denominational scheme of its own, the Free

190. *Dundee Advertiser*, 27 July 1855.
191. Robert S. Candlish, *Appeal to the people of the Free Church of Scotland on behalf of the education scheme* (Edinburgh, 1855); *Scottish Guardian*, 27 July 1855.
192. *UPM*, x (May 1856), 235–6.
193. *Dundee, Perth, and Cupar Advertiser*, 29 July 1856.

Church would lose its influence over the direction of the education question. By pledging the Free Church schools to any future scheme, Candlish could make the case that any progress of their denominational scheme was 'progress in the direction of a thorough national system of education', regardless of whether he and his church were pursuing such a goal.[194]

Despite Candlish's desire to press on alone, 1857 also witnessed a rejuvenation of an alliance between members of the Free and United Presbyterian churches based on an apparent convergence of principle on the education question, especially surrounding religious instruction. These calls for co-operation coincided with George Sinclair's public resolutions for ecclesiastical union between the two churches, with a national education act touted as a possible benefit to be derived from such an event. In April 1857, a month before Sinclair's resolutions, Chalmers' son-in-law William Hanna noted that the 'fear-haunted' question of education was the area in which Scotland's major dissenting churches were 'already drawing nearest to one another'. This Hanna claimed was due to some of the 'ablest and wisest' ministers within the United Presbyterian Church coming out in favour of introducing the religious element into the national schools. According to Hanna, the ecclesiastical incorporation of the Free and United Presbyterian churches proposed by Sinclair would facilitate a 'common ground' on which both bodies could approach the government and secure an agreed national system – the prospect of which ensured that 'one cannot help desiring to see that union as speedily as possible accomplished'.[195] While Hanna's correlation between educational and ecclesiastical union failed to gain traction among the majority of dissenters, by the late 1850s there was an increasing perception that it was 'high time' for Scotland's non-established Presbyterians to coalesce into, at least, 'one grand educational power'.[196] At a meeting in Glasgow in January 1859, voluntaries refuted the suggestion emanating from the establishment that the United Presbyterian Church represented the chief obstacle to union on national education. The Established Churchman and Conservative politician Archibald Orr-Ewing had also claimed that the apparent willingness of the Free Church to co-operate with the national kirk on the common ground of education marked the first step to closer union between the two churches. However, this was dismissed by James Mitchell, who argued that the United Presbyterian Synod was in favour of Moncrieff and his proposals, while the Glasgow minister James Taylor emphasised that it was the Church of Scotland, and not the United Presbyterians, that stood in the way of unified Presbyterian action.[197]

---

194. *PGAFC, May 1857* (Edinburgh, 1857), 255, 260–2, 266.
195. *Fife Herald*, 16 April 1857.
196. Fraser, *Educational Enterprises*, 163; Fraser, *Educational Condition of Scotland*, 31.
197. *Paisley Herald and Renfrewshire Advertiser*, 22 January 1859; *Glasgow Herald*, 15 January 1859.

The apparent convergence between the Free and United Presbyterian churches in the late 1850s, however, seemed somewhat tentative, and failed to resemble the unified national movement aimed for by the NEA. For example, the campaign for reform led by Moncrieff in 1861 centred solely on the proposed abolition of the religious tests for teachers in the parochial and burgh schools, with no reference to any future plan. The bill aimed to transfer the examination of new teachers from the presbyteries to four university-based boards, in effect ending the requirement for teachers to sign the Confession of Faith, though adherence to the Bible and Shorter Catechism was retained.[198] By the early 1860s, Moncrieff realised that a successful national education scheme for Scotland could not be achieved as 'one gigantic scheme' and should instead be attempted 'bit by bit'. To Moncrieff, the prevalence of sectarian interest remained so great that any full national scheme 'congenial to the one would be torn in tatters by the other'. Therefore the Lord Advocate believed that agreement on 'one grand point', such as the abolition of the requirement to sign the Confession, would be an 'enormous gain', and potentially pave the way for more extensive reform.[199] Ultimately, Moncrieff's cautious approach was vindicated, as the bill received widespread support among Scotland's dissenters and passed through parliament, the first of Moncrieff's bills on non-university education to do so.

What the 1861 Act would eventually lead to, however, remained heavily disputed and continued to divide Scotland's dissenters. One member of the Free Synod of Moray argued that the bill, throwing the schools open to public competition, had the potential to foster the kind of positive co-operative rivalry proposed by Chalmers in his territorial operations of the previous decade, and benefit Scottish education in the long term.[200] The United Presbyterians, hardened by the experiences of the previous education debates and wary of Free Church intentions, were hesitant to support anything other than the piecemeal scheme of reform favoured by Moncrieff. One dissenting commentator wrote that the 'sole object' of the United Presbyterian Church was to assist in the abolition of religious tests. The church would not, however, pursue the creation of 'another so-called national system of education' based on a 'compromise' that would 'ignore the conscientious principles of dissenters and of the United Presbyterian Church'. Rejecting a call by the Social Science Association for Presbyterians to unite around the education question, the United Presbyterians stated their preference to wait for when matters were more 'matured' before becoming involved in any national organisation. Only then could the friends of national education unite to effect 'an ultimate and compre-

---

198. Drummond and Bulloch, *Church in Victorian Scotland*, 97–8.
199. *John O'Groat Journal*, 18 July 1861.
200. *Elgin Courier*, 26 April 1861.

hensive settlement on catholic and permanent principles' without 'doing violence' to the consciences of any portion of Scotland's population.[201] The failure of a further reform bill issued by Moncrieff a year later underlined this point. This 1862 bill built on the previous decade's attempts to create a national system, but also aimed to conciliate the Established Church, much to the annoyance of the Free Kirk, and proposed to continue Privy Council Grants for Episcopalians and Roman Catholics, contrary to the voluntary principles of the United Presbyterians. The failure of this bill only further served to emphasise that neither of the major dissenting churches was willing to sacrifice its denominational principles in the spirit of compromise.[202] Despite the success of the 1861 Act, union among Scotland's Presbyterian dissenters behind national education appeared as distant as ever.

While the education debates appeared to provide a path to closer union between the dissenting churches, they also illustrated the hazards and barriers preventing such an achievement. Unlike other attempts at co-operation, such as in the Evangelical Alliance and the anti-Maynooth coalition (which the education debates effectively killed off), a single, agreeable reference point for national education was never available to draw the Free and United Presbyterian churches together into even a loose working alliance on the matter. Much like the narrowness of the anti-Maynooth campaign, while Scotland's dissenters agreed that the dominance of the Established Church over the country's schools should be ended, they agreed on little else. Even support for a national system to replace the parochial schools, the basic requirement of the majority of the reformers, did not receive wholehearted support within Candlish's faction of the Free Church, and if it did, contained so many caveats and conditions as to make unified action almost impossible. Fundamental differences, within and between the churches, halted any of the numerous attempts at compromise and conciliation, and also epitomised the variations in principle evident in the shifting dissenting landscape in this period.

The major sticking point of religious instruction neatly summed up the various competing views within dissent on the role of the church and state in the lives of the Scottish people. While the Established Church clung grimly to its control of the religious education of Scotland's children, the Free and United Presbyterian churches represented the three main strands of dissenting thought indicative throughout this period. Their attempts to solve the education question, particularly regarding the role of religious instruction, were mostly based on the 'national', 'dissenting' and 'voluntary' values that increasingly characterised the different ideological

201. *Kelso Chronicle*, 7 June 1861.
202. Stevenson, *Fulfilling a Vision*, 117.

factions within Scottish dissent (though of course both churches contained extremists opposed outright to any national system, for conflicting reasons). First, the Candlish faction, in both their support of a national system and their own educational scheme, maintained the 'national' significance of Presbyterian religion associated with the establishment principle, and believed it was the state's duty to recognise and fund religious instruction in the national schools. The minority group within the Free Kirk, led by Guthrie and Begg, largely epitomised the 'dissenting' identity increasingly associated with the Free Church after 1843. Though maintaining that secular and religious education should be taught together, this group were willing to leave that question in the hands of the parents, without interference from the state, essentially combining the 'national' and 'voluntary' principles of the other two factions. Nevertheless, many within this party such as Begg remained staunchly averse to any support for voluntaryism, yet were willing to forgo this for the sake of a better system of education. Third, while the majority of United Presbyterians largely adhered to the voluntary belief that the state should not recognise religion in any form, their opposition to the exclusion clause favoured by the secularists and willingness to acquiesce to Free Church demands on religious instruction in the schools underpinned a lack of stubbornness and ability to compromise missing in the fringes of the group.

However, this policy of forbearance, evident in nearly all of the attempts at co-operation between the Free and United Presbyterian churches, was not without its problems. Despite the efforts of the National Education Association, the lack of a unified voice in the education debates ensured that any attempts at compromise and conciliation between the churches were greeted with hostility once certain intrinsic demands were not met by the other side. Ultimately, while offering a chance for Scotland's dissenters to co-operate against the common enemy – the Established Church – the partisanship of the debates, based on a willingness from each group to defend their own interests, hindered the increasing if erratic convergence and goodwill between the Free and United Presbyterian churches noted in the previous chapters. The debates also provided a telling indication of the support for a distinct dissenting identity in the aftermath of the Disruption. While the national education movement offered dissenters a common platform against the establishment and even a potential route to the dissenting national church envisioned by the likes of George Sinclair, the Free Church's own education scheme was also integral to its attempt to create its own 'national' church after 1843. Candlish and his supporters' initial decision to oppose a national education system was indicative of the Free Kirk's sectarian desire to cement their own national authority following the Disruption, regardless of calls for dissenting co-operation. However, that is not to conclude that the education debates offered little progress in the way of dissenting convergence. The support for an alliance by the likes of Begg, one of the fiercest anti-voluntaries to oppose union negotiations after 1863, provides clear evidence of a will among a strong constituency of Free Churchmen and United Presbyterians to present a united front, if not ecclesiastically, at least on almost all other national issues.

Conclusion

In 1863 the Free Church entered into negotiations with the United Presbyterian Church with the aim of achieving an incorporating union between the two denominations and, according to the United Presbyterian minister Daniel Kerr, creating a 'great unestablished Church in Scotland'.[1] Though these negotiations ultimately concluded without success in 1873, they paved the way for a renewed period of union within Scottish Presbyterianism. With the exception of relatively minor anti-unionist protests, this period pieced together almost two centuries of dispute and schisms, and would eventually culminate in the reunification of the Church of Scotland in 1929. Three years after the conclusion of their decade-long negotiations for union with the United Presbyterians, the Free Church in 1876 entered into union with a majority of the Cameronians of the Reformed Presbyterian Church who had hitherto remained outside of mainstream Presbyterianism since the Revolution Settlement. To mark the occasion, Robert Rainy declared that 'we are in an age of Presbyterian reunions'.[2] So it proved; the 1876 union, and the abolition of patronage two years previously, was followed by a prolonged period of co-operation between the Free and United Presbyterian churches as they campaigned together to disestablish the Church of Scotland. The joint dissenting agitation for disestablishment underlined the gradual shift towards voluntary principles that had occurred in the Free Kirk under the leadership of younger ministers such as Rainy, and set the tone for a new round of union negotiations between the two major Scottish dissenting churches that resulted in the formation of the United Free Church of Scotland in 1900.[3]

Though similar claims were made by Scotland's dissenters before 1900, the United Free Church, representing over 500,000 Scots (compared to the Established Kirk's 656,000 members), did indeed resemble a truly national dissenting church that could rival the Church of Scotland. However,

---

1. *Report of speeches on union with the Free Church delivered in the United Presbyterian Synod, Friday 15 May 1863* (Edinburgh, 1863), 4. Initial discussions for union also included the Reformed Presbyterians and the various fragments of English Presbyterianism. This ambitious but ultimately futile attempt to unite 'all unendowed Presbyterians in Great Britain' was led by the United Presbyterians' most prominent advocate for union, John Cairns (5–6).
2. *Union of the Free and Reformed Presbyterian Churches of Scotland; report of proceedings in the Free Church Assembly Hall, on Thursday 25 May 1876* (Edinburgh, 1876), 21.
3. Machin, 'Voluntaryism and Reunion', 222.

despite the fears of those in an otherwise resurgent establishment, rather than acting as a catalyst for a reinvigorated and potentially successful voluntary attack on the Kirk, the creation of the United Free Church (combined with sympathy generated by the property disputes with the continuing Free Church) instead 'contributed to the creation of an atmosphere favourable to union' between Scotland's estranged Presbyterians.[4] The pro-union atmosphere was further strengthened by the 1921 Church of Scotland Act. This Act of Parliament legalised the Articles Declaratory, which ambiguously defined the Kirk as a national church independent of the state and opened the door for the eventual reunion with the United Free Church in October 1929.[5] The modified and nominal form of establishment embodied in the Church of Scotland Act and the later 1925 Act on endowments offered the reunified Kirk both national recognition and real spiritual independence from the state. Despite being hijacked by a divisive Tory and anti-Irish Catholic agenda within the church leadership, the 1929 union, in theory at least, realised Chalmers' ideal and allowed for compromise between the various establishmentarian, dissenting and voluntary strands of Presbyterian thought.[6]

Though the likes of Rainy viewed it as an age of reunion, in contrast to the schisms that had dominated Scottish Presbyterianism before 1843, the period after 1863, especially within the Free and United Presbyterian churches, was not unprecedented. Instead, the developments within Presbyterianism which would eventually culminate in the 1929 reunion of the Church of Scotland were grounded in the twenty years of transition that followed the Disruption. As this study has shown, the major issues that dominated the ten years of union negotiations and beyond also played a major role in fostering, maintaining and impeding co-operation between the Free and United Presbyterian churches in the immediate aftermath of the Disruption. As Chapter Two demonstrated, during the initial aftermath of the Disruption, and by extension the Voluntary Controversy, the Free Church went to great lengths to highlight the differences between the new church and their United Presbyterian counterparts, especially regarding their views on the voluntary principle and the church–state connection. However, by 1863 much more emphasis was placed on the principles that united Scotland's dissenters, while those that divided them were made matters of 'forbearance'. As the Free Church General Assembly considered overtures for union in May 1863, one of the leading pro-unionists, Robert Buchanan, acknowledged that the Free and United Presbyterian churches both were Scottish, Calvinist, Presbyterian, upholders of the church's

---

4. Rolf Sjolinder, *Presbyterian Reunion in Scotland 1907–1921: its background and development* (Edinburgh, 1962), 109–11.
5. Kidd, *Union and Unionisms*, 242–4; Cameron, *Impaled upon a thistle*, 135–7.
6. S. J. Brown, 'The social vision of Scottish Presbyterianism and the union of 1929', *RSCHS*, xxiv (1990); Douglas M. Murray, *Rebuilding the Kirk: Presbyterian reunion in Scotland, 1909–1929* (Edinburgh, 2000); Machin, 'Voluntaryism and Reunion', 233.

spiritual independence and the principle of non-intrusion, unconnected with the state and relied upon practical voluntaryism.[7]

Nevertheless, according to a report on the prospects of church union delivered by a committee comprised of representatives of both churches in 1864, the debate over the role of the civil magistrate in religion remained the most significant and perhaps only point of difference between the two groups of dissenters.[8] The Free Church's support after 1843 for state churches, in theory at least, was due to a number of reasons. First, they maintained the belief that it was the state's duty to uphold the nation's Protestant values and recognise and endow its established churches, which ideally would provide the official religious and moral voice for the entirety of the country. This view of Britain as a confessional state was most evident in the Free Kirk's opposition to the government endowment of the Roman Catholic seminary at Maynooth (Chapter Five) and their support for state-sanctioned religious instruction in the proposed national schools (Chapter Eight). Second, Free Churchmen such as Chalmers believed that the national character of a church could only be achieved through state endowments (though not through state control). Chapter Two illustrated how the Free Church embraced practical voluntaryism in their bid to create a 'national' church outside of the establishment. However, this tended to localise the church, creating a stark division between its urban middle-class membership and the rural Highland poor, and moving it away from its original 'national' aspirations.

While the Free Kirk turned to practical voluntary methods out of necessity, it was the refusal of many within the church to accept theoretical voluntaryism, and the perceived secularism and threat of 'national atheism' associated with its support for disestablishment, that remained a persistent barrier to closer dissenting co-operation.[9] As Chapter Three outlined, despite their co-operation in societies such as the Evangelical Alliance, the establishmentarian and voluntary wings of Scottish dissent remained carefully separated. Though each led to calls for further dissenting union, the church unions of 1847 and 1852 did not attempt to cross this ideological divide. Furthermore, any attempts to instigate a debate on union between the Free and United Presbyterian churches before 1863 were marked by awkwardness and an unwillingness even among the strongest Free Kirk pro-unionists to engage in a debate that had the potential to irretrievably divide their membership.

While from the outset of the post-Disruption period the majority of United Presbyterians were eager to cultivate a shared purpose with their

---

7. *Monthly Record of the Free Church of Scotland*, xii (July 1863), 277.
8. Walker, *Chapters from the History of the Free Church*, 235; Kidd and Wallace, 'Biblical Criticism and Scots Presbyterian Dissent', 241.
9. William Balfour, *Voluntaryism of the United Presbyterian Church unchanged, and directly opposed to the distinctive principles of the Free Church of Scotland* (Edinburgh, 1869), 28–9.

new dissenting colleagues, it was the Free Church that appeared confused at best and divided at worst over how to deal with their new position outside of the establishment. Even when a majority of the Free Church leadership had been won around to the prospect of dissenting union by 1863, the old suspicions of voluntaryism remained within a significant minority of its membership and would ultimately prove the undoing of the negotiations. This theologically conservative, establishmentarian and anti-unionist faction of the Free Church, largely situated in the Highlands and led by James Begg and John Kennedy of Dingwall, successfully opposed the movement for union after 1863 and remained outside of the eventual 1900 union.[10]

Despite the anti-unionists' intransigent grip on what they viewed as the 'Disruption principles' of the Free Church after 1863, the meaning and role of the establishment and voluntary principles within Scottish dissent had changed considerably in the twenty years after the Disruption. While in 1843 Scotland's dissenters appeared to be separated by diametrically opposed stances on the church–state connection, by 1863 the establishment and voluntary ideals embodied by the two churches had become diluted and more moderate than the hard-line stances that characterised the Voluntary Controversy. The convergence that occurred between these two seemingly disparate ideals was central to providing the foundations on which dissenting union could be negotiated. According to Rainy's biographer, Patrick Carnegie Simpson, the voluntaryism of the United Presbyterians bore little resemblance to the hostile rhetoric of the 1830s.[11] The 1864 joint-committee report also argued that while voluntaryism remained a central tenet of the United Presbyterian Church, it was not a term of communion.[12] A similar shift occurred in the Free Church. As Chapter Two demonstrated, the Free Kirk's reliance on practical voluntaryism benefitted most the urban Lowland ministers of wealthy congregations who formed the bulk of the church's leadership in this period. These ministers defined the increasingly middle-class character of the Free Church after 1843 and later in the century would prove integral to the unionist and disestablishment movements within Scottish dissent. In 1863 the Edinburgh minister Charles Brown acknowledged that while the Free Kirk remained opposed to voluntaryism in its strictest, most secular form (a view he claimed, in stark contrast to Begg, had long since abated in Scotland), they were now effectively voluntaries.[13] Free Church unionists were also keen to downplay the significance of the church–state connection, claiming that the Disruption was based not on a commitment to the establishment principle but

---

10. McLeod, *The Second Disruption*.
11. Patrick Carnegie Simpson, *The Life of Principal Rainy* (London, 1909), 152–4.
12. Walker, *Chapters from the History of the Free Church*, 235.
13. *Monthly Record of the Free Church of Scotland*, xii (July 1863), 278–9.

only to the national recognition and spiritual independence of the Church.[14]

This shift in the stance of both the Free and United Presbyterian churches between 1843 and 1863 allowed for the creation of a distinct dissenting identity that would characterise the calls for union and define the principles of the proposed united church. Though differences remained over when state endowments were acceptable, the unionists of the Free and United Presbyterian churches favoured the construction of what would be in effect a 'national voluntary' church: one which operated outside of the establishment and relied largely upon voluntary funds, but was committed to the national recognition and promotion of Protestantism and religious values.[15] This proposed United Free Church would allow room for both the Free Kirk's aspirations to be a national institution, and the United Presbyterians' commitment to voluntaryism.[16] This study has shown that the dissenting identity favoured by the unionists after 1863 was indicative of a gradual shift within both churches after the Disruption towards a more moderate and broadly acceptable vision of dissent.

The formation of this dissenting identity was influenced by the external political and social developments of the 1840s and 1850s that, along with the Disruption, shaped the ecclesiastical relationship between the Free and United Presbyterian churches. The immediate aftermath of the Disruption witnessed the beginning of the Free Kirk's experiment with practical voluntaryism and, in the case of Peter Hately Waddell, a recognition that some support for theoretical voluntaryism and dissenting union was possible, if initially discouraged, within the new church. However, it was 1845 in particular that marked a pivotal year in influencing the future direction of Scottish dissent. The Poor Relief Act of that year, assessed in Chapter Seven, removed an important pillar of the Church of Scotland's control over Scottish society and placed Scotland's dissenters on an equal footing with the establishment, providing an opportunity for co-operation on social issues, in particular urban evangelisation. Peel's decision to increase the annual government grant to Maynooth College in 1845 also prompted the dissenting churches to unite together on the common platform of 'no-popery' outlined in Chapters Five and Six. As John Wolffe has argued, the negative prejudice of anti-Catholicism had the potential to act as a catalyst for Protestants to think positively about their own common ground and shared identity.[17] The anti-popery campaign of the mid-nineteenth century not only dominated Scottish politics for over a decade but facilitated the formation of a working dissenting alliance and the tentative creation of

14. Walker, *Chapters from the History of the Free Church*, 235; Kidd and Wallace, 'Biblical Criticism and Scots Presbyterian Dissent', 241–2.
15. Simpson, *Life of Principal Rainy*, 154; *Glasgow Herald*, 3 March 1864.
16. Fleming, *Story of Church Union*, 32–3.
17. John Wolffe, 'Unity in Diversity? North Atlantic evangelical thought in the mid-nineteenth century', *Studies in Church History*, xxxii (1996), 365.

a distinct dissenting and anti-erastian Presbyterian identity. The national education debates that followed from the late 1840s also provided common ground for dissenters against a common enemy – the Church of Scotland's control of the parish schools – and offered another opportunity for the Free and United Presbyterian churches to shape together a post-Disruption Scotland which no longer viewed the Kirk as its sole moral arbiter. Both the Maynooth and national education debates, and the dissenting alliances formed through these debates, influenced both positively and negatively the concurrent attempts at ecclesiastical union examined in Chapter Four. Finally, the formation of the Evangelical Alliance in 1845, spearheaded by Scotland's dissenters, provided the first tentative steps towards the convergence of principle that would characterise the two churches by the 1860s. While dissenting support for the Alliance faded by the late 1840s, it nevertheless instilled a desire among the Free and United Presbyterian churches to co-operate on the broad basis of dissent, anti-erastianism and evangelicalism, and acted as a precursor to the 'age of unions' that would follow.

These developments after 1845 were central to securing the shift within Presbyterian dissent from the hardened ecclesiastical ideologies of the pre-Disruption era to the more moderate dissenting and 'national voluntary' identity of the 1860s. While the Free Church attempted to marry their ambitions to create a national church with the realities of practical voluntaryism, their 1852 union with the Original Secession Church also sought a middle ground between the erastianism associated with the Established Kirk and the outright voluntaryism of the United Presbyterians. The ideal of a 'pure' Church of Scotland, of national standing but free from state intrusion, heralded at the 1852 union, would later become one of the cornerstones of the 'national voluntary' church envisioned by unionists after 1863. Though the Free Kirk's union with the Original Seceders can be framed simply as the new church's opportunity to position itself as the historic 'true' Church of Scotland, it also opened the door for a different kind of church that combined both the establishment and voluntary principles evident in Scottish dissent.

The Free Church's move from the establishmentarian position of the Disruption was also manifested in other ways. For instance, while the traditional anti-popery associated with the Free Kirk's campaign against the Maynooth endowment was based on the defence of Protestantism as Britain's national religion, the failure of the government to differentiate between truth and error led many Free Churchmen to argue against the principle of state endowments in general. The ambiguity surrounding the Free Church's position on Maynooth was pivotal in enabling a common position with the United Presbyterian Church to emerge against the grant which was neither fully establishmentarian nor voluntary, but distinctly dissenting. A similar narrative was formed during the national education debates. The perceived need to secure full dissenting support for a system of state-directed national education resulted in the Thomas Guthrie-led faction of the Free Church pursuing a quasi-voluntary approach. While Guthrie and his supporters emphasised the importance of religion in the proposed national schools, they also favoured a scheme that separated religious and secular education, and put religious instruction not under the control of the state but in the hands of the churches and parents. In both the Maynooth and education debates, a significant number of Free Churchmen increasingly became advocates for a model that recognised and defended the national importance of Protestantism in Britain but also was based on the voluntary exertions of the churches and not under the authority of the state. Though they did not always constitute a majority of Free Church opinion, these shifts nonetheless represented an increasing acceptance of the church's new dissenting position and common cause with their United Presbyterian counterparts, paving the way for the 'national voluntary' identity of Scotland's dissenters after 1863.

The United Presbyterian Church also underwent a significant ideological shift after the Disruption. The move from the extreme voluntaryism of the 1830s to a more moderate stance was in part in order to make co-operation based on common dissenting principles more palatable for even the most anti-voluntary of Free Churchmen. The 1847 union between the United Secession and Relief churches most neatly encapsulates this change and highlights the desire among the voluntary wing of Scottish dissent to cultivate a unified dissenting identity broad enough to attract Free Church support and eventually provide a pathway to further union. As Chapter Four illustrated, while the United Secession and Relief churches had been drawn closer together due to their united exertions during the previous decade's Voluntary Controversy, the 1847 union actually played down the importance of voluntaryism to both churches. Instead, the United Presbyterian union was a 'dissenting' one; the voluntary principle was not stipulated as a term of communion to the new church and the policies of non-intrusion and spiritual independence in opposition to the existing establishment, attractive to Free Church ears, were emphasised. The union's broad interpretation of dissent and its careful tempering of outright voluntary sentiment ensured that the new United Presbyterian Church did not alienate its Free Church counterpart and therefore left the door open for a further union based on similar dissenting characteristics. The desire to maintain Free Church support was central to the United Presbyterian approach to dissenting co-operation in this period. Though their opposition to Maynooth was largely based on the voluntary hostility to all state endowments of religion, many United Presbyterian ministers and politicians played up the 'no-popery' aspect of the campaign in order to smooth co-operation with their Free Church colleagues in the electoral alliance and obscure any lingering divisions over the church–state connection. The United Presbyterian support for religious instruction in the proposed national schools also helped to ease fears among Free Churchmen in the NEA wary of the perceived secular implications of voluntaryism. This dissenting stance on issues such as Maynooth and national education was key to influencing the further convergence among United Presbyterians and Free Churchmen on 'national' and 'voluntary' lines.

Of course, the aftermath of the Disruption was not simply one of convergence between the two major dissenting churches. Nevertheless, where convergence of principle was not possible, a policy of forbearance was enacted to placate opposing viewpoints and would remain in place even as the 1900 union approached. If matters of 'abstract principle', namely the role of state endowments, were a barrier to dissenting co-operation, they were for the most part ignored. Mostly this policy of forbearance was deemed necessary when dissenters were willing to unite against a common opponent – the Established Kirk, the Whig party, the Roman Antichrist – but differed over the reasons for that opposition. This was perhaps most evident in the anti-Maynooth political alliance discussed in Chapter Six. The electoral pact between the Free and United Presbyterian churches within the Scottish Liberal party was strongest when it solely focused either on the Maynooth grant or a common opposition to the Whig establishment. However, when it tried to assert a positive radical vision of Presbyterian politics, placing Maynooth as not solely a matter concerning anti-Catholicism but one that questioned the entire nature of the state's relationship with religion, cracks within the alliance started to appear that highlighted the lingering suspicions within Presbyterian dissent and the weakness of a single dissenting political voice.

Similarly, the national education debates also emphasised this dissenting policy of forbearance. The NEA, though broadly representing the dissenting interest, was not a homogeneous unit and contained many disparate views, particularly on the role of the state in religious education, that divided opinion between the Free Church and United Presbyterian members of the society and within the Free Kirk itself. Instead, the dissenting members of the NEA were united solely in their opposition to the existing system of education in Scotland, and the Church of Scotland's control over the parish schools. While they agreed that the Scottish education system was in need of reform, there was little agreement on what that reform should entail.

The policy of forbearance, which essentially meant turning a blind eye to points of difference that would hamper a common goal, was particularly effective in securing the church unions of 1847 and 1852, and allowed for tentative discussions at least to emerge in the 1850s on the topic of union between the Free and United Presbyterian churches. This approach would also be central to the union negotiations of the 1860s. While both churches claimed to recognise their 'honest and conscientious differences' over voluntaryism and ecclesiastical government, they also argued that these divisions had no bearing on the 'fundamental truths' that united the churches.[18] In effect, by attempting to reduce the divisions over the church–state connection to a 'minor' point of difference, Scotland's Presbyterians gave themselves the freedom to craft a broad yet slightly ambiguous dissenting identity in which different personal views and principles could be accepted.[19]

Though it is clear that a broad and moderate dissenting identity was formed which encompassed the two major strands of dissenting thought, it is also apparent that co-operation between Scotland's Presbyterian dissenters was successful as long as it remained on terms acceptable to each of the churches. Despite the otherwise successful efforts to move dissent to the middle ground, hard-line establishment and voluntary outlooks remained entrenched within pockets of both churches, even among those who were earnest advocates of dissenting co-operation. For instance, James Begg was instrumental in aligning the two churches together in political and social issues (and was once viewed by Hugh Miller as among the most progressive Free Churchmen on the issue of co-operation) but refused to countenance union negotiations when he felt that the Free Kirk's founding principles were under threat.[20] Likewise, the 1847 United Presbyterian union was opposed by a small sub-section of ultra-voluntaries led by John Craig who believed that the moderate dissenting and 'seceding' rhetoric of the new church was an affront to the voluntaryism of his Relief Synod. Though by 1863 the relationship between the Free and United Presbyterian churches was closer than ever, the hardening of the more fanatical positions within the two denominations, uneasy at the moderation of their principles in the name of dissent, provided perhaps the most significant barrier to the attempts at union in the 1860s and 1870s.

While Begg and Craig undoubtedly represented the extremes of their respective parties, the denominational agendas and sectarian ambitions of the pre-Disruption period were also evident among dissenters who would later become identified with pro-union sentiments. For example, the church historian J. R. Fleming in 1929 praised the Free Church leader Robert Smith Candlish as a pioneer of the union movement.[21] However, Candlish was often criticised by United Presbyterians and even members of his own church for favouring the ambitions of the Free Church to the detriment of the other dissenting churches and, in the case of education, Scotland itself. Though many within both churches were keen advocates for co-operation in the social work of urban mission, the drive to evangelise Scotland's cities was sometimes appropriated as an opportunity to claim

---

18. *Contemplated Union between the Free Church of Scotland and the United Presbyterian Church* (1863), 1.
19. *Report of speeches on union with the Free Church*, 4, 14–15; Fleming, *Story of Church Union*, 32–3.
20. *The Future Church of Scotland: an essay in favour of a National Presbyterian Church* (Edinburgh, 1870), 304.
21. Fleming, *Story of Church Union*, 33.

large parts of the country for a particular church, especially in the increasingly level playing field of the post-Disruption era.

The perception of this level playing field also resulted in competition among the two major dissenting churches and the Established Kirk to claim Scotland's Reformation heritage (Chapter Five). While by the 1860s the majority of Free Churchmen and United Presbyterians had embraced the 'national voluntary' dissenting identity formed after the Disruption, the location of the 'true' Church of Scotland remained a point of contention, as both churches associated themselves with the historic Kirk and its national claim. However, as the century progressed the dissenting identity formed between 1843 and 1863 enabled the Free and United Presbyterian churches to position themselves, at least in theory, as the 'free' national church. As Callum Brown and Iain Hutchison have argued, the late nineteenth century was a period of sluggish growth for the dissenting churches – driven, ironically, in part by a preoccupation with union negotiations and the disestablishment controversy – and instead witnessed a reversal of fortunes for a resurgent Church of Scotland.[22] Nevertheless, beyond this sectional squabbling the energy and enthusiasm of dissenting involvement in Scotland's ecclesiastical, political and social issues, and the creation of their 'national voluntary' Presbyterian ideal, saw them provide a truly national alternative to the Established Kirk for the remainder of the century, and one which would complement the reinvigorated national church as reunion approached.

This study has shown that the development of Scottish Presbyterianism after 1863, though certainly not inevitable, was grounded in the period of transition that followed the 1843 Disruption. Linking the two distinct and prolonged epochs of Presbyterian schism and reunion, the period between 1843 and 1863 highlighted the complexities of intra-Presbyterian relations and the shifting role of dissent. For instance, the budding and tentative co-operation that emerged between the two major dissenting churches was fraught with difficulty while, contrary to Drummond and Bulloch's assertion, the Free Church 'drift' to voluntary principles was far from inevitable. Nevertheless it is apparent that a common middle ground, incorporating the national and voluntary ambitions of the respective churches, was certainly found by Scotland's Presbyterian dissenters as they sought to challenge the existing establishment and claim their own position within the religiously pluralist landscape of post-Disruption Scotland. The shared dissenting interest formed in social and political matters proved integral to the ecclesiastical convergence that culminated in the opening of union discussions in 1863. Though common ground was achieved initially through a narrow and negative opposition to mutual enemies, this period also saw the beginnings of a positive affirmation of Scottish dissenting identity. This was built upon the urban middle-class character of both churches' Lowland

---

22. Brown, *Social History of Religion*, 64–5; Hutchison, *Industry, Reform and Empire*, 141.

leadership and its support, in the most part, for practical voluntaryism, a liberal-radical brand of politics, national education and church-focused urban mission. However, this was certainly not an identity that represented the entirety of both churches and by 1863 Scottish dissent remained a broad umbrella of various principles and character.

While the Disruption can be viewed as a fight for the character of Presbyterianism in Scotland, the twenty years that followed witnessed an acceptance of multiple Presbyterian identities, each with their own claim to representing the true Church of Scotland. It was due to this new egalitarian landscape that a broad dissenting identity emerged that was able to incorporate the various strands of Presbyterian thought that made up the Free and United Presbyterian churches and effectively challenge the Established Kirk, which itself would regain its confidence and position within Scottish society by the end of the nineteenth century. The emphasis on unity in diversity and the creation of a moderate 'national voluntary' form of Presbyterian dissent would influence Scottish Presbyterianism for much of the following century.

Appendix

Acting Committee of the Scottish Reformation Society, 1851

Member	Denomination
R. S. Candlish	Free Church of Scotland
T. J. Crawford	Church of Scotland
G. D. Cullen	Independent
William Cunningham	Free Church of Scotland
D. T. K. Drummond	Edinburgh English Church
W. H. Goold	Reformed Presbyterian Church
R. M. MacBrair	Wesleyan Methodist
Thomas McCrie	Original Secession (joins Free Church, 1852)
Andrew Thomson	United Presbyterian Church
William Thomson	United Presbyterian Church
W. K. Tweedie	Free Church of Scotland
Daniel Ainslie	Church of England
Henry Craigie	Scottish Episcopal Church
Hugh Handyside	Free Church of Scotland
John F. Hawkins	Free Church of Scotland
John Gibson Jr (Treasurer)	Free Church of Scotland
George Lyon (Secretary)	Free Church of Scotland
James McLaren	Free Church of Scotland
John McNab	United Presbyterian Church
Prof. Menzies	Church of Scotland
Sheriff Monteith	Free Church of Scotland
William L. Alexander	Congregationalist

Editorial committee of the *Bulwark*, 1851

William Cunningham (revising editor)	Free Church of Scotland
William L. Alexander	Congregationalist
James Begg	Free Church of Scotland
D. T. K. Drummond	Edinburgh English Church
Robert MacBrair	Wesleyan Methodist
Thomas McCrie	Original Secession/Free Church
William Stevenson	Church of Scotland
Andrew Thomson	United Presbyterian Church

Bibliography

PRIMARY MATERIAL

Manuscript Sources

National Library of Scotland
Black and Tait Letters
Brown (John) Papers
Letter-books of the Home Mission Secretary and of the clerks in the Foreign Mission Office of the United Presbyterian Church
Letters and papers chiefly addressed to Duncan McLaren, Lord Provost of Edinburgh
McLaren Papers

New York Public Library
Lenox Papers

New College Library, Edinburgh
Chalmers Papers
New College Missionary Association Correspondence

Newspapers and Journals
Aberdeen Herald
Aberdeen Journal
Aberdeen Press
Ayr Advertiser
Belfast News-Letter
Bradford Observer
Bristol Mercury
British Quarterly Review
Bulwark, or Reformation Journal
Bury and Norwich Post, and East Anglican
Caledonian Mercury
Canadian United Presbyterian Magazine
Christian Journal of the United Presbyterian Church
Christian Observer
Christian Pioneer
Christian Reformer; or Unitarian magazine and review

Christian Times
Christian Witness, and Church Member's Magazine
Congregational Magazine
Covenanter
Daily Express
Daily News
Dublin University Magazine: a literary and political journal
Dumfries and Galloway Standard
Dumfries Herald
Dundee Advertiser
Dundee Courier
Dundee, Perth, and Cupar Advertiser
Dundee Warder
Ecclesiastical Gazette; or monthly register of the affairs of the Church of England, and of its religious societies and institutions
Eclectic Review
Economist
Edinburgh Advertiser
Edinburgh Evening Courant
Edinburgh Evening News
Edinburgh Evening Post
Edinburgh News
Elgin Courier
Evangelical Christendom: its state and prospects
Falkirk Herald
Fife Herald
Fife Journal
Free Church Magazine
Glasgow Argus
Glasgow Chronicle
Glasgow Citizen
Glasgow Constitutional
Glasgow Courier
Glasgow Gazette
Glasgow Herald
Greenock Advertiser
Herald of the Churches; or monthly record of Ecclesiastical and Missionary Intelligence
Home and Foreign Record of the Free Church of Scotland
Huddersfield and Holmfirth Examiner
Inverness Courier
John O'Groat Journal
Kelso Chronicle
Law Times: the journal and record of the Law and the Lawyers
Leeds Mercury
Leeds Times

Lloyd's Weekly Newspaper
London *Daily News*
London Standard
MacPhail's Edinburgh Ecclesiastical Journal, and Literary Review
Monthly Record of the Free Church of Scotland
Montrose, Arbroath and Brechin Review
Morning Advertiser
Morning Chronicle
Morning Herald
Morning Post
Newcastle Courant
Nonconformist
North British Review
Northern Warder and General Advertiser for the counties of Fife, Perth and Forfar
Original Secession Magazine
Paisley Herald and Renfrewshire Advertiser
Patriot
Perthshire Advertiser
Poor Law Magazine and Parochial Journal
Presbyterian
Presbyterian Review
Preston Chronicle
Protestant Magazine, published under the direction of the committee of the Protestant Association
Punch, or the London Charivari
Quarterly Review
Reformers' Gazette
Scotsman
Scottish Congregational Magazine
Scottish Guardian
Scottish Herald
Scottish Press
Sheffield and Rotherham Independent
Signal
Spectator
Standard
Stirling Observer
The Times
United Presbyterian Magazine
United Secession Magazine
United Secession and Relief Magazine
Wesleyan Methodist Magazine
Witness

Government Publications

Census of Great Britain, 1851. Religious worship, and education. Scotland [Cd. 1764], H.C. 1854, lix.

Census of Great Britain in 1851; population tables [Cd. 1632], H.C. 1852, lxxxvi.

Correspondence from July, 1846, to February, 1847, relating to the measures adopted for the relief of the distress in Scotland [Cd. 788], H.C. 1847, liii.

Education Commission (Scotland). First Report by Her Majesty's Commissioners appointed to inquire into the schools in Scotland [Cd. 3483], H.C. 1865, xvii.

Hansard's Parliamentary Debates, third series, 1830–91 (vols i–ccclvi, London, 1831–91).

Legitimacy (Scotland). List of all cases that have been decided in the House of Lords on appeal from the Court of Session, Scotland, from the 1st January 1839 to 7th June 1849, in reference to rights of property in which the legitimacy of any party was raised as a point for decision, H.C. 1849 (389), xlv.

Poor Law Inquiry (Scotland), Analytical Index to the report and evidence contained in appendices parts I, II, and III. Part VII [Cd. 544], H.C. 1844, xxvi.

Reports from Committees: Sites for Churches (Scotland), H.C. 1847 (9), xiii.

Report from Her Majesty's Commissioners for inquiring into the administration and practical operation of the Poor Laws in Scotland [Cd. 557], H.C. 1844, xx.

Report from the Select Committee on King's Printers' Patent (Scotland), H.C. 1837 (9), xiii.

Denominational and Society Publications, Records and Minutes

Acts of the General Assembly of the Free Church of Scotland, 1843–1847 (Edinburgh, 1847).

Acts of the General Assembly of the Free Church of Scotland, 1848–1852 (Edinburgh, 1852).

Address by the Scottish Board of Dissenters (Edinburgh, 1846).

Bicentenary of the Assembly of Divines at Westminster, held at Edinburgh, July 12 and 13, 1843 (Philadelphia, 1845).

British Anti-State Church Association, *Proceedings of the first Anti-State-Church Conference, held in London, April 30, May 1 & 2, 1844* (London, 1844).

Building Committee of the Free Church of Scotland, *Communication to the friends of the Free Church of Scotland* (Edinburgh, 1845).

Catechism on the principles and constitution of the Free Church of Scotland (Edinburgh, 1845).

Christian Union. A full report of the proceedings of the great meeting held at Exeter Hall, 1 of June, 1843, to promote and extend Christian Union (London, 1843).

Conference on Christian Union. Narrative of the proceedings of the meetings held in Liverpool, October 1845 (London, 1846).

Edinburgh Irish Mission, *Missions for the conversion of Romanists in the large towns of England and Scotland explained and recommended, being the report of the Edinburgh Irish Mission for the year 1851, with the list of subscriptions* (Edinburgh, 1851).

Evangelical Alliance, *Report of the proceedings of the conference, held at Freemasons' Hall, London, from August 19 to September 2 inclusive, 1846* (London, 1847).
Free Church of Scotland, *Report of the Financial Committee to the General Assembly of 1843* (Edinburgh, 1843).
——, *Pastoral Address of the General Assembly, met at Edinburgh, in the year 1845, to the people under their charge* (Edinburgh, 1845).
——, *A report of the proceedings in the General Assembly, on Wednesday, May 27, 1846, on the subject of Christian Union* (Edinburgh, 1846).
Free Church of Scotland Sustentation Fund Committee, *To the office-bearers of the Free Church* (Edinburgh, 1846).
Great Church Meetings in Glasgow. Addresses delivered at the formation of a Young Men's Evangelical Church of Scotland Society and address of the Rev. Dr Chalmers on the Free Presbyterian Church in Scotland (Glasgow, 1843).
Gillespie centenary: report of the centenary meeting held in Tanfield Hall, Edinburgh (Edinburgh, 1852).
National Education Association of Scotland (Edinburgh, 1850).
Pastoral Address to the congregations of the United Presbyterian Church (Glasgow, 1847).
Popery: its progress and position in Great Britain, and the relative duty of Protestants; being the ninth report of the Scottish Reformation Society (Edinburgh, 1860).
Position of Popery in Great Britain, and the means in Scotland for resisting it; being the Report of the operations of the Scottish Reformation Society for 1862 (Edinburgh, 1863).
Proceedings of the General Assembly of the Free Church of Scotland, May 1843 (Edinburgh, 1843).
Proceedings of the General Assembly of the Free Church of Scotland, held at Glasgow, October 17, 1843 (Glasgow, 1843).
Proceedings of the General Assembly of the Free Church of Scotland, held in Edinburgh, May 1844 (Edinburgh, 1844).
Proceedings of the General Assembly of the Free Church of Scotland, May 1845 (Edinburgh, 1845).
Proceedings of the General Assembly of the Free Church of Scotland, May 1847 (Edinburgh, 1847).
Proceedings of the General Assembly of the Free Church of Scotland, held in Edinburgh, May 1851 (Edinburgh, 1851).
Proceedings of the General Assembly of the Free Church of Scotland, 1853 (Edinburgh, 1853).
Proceedings and debates in the General Assembly of the Free Church of Scotland, held at Edinburgh, May 1857 (Edinburgh, 1857).
Proceedings of the General Assembly of the Free Church of Scotland, 1858 (Edinburgh, 1858).
Programme of the proceedings at the soiree in celebration of the union between the United Secession and Relief Churches, to be held in Tanfield Hall, Canonmills, on Thursday, 13 May 1847 (Edinburgh, 1847).

Proposed Evangelical Alliance. An address on behalf of the London branch of the provisional committee (London, 1845).
Report by the Committee on the Destitution in the Highlands and Islands, appointed by the Commission of the General Assembly of the Free Church of Scotland, November 1846, to the General Assembly, May 1847 (Edinburgh, 1847).
Report of the Education Committee of the Free Church of Scotland: Submitted to the General Assembly on 6 June 1849 (Edinburgh, 1849).
Report of the proceedings of the public meeting of the friends of National Education, in the Music Hall, Edinburgh, on Wednesday, January 25, 1854 (Edinburgh, 1854).
Report of the speeches delivered at the great meeting of Scottish Dissenters, held in the music hall, Edinburgh, on Wednesday evening, the 2 July 1845 (Edinburgh, 1845).
Report of speeches on union with the Free Church delivered in the United Presbyterian Synod, Friday 15 May 1863 (Edinburgh, 1863).
Scottish Central Board for Vindicating the Rights of Dissenters, *Statement relative to Church Accommodation in Scotland* (Edinburgh, 1835).
——, *Remarks on the First Report of the Commissioners of Religious Instruction, Scotland* (Edinburgh, 1837).
Subordinate Standards, and other authoritative documents of the Free Church of Scotland (Edinburgh, 1851).
Summary of Principles of the United Presbyterian Church (Scotland) (Toronto, 1856).
Thelwall, A. S. (ed.), *Proceedings of the Anti-Maynooth Conference of 1845* (London, 1845).
Union of Synod of United Original Seceders with the Free Church of Scotland. Proceedings of the General Assembly in the case (Edinburgh, 1852).
Union of the Free and Reformed Presbyterian Churches of Scotland; report of proceedings in the Free Church Assembly Hall, on Thursday 25 May 1876 (Edinburgh, 1876).

Contemporary Books, Pamphlets and Articles
[Adelphos], *The Common Fund versus the Sustentation Fund: earnestly addressed to all those who desire the stability of the Free Church of Scotland* (Edinburgh, 1847).
Aldis, John, *Six Lectures, on the importance and practicability of Christian Union, chiefly in relation to the movements of the Evangelical Alliance* (London, 1846).
Alison, W. P., *Remarks on the Report of Her Majesty's Commissioners on the Poor Laws of Scotland* (Edinburgh, 1844).
Angus, Henry, *The Spirituality of the Christian Church: a sermon preached at the opening of the Synod of the United Presbyterian Church, at Edinburgh, May 12, 1851* (Edinburgh, 1851).
Anon., *A word to Free Churchmen on union with Voluntaries* (Edinburgh, 1845).

Appeal in reference to the extension of the Edinburgh Irish Mission and Protestant Institute, addressed to the friends of Protestantism (Edinburgh, 1851).

Association for the Maintenance of National Religion, *Dr Chalmers On Voluntaryism versus the present Free Church majority* (n.d.).

Balfour, William, *Voluntaryism of the United Presbyterian Church unchanged, and directly opposed to the distinctive principles of the Free Church of Scotland* (Edinburgh, 1869).

——, *The Establishment Principle Defended: a reply to the statement by the Committee of the United Presbyterian Church on Disestablishment and Disendowment* (Edinburgh, 1873).

Balmer, Robert, 'The Scripture Principles of Unity', in *Essays on Christian Union* (London, 1845), 21–104.

Bayne, Peter, *The Life and Letters of Hugh Miller* (2 volumes, London, 1871).

Beecher, Edward, *The Papal Conspiracy Exposed; or, the Romish Corporation dangerous to the political liberty and social interests of man* (Edinburgh, 1856).

Begg, James, *Circular on the late convenor, John Hamilton, and the need to replenish the Building Fund* (Edinburgh, 1848).

——, *Pauperism and the Poor Laws; or, Our sinking population and rapidly increasing public burdens practically considered* (Edinburgh, 1849).

——, *National Education for Scotland practically considered; with notices of certain recent proposals on that subject* (Edinburgh, 1850).

——, *How Every Man May Become His Own Landlord; or, a way by which to elevate the condition of the masses of Britain, and develop the resources of the country* (Edinburgh, 1851).

——, *A Handbook of Popery; or, text-book of missions for the conversion of Romanists* (Edinburgh, 1852).

——, *Reform in the Free Church: or the true origin of our recent debates* (Edinburgh, 1855).

——, *Scotland's Demand for Electoral Justice; or, the forty shilling freehold question explained* (Edinburgh, 1857).

——, *Free Church Presbyterianism in the United Kingdom: its principles, duties and dangers* (Edinburgh, 1865).

——, *Happy Homes for Working Men, and how to get them* (London, 1866).

——, *The late Dr Chalmers on the Establishment principle and Irish Protestantism, with some 'forgotten chapters' of Free Church history* (Edinburgh, 1868).

——, *The proposed disestablishment of Protestantism in Ireland* (Edinburgh, 1868).

——, *The Union Question* (Edinburgh, 1868).

——, *Memorial with the opinions of eminent counsel in regard to the Constitution of the Free Church of Scotland, and remarks on our present state and prospects* (Edinburgh, 1874).

——, *The Apostolic Commission Applied to Present Circumstances* (Edinburgh, 1876).

——, *Voluntaryism indefensible; or, a nation's right and duty to profess and practise Christianity* (Edinburgh, 1879).
Blackburn, John, *The three conferences held by the opponents of the Maynooth College Endowment Bill, in London and Dublin, during the months of May and June, 1845* (London, 1845).
Blanchard, Jonathan and N. L. Rice, *A debate on slavery: held in the city of Cincinnati, on the first, second, third, and sixth days of October, 1845, upon the question: is slave-holding in itself sinful, and the relation between master and slave, a sinful relation?* (Cincinnati, 1846).
Brown, Archibald, *Free Churchmen and Seceders: or, an examination of plans proposed for union between them* (Edinburgh, 1851).
——, *Free Church door for the Seceders; or Dr Candlish's altered overture, as passed in the late Free Church Assembly, and lauded in the 'Original Secession Magazine', considered* (Edinburgh, 1852).
——, *The Free Church tending to voluntaryism: letter to the Rev. R. S. Candlish, D. D., occasioned by his proclamation, 'The Secession is extinguished in Scotland'* (Edinburgh, 1853).
Brown, John, *What ought the Dissenters of Scotland to do in the present crisis?* (Edinburgh, 1840).
——, *Discourses and sayings of our Lord Jesus Christ, illustrated in a series of expositions* (3 volumes, New York, 1854).
Brown, Thomas, *Annals of the Disruption* (Edinburgh, 1884).
Buchanan, Robert, *Circular letter on Sustentation Fund* (Edinburgh, 1848).
——, *The Ten Years' Conflict: being the history of the Disruption of the Church of Scotland* (2 volumes, Glasgow, 1849).
——, *The Schoolmaster in the Wynds; or, how to educate the masses* (Glasgow, 1850).
——, *The Finance of the Free Church of Scotland: its origins, objects, methods, and results* (London, 1870).
Cairns, John, *Memoir of John Brown* (Edinburgh, 1860).
Candlish, R. S., *Notes on Rev. John Cumming's letter to the Marquis of Cholmondeley on the present state of the Church of Scotland* (London, 1843).
——, 'Christian Union in connection with the propagation of the Gospel', in *Essays on Christian Union* (London, 1845), 105–46.
——, *Educational Scheme of the Free Church* (Edinburgh, 1846).
——, *Letter to the Marquis of Lansdowne, on the reform and extension of the Parish School System of Scotland* (Edinburgh, 1851).
——, 'Education in the Free Church of Scotland', in C. Van Rensselaer (ed.), *Home, the school, and the church; or, the Presbyterian education repository* (4 volumes, Philadelphia, 1852), ii, 78–85.
——, *Past Memories and Present Duties; or, Chalmers' Territorial Church, Fountainbridge, opened, on Sabbath, January 8, 1854: a narrative and sermon* (Edinburgh, 1854).
——, *Appeal to the people of the Free Church of Scotland on behalf of the education scheme* (Edinburgh, 1855).

——, *The Church's Unity in Diversity* (Edinburgh, 1862).
Chalmers, Thomas, *The Christian and Civic Economy of Large Towns* (3 volumes, Glasgow, 1823).
——, *Lectures on the Establishment and Extension of National Churches, delivered in London, from April 25 to May 12, 1838* (Glasgow, 1838).
——, *Sermon preached before the Convocation of Ministers in St George's Church, Edinburgh, on Thursday the 17 of November, 1842* (Edinburgh, 1842).
——, *Considerations on the economics of the Free Church for 1844* (Glasgow, 1844).
——, 'How such a union may begin, and to what it may eventually lead', in *Essays on Christian Union* (London, 1845), 3–20.
——, *On the Economics of the Free Church of Scotland* (Glasgow, 1845).
——, *Churches and Schools for the Working Classes* (Edinburgh, 1846).
——, *On the Evangelical Alliance: its design, its difficulties, its proceedings and its prospects: with practical suggestions* (Edinburgh, 1846).
Chalmers of Longcroft, Thomas, *The Sustentation Fund in danger: its disease and its cure* (Edinburgh, 1854).
Cleland, James, *Enumeration of the inhabitants of the city of Glasgow and county of Lanark for the government census of 1831* (Glasgow, 1832).
Cockburn, Henry, *Journal of Henry Cockburn, being a continuation of the memorials of his time, 1831–1854* (2 volumes, Edinburgh, 1874).
Common sense v. bigotry; or, reasons for supporting the parliamentary grant to Maynooth, by a clergyman of the Church of England (London, 1845).
Contemplated Union between the Free Church of Scotland and the United Presbyterian Church (1863).
Cowan, Charles, *Reminiscences* (privately, 1878).
Craig, John, *Relief Principles: reasons for declining to enter the United Presbyterian Church. An address to the Relief Church, Provost Wynd, Cupar-Fife* (Cupar, 1847).
Cunningham, William, Robert S. Candlish, A. E. Monteith and Alexander Wood, *Proposal for a system of National Education in Scotland* (Edinburgh, 1851).
Defence of the Rev. William Marshall, before the United Associate Synod, on Tuesday, 12 May, 1846 (Edinburgh, 1846).
Earnest Appeal in Behalf of the Sustentation Fund (Edinburgh, 1849).
Education Question in Scotland (Cupar-Fife, 1853).
Fletcher, Joseph, *Education: National, Voluntary, and Free* (London, 1851).
Fraser, William, *The State of our Educational Enterprises: a report of an examination into the working, results, and tendencies of the chief public educational experiments in Great Britain and Ireland* (Glasgow, 1858).
——, *The Educational Condition of Scotland: a national disgrace* (Paisley, 1859).
French, John and John Brown, *Reasons for the union of Christian churches, and the love of the brotherhood: two addresses, delivered by appointment, at a joint meeting of the ministers and elders of the United Secession and Relief*

Presbyteries of Edinburgh, on 25 February and 11 March 1845 (Edinburgh, 1845).
Future Church of Scotland: an essay in favour of a National Presbyterian Church (Edinburgh, 1870).
Fyfe, J. R. and William Skeen, *Report of the speeches delivered at the Conference of Ministers and Members of Dissenting Churches . . . to express their opinion of the injustice and immoral tendency of the Corn and Provision Laws* (Edinburgh, 1842).
Gillies, Archibald, *Free Churchmen and Voluntaries: may they honourably and consistently seek a union?* (Glasgow, 1853).
Goold, W. H., *The Maynooth Endowment, a sin and a blunder: being a speech delivered at the second annual meeting of the Scottish Reformation Society, in the Music Hall, December 9, 1851* (Edinburgh, 1852).
Gordon, Thomas, *Education in Scotland: its actual amount, embracing the results of the census* (Edinburgh, 1854).
Gray, Andrew, *National Education: second speech by the Rev. Andrew Gray, delivered in the Free Church Presbytery of Perth, on the 30 January 1850* (Perth, 1850).
Gray, James, *Day and Duty: the late Disruption of the Church of Scotland, and the present duty of the Free Church and of the Original Seceders* (Edinburgh, 1843).
Guthrie, D. K. and C. J. Guthrie, *Autobiography of Thomas Guthrie, D.D., and memoir by his sons* (2 volumes, New York, 1875).
Guthrie, Thomas, *A Plea for Ragged Schools; or, Prevention better than cure* (Edinburgh, 1849).
[Hamilton, James], *Farewell to Egypt: or, the departure of the Free Church of Scotland out of the Erastian Establishment* (London, 1844).
Handyside, Hugh, *To the Office-bearers of the congregations of the Free Church* (Edinburgh, 1845).
Hanna, William, *Memoirs of the life and writings of Thomas Chalmers* (4 volumes, Edinburgh, 1852).
—— (ed.), *A selection from the correspondence of the late Thomas Chalmers, D.D., LL.D.* (New York, 1853).
Hetherington, W. M., *History of the Westminster Assembly of Divines* (Edinburgh, 1843).
——, *National Education in Scotland, viewed in its present condition, its principles and its possibilities* (Edinburgh, 1850).
——, *History of the Church of Scotland; from the introduction of Christianity to the period of the Disruption in 1843* (New York, 1856).
Jack, George, *Free Church and Original Secession: Address to the congregation of United Original Seceders, Dundee* (Dundee, 1852).
Jamie, David, *John Hope, philanthropist and reformer* (Edinburgh, 1907).
Johnstone, James, *Church union considered and Presbyterian Church of Victoria case discussed: embracing the subjects Latitudinarianism in the Free Church, and heresy in the United Presbyterian Church* (Edinburgh, 1860).

[Junius], *The Church in Danger: a letter to the Rev. James Begg D.D.* (1849).
Kidston, William, *Summary of principles of the United Secession Church, agreed upon September 14, 1820* (Edinburgh, 1820).
King, David, 'Union among Christians viewed in relation to the religious parties of Scotland', in *Essays on Christian Union* (London, 1845), 229–80.
——, 'Historical Sketch of the Evangelical Alliance', in Edward Steane (ed.), *The Religious Condition of Christendom, exhibited in a series of papers, prepared at the instance of the British organisation of the Evangelical Alliance* (London, 1847), 30–76.
Letter to Dr Chalmers, on the organisation of a Free Presbyterian Church, by the son of a clergyman (Edinburgh, 1843).
Lewis, George, *Scotland a Half Educated Nation, both in the quantity and quality of her educational institutions* (Glasgow, 1834).
Lewis, James, *Finance of the Free Church of Scotland: Suggestions on the principles of distribution, for the consideration of the fathers and brethren of the Free Assembly* (Edinburgh, 1843).
Macaulay; the historian, statesman, and essayist. Anecdotes of his life and literary labours, with some account of his early and unknown writings (London, 1860).
MacColl, Dugald, *Among the Masses; or Work in the Wynds* (London, 1867).
MacEwen, A. R., *Life and Letters of John Cairns, D.D., LL.D* (London, 1895).
MacGillivray, Archibald, *Letter to Sir George Sinclair, Bart, of Ulbster, on the extensive prevalence of religious error, and the sinfulness and danger of latitudinarian schemes of union* (Glasgow, 1859).
M[acGregor], J[ohn], *Popery in A.D. 1900* (London, 1851).
Mackie, J. B., *The Life and Work of Duncan McLaren* (2 volumes, London, 1888).
Macvicar, J. J. G., *The Catholic Spirit of True Religion* (London, 1840).
Marshall, Andrew, *Ecclesiastical establishments considered: a sermon, preached on the evening of Thursday, 9th April, 1829, in Greyfriars Church, Glasgow* (Glasgow, 1829).
Maynooth endowment vindicated: on the grounds of religious principle, by a clergyman of the Church of England (London, 1845).
McClintock, John and James Strong, *Cyclopaedia of Biblical, Theological, and Ecclesiastical Literature* (New York, 1894).
McCorkle, Robert, *The Scottish Reformation: its testimony against popery and prelacy* (Edinburgh, 1863).
McCrie, Thomas, *Life of Thomas M'Crie, D.D.* (Edinburgh, 1840).
——, *Thoughts on union with the Free Church of Scotland, specially addressed to his own congregation* (Edinburgh, 1852).
McCrie, William, *Union with the Free Church. Observations upon the pamphlet of the Rev. Matthew Murray of Glasgow, on the position, principles, and present duty of Original Seceders* (Edinburgh, 1849).

McKerrow, John, *History of the Secession Church* (2 volumes, Edinburgh, 1839).
McLaren, Duncan, *History of the resistance to the Annuity Tax, and of the origin and application of seat rents for payment of ministers' stipends* (Edinburgh, 1836).
——, *Substance of a speech regarding the Bishops' Teinds, delivered at a public meeting of the Central Board of Dissenters* (Edinburgh, 1838).
——, *Substance of a speech delivered at a public meeting of Dissenters, held in Edinburgh on the 14th July 1841, to devise measures for protecting the civil rights of Dissenters from the unjust encroachments of the High Church party and their abettors in parliament* (Edinburgh, 1841).
——, *The Corn Laws Condemned on account of their injustice and immoral tendency* (Edinburgh, 1842).
——, *Substance of a speech delivered at the meeting of the Edinburgh Anti-Corn Law Association, on the 9 May 1844* (Edinburgh, 1844).
——, *Who has 'perverted' and 'distorted' Mr Macaulay's letter? A letter to the editor of the Scotsman* (Edinburgh, 1844).
——, *Evidence given before the Select Committee of the House of Commons, respecting the Annuity-Tax* (Edinburgh, 1851).
Memorial on Education, to the General Assembly of the Free Church, by the son of a clergyman (Edinburgh, 1844).
Memorials of the Union of the Secession and Relief Churches, now the United Presbyterian Church, May 1847 (Edinburgh, 1847).
Merle d'Aubigné, J. H., *Germany, England, and Scotland; or, recollections of a Swiss minister* (New York, 1848).
Miller, Hugh, *The Headship of Christ, and the rights of the Christian people; a collection of essays, historical and descriptive sketches, and personal portraitures*, ed. Peter Bayne (Boston, 1872).
——, 'The Position and Duty of the Free Church', in *Free Church Tracts No. 11* (Edinburgh, 1872).
——, 'Thoughts on the Educational Question', in John Davidson (ed.), *Leading Articles on Various Subjects, by Hugh Miller* (Edinburgh, 1872), 1–104.
Moncrieff, Henry Wellwood, *The Practice of the Free Church of Scotland in her several courts* (Edinburgh, 1877).
Murray, Matthew, *Remarks on the position and principles, and present duty of Original Seceders in relation to National Covenants, ecclesiastical standards, church communion, &c.* (Edinburgh, 1849).
——, *Reply to a pamphlet entitled 'Union with the Free Church'* (Edinburgh, 1849).
——, *Strictures on the Rev. William White's reply to the letter of the Rev. M. Murray, on the question of union with the Free Church of Scotland* (Glasgow, 1852).
Nicholls, George, *A History of the Scotch Poor Law, in connection with the condition of the people* (London, 1856).
Nicholson, Alexander (ed.), *Memoirs of Adam Black* (Edinburgh, 1885).

Objections to the principles of the proposed Evangelical Alliance, stated in the speeches of the Rev. Andrew King, A.M., and Rev. James Gibson, A.M., in the Free Presbytery of Glasgow, February 4, 1846 (Glasgow, 1846).

Oliver and Boyd's New Edinburgh Almanac and National Repository for the year 1851 (Edinburgh, 1851).

Rainy, Robert and James Mackenzie, *Life of William Cunningham* (London, 1871).

Reasons for declining to vote in favour of Mr Macaulay, as M.P. for the City of Edinburgh, By an Elector (Edinburgh, 1852).

[Reid, Robert], *Glasgow: Past and Present* (3 volumes, Glasgow, 1884).

Remarks on the Sustentation Fund of the Free Church of Scotland, including a plan for promoting church extension without encroaching on the Equal Dividend Fund (Edinburgh, 1855).

Report of speeches delivered by the Rev. Edward A. Thompson, Dundee, and Mr W. M'Crie, Edinburgh, in support of an overture of union with the Free Church, before the Synod of United Original Seceders, Edinburgh, May 1850 (Edinburgh, 1850).

Ritchie, John, *True-Citizen-Christianity; the substance of a speech delivered by the Rev. John Ritchie, A.M., D.D. at a meeting of the citizens of Edinburgh, held in South College Street Church, for consideration of the Maynooth Grant, 17 April 1845* (Edinburgh, 1845).

Robertson, Andrew, *History of the Atonement Controversy in connexion with the Secession Church, from its origin to the present time* (Edinburgh, 1846).

Robertson, James, *Ought the Non-Intrusionists to join with the United Secession? A letter addressed to the Rev. Dr Candlish, by a minister of the United Secession Church* (Edinburgh, 1843).

Robertson, John, *Review of the account of the late conference of the members of the Original Secession Synod, given in the March number of the 'Original Secession Magazine'* (Edinburgh, 1852).

Roman Catholic Endowment: a correspondence between the Right Hon. The Lord Advocate and James Harper, D.D., Leith (Edinburgh, 1857).

Sandison, John, *Review of discussions on union between the Original Secession and Free Church* (Edinburgh, 1852).

Scheme of a Confession of Faith and Church Government, adopted by a Reforming Protestant Congregation at Girvan (Glasgow, 1844).

Scheme of union betwixt the United Associate and Relief Churches (Edinburgh, 1840).

Scott, David, *Annals and Statistics of the Original Secession Church: till its disruption and union with the Free Church of Scotland in 1852* (Edinburgh, 1886).

Simpson, P. C., *The Life of Principal Rainy* (London, 1909).

Sinclair, Sir George, *A letter addressed to the non-established Presbyterian communions of Scotland* (Edinburgh, 1854).

Skeats, Herbert, *A History of the Free Churches of England, from A.D. 1688–A.D. 1851* (London, 1868).

Smeaton, W. H. O., *Thomas Guthrie* (Edinburgh, 1900).
Smith, Thomas, *Memoirs of James Begg* (2 volumes, Edinburgh, 1885).
Smith, Walter, *Recent sermons on the Headship: Reviewed* (Edinburgh, 1860).
Statement explanatory and defensive of the position assumed by certain ministers and elders of the Free Church of Scotland: in consequence of the decision of last General Assembly in regard to the present scheme of union (Edinburgh, 1867).
Struthers, Gavin, *The History, of the rise, progress, and principles of the Relief Church* (Glasgow, 1843).
——, 'Party Spirit: its prevalence and insidiousness', in *Essays on Christian Union* (London, 1845), 387–411.
Stuart, A. M., *An inquiry into the character of the present educational connexion between the Free Church and the government* (Edinburgh, 1848).
Thin, James, *Memorials of Bristo United Presbyterian Church* (Edinburgh, 1879).
Thompson, George and H. C. Wright, *The Free Church of Scotland. Substance of speeches delivered in the Music Hall, Edinburgh, during May and June 1846* (Edinburgh, 1846).
——, *The Free Church of Scotland and American Slavery* (Edinburgh, 1846).
Thomson, Andrew, *Life of Principal Harper, D.D.* (Edinburgh, 1882).
Thorburn, David, *The Sustentation Fund of the Free Church of Scotland: being a plea for a return to the principles on which the fund was established* (Edinburgh, 1852).
Tyndal, John, *Free and United Presbyterian union opposed to the principles of the Reformation: review of speeches on union in the Free Church General Assembly of 1863* (Edinburgh, 1864).
Union of Synod of United Original Seceders with the Free Church of Scotland. Proceedings of the General Assembly in the case (Edinburgh, 1852).
Union of the Free and Reformed Presbyterian Churches of Scotland; report of proceedings in the Free Church Assembly Hall, on Thursday 25 May 1876 (Edinburgh, 1876).
Voice from the Church, being a review of the resolutions and speeches at the public meeting on National Education (Edinburgh, 1854).
Waddell, P. H., *A Letter to Thomas Chalmers, D. D., and Rev. Thomas Guthrie, on the question of co-operation with Dissenters* (Glasgow, 1843).
——, *Orthodoxy is not Evangelism: being a letter of remonstrance, in the name of Christ, to all Orthodox ministers, preachers, and professors of the Gospel, in the Establishment, or out of it* (Glasgow, 1843).
——, *Protestant Delusion in the Nineteenth Century; being another letter of remonstrance to all Orthodox ministers, preachers, and professors of the Gospel* (Glasgow, 1843).
——, *The Girvan Petitions; or the Voluntary Question in the Free Church: being an account of the recent schism in the Free Church congregation at Girvan* (Glasgow, 1844).
——, *Church of the Future; arguments and outlines* (Edinburgh, 1861).

Walker, Norman, *Chapters from the history of the Free Church of Scotland* (Edinburgh, 1895).
Wallace, E. B., *A Lecture on the Right Relation between Church and State; delivered to the Girvan Mechanics' Institution* (Ayr, 1844).
Wallace, J. A. (ed.), *Testimonies in favour of the principles and procedure of the Free Church of Scotland* (Edinburgh, 1844).
Wardlaw, Ralph, *The Sentiments and Conduct of Dissenters towards their Non-Intrusion Brethren in the Established Church* (Edinburgh, 1843).
Wellwood, John, *Norman MacLeod* (Edinburgh, 1897).
White, Alexander, *History of Broughton Place United Presbyterian Church, with sketches of its missionary operations* (Edinburgh, 1872).
White, William, *Reply to a letter from the Rev. Matthew Murray, Glasgow, to the editor of the Original Secession Magazine, on the question of union with the Free Church of Scotland* (Edinburgh, 1852).
Wilson, J. H., *City Missions and how to work them* (London, 1849).
——, *Our Moral Wastes, and how to reclaim them* (London, 1859).
Wilson, Robert, *The Consummation: an ode on the auspicious union of the United Secession and Relief Churches, May 13, 1847* (Edinburgh, 1847).
——, *Elegy on the death of Thomas Chalmers, D. D.* (Glasgow, 1847).
Wilson, William, *Memorials of Robert Smith Candlish, D.D.* (Edinburgh, 1880).
[Wright, James], *Letter to Thomas Chalmers, D.D., L.L.D., on the present position of the Free Church of Scotland. By a Free Church Presbyterian* (Edinburgh, 1844).
——, *Letter to Thomas Chalmers, D.D., L.L.D., on 'Co-operation without Incorporation'. By a Free Church Presbyterian* (Edinburgh, 1845).
——, *The Evangelical Alliance, the embodiment of the spirit of Christendom. Addressed to the moderator of the Free Church* (Edinburgh, 1847).
Wylie, J. A. (ed.), *Tercentenary of the Scottish Reformation as commemorated at Edinburgh, August 1860* (Edinburgh, 1860).

SECONDARY MATERIAL

Books

Ansdell, Douglas, *The People of the Great Faith: the Highland Church, 1690–1900* (Stornoway, 1998).
Ash, Marinell, *The Strange Death of Scottish History* (Edinburgh, 1980).
Bebbington, D. W., *Evangelicalism in Modern Britain: a history from the 1730s to the 1980s* (London, 1989).
Beveridge, Craig and Ronnie Turnbull, *Scotland after Enlightenment: Image and Tradition in Modern Scottish Culture* (Edinburgh, 1997).
Boyd, Kenneth, *Scottish church attitudes to sex, marriage and the family, 1850–1914* (Edinburgh, 1980).
Brown, Alice, David McCrone and Lindsay Paterson, *Politics and Society in Scotland* (London, 1996).

Brown, C. G., *The Social History of Religion in Scotland since 1730* (Cambridge, 1987).
——, *The People in the Pews: Religion and Society in Scotland since 1780* (Glasgow, 1993).
——, *Religion and Society in Scotland since 1707* (Edinburgh, 1997).
Brown, S. J., *Thomas Chalmers and the Godly Commonwealth in Scotland* (Oxford, 1982).
——, *The National Churches of England, Ireland, and Scotland 1801–1846* (Oxford, 2001).
Bruce, Steve, *No Pope of Rome: Anti-Catholicism in modern Scotland* (Edinburgh, 1985).
Butler, Perry, *Gladstone: church, state and Tractarianism, a study of his religious ideas and attitudes 1809–1859* (Oxford, 1982).
Cameron, E. A., *Impaled upon a thistle: Scotland since 1880* (Edinburgh, 2010).
Cheyne, A. C., *The Transforming of the Kirk: Victorian Scotland's Religious Revolution* (Edinburgh, 1983).
——, *Studies in Scottish Church History* (Edinburgh, 1999).
Clark, J. C. D., *English Society 1660–1832: religion, ideology and politics during the ancient regime* (Cambridge, 2000).
Coleman, J. J., *Remembering the Past in Nineteenth-century Scotland: Commemoration, Nationality and Memory* (Edinburgh, 2014).
Colley, Linda, *Britons: Forging the Nation 1707–1837* (New Haven, 2009).
Coohill, Joseph, *Ideas of the Liberal Party: Perceptions, Agendas and Liberal Politics in the House of Commons, 1832–52* (Chichester, 2011).
Cowan, Ian, *The Scottish Covenanters, 1660–1688* (London, 1976).
Cowan, R. M. W., *The Newspaper in Scotland, 1815–60* (Glasgow, 1947).
Currie, Robert, Alan Gilbert and Lee Horsley, *Churches and Church-Goers: Patterns of Church Growth in the British Isles since 1700* (Oxford, 1977).
Dawson, Jane, *Scotland Re-formed, 1488–1587* (Edinburgh, 2007).
Devine, T. M., *The Great Highland Famine: Hunger, Emigration and the Scottish Highlands in the Nineteenth Century* (Edinburgh, 1988).
——, *The Scottish Nation: a Modern History* (London, 2012).
Doyle, Mark, *Fighting like the Devil for the sake of God: Protestants, Catholics and the origins of violence in Victorian Belfast* (Manchester, 2009).
Drummond, A. L. and James Bulloch, *The Scottish Church 1688–1843: The age of the Moderates* (Edinburgh, 1973).
——, *The Church in Victorian Scotland 1843–1874* (Edinburgh, 1975).
Dyer, Michael, *Men of Property and Intelligence: The Scottish Electoral System prior to 1884* (Aberdeen, 1996).
Ferguson, William, *Scotland 1689 to the Present* (Edinburgh, 1968).
Fleming, J. R., *The Story of Church Union in Scotland: its origins and progress 1560–1929* (London, 1929).
Flinn, Michael (ed.), *Scottish population history from the seventeenth century to the 1930s* (Cambridge, 1977).

Fry, Michael, *Patronage and Principle: A Political History of Modern Scotland* (Aberdeen, 1987).
Gallagher, Tom, *Glasgow, The Uneasy Peace: Religious tension in modern Scotland* (Manchester, 1987).
Gash, Norman, *Politics in the age of Peel* (London, 1969).
Handley, J. E., *The Irish in Scotland, 1798–1845* (Cork, 1945).
Harvie, Christopher, *Scotland and Nationalism: Scottish Society and Politics, 1707–1977* (London, 1977).
Hempton, David, *Methodism and Politics in British Society 1750–1850* (London, 1984).
Hillis, Peter, *The Barony of Glasgow: a window onto Church and people in nineteenth-century Scotland* (Edinburgh, 2007).
Hilton, Boyd, *The Age of Atonement: the Influence of Evangelicalism on Social and Economic Thought, 1785–1865* (Oxford, 1988).
Holmes, Andrew R., *The Irish Presbyterian Mind: Conservative Theology, Evangelical Experience, and Modern Criticism, 1830–1930* (Oxford, 2018).
Howe, Anthony (ed.), *The Letters of Richard Cobden, vol. ii, 1848–1853* (Oxford, 2010).
Howe, Anthony and Simon Morgan (eds), *The Letters of Richard Cobden, volume iii, 1854–1859* (Oxford, 2012).
Hume Brown, Peter, *History of Scotland to the present time* (3 volumes, Cambridge, 1911).
Hutchison, I. G. C., *A Political History of Scotland 1832–1924, Parties, Elections and Issues* (Edinburgh, 1986).
——, *Industry, Reform and Empire: Scotland, 1790–1880* (Edinburgh, 2020).
Jackson, J. A., *The Irish in Britain* (London, 1963).
Kehoe, S. K., *Creating a Scottish Church: Catholicism, gender and ethnicity in nineteenth-century Scotland* (Manchester, 2010).
Kidd, Colin, *Union and Unionisms: political thought in Scotland, 1500–2000* (Cambridge, 2008).
Kirk, James, *Patterns of Reform: continuity and change in the Reformation Kirk* (Edinburgh, 1989).
Lachman, D. C., *The Marrow Controversy 1718–1723* (Edinburgh, 1988).
Larsen, Timothy, *Friends of Religious Equality: Nonconformist Politics in Mid-Victorian England* (Woodbridge, 1999).
MacArthur, E. M., *Iona: the living memory of a crofting community, 1750–1914* (Edinburgh, 1990).
MacColl, A. W., *Land, Faith and the Crofting Community: Christianity and Social Criticism in the Highlands of Scotland, 1843–1893* (Edinburgh, 2006).
MacDonald, Alan, *The Jacobean Kirk, 1567–1625: sovereignty, polity and liturgy* (Aldershot, 1998).
Machin, G. I. T., *Politics and the Churches in Great Britain, 1832 to 1868* (Oxford, 1977).
——, *Politics and the Churches in Great Britain, 1869 to 1921* (Oxford, 1987).

Macinnes, Alan, *Charles I and the Making of the Covenanting Movement, 1625–1641* (Edinburgh, 1991).
MacLaren, Allan, *Religion and Social Class: The Disruption years in Aberdeen* (London, 1974).
Marwick, W. H., *Scotland in Modern Times: an outline of economic and social development since the Union of 1707* (London, 1964).
McCaffrey, J. F., *Scotland in the Nineteenth Century* (Basingstoke, 1998).
McFarland, E. W., *Protestants First: Orangeism in Nineteenth Century Scotland* (Edinburgh, 1990).
McIntosh, John, *Church and Theology in Enlightenment Scotland: the Popular party, 1740–1800* (East Linton, 1998).
McLeod, J. L., *The Second Disruption: the Free Church in Victorian Scotland and the origins of the Free Presbyterian Church* (East Linton, 2000).
Mechie, Stewart, *The Church and Scottish Social Development, 1780–1870* (London, 1960).
Morris, R. J., *Class and Class Consciousness in the Industrial Revolution 1780–1850* (London, 1979).
Morton, Graeme, *Ourselves and Others: Scotland 1832–1914* (Edinburgh, 2012).
Muirhead, A. T. N., *Reformation, Dissent and Diversity: The Story of Scotland's Churches, 1560–1960* (London, 2015).
Murray, D. M., *Rebuilding the Kirk: Presbyterian reunion in Scotland, 1909–1929* (Edinburgh, 2000).
Myers, S. G., *Scottish Federalism and Covenantalism in Transition: the theology of Ebenezer Erskine* (Cambridge, 2016).
Norman, Edward, *The English Catholic Church in the Nineteenth Century* (Oxford, 1984).
Obelkevich, James, *Religion and Rural Society: South Lindsey 1825–1875* (Oxford, 1976).
Parry, J. P., *Democracy and Religion: Gladstone and the Liberal Party 1867–1875* (Cambridge, 1986).
——, *The Rise and Fall of Liberal Government in Victorian Britain* (New Haven, 1993).
Paterson, Lindsay, *The Autonomy of Modern Scotland* (Edinburgh, 1994).
Paton, David, *The Clergy and the Clearances: The Church and the Highland Crisis, 1790–1850* (Edinburgh, 2006).
Paz, D. G., *The Politics of Working-Class Education in Britain, 1830–50* (Manchester, 1980).
——, *Popular Anti-Catholicism in Mid-Victorian England* (Stanford, 1992).
Pentland, Gordon, *Radicalism, reform, and national identity in Scotland, 1820–1833* (Woodbridge, 2008).
Rosie, George, *Hugh Miller: Outrage and Order* (Edinburgh, 1981).
Rosman, Doreen, *The Evolution of the English Churches 1500–2000* (Cambridge, 2003).
Routley, Erik, *English Religious Dissent* (Cambridge, 1960).

Roxburgh, K. B. E., *Thomas Gillespie and the origins of the Relief Church in eighteenth-century Scotland* (Bern, 1999).
Royle, Edward, *Modern Britain: a social history, 1750–2011* (London, 2012).
Scherer, Paul, *Lord John Russell: a biography* (London, 1999).
Sher, R. B., *Church and University in the Scottish Enlightenment: the Moderate literati of Edinburgh* (Princeton, 1985).
Sjolinder, Rolf, *Presbyterian Reunion in Scotland 1907–1921: its background and development* (Edinburgh, 1962).
Smout, T. C., *A History of the Scottish People 1560–1830* (Glasgow, 1972).
——, *A Century of the Scottish People 1830–1950* (London, 1986).
Stephen, Jeffrey, *Scottish Presbyterians and the Act of Union, 1707* (Edinburgh, 2007).
Stevenson, John, *Fulfilling a Vision: the contribution of the Church of Scotland to school education, 1772–1872* (Eugene, 2012).
Sykes, Alan, *The Rise and Fall of British Liberalism, 1776–1988* (London, 1997).
Thompson, E. P., *The Making of the English Working Class* (London, 1963).
Todd, Margo, *The culture of Protestantism in early modern Scotland* (London, 2002).
Vaudry, Richard, *The Free Church in Victorian Canada, 1844–1861* (Waterloo, ON, 1989).
Wallace, Valerie, *Scottish Presbyterianism and Settler Colonial Politics: Empire of Dissent* (London, 2018).
Whyte, Iain, *Send back the money: the Free Church of Scotland and American slavery* (Cambridge, 2012).
Withers, C. W. J., *Geography, Science and National Identity: Scotland since 1520* (Cambridge, 2001).
Wolffe, John, *The Protestant Crusade in Great Britain 1829–1860* (Oxford, 1991).
Wright, David and Gary Badcock (eds), *Disruption to Diversity: Edinburgh Divinity 1846–1996* (Edinburgh, 1996).

Chapters in Edited Collections

Anderson, R. D., 'The Scottish University Tradition: past and future', in Jennifer Carter and Donald Withrington (eds), *Scottish Universities: Distinctiveness and Diversity* (Edinburgh, 1992), 67–78.
Best, G. F. A., 'Popular Protestantism in Victorian Britain', in Robert Robson (ed.), *Ideas and Institutions of Victorian Britain: Essays in honour of George Kitson Clark* (London, 1967), 115–42.
Braber, Ben, 'Immigrants', in T. M. Devine and Jenny Wormald (eds), *The Oxford Handbook of Modern Scottish History* (Oxford, 2014), 491–509.
Brown, C. G., 'Religion and Secularism', in A. Dickson and J. H. Treble (eds), *People and Society in Scotland, vol. III, 1914–1990* (Edinburgh, 1992), 143–62.

Brown, S. J., 'Thomas Chalmers and the communal ideal in Victorian Scotland', in T. C. Smout (ed.), *Victorian Values* (London, 1992), 61–80.
——, 'The Ten Years' Conflict and the Disruption of 1843', in Stewart J. Brown and Michael Fry (eds), *Scotland in the age of the Disruption* (Edinburgh, 1993), 1–30.
——, 'William Robertson (1721–1793) and the Scottish Enlightenment', in S. J. Brown (ed.), *William Robertson and the expansion of empire* (Cambridge, 1997), 7–35.
——, 'Religion in Scotland', in H. T. Dickinson (ed.), *A Companion to Eighteenth-Century Britain* (Oxford, 2002), 260–70.
——, 'Religion and Society to c. 1900', in T. M. Devine and Jenny Wormald (eds), *The Oxford Handbook of Modern Scottish History* (Oxford, 2014), 78–98.
——, 'Protestant Dissent in Scotland', in Andrew C. Thompson (ed.), *The Oxford History of Protestant Dissenting Traditions, Volume II: The Long Eighteenth Century, c. 1689–c. 1828* (Oxford, 2018), 139–59.
Checkland, Olive, 'Chalmers and William Pulteney Alison: a conflict of views on Scottish social policy', in A. C. Cheyne (ed.), *The Practical and the Pious: Essays on Thomas Chalmers* (Edinburgh, 1985), 130–40.
Clark, I. D. L., 'From Protest to Reaction: the Moderate regime in the Church of Scotland, 1752–1805', in N. T. Phillipson and Rosalind Mitchison (eds), *Scotland in the Age of Improvement: essays in Scottish history in the eighteenth century* (Edinburgh, 1970).
Collins, Brenda, 'The origin of Irish immigration to Scotland in the nineteenth and twentieth centuries', in T. M. Devine (ed.), *Irish Immigrants and Scottish Society in the Nineteenth and Twentieth Centuries* (Edinburgh, 1991), 1–18.
Furgol, M. T., 'Chalmers and Poor Relief: an incidental sideline?', in A. C. Cheyne (ed.), *The Practical and the Pious: Essays on Thomas Chalmers* (Edinburgh, 1985), 115–29.
Hanham, H. J., 'Mid-Century Scottish Nationalism: Romantic and Radical', in Robert Robson (ed.), *Ideas and Institutions of Victorian Britain: Essays in honour of George Kitson Clark* (London, 1967), 143–79.
Hillis, Peter, 'The Sociology of the Disruption', in S. J. Brown and Michael Fry (eds), *Scotland in the age of the Disruption* (Edinburgh, 1993), 44–62.
Holmes, A. R., 'Religious Conflict in Ulster, c. 1780–1886', in John Wolffe (ed.), *Protestant–Catholic Conflict from the Reformation to the Twenty-First Century: the dynamics of religious difference* (Basingstoke, 2013), 101–31.
Kidd, Colin, 'Sentiment, Race and Revival: Scottish identities in the aftermath of Enlightenment', in Laurence Brockliss and David Eastwood (eds), *A Union of Multiple Identities: the British Isles, c. 1750–c. 1850* (Manchester, 1997), 110–26.
——, 'Union and the ironies of displacement in Scottish literature', in Gerard Carruthers and Colin Kidd (eds), *Literature and Union: Scottish Texts, British Contexts* (Oxford, 2018), 1–40.

Kidd, Colin and James Coleman, 'Mythical Scotland', in T. M. Devine and Jenny Wormald (eds), *The Oxford Handbook of Modern Scottish History* (Oxford, 2014), 62–77.

Kidd, Colin and Valerie Wallace, 'Biblical Criticism and Scots Presbyterian Dissent in the age of Robertson Smith', in Scott Mandelbrote and Michael Ledger-Thomas (eds), *Dissent and the Bible in Britain* (Oxford, 2013), 233–55.

Machin, G. I. T., 'Voluntaryism and Reunion 1874–1929', in Norman Macdougall (ed.), *Church, Politics and Society: Scotland 1408–1929* (Edinburgh, 1983), 221–38.

——, 'Disestablishment and Democracy, c. 1840-1930', in Eugenio F. Biagini, *Citizenship and Community: Liberals, radicals and collective identities in the British Isles, 1865-1931* (Cambridge, 1996), 120–48.

MacLeod, Donald, 'Chalmers and Pauperism', in Stewart J. Brown and Michael Fry (eds), *Scotland in the Age of the Disruption* (Edinburgh, 1993), 63–78.

McCaffrey, J. F., 'Political Issues and Developments', in W. Hamish Fraser and Irene Maver (eds), *Glasgow, Volume II: 1830 to 1912* (Manchester, 1996), 186–226.

Parsons, Gerald, 'Reform, Revival and Realignment: The Experience of Victorian Anglicanism', in Gerald Parsons (ed.), *Religion in Victorian Britain, Volume I: Traditions* (Manchester, 1988), 14–66.

——, 'Church and State in Victorian Scotland: Disruption and Reunion', in Gerald Parsons (ed.), *Religion in Victorian Britain, Volume II: Controversies* (Manchester, 1988), 107–23.

Raffe, Alasdair, 'Scotland Restored and Reshaped: politics and religion, c. 1660–1712', in T. M. Devine and Jenny Wormald (eds), *The Oxford Handbook of Modern Scottish History* (Oxford, 2014), 251–67.

Rowell, Geoffrey, 'The ecclesiology of the Oxford Movement', in Stewart J. Brown, Peter B. Nockles and James Pereiro (eds), *The Oxford Handbook of the Oxford Movement* (Oxford, 2017), 216–30.

Sefton, Henry, 'Neu-lights and Preachers Legall: some observations on the beginnings of Moderatism in the Church of Scotland', in Norman Macdougall (ed.), *Church, Politics and Society: Scotland 1408–1929* (Edinburgh, 1983), 186–96.

Sher, Richard and Alexander Murdoch, 'Patronage and party in the Church of Scotland, 1750–1800', in Norman Macdougall (ed.), *Church, Politics and Society: Scotland 1408–1929* (Edinburgh, 1983), 197–220.

Stevenson, John, 'Scottish Schooling in the Denominational Era', in Robert Anderson, Mark Freeman and Lindsay Paterson (eds), *The Edinburgh History of Education in Scotland* (Edinburgh, 2015), 133–52.

Sutherland, Philomena, 'Sectarianism and Evangelicalism in Birmingham and Liverpool, 1850–2010', in John Wolffe (ed.), *Protestant–Catholic Conflict from the Reformation to the Twenty-First Century: the dynamics of religious difference* (Basingstoke, 2013), 132–65.

Wallace, Valerie and Colin Kidd, 'Between Nationhood and Nonconformity: The Scottish Whig-Presbyterian novel and the denominational press', in Gerard Carruthers and Colin Kidd (eds), *Literature and Union: Scottish texts, British contexts* (Oxford, 2018), 193–220.
Withrington, D. J., 'Adrift among the reefs of conflicting ideals? Education and the Free Church, 1843–55', in Stewart J. Brown and Michael Fry (eds), *Scotland in the age of the Disruption* (Edinburgh, 1993), 79–97.
Wolffe, John, 'Change and Continuity in British Anti-Catholicism, 1829–1982', in Frank Tallett and Nicholas Atkin (eds), *Catholicism in Britain and France since 1789* (London, 1996), 67–86.
Wormald, Jenny, 'Reformed and Godly Scotland?', in T. M. Devine and Jenny Wormald (eds), *The Oxford Handbook of Modern Scottish History* (Oxford, 2014), 204–19.
Young, John, 'The Covenanters and the Scottish Parliament, 1639–51: the rule of the godly and the "Second Scottish Reformation"', in Elizabethanne Boran and Crawford Gribben (eds), *Enforcing Reformation in Ireland and Scotland, 1550–1700* (Aldershot, 2006).

Journal Articles

Aspinwall, Bernard, 'Popery in Scotland: Image and Reality, 1820–1920', *Records of the Scottish Church History Society*, xxii (1986), 235–57.
Barnes, R. P., 'Scotland and the Glorious Revolution of 1688', *Albion*, iii (1971), 116–27.
Bebbington, D. W., 'Religion and national feeling in nineteenth century Wales and Scotland', *Religion and National Identity*, Studies in Church History, xviii (1982), 489–503.
Brown, S. J., 'The Disruption and Urban Poverty: Thomas Chalmers and the West Port Operation in Edinburgh, 1844–7', *Records of the Scottish Church History Society*, xx (1978), 65–89.
——, 'The social vision of Scottish Presbyterianism and the union of 1929', *Records of the Scottish Church History Society*, xxiv (1990), 77–96.
——, 'Religion and the Rise of Liberalism: The First Disestablishment Campaign in Scotland, 1829–1843', *Journal of Ecclesiastical History*, xlviii (1997), 682–704.
——, 'The Christian Socialist movement in Scotland c. 1850–1930', *Political Theology* (November 1999), 59–84.
Bruce, Steve, 'Militants and the Margins: British Political Protestantism', *Sociological Review*, xxxiv (1986), 797–811.
Burrell, S. A., 'The Apocalyptic Vision of the Early Covenanters', *Scottish Historical Review*, xliii (1964), 1–24.
Burstein, Miriam Elizabeth, '"In Ten Years There Is an Increase of 450 Priests of Antichrist": Quantification, Anti-Catholicism, and the *Bulwark*', *Journal of British Studies*, lvi (2017), 580–604.
Cahill, Gilbert, 'Irish Catholicism and English Toryism', *The Review of Politics*, xix (1957), 62–76.

——, 'The Protestant Association and the anti-Maynooth agitation of 1845', *The Catholic Historical Review*, xliii (1957), 273–308.

Cameron, K. J., 'William Weir and the Origins of the "Manchester League" in Scotland, 1833–39', *Scottish Historical Review*, lviii (1979), 70–91.

Enright, W. G., 'Urbanisation and the Evangelical Pulpit in Nineteenth-Century Scotland', *Church History*, xlvii (1978), 400–7.

Ferguson, William, 'The Reform Act (Scotland) of 1832: intention and effect', *Scottish Historical Review*, xlv (1966), 105–14.

Forsyth, Neil, 'Presbyterian historians and the Scottish invention of British liberty', *Records of the Scottish Church History Society*, xxxiv (2004), 91–110.

Hillis, Peter, 'Presbyterianism and Social Class in mid-nineteenth century Glasgow: a study of nine churches', *Journal of Ecclesiastical History*, xxxii (1981), 47–64.

——, 'Education and Evangelisation: Presbyterian missions in mid-nineteenth century Glasgow', *Scottish Historical Review*, lxvi (1987), 46–62.

Holmes, A. R., 'Presbyterian religion, historiography, and Ulster Scots identity, c. 1800 to 1914', *Historical Journal*, lii (2009), 615–40.

——, 'Covenanter Politics: Evangelicalism, Political Liberalism and Ulster Presbyterians, 1798–1914', *English Historical Review*, cxxv (2010), 340–69.

——, 'The Scottish Reformations and the Origin of Religious and Civil Liberty in Britain and Ireland: Presbyterian Interpretations, c. 1800–60', *Bulletin of the John Rylands University Library of Manchester*, xc (2014), 135–53.

Hutchison, Gary, '"Party Principles" in Scottish Political Culture: Roxburghshire, 1832–1847', *Scottish Historical Review*, xcviii (2019), 390–409.

Kellas, J. G., 'The Liberal Party and the Scottish Church Disestablishment Crisis', *English Historical Review*, lxxix (1964), 31–46.

Kidd, Colin, 'Conditional Britons: the Scots Covenanting tradition and the eighteenth-century British state', *English Historical Review*, cxvii (2002), 1147–76.

Machin, G. I. T., 'The Maynooth Grant, the dissenters and disestablishment, 1845–1847', *The English Historical Review*, lxxxii (1967).

——, 'The Disruption and British politics 1834–43', *Scottish Historical Review*, li (1972), 20–51.

Maclear, J. F., 'The Evangelical Alliance and the Antislavery Crusade', *Huntington Library Quarterly*, xlii (1979), 141–64.

Mallon, Ryan, 'Scottish Presbyterianism and the National Education Debates, 1850–62', *Studies in Church History*, lv (2019), 363–80.

——, 'A Church for Scotland? The Free Church and Scottish Nationalism after the Disruption', *Scottish Church History*, xlix (2020), 1–24.

Mason, R. A., 'Usable Pasts: History and Identity in Reformation Scotland', *Scottish Historical Review*, lxxvi (1997), 54–68.

McCaffrey, J. F., 'Roman Catholics in Scotland in the nineteenth and twentieth centuries', *Records of the Scottish Church History Society*, xxiii (1983), 275–300.

Millar, G. F., 'Maynooth and Scottish Politics: the role of the Maynooth Grant issue, 1845–1857', *Records of the Scottish Church History Society*, xxvii (1997), 220–79.

Pentland, Gordon, 'Scotland and the creation of a National Reform Movement, 1830–1832', *Historical Journal*, xlviii (2005), 999–1023.

Raffe, Alasdair, 'Presbyterianism, Secularisation, and Scottish Politics after the Revolution of 1688–1690', *Historical Journal*, liii (2010), 317–37.

Ritchie, Daniel, 'Abolitionism and Evangelicalism: Isaac Nelson, the Evangelical Alliance, and the transatlantic debate over Christian fellowship with slaveholders', *The Historical Journal*, lvii (2014), 421–46.

——, 'Antislavery Orthodoxy: Isaac Nelson and the Free Church of Scotland, c. 1843–65', *Scottish Historical Review*, xciv (2015), 74–99.

Ritchie, Elizabeth, '"Alive to the advantages of education". Problems in using the *New Statistical Account* to research Education: A Case Study of the Isle of Skye', *Northern Scotland*, vii (2016), 85–92.

——, 'The People, the Priests and the Protestants: Catholic Responses to Evangelical Missionaries in the Early Nineteenth-Century Scottish Highlands', *Church History*, lxxxv (2016), 275–301.

Shaw, Ian, 'John Paton and Urban Mission in Nineteenth-Century Glasgow', *Records of the Scottish Church History Society*, xxxv (2005), 163–92.

Smith, R. M., 'The United Secession Church in Glasgow 1820–1847', *Records of the Scottish Church History Society*, xxxiv (2004), 48–90.

Szechi, Daniel, 'Defending the True Faith: Kirk, State, and Catholic Missioners in Scotland, 1653–1755', *Catholic Historical Review*, lxxxii (1996), 397–411.

Taylor, Anthony, 'Palmerston and Radicalism, 1847–1865', *Journal of British Studies*, xxxiii (1994), 157–79.

Wallace, Valerie, 'Benthamite Radicalism and its Scots Presbyterian Contexts', *Utilitas*, xxiv (2012), 1–25.

Wallis, Frank, 'The Revival of the Anti-Maynooth Campaign in Britain, 1850–52', *Albion*, xix (1987), 527–47.

Withrington, D. J., 'The Free Church Educational Scheme, 1843–1850', *Records of the Scottish Church History Society*, xv (1964), 103–15.

——, 'Non-Church-Going, c. 1750–c. 1850: a preliminary study', *Records of the Scottish Church History Society*, xvii (1972), 91–113.

——, 'The 1851 Census of Religious Worship and Education: with a note on church accommodation in mid-nineteenth century Scotland', *Records of the Scottish Church History Society*, xviii (1974), 133–48.

——, 'The churches in Scotland, c. 1870–c. 1900: towards a new social conscience?', *Records of the Scottish Church History Society*, xix (1976), 155–68.

——, 'The Disruption: a century and a half of historical interpretation', *Records of the Scottish Church History Society*, xxv (1993), 118–53.

——, 'The making of the Veto Act, 1833–34, *Records of the Scottish Church History Society*, xxviii (1998), 101–28.

Wolffe, John, 'The Evangelical Alliance in the 1840s: An attempt to institutionalise Christian Unity', *Voluntary Religion:* Studies in Church History, xxiii (1986), 333–46.

——, 'Unity in Diversity? North Atlantic evangelical thought in the mid-nineteenth century', *Unity and Diversity in the* Church, Studies in Church History, xxxii (1996), 363–76.

Unpublished Theses

Campbell, K. A., 'The Free Church of Scotland and the Territorial Ideal, 1843–1900' (PhD thesis, University of Edinburgh, 1999).

Furgol, M. T., 'Thomas Chalmers' Poor Relief theories and their implementation in the early nineteenth century' (PhD thesis, University of Edinburgh, 1987).

Jones, Andrew, 'The Continuation, Breadth, and Impact of Evangelicalism in the Church of Scotland, 1843–1900' (PhD thesis, University of Edinburgh, 2018).

Lumsden, C. C., 'Class, gender and Christianity in Edinburgh 1850–1905: a study in denominationalism' (PhD thesis, University of Edinburgh, 2012).

Marrs, C. J., 'The 1859 religious revival in Scotland' (PhD thesis, University of Glasgow, 1995).

Stephen, J. R., 'The Presbyterian response to the famine years 1845 to 1855 within Ireland and in the Highlands of Scotland' (MLitt(R) thesis, University of Glasgow, 2011).

Williams, J. C., 'Edinburgh Politics: 1832–1852', (PhD thesis, University of Edinburgh, 1972).

Index

Aberdeen, 4th Earl of, 33, 253
Aitken, John, 101
Alexander, William Lindsay, 157–8, 230
Alison, William Pulteney, 195
Anderson, Alexander, 206–7
Anderson, David, 37, 91–2
Anderson, James, 178, 181
Anderson, Jonathan, 43
Anderson, William, 93–5, 213
Annuity Tax, Edinburgh, 33, 155
Anti-Burghers *see* General Associate Synod
anti-Catholicism, 12–13, 15, 115–51, 152, 187, 266; *see also* 'popery'; Roman Catholicism
Anti-Maynooth Committee, 80, 125–6
Anti-State Church Association, 47, 77–8, 79, 125–6, 252, 254
Australia, Presbyterianism in, 103–4
Aytoun, James, 173

Badenoch, George, 130
Baine, Walter, 135
Balmer, Robert, 78, 80
Baptists, 30, 49, 124, 203
Baxter, W. E., 131
Bebbington, D. W. (historian), 28
Begg, James, 8–9, 35, 61, 62–3, 73, 86, 98, 265, 270
  and anti-Catholicism, 126–31, 133, 134, 141–5, 148–50, 176, 181
  and education, 223, 227–9, 231–3, 235–40, 245, 256, 260
  and political and national reform, 159, 185–7
  and social reform, 210–11, 215–17
  see also Free Church of Scotland, anti-unionism
Belfast News-Letter, 42–3
Black, Adam, 45, 69, 107, 162, 181–3, 186, 196, 200, 203, 241, 249, 252–3
Blackwood, James, 126

Blakeney, Richard Paul, 131
Bonar, John, 60
Bright, John, 173–5, 183
British Reformation Society, 144, 146
British Quarterly Review, 123, 160
Brown, Archibald, 96, 100–1
Brown, C. G. (historian), 5, 14, 15, 29, 222, 271
Brown, Charles, 265
Brown, John, 36, 44, 77, 133, 154
  and the Atonement Controversy, 78–9
  and the Evangelical Alliance, 67, 81, 83, 86
  and national education, 240, 247, 251
  and union with the Free Church, 70, 103, 104, 105, 108–9, 248
  and United Presbyterian union, 90, 92, 93–4
  and urban mission, 192, 203, 206–7
  see also United Presbyterian Church; United Secession Church; voluntaryism
Brown, Peter, 37, 71
Brown, Robert, 205
Brown, S. J. (historian), 1–2, 9, 14, 32, 39, 56, 226
Brown, Thomas, 36
Brown-Douglas, Francis, 106, 149, 181–3
Buchanan, Robert, 35, 36, 54, 60, 69, 82, 124, 211, 213, 237, 247, 249, 252, 263
Bulwark, or Reformation Journal, 141, 142–3, 144, 145, 148, 171, 181; *see also* Scottish Reformation Society
burgess oath, 26, 27–8, 30, 88, 93; *see also* General Associate Synod
Burnet, John, 77

Cairns, John, 106, 182, 240–1, 247, 249, 262
Calvin, John, 22

Calvinism, 21, 22, 24, 29, 84, 88, 92, 193, 237, 263–4; *see also* Westminster Confession of Faith
Cameronians, 23, 68, 119, 262; *see also* Reformed Presbyterian Church
Campbell, John, 1st Baron Campbell, 40
Campbell, John, 2nd Marquess of Breadalbane, 126
Canada, Presbyterianism in, 103–4, 148
Candlish, Robert Smith, 35, 42, 45–7, 49, 51, 58, 63, 74, 77, 198, 209, 211, 213, 270
  and anti-Catholicism, 124–5, 131, 134, 137, 141, 145
  and church union, 69–71, 75, 80, 81, 83, 84–5, 95, 96–7, 100, 101, 106, 108, 110
  and education, 178, 224–8, 231–9, 241, 245–6, 249, 252, 256–7, 259–60
  and voluntaryism, 45, 52–3, 59, 62
Carmichael, Alexander Gibson, 164
Carnegie Simpson, Patrick, 265
Central Board of Management for Highland Relief, 209
Chalmers, Thomas, 1, 14, 15–16, 31, 33, 35–6, 48, 74, 121, 165, 180, 224, 227, 238, 263, 264
  and church union, 68–70, 76–7, 79, 81–2, 97
  and establishment and voluntary principles, 8, 38–9, 40–6, 50, 52–64
  and urban mission, 33–4, 191–7, 198–207, 209–10, 211–15, 215, 258
  see also godly commonwealth
Chalmers of Longcroft, Thomas, 62
Chambers, William, 216
Chapels Act (1834), 33, 35
chapels of ease, 31, 33, 58, 90
Charitable Bequests Act (1844), Ireland, 115
Chiniquy, Charles, 148
Chisholm, Alexander, 206
Church of England, 17, 21, 47, 49, 75, 77, 82, 85, 123, 126, 131, 206
Church of Ireland, 82, 132, 136, 146, 156, 165, 220
Church of Scotland, 1, 2, 4–5, 6, 11, 23, 25, 27, 30–1, 34, 38, 40, 43–4, 52, 68, 90, 99, 102, 107, 109–10, 149, 154–6, 159, 266, 271

  and anti-Catholicism, 118, 124, 129, 145–6
  Articles Declaratory *see* Church of Scotland Act (1921), 263
  Christian unity, 75, 81–3, 85
  education, 17, 219, 220–3, 225, 229, 230, 236, 240–1, 244–6, 248–9, 257, 267
  Middle party, 109
  Moderate party, 7, 23–5, 35, 159
  Popular party, 24, 28, 31, 33; *see also* Non-Intrusionists
  reunion, 1929, 10, 262–3
  urban mission, 191, 194–5, 198–9
  see also Disruption of the Church of Scotland; schools, parish; poor relief
Church of Scotland Act (1921), 263
church unions
  Free Church and Original Secession (1852), 12, 87, 95–102, 111, 179, 264, 267, 269
  Free Church and Reformed Presbyterians (1876), 23, 145, 262
  United Free Church union (1900), 9, 262, 265, 269
  United Presbyterian union (1847), 2, 12, 87, 88–95, 136, 264, 268–70
Claim of Right (1842), 35, 73, 135, 159, 163, 253
Clark, William, 215
Cobden, Richard, 158, 173, 175, 185, 251
Cockburn, Henry, 32, 139, 168, 173
Coleman, James (historian), 6, 7
Collins, William, 159
Congregational Union of Scotland, 4, 30, 44, 45, 79, 107, 126, 142, 200, 210, 230, 247
Conservative party, 122, 135, 152, 156, 159–61, 163–4, 170, 183–4, 257, 263
Cooke, Henry, 41
'co-operation without incorporation', 68–75, 192
Corn Laws, 122, 153–4, 156, 160
Covenanters, 7, 22, 23, 26, 96–9
Cowan, Charles, 106, 164–9, 171, 175, 177, 180, 182–3, 186–7
Craig, John, 91, 270
Crum-Ewing, Humphrey, 184
Cullen, G. D., 126
Cunningham, William, 35, 63, 75, 86,

124, 136, 145, 147, 226, 234–6, 241, 246, 247–8, 249–50, 252

Dalglish, Robert, 184
Derby, 14th Earl of, 170, 177, 184
disestablishment, 2, 3, 9, 10, 32–3, 37, 41, 48, 77, 79, 123, 132–3, 136, 146, 154, 162, 220, 262, 264, 265, 271
Disruption of the Church of Scotland, 1–2, 4–5, 35–7, 38–9, 42, 44; *see also* Ten Years' Conflict
dissent, Scotland (definition), 3–4, 92–3, 260, 266
Dove, Patrick, 186
Duncan, David, 253
Duncombe, Thomas, 132
Dundas, Henry, 159
Dunlop, Alexander Murray, 35, 106, 124, 135–6, 164–5, 169, 171–2, 187, 247
Dunlop, Henry, 106

Ecclesiastical Titles Act (1851), 115
economic depression, 48, 59, 121, 195
Edinburgh Association for Promoting Voluntary Church Principles, 78
Edinburgh City Mission, 201, 203, 205
Edinburgh Co-operative Building Society, 216
Edinburgh Society for the Support of Gaelic Schools, 222
Education Act (Scotland) (1861), 242, 258–9
Education (Scotland) Act (1872), 242
education, Privy Council grants, 226–8, 230–1, 244, 259
elections, general
  (1832), 154
  (1836), 156
  (1841), 157–8
  (1847), 163–9
  (1852), 169–81
  (1857), 183–5
Elphinstone, James, 172
Enlightenment, 23, 24, 193
entrepreneurial radicalism *see* Free Trade; radicalism
Episcopalians, 21, 23, 24, 30, 142, 148, 259
erastianism, 1, 4, 17, 27, 33, 40, 42, 71–2, 76, 82, 83, 85, 102, 130–1, 152, 155, 232, 267

Erskine, Ebenezer, 26, 37, 88, 93, 95
Essays on Christian Union, 79–80, 200
establishment principles, 4, 8, 12, 38–41, 46, 51–2, 71–3, 91, 95, 99, 116, 127, 256, 267
Evangelical Alliance, 12, 64, 67, 80–6, 90, 105, 111, 124, 140, 200, 206–7, 247, 267
evangelicalism, 4, 13, 28, 88, 117–18, 193
Ewan, James, 201
Ewart, William, 174
Excise Reform Association, 169

Factory Education bill (1843), 17, 220
Famine
  Great Highland, 74, 121, 207–10
  Irish, 116, 120
Fleming, John, 233
Fleming, J. R., 270
Forbes, Robert, 49
Fordyce, Dingwall, 164
Forrest, David, 206
Forrest, James, 138, 159
Fraser, William, 228
Free Church Magazine, 43, 46, 56, 61, 82, 91, 159, 179–80, 224
Free Church of Scotland, 1–2, 38–9
  Act and Declaration (1851), 98–9
  anti-unionism, 8–9, 109–10, 262, 265, 270
  Chalmers Endowments scheme, 212
  claim to be the national church, 6–7, 36, 42–5, 43, 99–100, 103, 106, 267
  colleges controversy, 63
  education scheme, 223–8, 231–2, 234, 256
  'gathered church' mentality, 197–200, 210
  General Fund, 42, 53–63
  middle-class character, 16, 197, 204, 264, 271–2
  'practical voluntaryism', 11, 47–64, 264–5
  see also church unions; Claim of Right; Disruption of the Church of Scotland; dissent; establishment principles; evangelicalism; General Assembly; New College; Non-intrusionists; spiritual independence
Free Church of Scotland (Continuing), 265

Free Trade, 14, 117, 135, 139, 153, 154, 169, 174
Free Presbyterian Church of Scotland, 9
freehold movement, Scotland, 186–7
French, John, 90, 187, 216

Gaelic School Society, 85
General Assembly, Free Church of Scotland
  (May 1843), 43, 46, 53, 224
  (October 1843), 43, 44, 50, 54, 56, 61, 70, 95, 125, 223, 225
  (1844), 60, 71, 196
  (1845), 39–40, 42, 76, 81, 124
  (1846), 84, 136, 205
  (1847), 96–7, 227
  (1848), 63
  (1850), 233, 245
  (1851), 98
  (1852), 100, 143
  (1853), 59, 212, 235
  (1857), 108, 256
  (1860), 147–8
  (1862), 110
  (1863), 263–4
  (1895), 212
General Associate Synod, 26, 29–30
Gibson, James, 84, 107, 235
Gibson, John, 144, 146
Gibson-Craig, William, 157
Gillan, Robert, 110
Gillespie, Thomas, 27, 37, 88–9, 93
Gladstone, William Ewart, 115, 162
Glasgow City Mission, 214
Glasgow Education Society, 220–1
Glasgow Protestant Laymen's Association, 128, 141, 142
Glasites, 30
godly commonwealth (definition), 15–16, 22, 191–5
Goold, William, 134, 145, 170
Goudy, Alexander, 43
Graham, Sir James *see* Factory Education bill (1843)
Gray, Andrew, 211, 239
Gray, James, 96
Grey, Charles, 2nd Earl, 153
Gunn, William, 223, 231, 233–4, 239, 245–6, 256
Guthrie, Thomas, 35, 44, 50, 69, 135, 136, 148, 196, 211, 214
  and education, 222–3, 225, 227–9, 231–5, 238–40, 243, 246, 248, 253–4, 256, 260, 268

Hanham, H. J. (historian), 14
Hanna, Samuel, 41
Hanna, William, 41, 52, 106, 108, 201, 211, 257
Harper, James, 44, 70, 83, 185, 200, 242, 247, 253
Hastie, Alexander, 164, 172, 181, 184
Hastie, Archibald, 184
Henderson, John, 79–80, 215
Hetherington, William Maxwell, 36, 43, 82, 85, 96, 102, 131, 196–7, 222, 234, 237, 241
Heugh, Hugh, 70
Highlands, 8–9, 36, 57, 74, 120–1, 153, 193, 197, 208–9, 222, 225, 265
  Clearances, 36
  see also Famine
Home Rule, Scotland, 187
Hope, John, 145–6; *see also* Scottish Protestant Society
housing, working class, 192, 215–16
Hume, Joseph, 157
Hutchison, I. G. C. (historian), 3, 15, 153, 271

Independent Liberal Committee, 165–8, 173, 175–6, 182–3
  'ultra' faction, 174, 176–7
  see also McLaren, Duncan; Scottish Central Board of Dissenters
industrialisation, 29, 31, 121, 193, 220, 221; *see also* urbanisation
Irish immigration to Scotland, 30, 116–17, 120–1

Jack, George, 99
Jacobitism, 23, 119–20
James, John Angell, 79
Johnston, George, 135, 252, 254
Johnston, William, 175, 182
Johnstone, James, 110

Kennedy of Dingwall, John, 9, 265
Kerr, Daniel, 262
Kidd, Colin (historian), 6, 9, 13
Kidston, William, 93
King, Andrew, 83
King, David, 80, 82, 89, 94, 213
Knox, John, 119, 148, 221, 222, 224

Laing, Samuel, 172–3, 174
Laird, Henry, 73
Lansdowne, 3rd Marquess of, 236, 246
Larsen, Timothy (historian), 14, 48
Law, James, 73
Leitch, Alexander, 148
Lenox, James, 40, 62, 201, 204, 207
Lewis, George, 221
Lewis, James, 55, 57
Liberal party, 14, 134, 140, 152, 158–64, 166, 171–4, 183, 243, 269; *see also* radicalism; Whigs
liberalism *see* voluntaryism and political liberalism
Lindsay, William, 133, 149, 213, 216
Loch, James, 172
Lyon, George, 144

Macaulay, Thomas Babington, 139–40, 156–7, 164, 165–9, 173, 177–8, 179, 181–2
MacColl, Dugald, 211, 213
McCosh, James, 41, 54–5
McCrie Snr, Thomas, 29, 96, 104
McCrie, Thomas (son of the historian), 76–7, 80, 98–9, 101, 144
McCrie, William, 97–8
MacDonald, John, 225
McDouall, Robert, 138
MacDuff, John, 249
Macfarlane, Patrick, 39, 49, 124, 136–7, 205
MacGill, Hamilton, 215
McGillivray, Angus, 84
MacGillivray, Archibald, 110
MacGregor, John (MP for Glasgow), 164, 169, 172
MacGregor, John (philanthropist, traveller and secretary of Protestant Alliance), 140–1
MacKellar, Angus, 71
Mackelvie, William, 88–9, 93
McKerrow, John, 30, 89
Maclagan, James, 83
McLaren, Duncan, 15, 106, 138
 and anti-Catholicism, 123, 133, 146–7
 and radical politics, 155–8, 165–6, 173–80, 182–3
 and reform movements, 186–7, 215–17
 and voluntaryism, 33, 133
 see also Independent Liberal Committee; radicalism

MacLeod, Norman, 109–10, 124, 146, 246–7
McNab, Robert, 107
MacPherson, Finlay, 201
McRae, Donald, 214
Macvicar, John Gibson, 80
Maitland, Thomas, 138–9
Malthus, Thomas Robert, 194
Marshall, Andrew, 32–3, 78–9, 92, 158, 250
Maule, Fox (later Lord Panmure), 108, 124, 129, 229–31, 234, 238–9, 247, 252, 255
Maxwell, M. C., 138
Maynooth College controversy, 5, 12, 13, 80, 115
 electoral alliance, 135–40, 160–85
 Protestant opposition to grant, 14, 15, 116–17, 121–7, 129, 142, 146
 support for grant, 123
 voluntary opposition to grant, 131–4, 138
 see also 'popery'; Roman Catholic Church
Melbourne, Lord, 156, 157
Melgund, Lord, 169, 171–2, 227, 241, 242, 244–6, 250
Melville, Andrew, 21
Merle d'Aubigné, Jean-Henri, 76
Methodists, 30, 47, 48, 124, 142
Miall, Edward, 77, 162, 181, 254
Miller, Hugh, 46, 75–6, 131, 137, 175, 182, 187, 225, 231, 234, 270
Miller, John, 148, 178
Miller, William, 148, 185
Mitchell, James, 257
Moncrieff, James, 105, 183, 184, 185, 242, 246–8, 250–9
Monteith, Alexander, 234
Morison, James, 78
Murray, Matthew, 97–9

National Association for the Vindication of Scottish Rights, 187
National Club, 161
National Covenant (1638), 22–3, 96
national education bills, Scotland, 105, 242–59
National Education Association of Scotland, 220, 229–30, 237, 239–40, 242, 246–9, 252–3, 258, 268–9

New College, Edinburgh, 56, 63, 106, 148, 233
New Light, 28–30, 88
nonconformity in England, 32, 47–50, 52, 77, 103, 124, 150, 160–1, 220, 222
non-intrusion, principle of, 1, 8, 34–5, 106, 264; see also spiritual independence
Non-intrusionists, 1, 7–8, 35–6, 38, 40–1, 71, 89, 117, 129, 138, 159, 163

O'Connell, Morgan, 122
Old Light, 28–9, 30, 92, 95
Original Secession Church, 5, 12, 30, 68, 71–2, 76–7, 92, 129; see also church unions
Original Secession Magazine, 97, 105
Orr-Ewing, Archibald, 257
Oxford Movement, 47, 75, 76, 82

'papal aggression', 12–13, 115–18, 121, 126, 127–8, 140, 142, 152, 169–71, 188
Paterson, Nathaniel, 49
patronage, 24, 25–7, 33–5, 41, 88, 91, 109–110
Patronage Abolition Act (1874), 9, 262
Patronage Act (1712), Scotland, 24–5, 135
Peddie, James, 106, 187, 251
Peddie, William, 206, 216
Peel, Sir Robert, 5, 35, 41, 80, 115, 118, 122–3, 124–5, 129, 134, 136–7, 156, 159–60, 163, 165, 170, 266
Police (Scotland) Act (1833), 154
Poor Law (Scotland) Act (1845), 5, 15, 191, 195–7, 266
poor relief, 5, 22, 191, 194–6, 199
'popery', 22–3, 84, 116–17, 119–21, 124, 125, 127–31, 133–4, 141
Presbyterian church government, 11, 21–2, 72
Presbyterian Church in Ireland, 41, 43, 47, 132
Protestant Alliance, 128, 140–2
Protestant Institute, 143–4, 147, 149; see also Scottish Reformation Society
protestant unity see *Essays on Christian Union*; Evangelical Alliance
Purves, David, 73

radicalism, 14–15, 32–3, 153–8, 160–4, 166, 171, 173–4, 177–8, 182–4, 187, 269
ragged schools, Edinburgh, 214–15, 228, 239
Rainy, Robert, 9, 75, 80–1, 86, 87, 108, 127–8, 262–3
Reform Acts (1832), 32, 153–4, 155, 164
Reformation, Protestant, 3, 13, 117–18, 130, 143; see also Scottish Reformation
Reformed Presbyterian Church, 5, 23, 68, 72, 79, 92, 96, 104, 109, 134, 143, 144, 149, 262; see also Cameronians; church unions
regium donum, 53, 132, 133, 162, 176
Relief Church, 2, 27–8, 32, 37, 81, 87
 opposition to United Presbyterian union, 91–3
 relationship with Established Church, 90–1
 relationship with Free Church, 58–9, 67–80
 toleration, 27
 see also Annuity Tax, church unions, disestablishment, dissent, evangelicalism, Scottish Central Board of Dissenters, seceders, voluntaryism
Religious Freedom Society, Aberdeen, 165
religious revival, 30–1, 73–4, 211, 214
Renton, Henry, 149–50, 252
Representation and Appeal of the Original Seceders, 100–2; see also church unions
resolutions for Presbyterian union (1857), 106–11
Revolution of 1688, 4, 23, 92, 119, 130, 262
Rice, Nathan, 45
Ritchie, John, 133, 200
Robertson, James, 71, 202
Robertson, William, 23–4, 27
Robie, James, 174
Robson, John, 210, 213
Roman Catholicism
 Emancipation Act (1829), 31–2, 121, 129
 in Ireland, 123, 124, 126, 132, 147, 165

in Scotland, 23, 30, 117, 119–21, 172, 177, 201, 225, 226–7, 251
restoration of hierarchy (1850) *see* 'papal aggression'
see also anti-Catholicism; Maynooth College; 'popery'
Roper, H. I., 49
Roxburgh, John, 214
Russell, Lord John, 115, 156, 160, 163, 166, 170, 172, 183, 244

Sabbath School Union, 214
St John's parish, Glasgow, 31, 34, 193–5, 211
Sandison, John, 99
schools, parish, 5, 17, 221–2, 224, 229–30, 237, 240, 244, 251, 253, 267, 269
schools, religious instruction in, 178, 183, 229, 235–43, 245, 249, 250–5, 257, 259–60, 264, 268
Scotsman, 107, 131, 138, 172–3, 175–6, 181, 183, 185
Scottish Central Board of Dissenters, 33, 77, 137, 154–5, 157–9, 165, 173–4, 177
Scottish Guardian, 58, 242, 247, 255
Scottish Press, 179, 180, 232
Scottish Protestant Society, 145
Scottish Reformation, 22, 100, 119, 221, 271
    1860 tercentenary, 118, 147–50
Scottish Reformation Society, 126, 130, 131, 140, 141–7, 148–50, 170, 171, 176, 184
Scottish rights movement, 186–7
Scottish Social Reform Association, 186, 216
Scottish Society for the Propagation of Christian Knowledge, 222
Scully, Vincent, 131
seceders, eighteenth-century, 7, 8, 21, 26–31, 37, 88, 91, 93, 95
Second Reformation, Scotland, 96, 99, 100, 101
secularism, 5, 32, 236, 240, 249, 264
'Send Back the Money' controversy, 49, 209; *see also* slavery
Shaftesbury, 7th Earl of, 140–1
Sinclair, Sir George, 104–7, 109–11, 135, 178, 248, 253, 257, 260
slavery, 45, 154

Smith, Adam, 194
Smith, J. B., 178
Smith, Sir Culling Eardley, 124, 139, 157
Smyth, John, 107
Solemn League and Covenant (1643), 22, 23, 80, 96
spiritual independence, 1, 4, 22, 25, 34, 41, 47, 70, 106, 127, 129, 130, 239, 263–4, 268; *see also* non-intrusion
Spooner, Richard, 162
Stevenson, William, 145
Stuart, Alexander Moody, 227
Stuart, Cohen, 148
Struthers, Gavin, 67, 79, 88, 93
Struthers, Thomas, 70
Sykes, W. H., 164
Symington, Andrew, 68, 104

Taylor, James, 257
Tasker, William, 202–5, 211, 212
Ten Years' Conflict, 2, 6, 8, 10, 33–5, 39, 41–2, 104, 129, 154, 156, 159, 163, 220; *see also* Disruption of the Church of Scotland; Voluntary Controversy
territorial home missions *see* urban missions
The Times, 43, 46, 122, 255
tithes, 155
Thorburn, David, 60
Todd, David, 167–8
Tories *see* Conservative party

Union, Acts of (1707), 1, 23, 25, 35, 117, 119, 129, 187, 221
United Free Church of Scotland, 9, 262–3, 266
United Presbyterian Church, 2–3, 88–95
    adherence to, 5
    Canongate mission, 206–7
    theology, 9, 92
    see also church unions; disestablishment; dissent; evangelicalism; Scottish Central Board of Dissenters; voluntaryism
United Presbyterian Magazine, 75, 101, 103, 105–6, 110, 132, 149, 161–2, 185, 213–14, 215, 241, 248, 256
United Secession Church, 30–1
    Atonement Controversy, 78, 80, 89, 92, 250

United Secession Church (*cont.*)
  see also Annuity Tax; church unions; disestablishment; dissent; evangelicalism; Scottish Central Board of Dissenters; seceders; voluntaryism
United Secession Magazine, 37, 45, 46, 59, 71, 73, 76, 89, 91, 125, 136, 200
Universities (Scotland) Act, 1853, 246
urban mission, 121, 192, 198–215, 217
urbanisation, 31, 220

Veto Act (1834), 33, 34, 35
Voluntary Church Association, 33
Voluntary Controversy, 3, 8, 10, 11, 31–6, 44, 67, 70, 78, 79, 89, 90–1, 137, 138, 155–8, 215, 252, 265, 268
voluntaryism (definition), 3, 28–9
  and political liberalism, 14, 134, 154–60

Waddell, Peter Hately, 50–2, 64, 266
Wallace, Ebenezer, 52
Wallace, Valerie (historian), 6, 14
Wardlaw, Ralph, 44, 47, 79
Wellington, 1st Duke of, 122
Welsh, David, 1, 39, 45, 69, 224
Wesleyan Methodists, 47–8

West Port, Edinburgh, 16, 200–6, 210, 212, 213, 215; *see also* urban mission
Westminster Assembly, Bicentenary of, 53, 68–9, 76, 79
Westminster Confession of Faith, 9, 22, 50–1, 72, 78, 258
Whigs, 14, 34, 124, 135, 138–9, 152, 153, 157, 159, 160, 163–4, 171–2, 177–8, 183–4, 220
  voluntary opposition, 15, 131, 154, 155–60, 161–2, 164–9, 170, 174, 176, 182, 187–8; *see also* Liberal party
White, William, 97, 98
Whitefield, George, 27
Wild Party, Church of Scotland, 35; *see also* Non-intrusionist party
Wilson, George, 247
Wilson, James Hall, 210, 214
Wilson, James Hood, 211, 212
Wilson, Josias, 41
Wilson, Robert, 74
Witness, 46, 49, 137, 175, 204, 243
Wright, James, 72, 84
Wylie, James Aitken, 129, 133, 141, 144, 145, 149

Young, David, 132

EU representative:
Easy Access System Europe
Mustamäe tee 50, 10621 Tallinn, Estonia
Gpsr.requests@easproject.com